# TASTE, TRADE AND TECHNOLOGY

Modern Economic and Social History Series

General Editor: Derek H. Aldcroft

Titles in the series include:

# Taste, Trade and Technology

## The Development of the International Meat Industry since 1840

### RICHARD PERREN

## ASHGATE

© Richard Perren, 2006

Published by
Ashgate Publishing Limited
Gower House
Croft Road
Aldershot
Hants GU11 3HR
England

Ashgate Publishing Company
Suite 420
101 Cherry Street
Burlington
Vermont, 05401–4405
USA

Ashgate website: http://www.ashgate.com

British Library Cataloguing in Publication Data
Perren, Richard
    Taste, Trade and Technology: The Development of the International Meat Industry since
    1840. – (Modern economic and Social History)
    1. Meat industry and trade – History – 19th century. 2. Meat industry and trade – History
    – 20th century. 3. International trade – History – 20th century. 4. International trade –
    History – 19th century
    I. Title
    338.4'76649'009

US Library of Congress Cataloging in Publication Data
Perren, Richard.
    Taste trade and Technology: The Development of the International Meat Industry since
    1840 / Richard Perren.
        p.    cm. – (Modern Economic and Social History Series)
    Includes bibliographical references and index.
    1. Meat industry and trade – History. 2. Meat industry and trade – Government policy.
    I. Title. II. Series:  Modern Economic and Social History Series.

HD9410.5.P45 2006
382'.416–dc22                                                                            2005032871

ISBN-10: 0-7546-3648-8

This book is printed on acid-free paper.

Printed and bound in Great Britain by MPG Books Ltd, Bodmin, Cornwall.

# Contents

# List of Tables

# Preface

What this book does is to suggest some reasons for the broad outlines of the vast change in public image in an industry that hardly existed in 1840, but has since come to include three continents. In the past there have been a number of very fine studies that have concentrated on the details of meat production and marketing in individual countries over shorter periods of time. They have analysed in detail the particular problems involved, as well as the relationships between farmers, meat traders, processors, and governments. However, there has been no continuous study of the industry on the global scale that it has now assumed, detailing the changing relationships between the countries that became involved in it, or between the firms carrying out that trade and the consumers they supply. This is a modest attempt to cover at least some aspects of that process and possibly to stimulate further work on it.

I would like to thank Professor Allan Macinnes of Aberdeen University for first suggesting that this book it would be good idea, and for his encouragement in its early stages. I would also like to thank the University of Aberdeen grants of study leave and reductions in teaching loads to complete it. For my research into this industry I have relied on sources that are available in the United Kingdom and I am therefore extremely grateful for the help given by the staff at a number of institutions. I would like to thank the library staff at Aberdeen University, the British Library at its Euston and Colindale branches, and the National archives at Kew for their help and assistance in finding material. I would also like to thank Dr David Ditchburn and other colleagues in the History Department at Aberdeen University for their help and encouragement. At other institutions I also wish to thank Professor Margaret Walsh of Nottingham University, Dr Peter Wardley of Plymouth University, Dr David Higgins of Sheffield University, and Professor Ian MacLachlan of the University of Toronto for their assistance in providing me with helpful information and references.

Richard Perren

*September 2005*

# Modern Economic and Social History Series
## General Editor's Preface

Economic and social history has been a flourishing subject of scholarly study during recent decades. Not only has the volume of literature increased enormously but the range of interest in time, space and subject matter has broadened considerably so that today there are many sub-branches of the subject which have developed considerable status in their own right.

One of the aims of this series is to encourage the publication of scholarly monographs on any aspect of modern economic and social history. The geographical coverage is world-wide and contributions on the non-British themes will be especially welcome. While emphasis will be placed on works embodying original research, it is also intended that the series should provide the opportunity to publish studies of a more general thematic nature which offer a reappraisal or critical analysis of major issues of debate.

Derek H. Aldcroft
University of Leicester

# List of Abbreviations

| | |
|---|---|
| APHIS | Animal and Plant Health Inspection Service (Part of USDA) |
| BSE | Bovine Spongiform Encepalopathy |
| CAP | Common Agricultural Policy |
| CJD | Creutzfeldt-Jacob Disease |
| DEFRA | Department for Environment Food and Rural Affairs |
| EC | European Community |
| EU | European Union |
| EUFMD | European Commission for the Control of Foot-and-Mouth Disease |
| FAO | Food and Agriculture Organization of the United Nations (founded in 1945) |
| FAOSTAT | Provides access to the statistical databases of the FAO |
| FAS | Foreign Agricultural Service (Responsible for USDA's international activities) |
| FMD | Foot-and-Mouth Disease |
| GATT | General Agreement on Tariffs and Trade |
| LIPC | Livestock Industry Promotion Committee (for Japan) |
| MLC | Meat and Livestock Commission |
| OIE | Office International des Epizooties (located in Paris) |
| PANAFTOSA | Pan-American Foot-and Mouth Disease Center |
| PSE | Producer Subsidy Equivalent |
| USDA | United States Department of Agriculture |
| USSR | Union of Soviet Socialist Republics |
| vCJD | [New] Variant Creudzfeldt-Jacob Disease (i.e., the human form of BSE) |

# Introduction

This study is an attempt to explain and analyse some of the changes in this important sector of the food industry and important component of the international food chain. This is a topic that involves the evolution of the international economy and the part played by the investment of capital, technology, and the enterprise of individuals. It also has relevance to the evolution of patterns of development of the agricultural exporting regions of the New World, and the changing patterns of personal consumption in the post-industrial world.

In its early history the industry depended heavily on the immediate post-colonial relationships between Europe and the areas of recent European settlement. This was a process that also involved strong competition between various meat producers and this was partly driven by the product, price and quality differences. The meat exported from English-speaking North America and from Australia and New Zealand found a ready market in Britain, but there was no such Hispanic or European market for meat from the predominantly Spanish-speaking meat producing states of the River Plate. While the United Kingdom always remained the one market open to all overseas food producers, most of mainland Europe responded to the wishes of its farmers and eventually placed severe restrictions on most imported meat. The industry was thus a very much an Anglo-centric one, highly dependent on the prosperity and the demand of just one market for its growth. In the case of Oceania and North America there were pre-existing cultural and political links to the British market. But it was also one on which the predominantly Spanish-speaking meat exporting countries of South America also came to depend, as they loosened some of their economic ties with their old colonial overlords. It was state of affairs that lasted well beyond 1914, and only after the 1950s, when Britain finally forged stronger economic links with Europe, was it necessary for all of the traditional meat exporting countries to widen their customer base.

In many ways the industry was also a significant industrial pioneer. It presented some of the earliest examples of large volume production and the development of assembly line techniques. It was an industry ideally suited to serving a mass market as the economies of scale and the lowering of costs to be made by gigantic processing plants handling thousands of animals became apparent. It was in the massive processing plants of the industrial pioneers that many of the techniques of the large industrial plants of the late nineteenth and early twentieth centuries were pioneered. It was also one of the earliest industries to be dominated by the multinational enterprise as United Kingdom and United States firms extended their spheres of operation to exploit new areas of supply and gain access to new markets. In addition, its supply networks and product lines underwent constant innovation and refinement in the attempts to supply a constantly changing and expanding market.

But it has also been an industry that has always attracted fierce criticisms. In their attempts to cut cost and raise their profits, meat packers have been variously accused of conspiring together against farmers, exploiting their workers, disregarding good hygiene practices, and hazarding the health and welfare of the consumer. Some of what has been written about the industry on this subject is strongly polemical and while some reference is made to it, this study will not attempt to enter into or take sides in this debate. At times all large industries have been accused of unethical or unfair businesses practises, but in such cases mechanisms either exist or eventually evolve to bring about any necessary regulation. Rather than take sides, the object of this book will be to provide further discussion of some of the effects of animal health and food hygiene regulations on meat producers. This is an area where the competing demands of the various interest groups involved in the food businesses have had to be negotiated. This part of the study will add to the stock of information about how governments reacted to the competing demands of agriculturists, veterinarians, doctors, businesses, and also consumers. These debates really came to the fore after 1850 and challenged the growing domination of big business over the industry. They were an on-going feature and the nature of the concerns raised changed as the industry evolved. At the end of the nineteenth century politicians and farmers were worried by the spectre of big business and the way it used its power, but by the end of the twentieth consumer groups were questioning the effectiveness of meat inspection and the danger to humans of eating meat from cattle that might have BSE.

Part of the study will deal with the reactions of the food industry to the stimulus of wars. New food preservation and transport technologies since 1850 have been able to overcome the problem of discontinuities in the supply of all forms of perishable foodstuffs. The meat industry in the nineteenth and twentieth centuries provides one of the best instances of how these developments allowed both armies and civilian populations to experience radical changes to their supply of foodstuffs in wartime. It did so because it was an important innovator in the process of food distribution in the industrialising and post-industrial economy. In the early nineteenth century meat was for many a luxury item and only available in limited number of product forms. But by the late twentieth the industry determined and orchestrated much (though not all) of the changing tastes in meat consumption in the Western world and also catered for the rise in demand for meat among the newly industrialising countries of Asia.

This book is divided chronologically into three parts in which the themes already mentioned are explored. Starting with Part 1, in the mid-nineteenth century Europe was experiencing a chronic shortage of meat. It was most apparent in Britain, as can be gathered from contemporary accounts, price and food consumption data. The regions of recent settlement in the New World and New

Zealand and Australia were seen as having the potential for livestock farming but with small populations and the lack of effective preservation and transport technology it was impossible to exploit them effectively. The building up of an efficient meat exporting industry required investment, which was part of the general process of economic development. This study will focus on the nature of the firms involved in this trade, the part played in the industry's development by foreign investment, much of it British, and the encouragements given by governments. The source material used in this and all sections will be; newspapers, trade and technical journals and government publications from all countries involved in the industry. The effect of these developments was that by 1914 Britain, by relying heavily on imports of frozen and chilled meats, had raised its per capita consumption by 50 per cent and had become the chief market for internationally traded meat.

Part 2 deals with the changes imposed on the international meat industry in the First World War and how it responded to them. It will then concentrate on events after the return to peace and the changes that took place between the wars. Attention is given to the factors behind the accumulation of agricultural surpluses, and how these and industrial depression in Britain and other meat importing countries caused prices to fall. The increase in trade barriers in the form of tariff protection, quotas, and the British policies of Imperial preference in the 1930s further worsened the situation and caused further marketing difficulties for meat producers and processors. The changes brought about during the Second World War and in its immediate aftermath are also considered and compared with those of the First World War. Although both conflicts placed severe strains on all food supplies their nature and severity in each war varied, as did the ways in which countries tried to overcome them. For the meat industry the pressures placed upon it by governments at war desperate to secure strategic supplies, also had consequences in the years immediately after. This was especially so after 1945 when the task of reconstruction required so much in the way of resources that demand for meat did not fully return to pre-war levels until the 1950s.

In Part 3, the period since the 1950s is examined to understand some of the shifts that have taken place in the industry over the last fifty years or so. The impact of developments in world trade and various agreements on the international meat trade, plus the increased concentration in Europe on agricultural self-sufficiency as a result of the Common Agricultural Policy, will be assessed. Together they forced a re-structuring and diversification of markets, particularly as the whole of Western Europe including the United Kingdom was able to supply an increased amount of its meat requirements from domestic sources, and became less reliant on former overseas sources of supplementary meat. Also, part of this section will deal with the debate occasioned by increasing concern over animal rights and its effects on the international transport of livestock. Another area that will receive attention will be the end of rising meat consumption per head in the advanced industrial nations, as well as growing health concerns about red meat. Part of the industry's reaction to counteract this was to pay greater attention to new ways of presenting and marketing its products. Some attention will be given to the increasing markets for meat in the newly industrialising countries of Asia and the response of the industry to this shift away from the former heavy reliance on English-speaking customers in the Western world.

The study begins with Western Europe suffering from a chronic meat shortage and ends with it producing an embarrassing surplus. In the nineteenth century regions of recent settlement remedied its shortages, promoted by the general progress of settlement and development, and the rise in real incomes. But after the traumas of war and depression in the first three-quarters of the twentieth century, that phase of the industry had come to an end by the last quarter of the twentieth century. After the 1960s meat producers found to their cost that increasing incomes in the Western world were no longer matched to the same extent by increased consumption of meat. This change in its traditional markets prompted the industry to search for new ones in Asia, and begin to re-think its marketing methods in the West. From starting its development in the seller's market of the nineteenth century, the industry found to its cost that by 2000 it was operating in a highly discriminating buyer's market.

# PART 1
## 1840 to 1914

# Chapter 1

# New Suppliers

## The Growth of Unsatisfied Demand

Relationships within the international meat industry are best understood in terms of two complementary sets of regions: one of them is the regions of surplus production and insufficient demand, while the other comprises those of deficit production and surplus demand. These regions have not always remained constant and have been subject to changes, some of which have been long term and permanent, but others short term and temporary. The long-term shifts have been the result of population changes and economic growth. But the short-term shifts have mainly been brought about by international conflict and national politics.

For all of the nineteenth century Western Europe was an area of insufficient production and surplus demand. The dramatic growth of population was relieved to some extent by emigration, but even so in some countries definite shortages of foodstuffs started to emerge. They were most pronounced in Great Britain where population increased from approximately 10.5 million in 1800 to 41 million by 1911. Ireland also grew rapidly from 6.8 million in 1791 to about 8.5 million on the eve of the famine, which checked the rate of natural increase and encouraged emigration after 1848. The rate of increase was generally not so rapid for the rest of Europe. For the countries of the West, that is modern Austria, France, Belgium, Holland and Scandinavia, population rose from approximately 59 million to 155 million from 1800 to 1910.[1] As these were the countries that experienced the greatest advances in industrialization and economic growth, the potential increase in the market for meat, and all other foodstuffs was immense. Southern Europe did not exhibit the same appetite for meat, as the terrain would only support much lower densities of livestock than Northern Europe and so Mediterranean diets always involved much lower meat consumption. Again, the low levels of economic growth and lack of modern industry South of the Alps preserved traditional patterns of diet with their high levels of cereal consumption.

The growth of world trade in meat and livestock after 1850 depended on the increase in effective demand and the development of technology to allow that demand to be satisfied. On the demand side it has to be noted that the demand for food is relatively inelastic, that is the proportion of a family's income spent on total food shrinks as its income rises.[2] But as incomes rise there is a change in the type of food purchased. Families with low incomes have to devote a high proportion of their food expenditure to cheap energy giving cereals, but those with high incomes can afford to trade up and spend more on the expensive high protein animal food products.[3] The rise in personal incomes as a result of industrial and commercial development from 1850 up to 1914 meant considerable trading up to high value food products, among them meat. There was thus a growing market for all types of meat, but especially the better qualities.

Industrial growth was accompanied by increasing urbanisation and, as urban incomes are higher than rural incomes, the transfer of population from the countryside to the town reinforced the growth of demand. People living in the countryside supply a certain amount of their own foodstuffs, but modern urban consumers expect to purchase all their food requirements. The rise of the Western European consumer society was thus a vital part of the increase in the size of the market. The measurement of price and income elasticity for meat is not easy, because it is not a homogeneous commodity and different types and qualities are substitutes for each other. However, Capie's econometric study of British consumption patterns in the 1920s and 1930s reveal price and income elasticity of meat greater than unity.[4] This means that a 1 per cent rise in incomes, or a 1 per cent fall in meat prices, caused consumption of meat to increase by more than 1 per cent, a relationship that held true throughout the nineteenth century.

There are signs that some parts of Western Europe were experiencing food shortages by the 1840s. There was widespread evidence of malnutrition among conscripts into the French army from Alsace between the 1830s and the end of the 1850s, only becoming less frequent from the 1860s.[5] The country that felt the shortage of meat most of all was probably Britain. After 1850 the meat supply situation there became progressively more difficult. One farming magazine, published in the mid-1860s, blamed Britain's high mutton prices on the heavy mortality amongst the sheep breeding flocks in the severe winters of 1860 and 1861, and high beef prices on the heavy incidence of imported livestock disease amongst cattle.[6]

F.M.L. Thompson has recently observed that British farmers 'seem to have bumped up against some kind of beef productivity [barrier] as early as the 1850s', and E.J.T. Collins has recently described these years as the 'mid-Victorian meat famine'.[7] Collins, Thompson, and the present author agree that between the 1840s and 1870s there was almost no increase in home meat output, whereas we know that census-based estimates for England and Wales between 1840 and 1875 show that population was growing at 1.21 per cent per annum. Price evidence also shows a steady upward trend in English and Scottish meat prices from as early as 1828 to 1865.[8] By the 1860s meetings were held in various places to discuss the 'meat question' and in 1863 the Society of Arts had offered a medal and a £70 prize for an invention that allowed the long distance transport of fresh meat.[9] The outcry rose to fever pitch at the height of the industrial boom of the 1870s. The *Agricultural Gazette* of 1 November 1873 reported that Britain's 'meat supply is becoming the most important problem of the day, and its satisfactory solution is almost impossible.'[10]

The constraints upon increase in output to meet this rising Western European demand were the availability of land to extend livestock farming and the cost to other branches of agricultural production. From the Middle Ages to the eighteenth century there was already a substantial, though variable, east-west European trade in animals and animal products. At the end of the fifteenth century the North German towns received cattle from the plains of Hungary, and as far as the Black Sea coast, when this route was not blocked by the Turks, and there was also a trade from Poland and Russia. In the sixteenth century large numbers of 'Friesian cattle' were driven from the Danish North Sea marshlands to markets in Holland and north and central Germany.[11] The coming of the railways after 1840 had speeded up the transport process so that by 1866 the ports of Hamburg and Rotterdam were the terminal stations of a great network of main German railway lines and branch lines that ran into Hungary, Poland and Galicia, and by the end of the decade they were expected to extend as far as the Bessarabian frontier.[12] Along these cattle, sheep and pigs could be brought from the furthest regions to feed the main great population centres of Northern Europe.

But by the start of the nineteenth century this trade was already approaching the limits set by livestock supplies and available land to feed them, even without the further barriers imposed by periodic outbreaks of conflict in the region, such as the Crimean War which was thought to have reduced the numbers of European sheep coming to Britain between 1853 and 1856.[13] *The Economist* commented on the high price of meat as early as 1853, observing that there was no need for the British farmer to be afraid of imports of foreign livestock as they were having no effect in keeping down meat prices.[14] Meat was dear in the mid-1860s because the working class were earning good wages and creating 'a largely increased and effective demand for meat.' Nor was much relief to be expected from the steady increase in supplies of imported meat as 'foreign stock both in condition and quality are much inferior to English … and the climate of Europe – hot in summer and severely cold in winter – presents obstacles to stock breeding and feeding not easily to be overcome.'[15] Although the railways – and steamships – speeded up the process of supplying meat to Northern Europe and reduced the weight losses caused by when drovers walked the animals overland, they did not cause any substantial increase in the area of supply. For that to occur, completely fresh regions of meat supply outside Europe had to be brought into production.

**Characteristics of New Suppliers**

There were four important overseas sources of meat in the nineteenth century, the United States and to some extent Canada, the South American countries of Argentina and Uruguay, Australia, and New Zealand. Together they made up the substantial proportion of the regions that saw the migration of nearly 50 million Europeans who emigrated to the Americas, Australia, New Zealand and Africa during the nineteenth and early twentieth centuries, and only Africa was not a serious contributor to this aspect of international trade. Thus the establishment and progress of this stage of the international meat industry was very much a matter of general European imperial and colonial development. But they all achieved their necessary levels of economic growth to become suppliers of meat, along with other primary products, in rather different ways. As they did not each start from the same set of preconditions their early strategies for economic development were different. If one were to generalize it seems that all the countries of recent settlement had to undergo three elements of internal change to establish the domestic conditions necessary for them to set up as exporters of meat and other products. It would be misleading to see these as precise chronological stages because all overlapped in time rather than following on in succession. But they all eventually required the following:

- the establishment of a firm and stable system of internal politics and government, to guarantee property rights, and reassure settlers and investors that their assets would be protected;
- the necessary military power to guard against any threat of hostility from indigenous peoples;
- the presence of a sufficiently large settler population to establish an internal market and reinforce the rule of law.

Together, these provided a necessary environment to attract sufficient businessmen endowed with the entrepreneurial spirit and venture capital, necessary to establish a network of modern transport systems and meat processing plants.

But each of the regions that were to become important international meat suppliers did so for rather different reasons and in different ways. Geography and climate varied, as did patterns of settlement before the nineteenth century, and each had inherited its own particular cultural and political forms. Each looked distinctly unpromising in 1840. All were thinly settled, and still in the process of subduing their indigenous inhabitants. Australia was still not a nation, only a series of widely scattered small colonies hardly linked at all overland, and both they and New Zealand had only small urban centres. The United States was already in the early stages of establishing its transport system, while large parts of Argentina and Uruguay, the main South American meat producers, were still characterized by lawlessness and terror. In Australia and New Zealand the problems of internal political stability were never serious. The United States only suffered one serious disruption of civil war in the 1860s, though this was speedily overcome. But in South America political instability and poor government was far more serious, and because they were longer-lasting and took longer to overcome, they had a significant effect in holding back the progress of all aspects of development.

The aftermath of political independence from Spain in the 1820s left Argentina and Uruguay with more than thirty years of political instability as local warlords fought for power and largely disregarded their weak central governments. Although it is possible to identify elements of this situation in other regions of recent settlement it was never encountered to the same extent in any of the other meat producing regions. For these two countries, the full exploitation of their agricultural resources and integration into the European economic system required three things. Firstly, the establishment of international peace in the basin of the River Plate, which was only achieved by a series of external treaties which involved the interested nations of South America and Europe. Secondly, in Argentina there had to be an internal settlement of the regional struggle between the province of Buenos Aires, fighting to establish and retain central power, and the rest of the country who wanted provincial rights. Internal stability was accomplished after 1861 with a federal compromise, with Buenos Aires at the centre and the interior provinces represented there. Thus from 1862 the country was firmly unified when Bartolomé Mitre became president, under an effective central power which established a framework of national political and economic organisation, assisting the growth of institutions with an Argentine dimension like the National Bank, a modern press, a postal service and the railway system. Such institutions were also made possible by meeting the third requirement of national growth, further investment. Previously the barrier to this had been the Argentine government's default in 1824 on the payments for a British loan of £1 million. In 1857 the government in Buenos Aires agreed to repay this debt plus the accumulated interest, so that in the second half of the nineteenth century Argentina became connected once again with the ever-increasing international flow of capital.[16]

Finally, the full development of both countries' agricultural systems and their integration into the European economic system required the establishment of international peace in the basin of the River Plate, which was achieved by a series of treaties involving the interested nations of South America and Europe. Thus from 1869 both countries were firmly unified and central power and national political and economic organization survived and were able to take root.

Uruguay, the other South American meat exporter, though necessarily on a much smaller scale than Argentina as it only contains one fifteenth of the land area, was also chiefly a beef producer and its political and economic conditions in the 1840s were, if anything, even more unpromising than Argentina's. Its initial settlement in the sixteenth century as a Spanish colony was followed by small amounts of emigration from southern Europe. Uruguay was divided after it separated from Argentina in 1828 by the same sorts of warring factions like those of its larger neighbour. At times it was also drawn into Argentine politics as well. The *Colorado* party under Fructuoso Rivera came to represent the city of Montevideo and the *Blanco* party commanded by Manuel Oribe secured the support of the landowners from the surrounding countryside. It was also subsidised by the disruptive and reactionary Argentine dictator Juan Manuel de Rosas (1829–52) who was a great landowner and commanded the Argentine rural militia. Politics there was much the same too as Uruguay and tended to be controlled by a succession of often militarily based rural strongmen, or *caudillos*, until they either died or more often were violently removed by their successors. Peace in Uruguay was eventually secured by 1870, not so much by military victory, but by war-weariness on all political sides.[17]

From 1852 to 1880 as Argentina underwent a period of political consolidation under regimes of less violence and greater political stability the native Indians were ruthlessly suppressed thus removing their threat to the further exploitation of some of the country's territories. The question of Buenos Aires' position within the nation was eventually settled by the constitutional decision to make it a federal territory and the nation's capital, and have a separate capital for its surrounding province of Buenos Aires at La Plata. But immigration was still largely the key to any further development. Even as late as 1869 Argentina's population of little more than one and a half million inhabited an area of over a million square miles. Such a thinly scattered population dictated that most farming was little more than subsistence, although some ranchers did produce salted meat and hides on a commercial scale. Lack of people was one obstacle to further settlement and more intensive exploitation, but levels had been kept low, not only by the earlier internal political disorder but also because it was often reinforced by the presence of hostile Indians in the interior. Their suppression and removal was intermittent in the era of political instability, but was undertaken with renewed vigour by Domingo Sarmiento (1874–80) and was concluded by Julio Roca (1880–86).[18]

## Settlers and Supplies

One feature that accompanied the gradual establishment of political stability in both these South American countries from the 1860s was the encouragement of European immigration, supported by a range of informative publications. In some cases books were sponsored directly by governments, but in others private individuals appeared to recount personal experiences. The publishing firm of Bates, Hendy, & Co., which specialised in books, pamphlets, maps, almanacs, and a bimonthly magazine about South America, did not confine itself to that continent alone.[19] It also produced guides to, and accounts of how to settle and survive in Australia, New Zealand, Canada, and South Africa. A number of these publications were directly aimed at intending farmers but there were also titles on South Africa and North America that covered gold mining. This genre of publications was aimed not only at potential emigrants but had others that claimed to be adapted for merchants and traders. The basic point is that all of these countries were desperate to supplement their initial patterns of sparse and scattered settlement. By all means possible they hoped to establish a critical mass of population to support the development of a wide variety of secondary industries, many of which, as in the case of meat, would then stimulate demand and further rounds of immigration and investment.

Although its first European settlements dated back to the sixteenth century, South America faced long-term historical difficulties in attracting migrants, as political instability had been endemic and particularly severe up to the middle of the nineteenth century. Before that time the lack of any really settled system of law and the effective protection of property rights not only held back settlement but also deterred investment to complete the process. Indeed, mass immigration had also been held back by an 'Iberians only' rule when the continent was under Spanish and Portuguese government. Some of the earlier accounts of the continent were so distinctly uninviting with so much prejudice and real difficulties to be overcome, that it is not surprising immigration only gathered any real momentum after 1870.[20] But after its slow start the flow of migrants from all parts of Europe into the River Plate region was, by 1914, sufficient to overcome the chronic labour shortages of the early nineteenth century. This was a key factor in the development of a substantial agricultural export economy that included meat as one of its important products, and also confirm South America's place as a substantial player in the greater Atlantic economy of the early twentieth century.[21]

But despite these early deterrents, even before 1860 the expansion of cattle ranching was responsible for population of the River Plate area. The rural population of the province of Buenos Aires rose by an astonishing 4.2 per cent a year between 1836 and 1855, which was faster than either Britain or America at that time. For Argentina as a whole, the population rose at just 2 per cent per annum.[22] But settlement in most of the rest of South America was still held back before the 1850s by the many hazards attaching to the process. However, by 1869 William Hadfield could write that since his first visit to the region in 1853: '... a large amount of English capital has been invested in various enterprises connected with Brazil and the River Plate, particularly for the construction of railways, the formation of banks, and the promotion of steam navigation on the great rivers communicating with the interior.'[23] Governments now entered into contracts with individuals and companies to promote immigration and settlement from Western Europe. And there were some agreements, under which private companies were granted large tracts of land in the interior provinces that were specifically targeted for pastoral settlement.[24] Although not all schemes were soundly based, or eventually successful, net immigration to Argentina, which was only 11,000 in 1857–60, rose to 638,000 in the 1880s and 1.1 million in the decade before 1911. Under this stimulus and natural increase the country's total population rose from an estimated 1.1 million in 1850, 1.7 million at the first census in 1869, to 4.7 million in 1900 and 7.8 million by 1914.[25] Over the sixty-four years after 1850 up to the outbreak of the First World War this represented an annual increase of 3.1 per cent.

The population of Uruguay, the second important South American meat exporter, naturally grew out of a similar background of political and economic stability. In the 1860s the population was about 300,000, half of whom lived in its maritime capital of Montevideo. Civil strife had been endemic from the country's successful claim of independence from Spain in the 1820s to the 1860s. Established as a buffer state between Argentina in the South and Brazil in the north, its main output was cattle and the government was basically unable to impose its authority on a scattered society of ranchers. 1857 the first nationally owned bank, the Banco Comercial, was founded and by the 1860s the establishment of a middle class of merchants and wealthy landowners was beginning to integrate the country into the world economy.[26] In 1850 the population was estimated at 132,000 and in 1881 at 450,000, rising to 915,000 in 1900 and 1.3 million in 1914. Immigration made some contribution to this increase but was low compared to natural increase, as Uruguay could not compete with the attractions of its much larger and more prosperous neighbour Argentina as a destination. In the decade or so before the First War the ratio of new immigrants to population was only a tenth of Argentina's, and many Europeans who landed at Montevideo were simply there en route to Buenos Aires.[27]

As Australia and New Zealand initially had stable colonial government under British rule and achieved self-government in the 1860s, the growth of settlement after 1840 did not involve revolution or require the imposition of political stability through civil war. In both countries native populations were something of an impediment to early settlement by hampering the acquisition of land by immigrants, but were overcome by a combination of military and police action and imposed treaties. New Zealand's immigrant population in 1851 was around 27,000 plus between 100,000 and 150,000 Maoris. By 1871 the immigrant population reached 256,000, drawing most of its recruits from England,[28] and further growth in the 1870s and 1880s took the population to 627,000 by 1891, boosted by various colonial government-assisted immigration schemes. Later immigration added Irish and Scots to the English settlers and other groups were from Europe. As in other countries the indigenous people were seen as impediments to development, especially where Maoris occupied prime agricultural areas.[29]

Although the treatment of indigenous people was by no means as bad as Australia, where 'the Aboriginal was despised as a rural pest', relations with the Maoris worsened in the 1850s. As he was 'respected as a warrior' the Maori as a cultivator could not easily be driven from his land as the Aboriginal hunter-gatherer.[30] Disputes over land sales and relentless settler pressure on the government and Maoris for the release of more good land caused serious outbreaks of fighting in the North Island over the issue in the 1860s. By 1870 an uneasy peace had returned, land sales were enforced, some unfair confiscations took place, and by 1900 the Maoris lost most of their best native land.[31] The direct effects of the fighting on population numbers was only serious for the tribes that had actually been engaged in it, but the general effects of the whole dispute, and loss of status and resources, on native morale meant the Maori numbers appear to have reached their nadir of 42,113 in 1896 before starting to recover. Although around the turn of the century there was a widespread belief among Europeans that the Maoris were nearing extinction, this was not the case. In 1901 there were 45,549 Maoris, and in the first Maori census of 1906 they were reckoned at 47,731 persons.[32]

Other colonial states, Australia in particular during the pastoral boom of the 1850s and then gold miners from Australia and America in the 1860s, also played a part in the enlargement of European society overseas. Australia, which had a smaller indigenous population but a more hazardous agricultural climate, also competed with New Zealand in the 1850s as a destination for English migrants on assisted passages. Its population in 1840 was 190,000 rising spectacularly under the additional stimulus provided by the discovery of gold from 400,000 in 1850 to

1,146,000 by 1860. Thereafter, its population growth was slightly faster than New Zealand's, reaching 3,151,000 by 1890.[33] The Australian colonial settler economy was initially smaller than the Aboriginal one. Comparisons are difficult because they each valued different things but certainly after the discovery of gold in 1851 the colonial economy grew and the Aboriginal one declined. The Aboriginal economy declined absolutely because the Aboriginal population fell. Deliberate killing took place often enough, but the major causes of decline were the diseases such as measles, smallpox and tuberculosis that the colonists brought with them. In 1860 the indigenous population was probably only a half of what it had been in 1788. Access to natural resources was restricted as Aboriginals were cleared from lands of white settlement and this, along with the effects on fertility of also imported venereal disease, prevented the natural recovery of numbers. In 1850 the colonists outnumbered Aboriginals by four to one, and in 1860 by five to one. Once the scale of 1860 had been reached it only took small increases in colonial numbers to swamp the Aboriginal population; by 1890 there were twenty times as many colonists as Aboriginals.[34]

Both the United States and Canada already had an established and stable political framework at the start of the nineteenth century. Although the Civil War disturbed this for the United States in the 1860s, further settlement and the development of pastoral farming was predominantly a question of attracting individuals and capital. The United States population in 1790 was already 4 million, and had risen to 10 million by 1820. In the 1830s and early 1840s there was a substantial rise in US immigration from England, Ireland and Germany. The potato famine of 1845–47 increased the flow of Irish emigrants and the rise in their numbers lasted into the 1850s. The failure of the European national and democratic revolutions in 1848 had a similar effect on emigration levels from Germany. The effect of these movements, and natural increase, trebled the US population to 31.5 million by 1860.[35] Canada, which did become a minor international meat trader, and occupied a somewhat similar position in relation to its giant neighbour as Uruguay did to Argentina, had a population of only 2.4 million in 1850. In the next decade this advanced to 3.2 million by 1860, but here emigration only accounted for a quarters of the additional number and the rest was by natural increase. Climatic factors meant Canada was never a popular initial destination for its predominantly British immigrants and even from among those it experienced a net outflow of migrants, particularly to the more prosperous United States, particularly after the Civil War and until the start of the twentieth century. By 1890 it was estimated that about a million ex-Canadians, or 17 per cent of its population then were living in the United States.[36]

In the United States, as in all the other regions of western settlement, the displacement and swamping of the indigenous population followed a similar course, with the difference that in the United States the process started even earlier. There the westward movement started soon after the first European colonists appeared, starting in the 1540s in the south with the Spanish and followed in the seventeenth century by the English and French in the north. After 1763 the French withdrew from Canada, giving the British a brief, though far from undisputed, control of the north. At the start the Appalachians were the first serious frontier that needed to be crossed, but as pressure mounted from the east later incursions further westwards were made. The process was taken further from 1783 to 1812 when the new United States government asserted its political control over the country beyond those mountains and French land east of the Mississippi. In all of these years there was a relentless displacement of the indigenous inhabitants – the Indians – and after 1812 their last hope of blocking the absolute control of trans-Appalachia by the United States had gone.[37] Relations with the Indians continued to be wary and combative, but the government's general success in subduing native opposition made life a lot easier for the first waves of new white settlers.

By 1800 the United States government had established the principle that Indian rights to land could be extinguished only by treaties, and although the principle was never entirely discarded it was greatly bent by governmental and popular practice. The treaties were reinforced by the establishment of military forts, the removal of Indians from areas where their presence was inconvenient, and in the years from 1840 to 1890 finally confining them to reservations. In the 1830s Alexis de Tocqueville had noted, 'It is impossible to destroy men with more respect for the laws of humanity.' Advances into the frontier meant practices like deforestation and unlimited animal kill-offs – of which the destruction of the bison is probably the most noted – put native peoples' resources at risk and eventually removed their economic independence.[38] Although their self-supporting indigenous economies were also vulnerable to the periodic natural crises of fire, flood, drought and famine as well as destructive outbreaks of inter-tribal wars, they were universally replaced by capitalist production systems organised for profit and maximum output. At times the new systems put the environment under greater risk from things like erosion when weak soils were ploughed to grow grain, or from flood and landslides when the river courses were altered, or timber cut from mountainsides. In doing these things, frontier settlement by Europeans in the United States, Argentina, Australia and New Zealand also had the certain and undesirable effect of creating a largely dispossessed and resentful native underclass.

**Agriculture and Exports**

The early agricultural history of all new settlements and colonies was initially a matter of supplying a growing settler population, but often it rapidly passed beyond this stage as agricultural exports became a way of earning foreign exchange to pay for imports. But again the ways in which this happened and the extent of its importance varied for each of the great international meat suppliers of the nineteenth century. In South America the cattle farming was predominant, but in Australia and New Zealand climate and soil were more suitable for sheep. Argentina, Uruguay, Australia and New Zealand were all to remain very important meat and other agricultural primary product exporters. For the United States the position was somewhat different as it produced both cattle and hogs for export with no emphasis on sheep, but failed to remain a substantial exporter of its own meat much beyond 1900. It was a far more diversified economy than any of the others, and this was reflected in its patterns of trade.

But in the early part of the nineteenth century livestock farming in North and South America was initially very largely a task of supplying the domestic market with animal products, whereas much of the early growth of livestock numbers in Australia and New Zealand was geared to the export of fine Merino wool. In the 1820s it was already profitable to ship Australian wool to the English textile mills and the period from 1820 to 1851 has been described as Australia's 'pastoral age'. The expansion of wool exports was a vital factor in freeing this former convict colony from its dependence on the British government subsidies, establishing private enterprise as more than an appendage, and encouraging a significant flow of free immigrants to provide an economically motivated labour force. As a result, sheep numbers in New South Wales rose from 139,000 in 1822 to 12 million in 1850, to make wool Australia's principal export until it was overtaken by gold in 1853. New Zealand's wool industry developed rather later, from the end of the 1840s with sheep shipped from Australia and pastured on the open plains and downs of the east coast of the two islands. As with Australia, wool was the main export in the 1840s and 1850s, but it was also for a time overtaken by the gold first discovered on the South Island in the 1850s and exported in significant quantities in the 1860s and early 1870s, before supplies declined.[39]

In all regions of recent settlement livestock farmers were constantly on the search for further markets for the full range of livestock products. Settlement and indigenous population growth meant growth of the domestic market but these could be limited, and not all forms of settlement assisted the farmers. Fortuitous events were also an important factor in forming the path of development and no event was more fortuitous than gold discoveries in both Australia and New Zealand. The first discoveries in New South Wales and then in Victoria meant the Australian economy experienced a boom in the 1850s of a size that has not been equalled since. The initial discoveries in both countries were alluvial and did not need great amounts of capital to exploit so they attracted large numbers of immigrant fortune hunters. The influx of male gold workers to New Zealand in the 1860s further exaggerated the sexual imbalance of its population, just as it had done for Australia's. In 1861–65 there was a net New Zealand immigration of 93,000, of which 63,000 were males.[40] But the exploitation of gold reserves in both colonies conflicted with the interests of farmers. In the short term gold competed with farming for labour, and in the long-term the gold workers who remained after that work had subsided competed with sheep farmers for land.

In the 1840s a framework of extensive farming had been established as sheep pastures were extended beyond the approved frontiers of settlement by the process of squatting on unoccupied and unallocated land. All governments in countries of recent settlement, both in North America and the Southern Hemisphere, had strong reservations about the constant extension of the farming area. Although a potential source of greater farm exports, they disliked it mainly because it increased the area that had to be policed, more often than not raising the possibility of conflict with native peoples, and threatening to become a further burden on finance. But in the long run they had to accept it as well as try to arbitrate between outraged dispossessed native people and land-hungry white farmers. However, this form of settlement did little to extend the size of domestic markets, as these remained centred on the coastal settlements.[41] It also meant that in the generation before 1851 sheep farming in both Australia and New Zealand came to depend on a large supply of labour to patrol and manage extensive sheep runs.

The subsequent increases in immigration as a result of gold discoveries did provide some enlargement of local markets and enhanced the prices for livestock products, but it also had the effect of raising the level of wage costs and caused shortages of labour by enticing hands away from sheep holdings. The Australian flocks needed constant shepherding to guard against losses from dingoes and other predators and also to tend them at the vulnerable lambing time. But as a result of the gold, between 1851 and 1861 the total number of workers engaged in New South Wales sheep farming fell by over a quarter from 11,000 to 8,000. Before the gold rush shepherds were paid £25 a year, but by 1852 they were asking double that amount. The gold relegated agriculture from its position of chief export earner to a subordinate position in the economy and the growth of the export sector of the pastoral industry was severely checked. During the 1850s many farmers turned their attention towards supplying the expanded domestic market for meat, encouraged by high meat prices and discouraged from increasing wool exports by the failure of wool prices to keep pace with rising labour costs. Although this situation did not last when the decline in gold mining allowed wool to re-emerge as Australia's chief export in the 1860s and 1870s, wool growing was never again as important as it had been before 1850.[42]

In the 1850s New Zealand derived some advantages from the Australian gold rush because this increased the demand for her farm exports. But it also experienced some labour losses as men left New Zealand for the diggings and there were further labour shortages with the exploitation of its own gold deposits in the 1860s, which also attracted Australian diggers. The effects of labour losses were not as severe in New Zealand. Its milder climate and absence of natural predators meant its sheep flocks required less close shepherding, and although Australia partly offset shortages of labour in the short term by increased use of fencing, this also represented an extra cost.[43]

But for both countries gold was an important short-term factor that helped increase the population base and extend the long-term business and commercial development acting as a springboard for further diversification of their farm exports. From 1841 to 1879 the North Island city of Auckland was starting to build up a thriving business community, based on land speculation, timber firms, and the need to meet government orders for buildings and supplies required in the efforts to counter the Maori uprisings in the 1860s.[44] But as the mining boom eased there was a need for both countries to find new markets for their farm goods to sustain their economic development. There was no absolute fall in the population of either country, but the rate of demographic growth slowed for all Australia. The development of mining, unlike that of commercial farming, did not provide a great impetus for the rise of services or the agricultural processing industries and, after the initial rushes had subsided, it did not need a large labour force. Although it encouraged national population movements, it was unable to provide a prolonged increase in the growth of exports.

## The Establishment of Transport Networks

Initial internal transport development was a pre-requisite for all countries to enable their wider participation in international trade, and was vital for the export of many other products beside meat. In almost no case can one say that a single commodity was the sole reason why a road was built, a canal dug, or a railway line built. And where this was so it only applied to very short distances where there was a need to undertake a particularly specialised piece of work, like a logging road or a mineral railway track to exploit a particularly remote site distant from existing settlements and where there would otherwise have been no incentive to undertake this investment. The progress of transport systems in all four meat producing regions followed the general pattern of development with the United states taking the lead over South America, Australia and New Zealand. This can be seen in the history of railway construction shown in Table 1.1 below, where the Southern Hemisphere lagged markedly behind North America.

In 1840 the United States already had an effective road, river and canal system for the existing area of settlement, but further extension of that system was necessary to extend the settlement area. The most important long-distance part of the whole system was the Erie Canal, 363 miles long with 82 locks from Albany on the Hudson to Buffalo on Lake Erie. It was authorised by the New York State legislature in 1817 and completed in 1825. From the beginning this highly successful project opened up the prairies of the Midwest. It allowed their farm produce to flow eastward to New York, and manufactured goods to make the return journey westward, thereby giving New York predominance over other Atlantic seaboard ports. This network of waterways was responsible for the initial shift of the population west of the Appalachians, allowing almost 40 per cent of the population to live west of New York, Pennsylvania and the coastal states of the south by 1840. And although the early canals were later overshadowed by the railroads their initial reduction in costs over those of road transport was more dramatic than any subsequent differential between railways and canals.[45]

By 1840 there were over 3,300 miles of inland waterways and total canal investment was 125 million dollars. But although by then every state east of the Mississippi, except Illinois, Michigan, Mississippi and Tennessee had canals, 70 per cent of their total mileage was in Pennsylvania, Ohio and New York. In

*Taste, Trade and Technology*

addition to the major waterways several minor canals had also been built to overcome river obstacles, such as waterfalls or to link two busy rivers, lakes or bays. The expense of canals was greater than turnpikes and their construction, as with the Erie, usually involved the state government. One estimate puts the average direct state share in canal construction costs at 60 per cent and such involvement was not without risk, as in the financial panic of 1837 several, who had borrowed heavily to do this found themselves on the verge of bankruptcy.[46]

### Table 1.1  Public railway mileage, 1830–1910

| Year | United States | Argentina | Uruguay | Australia | New Zealand |
|------|--------------|-----------|---------|-----------|-------------|
| 1830 | 23 | – | – | – | – |
| 1840 | 3,327 | – | – | – | – |
| 1850 | 9,021 | 6[a] | – | – | – |
| 1860 | 30,626 | 24 | 12[b] | 864[c] | – |
| 1870 | 52,922 | 455 | 12 | 950 | 145[d] |
| 1880 | 93,262 | 1,437 | 268 | 3,632 | 1,181 |
| 1890 | 163,697 | 5,750 | 611 | 9,524 | 1,956 |
| 1900 | 193,346 | 10,419 | 1,075 | 13,231 | 2,300 |
| 1910 | 240,293 | 17,220 | 1,546 | 17,429 | 2,790 |

[a] 1857; [b] 1869; [c] 1869; [d] 1873

*Source:* Mitchell, B.R. (1983), *International Historical Statistics: The Americas and Australasia*, Macmillan, London, pp. 656, 568, 661–3, 666. This table excludes purely industrial lines not open to public traffic.

But the American railroad came into existence because poor geographic knowledge caused the first British colonists to site early settlements in what later came to be unfavourable locations with insufficient waterway communication with the interior. The uplands in central Massachusetts were already being abandoned for agricultural use when the railroad arrived in that region in the mid-1830s. Only when in the 1840s a railroad reached into the agricultural belt in the American Midwest could the ports of Boston, Baltimore and Charleston fully exploit their hinterlands. Railway construction, which started in the 1830s, was almost equal to the total length of canals by 1840. Table 1.1 above shows the 1840s saw further railway expansion so that by 1850 there were over 9,000 miles of line. In 1840 railways were mainly restricted to New England and the other northern states. Such early railroad ventures were not typical of the South. In the 1850s another 20,000 miles of rails were added to the system and all the states east of the Mississippi were connected in this decade, although the multiplicity of gauges meant there was a far from completely integrated network in place by the eve of the Civil War.[47] Unlike the canals, the capital for this building was predominantly private and mostly from abroad with public capital contributions in the Antebellum period averaging 25 per cent for the country as a whole.[48]

The Civil War restricted the expansion of the system but after its end in 1865 the completion of the country's railway network was resumed. While it may be argued whether a similar result could have been obtained from an extension of inland water transport in the east, the railway was absolutely essential for a transcontinental link. The 1860s saw the bridging of the east and west coasts when the Union Pacific and the Central Pacific lines met in Utah in 1869, followed by other lines in the 1870s to take further traffic. But there was also heavy building in the Great Plains states. Chicago became the main terminus for lines extending to the centres of the north, west and south. These lines then extended the branches from places like Omaha, Denver, and Minneapolis into the surrounding rich farm country of the region.[49]

In South America, constructed waterways played a smaller part than in the United States in the early extension of agricultural settlement, and the development of railways came later. For Argentina and Uruguay, the main meat producers of the River Plate, the Paraná and Uruguay rivers were the main early routes into the interior in the first part of the nineteenth century. But a generally slower pace of growth and continued lack of infrastructure restricted their use for both freight and passenger transport. In the 1840s this was a country still without roads or bridges, and tracks only on the main routes. At the personal level almost everything was done and supplied from horseback. Horses carried individuals and armies on their travels and beggars even begged from horseback; for these reasons alone horses were as important an item of agricultural output as cattle. Any freight transport was mainly by bullock carts that operated over the two main routes crossing Argentina. The first went west from Buenos Aires through the provinces of San Luis and Mendoza to Chile and the second to the north-west through the provinces of Cordoba, Santiago, Tucumán, Salta and Jujuy to Bolivia. Such journeys were lengthy and expensive, taking weeks or months to complete and adding 40 or 50 per cent to the cost of goods.[50]

Faced with such an unattractive prospect, there was nothing to attract more than a minority of settlers to the very interior provinces. Unlike the United States, throughout the nineteenth century there was comparatively little of the great westward movement of the country's population. This was not only a function of lack of initial infrastructure but also a reflection of the lower resources of the north western and southern provinces. In 1869 the four large eastern pampas provinces of Buenos Aires, Santa Fe, Entre Ríos, and Córdoba contained 54 per cent of the population, and this concentration became greater with 67 per cent in 1895, and 73 per cent living there by 1914.[51] Not surprisingly, most of the railway development, which was largely British financed, was also concentrated in the eastern provinces and few of the early lines extended beyond the pampa. Only in 1882 did an Andean branch of the system reach San Luis, and it was not until 1910 that Argentina and Chile were finally linked by rail. The majority of lines converged on Buenos Aires, and Rosario, the second port of Argentina, was not linked to Buenos Aires by rail until 1886. By 1884 the southern port of Bahía Blanco became the coastal terminus of the important rail system of the south-east region, and grew to become the country's third port through the cattle and wheat traffic. But in the eastern provinces the railways initiated a dramatic transformation with a really substantial advance in the pace of change in the boom years of the 1880s. As can be seen from table 1.1 above, a further 775 more miles of railway were added and towns sprang up along the tracks, particularly at watering places.[52]

Australian transport remained a matter of sea and horse or bullock cart overland by bad roads until the first railway lines in the various colonies were built, starting as tramways in the 1850s but really gathering force from the 1870s. Their principal initial purpose was getting primary produce from mining and timber sites inland to the coast. Without railways the Australian colonies could not possibly have supplied the markets of the world, and Butlin has identified a 'transport crisis' in the 1850s.[53] The first railway tracks were laid near Melbourne in 1854, but even by 1869 there were only 864 miles of railway open to public traffic in the entire sub-continent, as can be seen from Table 1.1 above. But despite this slow start, by 1890 the consensus within the colony was that railways had been built in every place where they were useful, and in quite a few where they were not.[54] Although they did not result in permanent employment, railway building also had the advantage of being one of a variety of projects that brought quite large groups of workers to a locality. In Queensland in 1866 navies brought to the colonies by the contractors Peto, Brassey, and Betts, were paid off with no prospect of further employment at the end of a period of construction on the Ipswich-Toowoomba railway line.[55] Many of these men went to swell the labour force of the cities, as well as those competing for more farming land.

But the resulting transport system was far from being an integrated one. Each state built their own railways, and did so with three different gauges of track. All six states were not finally linked by rail until 1917 and the track problem meant that six trains were needed to cross from East to West from Brisbane to Perth. The track gauges were not finally standardised until 1955, and the North South link from the Pacific to the Antarctic Ocean was not in place until 2003.[56] In some ways the final system matched the rather piecemeal development of a country whose separate states did not reach federation until 1900. In this economy some of the original private light gauge pioneer tracks, like those serving the sugarcane industry in Queensland and some of the logging interests, were made permanent. It was also an expensive system and Jackson urges the need for caution in estimating its short-term effects on the export economy, as there were still many pastoral areas that were still a long way from the nearest station in 1890. Yet in spite of these imperfections, a system was in place by then adequate for the needs of farmers, graziers, miners, and timber men, allowing not only exports, including meat, to reach the coast but also providing an important part of the transport needs of the Australian cities.[57]

New Zealand's transport needs were poorly served in the early part of the century, and only started to make some progress after 1870. Like Australia, the provision of this aspect of social overhead capital relied heavily on government expenditure. The man responsible for the start was Julius Vogel, who was the colony's Treasurer and real power in the colony until the mid-1880s. He had elaborate plans for its development financed by British government loans, largely because the prospects of profit were too uninviting for private finance.[58] Vogel argued that the only way to promote further development was to improve the whole of the colony's totally inadequate transport system. The road system was insufficient and its quality poor, there was less than two hundred miles of railway, and only seven hundred miles of telegraph lines. To fund the necessary improvements he proposed to borrow £10,000,000 over ten years, guaranteed with grants of government land to the lenders. Part of the money was also to be used to promote immigration to provide the necessary labour. Strong political opposition from the provinces was overcome, and the government's eventual borrowings were actually double the amounts first proposed. Although its public spending schemes were characterised by wastefulness and inefficiency, some progress was made before this particular project came to a halt with the failure of the City of Glasgow Bank in 1878.[59] But, as can be seen from Table 1.1 above, a start had been made and in the six years from 1873 to 1880 1,036 miles of railway were built. This was added to in the next ten years when a further 775 miles were built, and by 1910 New Zealand had a total of 2,790 miles of track.

Like Australia's, this was not at all a comprehensive national system, but one that still left large gaps with some districts completely lacking any rail service at all, and left to rely on roads for overland transport. Most lines were in Otago and Canterbury, the two richest provinces of the South Island; but the North Island had only eight unconnected fragments of line. The system remained incomplete 'because of the inability of the Government to borrow adequate sums, and this may be traced chiefly to the unprofitable character of the lines already built.'[60] In fact it was the roads and bridges built in the 1870s that had the greatest effect on regional communication and they accounted for around a third of all public expenditure in that decade.[61] Broadly, the 1870s continued the pattern that had started in the 1840s with New Zealand as an unstable dependent economy, as pointed out by G.F. Simkin in the 1950s.[62] It remained heavily reliant on Britain and London for finance and was also overwhelmingly committed to the British market to absorb its exports of primary products. The diversification of these exports was added to in the 1880s by the introduction of frozen meat, but although it added an extra source of import earnings the appearance of this particular agricultural product did not bring about any immediate shift away from the trading and financial pattern of the previous forty years.

## Urban Development

The development of urban centres was another essential pre-requisite for the start of the international meat business. Towns in America, Australia and New Zealand were among the first markets for the initial commercial meat processing plants. They also provided the necessary technical and financial support services for them, even if they did not always provide large enough domestic markets to justify the subsequent expansion of the industry. The earliest example was the United States where the meat packing industry of the Midwest matured from a simple mercantile operation in the early 1800s in which numerous farmer-packers killed and cured their own animals and sold surplus meat at local market-towns to a concentrated and centralised urban manufacturing industry.[63] The advantage of the US was that with the longest history of extensive European settlement, and abundant natural resources, it was able to develop inland urban centres, whereas the other meat exporters with much smaller populations lagged behind in this branch. Australia and New Zealand's towns were the last to develop, and in their case it was the European market that provided the major initial stimulus for the growth of their meat processing industries. Argentina was different in that Buenos Aires did provide a substantial – and in many ways a much more developed – urban market centre from the early years of the nineteenth century.

The centralisation of the great US meat packing industry around Chicago was in place before the Civil War, but in the mid-1840s there were a number of other cities that were also sizeable meat – mostly pork – processing centres. In that decade Cincinnati was responsible for a quarter of the pork packed in the Midwest and by the late 1850s the two largest pork-packing centres were Cincinnati and St. Louis with 18 and 12 per cent of total output, respectively. Chicago was a relative latecomer to the industry and with just 5.5 per cent of pork output in the 1850s and only by the mid-1860s was it the largest packing point with 28 per cent of output, while Cincinnati and St. Louis had declined to 17 and 5 per cent, respectively. Although in the 1840s there were a number of smaller rural centres like Madison, Chillicothe, Hamilton, Terre Haute, Peoria Quincy and Keokuk the larger cities were much better placed for gaining funds for expansion from the larger number of banks in places like Cincinnati, Louisville and St Louis. Indeed, in Cincinnati in the early 1840s some of the meat packers were also bank directors. The eventual dominance of Chicago was because, with the boom in US railway building from 1844 to 1854, it became the terminus of a number of railroads that gave it good communication with the flourishing hinterland of the western prairies. Its first line was the Galena and Chicago in 1848 and by 1859 railways had linked the city to both the Mississippi and Missouri rivers and there was over 4,500 miles of track entering the city. In 1850 it had a population of 30,000 but a decade later its development as a corn, cattle, hog and lumber market had boosted this to 109,000.[64]

Although Australia also had a relatively high percentage of urban population this was concentrated into a few of the coastal cities. In 1850 these contained 29 per cent of total population with only 5 per cent living in the smaller towns. The large urban concentrations were the main seaports, which before 1850 contained little in the way of manufacturing industry, which remained a small employer. The gold rushes of the 1850s relegated the pastoral industry to second place as the colonies' export earner, and as processing the country's alluvial gold was carried out by primitive methods and simple equipment this gave little stimulus to further industrial development.[65] But wool-growing itself had already provided an initial impetus for marketing, finance and technical support services which later enterprises, including the meat industry, were able to build on and make use of.[66] The gold rushes provided a further stimulus to urbanization and a limited amount of decentralisation. Most of the goldfields were in Victoria whose capital Melbourne (founded in 1835) grew at an average of 15.7 per cent in the 1850s, and by 1861 was the largest city of Australia with a population of 125,000. But also scores of towns sprang up near the diggings, which also made up a large urban population. By the 1871 Census these towns constituted significant markets, as they had a total population of 265,000 against Melbourne's 191,000.[67]

New Zealand was less of an urban centred colony than the Australian colonies and its rapid urban growth seems to have begun somewhat later. Halting beginnings can be seen in the 1840s and in the three decades before 1870 various urban centres were established, though some of them on a rather slender industrial and commercial base. In fact the whole economy was far more rural based than Australia's. As late as the 1890s only 28 per cent of the European population lived in the four main urban centres of Auckland, Wellington, Christchurch and Dunedin.[68] In contrast Australia already had 37 per cent of its population located in urban areas (of over 2,500) persons in the 1840s and by 1901 it had risen to 52 per cent, whereas for the United States in 1900 it was only 40 per cent.[69] Butlin has described the exceptional rate of urbanisation as: 'The outstanding characteristic of Australian economic history, ... overshadowing rural economic development and creating a fundamental contrast with the economic development of other "new" countries.'[70] New Zealand's urban development did provide a necessary network of financial and commercial services to exploit and develop the rural hinterland, but its overall rate of growth in the nineteenth century was probably the slowest of all the four meat-producing areas considered in this chapter.

In South America both Buenos Aires and Montevideo provided the necessary financial links and marketing skills as well as the general business environment to sustain and allow for the development of their countries' meat processing industries. Both cities provided the essential link between the interior regions and their wider European markets. In the earlier part of the nineteenth century the tensions that developed between the colonial capital cities and the interior provinces in the struggle for primacy had slowed down the progress of each set of interests, but these disputes were very largely resolved in both countries by 1870. In addition, both cities provided the necessary sophisticated internal market for something more than the export trade in non-processed, or just poorly processed, agricultural products to develop. Although cattle dominated the economies of both countries in the 1850s, their export trades still consisted of raw and semi-cured hides and dried meat. For anything more to grow out of the very limited livestock product range it was necessary to combine capital, enterprise, and the latest European developments in nineteenth-century technology, and draw upon the resources of the urban centre to exploit the resources of the *estancias* and pastoral hinterlands.


## Notes

1 Mitchell, B.R., 'Statistical Appendix', in C.M. Cipolla (ed.), *The Fontana Economic History of Europe, vol. 4 (2), The Emergence of Industrial Societies* (London, 1973) pp. 747–8.

2 This observation, known as 'Engel's law', was first published in 1857 by the German statistician Ernst Engel (1821–96) in a paper, reprinted in the 1895 *Bulletin of the International Statistical Institute*, 9(1), supplement 1 (1895).

3 Orr, J.B., *Food Health and Income: Report on A Survey of Diet in Relation to Income* (London, 1936), pp. 25, 30, 49, 65–7.

4 Capie, F., 'The Demand for Meat in England and Wales Between the Two World Wars', in D.J. Oddy and D.S. Miller (eds), *Diet and Health in Modern Britain* (London, 1985), pp. 69–74.

5 Hau, M. and J.M. Selig, 'Malnutrition in XIX$^{th}$ Century Alsace', *Journal of European Economic History*, 32(1) (2003): 64–7, 70–2.

6 Anon, 'On the Price of Butcher-Meat, and the Increase of Home Supplies of Cattle and Sheep', *Journal of Agriculture*, 25 (July 1865 to June 1866): 358–61.

7 Collins, E.J.T., 'Rural and Agricultural Change' in E.J.T. Collins (ed.), *The Agrarian History of England and Wales, vol. VII, 1850–1914, Part I* (Cambridge, 2000), pp. 107–16; F.M.L. Thompson, 'Agriculture and Economic Growth in Britain', in P. Mathias and J. Davies (eds), *Agriculture and Industrialization: From the Eighteenth Century to the Present* (Oxford, 1996), pp. 54–5.

8 Edwards, R. and Perren, R., 'A Note on Regional Differences in British Meat Prices, 1825–1865', *Economy and History*, 22(2) (1979): 134.

9 *Journal of the Society of Arts*, 15(737) (4 Jan. 1867): 100; 20(939) (18 Nov. 1870): 4.

10 Reported in Collins, 'Rural and Agricultural Change', p. 109.

11 Abel, W., *Agricultural Fluctuations in Europe from the thirteenth to the twentieth centuries* (London, 1980), pp. 70, 110–11, 170, 178, 188, 210–11.

12 [C] 3600 (PP 1866, vol. XXII), *Second Report of the Cattle Plague Commissioners*, p. ix.

13 Dodd, G., *The Food of London* (London, 1856), p. 227.

14 *The Economist* (23 July 1853), p. 813.

15 *The Economist* (21 Jan. 1865), p. 66.

16 Ferns, H.S., *Argentina* (New York, 1969), pp. 98–9; J. Lynch, 'From Independence to National Organization' in L. Bethell (ed.), *Argentina Since Independence* (Cambridge, 1993), pp. 40–1.

17 Lynch, 'From Independence to National Organization', pp. 559–61.

18 Smith, P.H., *Politics and Beef in Argentina: Patterns of Conflict and Change* (New York, 1969), p. 11.

19 Hadfield, W., *Brazil and the River Plate in 1869: By William Hadfield, Showing the Progress of those Countries since his Former Visit in 1853* (London, 1869). See the advertisement pages at the end of the book.

20 Stewart, I.A.D. (ed.), *From Caledonia to the Pampas: Two Accounts of Early Scottish Emigrants to the Argentine* (East Linton, 2000).

21 Taylor, A.M., 'Peopling the Pampa: On the Impact of Mass Migration to the River Plate, 1870–1914', *Explorations in Economic History*, 34 (1997): 100, 104–7.

22 Sánchez-Albornoz, N., 'The Population of Latin America, 1850–1930', in L. Bethell (ed.), *The Cambridge History of Latin America, vol. IV, c.1870 to 1930* (Cambridge, 1986), pp. 121–3.

23 Hadfield, p. 5.

24 Hutchinson, T.J., *The Paraná; with incidents of the Paraguayan War and South American recollections from 1861 to 1868* (London, 1868), pp. 176–86.

25 Díaz Alejandro, C.F., *Essays on the Economic History of the Argentine Republic* (New Haven 1970), pp. 421, 424; Sánchez-Albornoz, 'The Population of Latin America, 1850–1930', p. 122.

26 Oddone, J.A., 'The Formation of Modern Uruguay. c.1870–1930' in L. Bethell (ed.), *The Cambridge History of Latin America, vol.. V, c.1970 to 1930* (Cambridge 1986), pp. 453–6.

27 Consulate-General of Uruguay, *The Republic of Uruguay; Its Geography, History, Rural Industries, Commerce, and General Statistics* (London, 1883), p. 2; M.H.J. Finch, *A Political Economy of Uruguay Since 1870* (London, 1981), pp. 24–5; Sánchez-Albornoz, 'The Population of Latin America, 1850–1930', p. 122.

28 Hudson, P., 'English Emigration to New Zealand, 1839–1850: Information Diffusion and Marketing a New World', *Economic History Review*, 54(4) (2001): 680–98.

29 Lloyd Prichard, M.F., *An Economic History of New Zealand to 1939* (London: 1970), pp. 36–7, 132, 140–43; J. Graham, 'Settler Society' in W.H. Oliver, with B.R. Williams (eds), *The Oxford History of New Zealand* (Oxford, 1981), pp. 116–17.

30 Sorrenson, M.P.K., 'Maori and Pakeha', in W.H. Oliver, with B.R. Williams (eds), *The Oxford History of New Zealand* (Oxford, 1981), p. 169.

31 Sinclair, K., *A History of New Zealand* (London, 1980), pp. 145–7.

32 King, M., 'Between Two Worlds', in W.H. Oliver, with B.R. Williams (eds), The *Oxford History of New Zealand* (Oxford, 1981), p. 280; Condliffe, J.B., *New Zealand in the Making: A Study of Economic and Social Development* (London, 1936), pp. 289–90.

33 Davidson, N.B., *European Farming in Australia: An Economic History of Australian Farming* (Amsterdam, 1981), p. 116; R.V. Jackson, *Australian Economic Development in the Nineteenth Century* (Canberra, 1977), p. 29.

34 Jackson, R.V., 'The Colonial Economies: An Introduction', *Australian Economic History Review*, 18(1) (1998): 12–14.

35 Robertson, R.M., *History of the American Economy* (New York, 1973), pp. 227–8.

36 Census of Canada; N. Macdonald, *Canada: Immigration and Colonization, 1841–1903* (Aberdeen, 1966), pp. 182–7, 271–2.

37 West, E., 'The American Frontier', in C.A Milner II, C.A. O'Connor, and M.A. Sandweiss (eds), *The Oxford History of the American West* (New York, 1994), pp. 115–18, 123, 142–7.

38 Nugent, W., 'Comparing Wests and Frontiers', in C.A Milner II, C.A. O'Connor, and M.A. Sandweiss (eds), *The Oxford History of the American West* (New York, 1994), pp. 811, 813.

39 Davidson, pp. 95, 132; Gardner, W.J., 'A Colonial Economy' in W.H. Oliver, with B.R. Williams (eds), *The Oxford History of New Zealand* (Oxford, 1981), pp. 62–3; G.G.F. Simkin, *The Instability of a Dependent Economy: Economic Fluctuations in New Zealand 1840–1914* (Oxford, 1951), p. 25.

40 Maddock, R. and I.W. Maclean, 'Introduction: The Australian Economy in the Very Long Run', in R. Maddock and I.W. Maclean (eds), *The Australian Economy in the Long Run* (Cambridge, 1987), p. 10; Graham, 'Settler Society', p. 125.

41 Condliffe, pp. 108–15; P. Michael, *Settlers and the Agrarian Question: Foundations of Capitalism in Colonial Australia* (Cambridge, 1984), pp. 128–34.

42 Davidson, pp. 95–6, 119–120; Jackson, *Australian Economic Development in the Nineteenth Century*, pp. 10–11.

43 Lloyd Prichard, pp. 94–6.

44 Stone, R.C.J., *Makers of Fortune: A Colonial Business Community and its Fall* (Dunedin, 1973), pp. 5–28.

45 Fogel, R.W., *Railroads and Economic Growth: Essays in Econometric History* (Baltimore, 1964), pp. 8–9; M. Walsh, *The American Frontier Revisited* (London, 1981), p. 57.

46 Boorstin, D.J., *American Railroads* (Chicago, 1961), pp. 6–7.

47 Robertson, pp. 147–51.

48 Fishlow, A., *American Railroads and the Transformation of the Ante-Bellum Economy* (Cambridge, Mass.,1965), pp. 65 ff.

49 Robertson, pp. 271–5; A.M. Johnson and B.E. Supple, *Boston Capitalists and Western Railroads: A Study in the Nineteenth Century Railroad Process* (Cambridge, Mass., 1967), pp. 190–91.

50 Lynch, J., 'The River Plate Republics from Independence to the Paraguayan War', in L. Bethell (ed.), *The Cambridge History of Latin America, vol.. III, From Independence to c.1870* (Cambridge, 1985) pp. 618–19.

51 Díaz Alejandro, p. 27.

52 Wright, W.R., *British-Owned Railways in Argentina: Their Effect on Economic Nationalism 1854–1948* (Austin, 1974), pp. 52–4.

53 Butlin, N.G., *Investment in Australian Economic Development 1861–1900* (London, 1964), pp. 300–305.

54. de Garis, B.K., '1890–1900', in F.K. Crowley (ed.), *A New History of Australia* (Melbourne, 1974), p. 220.

55 Kingston, B., *The Oxford History of Australia, vol. 3, 1860–1900, Glad, Confident Morning* (Melbourne, 1988), pp. 33, 44–5, 46.

56 *The Times* (19 Sept. 2003), p. 23.

57 Jackson, *Australian Economic Development in the Nineteenth Century*, pp. 86–90.

58 Gardner, 'A Colonial Economy', pp. 71–2.

59 Sinclair, pp. 152–62.

60 Condliffe, p. 38, quoting H.D. Bedford, 'Monetary Difficulties of Early Colonisation in New Zealand', *Economic Journal* (June 1916).

61 Gardner, 'A Colonial Economy', p. 72.

62 Simkin.

63 Walsh, M., *The Rise of the Midwestern Meat Packing Industry* (Lexington, 1982), pp. 7, 14.

64 Ibid., pp. 20–22, 30–31, 50–51, 94–6; Fishlow, p. 104.

65 Jackson, *Australian Economic Development in the Nineteenth Century*, pp. 7–8.

66 Ville, S., 'Business Development in Colonial Australia', *Australian Economic History Review*, 38(1) (1998): 26–9.

67 Frost, L., 'The Contribution of the Urban Sector to Australian Economic Development before 1914', *Australian Economic History Review*, 38(1) (1998): 45–6.

68 Olson, E., 'Towards a New Society', in W.H. Oliver, with B.R. Williams (eds), *The Oxford History of New Zealand* (Oxford, 1981), p. 254.
69 Jackson, *Australian Economic Development in the Nineteenth Century*, pp. 93–4.
70 Butlin, p. 6.

# Chapter 2

# Technical Advance

Three complementary types of technical advance were required to allow the industry to grow from a position of insignificance in 1840 to the size and international importance it had assumed by 1914. In some ways these changes – like the improvement of livestock and product quality – were specific to the industry itself, but in other respects – like the introduction of low-cost long-distance transport – they were technical changes that had a much wider application.

## Farm and Livestock Improvement

In all four main production regions the improvement of livestock quality was necessary to meet the rising European demand for imported meat. This involved the import of improved breeds of sheep and cattle, chiefly from Britain where livestock improvement had been underway from the mid-eighteenth century. In some parts of northern Europe, notably Holland, parts of Germany and northern France similar improvements in the quality of livestock also took place, but it is significant that they did not become exporters of improved farm livestock to the same extent as Britain in the nineteenth century. However, the livestock improvement movement did not take off immediately as it was at first held back by other factors.

There were no indigenous cattle in the Americas, but by 1840 a variety of cattle had become established, based on animals shipped from different parts of Europe dating back to the earliest – typically the long-horned Spanish cattle found in the southern United States and South America – brought in by colonists from Southern Europe in the sixteenth century. These animals – sometimes referred to as 'razorbacks' – were large boned and rangy and suited to life on unimproved natural pastures. Settlement of French Canada and the British thirteen colonies in the seventeenth and eighteenth centuries saw other varieties of farm animals introduced by settlers from northern Europe who imported examples of their local breeds. But all these early introductions were either draught or dairy animals of mixed or uncertain ancestry.[1]

In the 1840s the great plains of Buenos Aires supported some 3 million cattle and they were the prime wealth of the province. But these were animals of inferior grade, raised on the open range under the care of a few herdsmen and yielded hides and coarse salt meat; there was no need for any breed improvement as that was all the market demanded.[2] The same lack of market opportunity held back livestock improvement in North America. Writing as late as 1878 James Macdonald observed that the production of good quality United States beef was confined to a comparatively small area of the county – the northern states of Illinois, Kentucky, Indiana and Ohio. After the Civil War these few states began to supply good quality meat to the Eastern cities like Philadelphia, Boston and New York, but demand from these places was still limited.[3] However, the beef from the long-horned Spanish cattle down in Texas, as well as that from the 'common cattle' of America was not the sort to find acceptance either here or in the British market. The percentage of bone and gristle to meat was too high, 'and the quality of that meat too coarse, to admit … American beef into the … markets of Great Britain'.[4]

Contemporaries agreed from the 1850s that the South American cattle were in need of improvement and from the mid-1850s a few Argentine *estancia* owners imported English cattle, mainly shorthorn bulls, to improve the native breeds. But such improvement was limited by the fact that in the 1850s the most valuable cattle product was the hide, followed by its grease and tallow. Even as late as 1867 it was reported that 'not long ago the cattle on the River Plate were prized for their hides alone, the flesh being wasted or disposed of at nominal prices'.[5] As shorthorn crosses did not produce a very much heavier weight of hide, they hardly justified the extra cost of introducing thoroughbred blood into the herds. The main advantage of thoroughbred cattle was that they produced more meat, but as this was a characteristic that also required conditions of domestication and high feeding, their introduction into the semi-wild herds of the Argentine pampas did not confer any particular advantage in an environment where animals found their food as best they could. Even though by the 1860s Buenos Aires was a city of 200,000 people and had developed well beyond a frontier town, and possessed substantial public buildings, theatres, opera house and concert hall, club houses, a cathedral and churches, there was at that time still little demand for better quality meat. Quantity and low price were supposed to make up for the lack of any real quality, although one writer did prophesy that 'the call from Europe for meat supplies, must sooner or later induce the possessors of well-bred herds to take steps to put their neats [steers] into a condition that will give beef of a quality more or less 'up to the mark' of European requirements'.[6] Although breed and cattle type improvement was theoretically possible in the 1860s – after all it had been achieved in Britain where breeders believed they were still in the process of further improvement – farmers overseas still faced a variety of local constraints that prevented the process from being generally accepted.

The first Shorthorn bulls and the first wire fences were brought into Argentina in 1844, and ten years later the breed was relatively popular. Once the wire fences made it easy to isolate improved animals from the common *criollo*, other breeds became more popular. Herefords and other cattle, Lincoln and Leicester sheep, mares and stallions followed.[7] But even at this point, the demand for good quality meat was still held back until the mid-1860s. This was not just because of local consumer inertia – it was also a consequence of the system under which the land was farmed. In mammals the bones are laid down first, then the muscles and finally the fat; and it is this last stage that produces meat that is tender and tastes well. Up to the 1860s the scarcity of good quality Argentine beef was caused by a lack of sufficient forage crops, which meant that cattle could not be finished with a stint of paddock feeding to produce the type of high quality meat that was veined or marbled with fat. Even when cattle were kept on the best of pastures, if they were fed on that alone they did not put on much fat and produced a meat said to lack richness, flavour, and delicacy. There was little serious investigation of ways to find good supplies of forage crops. In most cases the usual practice was to take separate crops of maize and wheat until soil fertility dropped so low that cultivation was unprofitable. When that point was reached the land was laid down to lucerne or alfalfa (*Medicago sativa*) which, although it was a legume and capable of restoring fertility for grain growing, was mown for hay year after year until the land was fully exhausted. When that point was reached it dropped out of cultivation and the farmer moved on to find fresh land; in the absence of any proper system of crop rotation, as a general rule the land appears to have been 'mined' rather than farmed. This system also meant the few cattle ranchers who produced good forage and had better managed paddocks on their own farms, and also used imported shorthorn and Hereford bulls to improve their herds found very little demand for the next generation of cross bull calves from other farmers. Once they had selected out those they needed for their own purposes, they were compelled to castrate the rest because there was no secondary market for these animals among the farmers who were not direct importers of British thoroughbred bulls.[8]

A further help to local agricultural improvement came in 1866 when the *Sociedad Rural Argentina* was formed. It was begun by a group of large *estancia* proprietors modelled on European and United States agricultural improvement societies first started in England. It concerned itself in all aspects of the country's farming such as breed improvement and compiling its herd and stud books, managing the country's great cattle and horse shows, as well as promoting the improvement of both fodder and arable crops. In 1876 the first unsuccessful shipment of frozen meat to Britain was conducted under the auspices of the *Sociedad Rural.*[9] Under the stimulus of supplying better quality beef to Europe, alfalfa spread rapidly in the two decades before the First World War. This crop greatly improved the productivity of the light porous soils of the middle Pampa that were unable to provide really good quality pasture. Normally four to seven acres of native grasses were required to support a full-grown steer, but just one and a half acres of alfalfa were needed to do the same.[10]

The export of British pedigree animals for herd and flock improvement was of course not only to Argentina: the three other meat-producing regions also took them. But as Argentina concentrated very heavily on producing beef for export, South America became the major destination for British pedigree cattle. This trade with the continent was built up slowly from the 1860s, reaching its peak from the 1890s so that South America became the chief buyer of British pedigree cattle after 1900. In the late nineteenth century the bulk of Argentine cattle were of the native type, partly improved. But the work done by breeders after 1890 largely replaced them with prime pedigree herds by 1910. These were so good that they contained animals able to produce chilled beef of a quality good enough to replace the dwindling supplies from the United States.[11] The data reproduced in Table 2.1 below compiled by H. Schwartz detailing progress in Argentina's main cattle producing provinces shows that very little had been done in this direction before the Argentine debt crisis of 1890. Apart from Buenos Aires, where the number of improved animals was still only 50 per cent in 1895, producers elsewhere had barely started to breed cattle for meat, not hides, before the early 1900s.

**Table 2.1 Distribution of cattle, and ratio of crossbred[a] to native cattle, by region of Argentina, 1895 and 1908**

| Region | 1895 | | 1908 | |
|---|---|---|---|---|
| | % of total cattle | Ratio of crossbred | % of total cattle | Ratio of crossbred |
| Buenos Aires | 38.9 | 1.0 | 35.6 | 9.8 |
| Santa Fe | 14.0 | 0.2 | 11.7 | 0.7 |
| Entre Rios | 11.6 | 0.2 | 10.8 | 1.4 |
| Córdoba | 9.5 | 0.1 | 9.1 | 0.2 |
| Corienntes | 14.5 | 0.02 | 14.7 | 1.0 |
| Rest of Argentina | 11.5 | - | 18.1 | - |

[a] The larger the number of crossbred animals the more complete the transition to beef.

*Source:* Schwartz, H., *In the Dominions of Debt: Historical Perspectives on Dependent Development* (Ithaca, 1989), p. 218.

E.H. Whetham's pioneering article on this trade shows that over the whole of the nineteenth century the largest numbers of pedigree cattle were probably sold to farmers in the northern states of the United States. Here there was greater interest in livestock improvement at an earlier date. The precise reasons are difficult to pinpoint, but it is likely to have had more to do with its earlier and faster rate of population increase, its more rapid urban growth, and higher income levels. Together with the effect of transport improvements in opening up the West, all these things widened the commercial opportunities for better systems of livestock farming. The number of animals exported from the United Kingdom 'not for food' increased in the 1880s and was reinforced by the extension in the number of British breed societies formed and herd and flock books established.[12] Early British exports of improved animals to the United States seem to have been Shorthorns. This is not surprising as the first breed society to be started in Britain was for Shorthorns in the 1820s and their first herd-book for the whole breed began in 1846. The Hereford society did not start until the 1840s, and their herd book began in 1875. But some United States farmers – like John Sanderson of Bernardston,

Massachusetts – were so enthusiastic about the commercial prospects of the Shorthorn breed, that they produced their own improved animals before the 1860s.[13]

The popularity of breeds varied and some were seen as being better suited to particular conditions and also, as the output of the industry became more sophisticated and varied, producing meat best suited to a particular purpose. In the United States the Shorthorn was the most popular and had the attraction of producing the heaviest carcases of good meat. However part of this was appearance, as a Shorthorn was also considered to look larger than a Hereford of the same weight. But Herefords were more popular than either Aberdeen Angus or Galloway cattle. The introduction of the Aberdeen Angus breed into the United States had been comparatively late, though it showed a marked readiness to fatten and mature earlier. The Galloways were always considered to be slower to fatten, and reach a smaller size than any of the other beef breeds, which no doubt explains why they were consigned to fourth place in the popularity of breeds.[14] But popularity had also something to do with the vigour of the marketing campaigns and relative levels of activity of the breed societies and individual livestock breeders in the United Kingdom.[15]

The improvement of sheep types was not in the first instance for meat, but for wool. The growing European demand and limited home supplies of this product was felt in all four major sheep producing countries, though probably least in the United States where the overwhelming commercial advantages were in cattle farming. Like cattle, the first unimproved sheep were introduced in the sixteenth century by the Spanish in South America and were known as *criollo*. These animals produced only coarse low value wool, so from the 1820s some Argentine *estancia* owners started to import Spanish Merinos to improve its quality. The almost total removal of English wool import duties provided a ready export market for the product. In the 1830s there were further imports of Merinos from Europe and the United States, and from Germany Saxony breeds were also imported.[16] At the same time sheep improvements took place in Uruguay, where in the 1830s improved French sheep were introduced, followed in 1840 by improved German Merinos (the latter known as Negretti), and French Rambouillet sheep in 1852. In addition, by the 1870s some English breeds such as Lincolns, Romney Marsh and Southdowns had also appeared, and as the Southdowns were considered better for mutton than wool they tended to be kept on holdings near to large meat markets.[17] But all of these new breeds demanded more capital and labour intensive methods of farming with improvement of pampas grasses, the fencing of fields and the construction of shelter and shearing sheds. Indeed, it seems that the improvements in wool production gathering pace from the 1840s were to predate the similar improvements for beef production that came about from the 1870s. But by the 1860s there were certainly strong contrasts emerging between the two branches of livestock farming.

In general, the sheep *estancias* were to be found nearer to Buenos Aires and the cattle *estancias* occupied lands further distant. Some of them contained both cattle and sheep, and there was a gradual encroachment of sheep on what had previously been pure cattle lands. The *estancia* plant consisted of the *estancia* house, with horse and animal *corrales*, and *puestos* or stations looked after by a herdsman or *puestero*. On these tracts of land the herdsmen looked after a flock of sheep or herd (*rodeo*) of cattle and lived in primitive residences that varied from an earth hut upwards to a more substantial wood cabin. On the cattle *estancias* the true type of the pampas gaucho was still to be found, a type rarely encountered in the sheep districts by the 1860s. They were men familiar with the plain on which they were born and lived, without ever having known or seen anything beyond it. These characters – generally single men – had no need for any sort of roofed accommodation, and their horse gear was their sole furniture. They spent the working day superintending the herd from their horse and rarely knew any other bed than their *recado* (saddle) stretched on the ground with their *ponchos* (cloaks) and saddlecloths as covering. On the cattle *estancias* there was a *capataz* or overseer to a certain number of *puestos*, and a general manager or *mayordomo* in charge of all. On the sheep *estancias* the flocks varied from twenty to a hundred thousand animals, and on the cattle *estancias* the rodeos varied from a few hundred to a few thousand semi-wild longhorn cattle. These animals were generally small to medium size, and of varied quality, according to the locality and nature of the terrain where they were reared and kept. In some districts, where the pasture quality was better, the cattle were larger in size and yielded a heavier hide and more grease, but they were usually poor milking animals.[18] In the 1860s, in spite of one or two early pioneers, the management of most estates still remained very far from the niceties of breed improvements.

In the context of herd and flock improvement it is also necessary to mention the use of wire fencing and improved fodder. The first requirement of all ranchers and estate owners was to maintain the effect of introducing animals from improved bloodlines. On the vast cattle ranges and sheep pastures of all newly settled countries secure fences were essential to prevent mixing of livestock from those estate owners who had invested in best pedigree European stud animals with those who had not made the investment. Because it fixed boundaries wire fencing also defined the precise limits of ownership, especially if it was reinforced by additional investment in improved fodder cultivation. But on unimproved *estancias* the intermingling did not matter as herds were sorted out and branded at calving times. However, fencing was an expense, although once undertaken it would theoretically cut labour costs by reducing the numbers of shepherds and herdsmen. Its effectiveness also depended on the extent of predators and other vermin. In Australia dingoes and rabbits after 1860 were problems.[19] For it to be successful, farmers also had the cost of clearing fenced land of competing wildlife.

Improvement in fodder required fencing and modern systems of farm management. On the *estancias* and ranches of the 1850s little attention was paid to improving the productivity of land that was in plentiful supply. But as increased population put limits on its availability, the pastoral industry needed to pay greater attention to more intensive systems of land management. The earliest advances in the nineteenth century seem to have been in the use of the legume alfalfa. The plant was first taken from Europe to South America and spread to the United States after 1850.[20] It was perhaps used most extensively in South America, and by the early twentieth century some Argentine *estancia* had tracts of over 60,000 acres sown to this legume.[21] In Australia where farmers soon realised that it was not profitable to feed sheep or cattle during droughts, there was comparatively little done to improve fodder crops, apart from fencing to prevent rabbit damage. Some perennial rye grass and white clover were introduced after 1900 and small areas of oats were grown in the south.[22] In New Zealand it was only after the 1890s that farmers became aware of the need to introduce more scientific systems of farming to land where the initial high fertility had disguised haphazard management. In this they were assisted by the Department of Agriculture set up in 1891, which worked closely with local associations to introduce new grass types and better use of fertilizer.[23] In the United States the great livestock feed of the nineteenth century was maize, a native plant of the Americas. Early on this had been fed to pigs but the prime zone for the production of good cattle lay between the 36th and 43rd parallels, and had more to do with this region being relatively free from the climatic extremes of the areas to the north and south.[24]

As all the standard histories of the meat industry argue, the major impetus to breed improvement was provided by the ocean transport of refrigerated meat.[25] For North America this began in the 1870s, and as refrigerated meat was accompanied by a trade in exports of live US beef cattle for slaughter in Europe, this trade also gave an added incentive to breed improvement. But improvement also became a universal process for all four regions and encompassing all types of meat producing animals. It continued throughout the rest of the nineteenth century and up to the present day in a continuous attempt to improve meat quality and increase wool and dairy output by widening the phenotype gene pool. In addition to doing this by going back to the origins of breeds in Europe, a cross trade of improved animals from the United States and other countries also developed and in some cases in the twentieth century Asian breeds were imported whenever they were considered to have characteristics farmers in other continents wanted to build into their herds and flocks.

In North and South America both the home market and the export trade dictated that cattle were most in demand, but in Australia and New Zealand where sheep predominated, nineteenth-century pedigree imports were mainly breeds famed either for particular wool, or else their lamb- and mutton-producing characteristics. There was certainly a need for improvement at the start of the long distance trade in meat products in the late-1870s, and all observers commented on the generally poor quality of the livestock in the United States and other countries. As we have already seen, James Macdonald, when sent to the United States by the *Scotsman* newspaper to report on the meat situation there, was very pessimistic about the quality of a large percentage of the American beef animals. When he returned to Edinburgh he had strong doubts as to whether sufficient quantities of meat suitable for European tastes would ever be forthcoming, at least in the short term.[26] It was these doubts that were central to the whole breed improvement in North and South America, but breed improvement itself also depended on better fodder crops, fenced pastures, and modern transport systems.

But as improvement was undertaken in the next quarter of a century the British versions of the various pedigree livestock societies and herd books were followed by overseas versions run as entirely separate and independent entities by local breeders. This overseas activity was partly driven by the policies of all the original breed societies in the United Kingdom to close their herd books at various dates to any animal born thereafter whose sire or dam had not been registered. A good example of this is the Hereford breed of cattle, which was immensely popular as a beef-raising animal in North and South America, as well as Australia and New Zealand. It was natural for overseas breeders to be just as aware of the desirability and price advantage of selling high quality thoroughbred livestock, and they decided to take advantage of this for themselves. In addition, they sometimes introduced further refinements to the original breed whenever they believed they could make it more suited to local conditions.

As it was the most popular breed, a great deal of status attached to a prime Hereford animal, and the breed's first herd book was begun in 1846 and then the Hereford Herd Book Society was founded in 1878. The Society set about stressing the good beef forming qualities as well as the familiar red hide and white face colour characteristics of this English West Midlands shorthorn breed, and closed its herd book in 1886, eight years after the Society's inauguration. Thereafter entries of cattle into its herd books were confined to those whose sire and dam had been recorded in previous volumes. The earliest Herefords were exported to the United States in 1817, and spread through Canada, Mexico and South America.[27] They arrived in Tasmania from England in 1826 and the Australian mainland in 1827. They were a popular choice of beef animal in Australia and more Herefords were imported from England, and later from the United States and Canada. In 1885 the first meeting of Australian Hereford breeders was held and the Australian Herd Book Society was formed to record the breeding of Australian Herefords and published the first volume of the Australian Herd Book in 1890.[28]

In the United States Hereford societies were established in more than one state. Although considered an excellent beef animal there as well, the horns of the Hereford were thought a disadvantage by some American cattlemen who sought out polled examples of the breed as easier to manage. In most countries the horned and polled examples were both simply referred to as Herefords but in the United States and Australia the polled animals developed as a separate breed. One of the pioneer breeders was Warren Gammon of Iowa who began in 1900 with a small number of polled sports selected from his own herd and advertised for similar animals among other United States breeders. By 1907 the polled breed had increased to the extent that it was possible to start an American register of the polled version of the breed. Interest in it spread and in 1920 the first polled Herefords were imported into Australia, where in 1933 a separate Australian Poll Hereford Society was also established.[29]

**Improvements in Traditional Meat Preservation**

Important though the above factors were for herd and flock improvement, they were permissive; the main development driving the whole process was technical change in the meat processing industry. In 1840 the export of meat was possible in three ways, either as live animals, or as dried meat, or as salted meat. All three methods had disadvantages. The first was only possible overland for moderate distances and required frequent stops and some time at the end of the journey for animals to recover and often regain weight walked off on the journey. If they were transported by sea for immediate sale this was again only possible for shorter distances as the cramped conditions on board nineteenth century sailing ships limited numbers carried and the length of voyage. The few breeding animals before 1800 that managed to survive the rigours of a voyage of some weeks to the New World, or some months to Australia and New Zealand, needed considerable time to recover from their ordeal. In the 1840s and 1850s there was a small short-distance trade of cattle, sheep, and pigs to Britain from Spain, Portugal, France, Belgium, Holland, the north German states, Denmark and Sweden.[30] The main feature of this very short distance sea trade was to use the ports as collecting centres for animals that had been driven there overland from distance. Once in the port environs they would then recover, or perhaps be held for some time until British livestock prices were right before the final leg of the journey. By the 1850s and with the general use of steamships, the voyage to any British port would be only a few days even from the furthest European port. But even so it was not unknown for some of these animals to be subjected to further feeding once landed.[31]

Every meat-preserving technique employed in the days before refrigeration was less than perfect, and displayed various disadvantages. Whatever preservation method was used meant some loss of quality over fresh meat, and hence a lower level of consumer acceptability and consequently fetched a lower price. The best example of this was the main beef export from South America before refrigeration, which was called *charqui*, or *tasajo*, by the American Indian, and was also known as biltong in South Africa. Europeans referred to it as jerked beef. Essentially this is a dry salting, or dry curing technique.[32] In South America this traditional product was prepared by slicing the best meat and placing it in a heap with salt; after some time it was taken out and hung on rails in the open air to dry and then covered with tarpaulins until ready for shipment.[33] This product had the advantage that it kept indefinitely in hot humid climates and was therefore easily transported and remained popular until the arrival of refrigeration. Prior to refrigeration the chief products of the South American slaughtering plants, or *saladeros*, remained the hides and tallow, which were meant to cover the cost of purchasing and processing the animal plus a small profit. Any increase in that profit came from bones, hoof and flesh.[34]

All meat preserved in this way loses much of its original quality; it is dry, unpalatable and its appearance is unappetising to Western European consumers. It does have the advantage that it will keep almost indefinitely in a hot climate, but will turn mouldy and putrefy if allowed to become damp. Various forms of this type of air-dried meat have been used by primitive societies for centuries. In some cases the process has been carried out over fires, giving rise to smoked meat. This form was known about in Europe and used to preserve and also add flavour to items like sausages, bacon and fish. But the largely air dried product of the American Indian, where strips of meat were exposed to the sun, sometimes known as pemmican, met with no favour in Western cultures.[35]

In the nineteenth century dried meat had only two export markets, in Brazil and Cuba, to feed to the slaves of the two great slave-owning economies of South America.[36] But it was a trade that led nowhere as this group of consumers had nothing in common with those in Europe. Their cultural background was different, they were not direct purchasers, and the slave and plantation owners responsible for feeding them did so with the cheapest foodstuffs. This was in all senses a captive market completely lacking in consumer choice among alternatives and no possibility of expansion through rising monetary incomes. It was also limited in size and declining in 1850 when British warships stopped the import of slaves from Africa. At that time the Brazilian slave population numbered well over a million, and the Cuban approximately 325,000. Its final demise came when slavery was abolished in Cuba in 1886 and Brazil in 1888.[37] Thereafter modestly rising income levels for even the poorest ex-slaves eventually released them from their former reliance on this item of diet. As late as 1910 Uruguay slaughtered 537,000 cattle for *charqui*, but in 1916 only 61,000 by which time the arrival of canning and freezing plants had finally banished the industry from Uruguay to the interior of Brazil.[38]

An early attempt to overcome the various disadvantages of the salted product was started in Uruguay at the Paysandu *saladero* in May 1865, using a technique developed by Professor John Morgan, President of the Dublin Royal College of Surgeons.[39] Immediately after slaughter the chest of the animal was opened and incisions made in each side of the heart to empty it of blood. A pipe was then inserted into the aorta and water pumped in under pressure to wash out the blood vessels followed by a mixture of brine and saltpetre around the entire circulatory system, including the smaller blood vessels so that the whole of the carcase contained this preserving fluid. In fact the method still involved the use of salt but here it was applied internally rather than the traditional method of external application. Afterwards the carcase was cut up to allow some of the water to evaporate and then placed in a current of warm air in a drying chamber. There was perhaps little that was really revolutionary about the method, as the consumer was still presented with salt meat, but it was claimed that it was more acceptable to the European customer than *charqui*. As the whole process was claimed to take no more than ten minutes for an ox, and less for smaller animals, it took less time than traditional dry salting but it did need more sophisticated equipment though none of any high order. The pressure required to force the brine and saltpetre into the carcase as well as the circulation of air in the drying chamber required either water or steam power, whereas the traditional methods needed neither. In this respect it took the *salederos* into the nineteenth century and beyond their former reliance simply on human muscle and natural warmth. Experimental consignments of 225 tons of the meat were sent from Paysandu to Liverpool in 1865 and 1866 where it was said to have had a ready sale. One commentator described it as 'inviting and palatable' and bearing a close resemblance to English corned beef – something that could never be said of the *charqui*.[40]

The salting and packing of meat in wooden casks and tubs was another form of preservation, but one not used by traditional societies who did not possess the tools and skills necessary for coopering. There was some trade in salted meat and it was traded internationally in larger quantities than dried meat. But though the quality of this product was slightly superior to dried meat it was still not highly regarded by most Europeans. Meat – usually beef and pork – preserved in this way was mostly pickled in brine, which did keep it moist but in some cases pork was packed in boxes between layers of dry salt. In the 1860s whenever the Chicago packing industry had a surplus of hog products it sent meat rubbed in salt to be packed loose in the hold of a ship to London or Liverpool between layers of dry salt. By the time the meat reached its destination it would be fully cured and often referred to as 'bacon'.[41] During the American Civil War great quantities of United States bacon were still exported to Britain and sold in great quantities at low prices. About three-quarters of this salt meat went to Liverpool and the rest to London. Generally the less salt the product the better it sold. Thus American barrelled port was not so salt as the bacon, which was called 'junk' and went for very low prices.[42] American beef was also very salt, and for this reason totally unacceptable to the British civilian consumer, and was purchased by the army and navy. In addition, large amounts of salted meat from Australia and South America were sent to Britain where they were described as 'a perfect drug on the market'.[43]

**Canning and Meat Extracts**

Meat canning was the final preservation method. Here we know most about the problems facing navies, though it is unlikely that those for merchant vessels on long voyages were very different. For navy rations on board ship, canned meat certainly represented a marked improvement over the traditional methods of preserving meat by pickling it in casks of brine at navy victualling yards. For all navies the main problem was one of getting contractors to maintain consistently good quality using traditional methods of preservation. This was also noticed in all sectors of the civilian meat industry, as when new technologies were first used here they too were initially just as inconsistent and unreliable as the traditional techniques. Part of the problem was caused by contractors using cheap foodstuffs to try and cut costs and increase their profits, but there were also technical difficulties, as well as providing adequate storage for provisions once on board ship. In the seventeenth century ships frequently had to return to port because there was no (edible) food on board to consume, and Samuel Pepys blamed the abuses of victualling contractors for much of the poor quality of shipboard food.[44] In the eighteenth century the quality of ship provisioning was improved and the administrators of the British Navy's Victualling Board which had since been set up were conscientious men who tried to raise the standard of naval victualling in an age when technology for preparing and preserving victuals in their original state for prolonged periods was non-existent. But as technology was against them there were still complaints. In the Seven Years' War (1756–63) British naval officers still complained that the Victualling Board had not taken enough care in packing salted beef, though the amounts of condemned pork and beef that had to be returned from sea as being unfit to eat or drink were less than for any other kind of foodstuffs, with the predictable exception of brandy.[45]

There was thus a ready market waiting for any improvements on the current technology. But in many respects it was similar to that for South American dried beef. Like the Cuban and Brazilian slaves, the ultimate consumers the ships' crews had no direct say in what they were fed, although like the slave-owners their employers, whether the navy or merchant ship owners, wanted a product that would maintain their employees' physical efficiency. Although the principles of food canning were known about and employed from the end of the eighteenth century, it had made limited commercial progress by 1840 and was mainly used to produce shipboard rations for the British and French navies. The main supplier of the British Navy was the London firm of Donkin and Hall and Gamble, who had a canning works in Blue Anchor Road, Bermondsey, and they supplied the Navy from 1813. This product had generally a good reputation, being often used on long voyages to the polar region or to the tropics, places where climatic conditions were extreme. The firm did not confine itself to canned meat but also prepared canned vegetable and concentrated broth, or 'portable soup', for its Naval contracts, but the vegetables were never popular with the Navy. The main effect of canned meat, and other food preserved in this way, was that it extended the range of naval activities by increasing the time ships might stay away at sea without provisioning. In the event of war it allowed blockading squadrons to remain at sea longer and without canned meat and other tinned provisions the great nineteenth-century attempts to open up the North West Passage would not have been possible.[46] Canned meat was certainly regarded as superior to the salt beef (or pork), which had been standard issue for long voyages for hundreds of years.

Official and public confidence in it took something of a knock in the 1850s when it was revealed some of the canned meat supplied to Franklin's expedition in H.M.S. *Erebus* and *Terror* by another firm run by the Hungarian, Stephen Goldner was found to be rotten There are different versions of exactly how much of the meat was rotten. Andrew Wynter puts it at no more than 18 canisters making up just 5 per cent of his meat.[47] But Drummond says that in 1849 111,000 lb of meat from Goldner's factory, situated in Galatz by the Danube in Moldavia, was condemned as unsound by the inspectors of H.M. Victualling Yards.[48] Part of the problem seems to have been that Goldner was under pressure from the Admiralty to supply the contract in a hurry and also to increase the size of the containers he used above what was normal at that time. Goldner may also have had problems in imposing good quality control measures as he was not always on site. Reports by the Yards' inspectors revealed that most of the bad meat was found in his large pack tins of between 9 lb and 32 lb, and almost none in the firm's small tins containing 6 lb of meat and under. In the case of the large containers it seems that the heating apparatus available at that time was not powerful enough to completely sterilize the meat in the centre of the large containers. One result of this failure, which received so much publicity that it became a national scandal, was for the Admiralty to set up its own canning factory in 1852 at Deptford. But there were other pioneering private firms engaged in this trade by that time, such as Cooper and Aves, Devaux & Co., both of London, and the Scottish firm Hogarth of Aberdeen, who seem to have avoided any complaints about their products. And even after the Goldner case the Admiralty still continued to use private contractors for all types of victualling.[49]

From the pioneering work done before the 1840s there were relatively few technical difficulties in establishing canning works outside Europe once their commercial opportunities became apparent. The new technique spread rapidly; and canned foods were used in Australia as early as 1815, and the process was taken from England to the United States in 1817 by William Underwood and was well established on both sides of the Atlantic by the 1830s. Production in Australia began on a modest scale in Sydney by Sizar Elliot, a ship's chandler in 1845–46. Others followed, employing more capital and a larger scale of production; in 1846 the Joseph family in Sydney and in July 1848 Henry, William and Richard Dangar at Honeysuckle Point on the Hunter River near Newcastle, New South Wales, imported the technology directly from London and had their employees trained at the Houndsditch factory of Ritchie and McCall.[50] In their first year of operations their firm exported 30 tons of canned meat to New Zealand and down the coast to Sydney. As their firm was larger than Elliot's and able to produce at lower costs, they forced the smaller firm to close. By 1851 their output had risen to 49,000 5 lb tins.[51]

However, rebuilding a market for the product was not always easy after the bad publicity of the Goldner scandal of 1852 and the revelations of the Parliamentary investigation.[52] After the scandal various alternatives to Europe as sources of supply were suggested. In 1853 when delivering the centenary address of the Royal Society of Arts, the Chairman of the Council asked why Australia only exported the wool and tallow of its sheep and not the mutton to feed Britain's hungry masses.[53] But to sustain the meat canning industry in continuous production required a readily available labour force as well as a more or less regular throughput of livestock. In the wake of the Goldner scandal the Dangars saw and acted on the opportunity to market their own product in England by negotiating to supply the Admiralty with canned Australian meat. It is probable this trade would have grown as the Admiralty's belief in the product survived the Goldner scandal but their early attempts to establish the industry did not find immediate success, principally because of labour shortages. The Dangars found they were unable to fulfil the contract when the gold rushes after 1851 siphoned off available labour and also pushed up the price of sheep making their business uneconomic and forcing them to close in 1855.[54]

Although they ultimately benefited the Australian economy by attracting more capital and labour, the gold discoveries of the 1850s represented a temporary set back to the country's meat exports by diverting resources to currently more profitable uses. It was not until the 1860s when the gold rush fever died down, and the pressure on wages and raw materials was reduced, that interest in Australian meat exports revived. In part there was a renewed interest from the British market when the cattle plague, which started in 1863, pushed up meat prices. From then on both Australia and the United States sent canned beef and mutton to Britain, but the lead was taken by Australia.[55] There were exports from the United States, but as it was dominated by the Civil War up to 1866, demand from the military absorbed most of the output of its canning industry.

The main person behind the revival of Australian canning in the mid-1860s was Charles Grant Tyndal. In 1865 he formed the Australian Meat Company, with a works at Ramoornie on the Orara River in September 1866. At first it used the English firm of John McCall, 137 Houndsditch as agents but later opened its own London selling office. Besides its British sales the firm also had a contract with the French government. In September 1868 a second firm, this time in Victoria, the Melbourne Meat Preserving Company, started production at Saltwater (Maribyrong) River under the management of Samuel Ritchie, Goldner's agent in London at the time of the British navy meat scandal.[56] The efforts of both Tyndal and Ritchie pushed up the amount of canned Australian meat received in London. The heyday of Victorian meat canning was in the early 1870s, reaching its peak of 6639 tons in 1872. By 1873 many others had entered the business, and the efforts of these newcomers to purchase stock pushed up the price of sheep to such an extent that high prices in England reduced demand.

The new companies, being smaller and unable to absorb this increase in the cost of raw materials as successfully as the industry's first entrants, had short lives before they were forced to close down. The Melbourne Meat Preserving Company suffered as well and experienced a further setback in 1879 with Joseph Ritchie's death. There was also competition from South America and New Zealand, and in 1899 the Melbourne company was wound up. After 1880 and the eclipse of the Victorian factories, the tonnage of meat from New South Wales canneries started to move up. Some blamed the Victorian livestock tax, introduced in 1877, for the demise of its canneries, but this does not seem to have been the main reason. K.T.H. Farrer takes the view that the difference between Victorian and New South Wales firms was that the former were operated by businessmen who expected them to pay a dividend at all times, whereas many of the latter were set up by livestock farmers, not to pay a dividend but to stabilise the price of stock by buying and canning when prices were low and doing little business, or any at all, when prices were high. When prices were low the farmer shareholders hoped that by buying and exporting surplus meat the firms would provide an extra outlet for their animals, and push prices up to the level when they could make a profit from the domestic market.[57]

Other meat canneries opened up in Queensland and South Australia under the same stimulus of high prices in Britain in the late 1860s caused by the Cattle Plague, as well as the artificial market in Europe created by the interruption of supplies during the Franco–Prussian War of 1870–71. Australia did well in this market as the military requirements of the Civil War absorbed much of the canned meat produced in the United States, and no South American meat was imported before 1871.[58] From the late 1870s the United States industry was free to export again but by then canned meat was a less attractive alternative in the face of increasing amounts of more palatable chilled and frozen meat. Nevertheless, its long storage life under the right conditions ensured that a market for the canned product remained in those situations where there was no access to the refrigeration technology necessary for chilled and frozen meat. The expansion of the meat canning industry in the 1870s made it available to a greater number of general consumers than in the 1850s when its use was mainly confined to institutional consumers. It is difficult to be sure just how adversely the Goldner scandal influenced public perception but greater public consumption did a lot to break down any persisting consumer prejudice. In the 1870s there were still complaints about the taste of the product, but over the rest of the nineteenth and twentieth centuries this was improved by further developments in canning methods. Canning technology also did a lot to lower the cost of packaging. In the 1870s the industry employed labour intensive batch production methods with each tin made, filled and sealed by hand. By the mid 1890s producers could pay closer attention to packaging and presentation, with automated production lines often using better packaging and smaller tins, and this had an important influence in increasing their markets.[59]

The early use of canning elsewhere was just as limited as it was in Europe and Australia. New Zealand did not have any pioneering firms and had to wait until later in the century for the industry to make a modest appearance there. Its early use of this sort of meat was limited by its smaller economy, and where low population meant a restricted market for the product in a country with the greatest abundance of fresh meat, it was supplied either by Britain or Australia. One problem facing both sets of the southern hemisphere colonies was that all the packaging materials had to be imported from Britain. Their industrial sectors were too limited to cope with iron smelting or steel or tinplate production, where the comparative advantage lay with Britain. Ocean transport added to the cost of containers in the colonies so that the crucial factor determining the competitiveness of all their canned foods was the price of the contents. Even in normal times labour was also more expensive than in Britain and this was increased in Australia in the 1850s and New Zealand in the 1860s by the gold discoveries. In these years the meat industries of both countries could make better profits by feeding the large numbers of agriculturally non-productive persons engaged in the diggings than by worrying about how to sustain the British navy's demand for tinned meat.

The most significant technical progress in the industry was made in the United States after the Civil War, when the Wilson Packing Company in Chicago began packing compressed cooked beef in tapered rectangular cans in April 1874. Fully cooking the meat before packing gave it a better flavour than the old process of heating raw meat in cans, and reducing the amount of liquid it contained made customers happier that they had bought only meat and had not been fobbed off with an uncertain amount of water. In 1875 Libby, McNeil and Libby also entered the trade and jointly patented the process with the Wilson Packing Company. But when the St Louis Beef Canning Company and others also used the same processes the Supreme Court refused to uphold these patents. This dramatically reduced the cost of entry and after 1875 a number of other firms entered the industry so that by 1910 the country had around 40 establishments engaged in canning meat. Although American methods were soon adopted in other countries, they do not seem to have been able to produce as good quality a product as the United States, or compete effectively on price.[60] As a result the United States, in addition to its exports of live cattle and refrigerated beef, was able to build up quite a wide export trade in canned beef and pork by the mid-1880s, which it shipped to nearly all the countries of Europe, as well as all places where the British and German navy and army were stationed.[61]

The early progress of the industry in South America was slower than in the United States because of its smaller industrial sector and limited market opportunities for diversification. There the earliest attempts at non-traditional methods of meat processing were not in canning anyway, but in the production of meat concentrates. In fact there was little particularly new about this item; in the eighteenth century 'portable soups' that were nothing more than a concentrated broth had been taken on his round the world voyage by Captain James Cook in 1772–73. The fat was first removed from the meat broth and that was then further concentrated into hard cakes by further evaporation. If kept dry the product had a more or less indefinite shelf life, though it was not known in the eighteenth century that it had little nutritional value. Cook, who like all others at the time and well into the nineteenth century regarded it as containing the concentrated goodness of the meat and used his supplies as a medicine. He gave it as a tonic soup to his sick crewmen mixed with pease flour three times a week.[62] Probably its main benefit was that it helped to add flavour to a rather unappealing ship's diet, and this served to stimulate the appetites of the invalids. It was certainly a product that had some popularity. It was palatable and built up a reputation as a tonic food when it was used on other voyages in the late eighteenth and early nineteenth centuries, and most early food canners added this item under one name or another to their range of products

But its first imports into Europe came from South America when the Liebig Company started to produce its 'Extractum Carnis' at Fray Bentos in Uruguay in 1863. Here the animals were killed, allowed to cool for 24 hours, the meat removed and mechanically minced before it was placed in water and steamed for an hour. It then passed into a reservoir where it was allowed to cool and strained under pressure before passing into another vessel where the fat was removed. The remaining gravy was then passed into another vessel with steam heating pipes for a further eight hours during which time the steam from the broth was drawn off. When it was sufficiently reduced in volume it was allowed to cool and partially harden and then packed in tins for export. It was expensive to manufacture as it took about 34 lb of meat to produce 1 lb of essence. The advantage of producing it in Uruguay was that the country had large numbers of poor unimproved cattle that would never have found a sale in London as fresh meat, if it were possible to get it there in that state, let alone as *charqui* beef, whereas a 1 lb tin of extract found a ready sale at 12s. 6d. A great deal of this product was sold in Germany, and in its initial years the firm had strong links with the German chemist, Justus von Liebig, who described the manufacturing process in his *Researches on the Chemistry of Food*, first published in Britain in 1847.[63]

The original Liebig firm was a Dutch one registered in, and with its central depot at Antwerp, but founded by a German engineer George Christian Giebert. Von Liebig was Director of its Scientific Department and one of his former assistants, Mr Seekamp was 'manager of the chemical branch of the manufactory at Fray Bentos', while another of his assistants worked at the central depot in Antwerp sending samples of the extract to the Liebig's laboratory for testing.[64] By the middle of 1864 the factory was sending 1,500 lb a month of the extract to Europe, along with such by-products as smoked tongues, salt beef, bone meal and dried blood. But in spite of its advocacy by the great man its process was similar to that employed by the many other makers of concentrated meat stock. The European link was broken either in or after 1866 when the Dutch company, lacking sufficient capital for expansion sold the estate and *saladero* adjoining the business to an English firm. The new firm was registered in London and its owners invested £150,000 in it and renamed it Liebig's Extract of Meat Company.[65] However, the product still retained its name and restorative medical image, but it is not known if the quality controls established by Liebig were maintained. But about the time the company changed hands, Liebig had been criticised for arguing that his own method of producing meat extract was superior to the one used in Australia.[66]

Liebig's product used beef but there were attempts in Australia to produce a similar product from mutton. The Australian item differed slightly in that the Uruguayan product contained no gelatine (or glue) as it was removed in the pressing, whereas the Australian product boiled bones and meat together and they were simply strained, which allowed the gelatine to remain after the tallow was removed. Britain first imported the Australian item in 1865, and by the early 1870s it was being sold in two qualities. The prime quality was for human consumption and the second was recommended for pigs or dogs. Augustus Voelcker, the consulting chemist to the Royal Agricultural Society of England, experimented with it as a pig food. His results are worth reporting as no similarly controlled experiments were carried out on humans and the pig has some physiological characteristics similar to humans. He found that when fed on a mixture of conventional farinaceous foods but substituting the extract for one of those foods, those animals did not gain as much weight as a control groups fed on solid food alone. However, when mixed with conventional solid foods it promoted a greater weight gain than in animals fed with just the solid foods. He cautiously concluded that although little was known about its precise physiological functions the experiment 'tends to indicate that meat extract materially assists in the assimilation of food, and in consequence possesses a certain physiological and possibly economic value'.[67]

By the end of the nineteenth century dietary science had advanced far enough to give more definite opinions about meat extracts, and they were not flattering. W. Tibbles, in the textbook *Foods*, concluded their cost was out of all proportion to their [food] value, although he conceded that some of them did appeal to the aesthetic sense. None of them contained less than 40 per cent water and for the highest it was over 80 per cent. But overall he believed they were expensive preparations, sold at a price far beyond their nutritive value, which was probably explained by the method of their manufacture; he might possibly have added human gullibility and the effects of vigorous advertising. Even so, it did not prevent them from being popular among a section of consumers as there were over a dozen different brands on sale in Britain in 1912.[68] As in the 1860s not all were imported, but they all had the advantage of being able to use cheap poor quality meat that would need some form of processing to make it acceptable to the public. Overseas manufacturers found them a useful way of processing abundant supplies of poor quality animals that were otherwise hard to dispose of in any other way than for their hides and fat, and selling as a by-product what was formerly wasted after the fat and tallow had been drawn off.

But canning and meat extracts were both compromises. Like dried and salted meat they destroyed the intrinsic qualities of fresh meat, and by doing so they made the whole process of livestock improvement largely superfluous. What the European market still required were imports of fresh meat from over long distances to satisfy consumer demand, and the only process that could come close to doing this involved the use of refrigeration.

**Refrigeration**

Here the first experiments in freezing and chilling were started in the 1860s but it was not until the 1870s that this aspect of the industry really began to move forward. The initial exports of significant amount of refrigerated meat to Europe came from the United States, and its trade in chilled meat to the British market became really large over the last three decades of the nineteenth century. Exports of frozen meat from Australia, New Zealand and Argentina began soon after in 1880s. It had long been known that lowering the temperature of many perishable foods was an effective way of keeping them fresh, and the most common way was to use of natural ice. In the eighteenth and early nineteenth centuries the wealthy built icehouses on their estates to store meat and other perishables for household use in the hot summer months. They were small chambers generally sited in shady locations close to the house and constructed largely below ground level then filled in the winter with ice that was often cut from their ornamental lakes. But this was a refinement that was confined to a very small section of society and it did nothing to promote the long distance transport of perishables.

The first pioneer of freezing meat for export was the Australian businessman Thomas Mort who in 1861 established the first Australian freezing works at Darling Harbour, Sydney. The establishment used ammonia compression refrigerating machinery and was housed in large rooms 75 feet square enclosed by brick walls 4 feet 6 inches thick. Meat was initially prepared for the Sydney market but in 1875 Mort decided to also export it to Britain. In 1876 the first trial shipment was actually packed aboard the Australian sailing ship *Northam*, which had been fitted with an ammonia compression freezing apparatus. But the flexing of the ship before it left harbour caused the freezing pipes to rupture and the whole cargo had to be unloaded and the attempt abandoned.[69] A year later another Australian refrigeration pioneer, James Harrison, sent an experimental cargo of Australian beef and mutton to London on the *Norfolk*; this time it was frozen on board by two tanks packed with ice and water but the tanks leaked before the end of the three-month voyage and the cargo was ruined.[70] At this time the barriers to the export of frozen meat were the unreliability of the refrigeration machinery onboard the ship and the length of the voyage from the southern hemisphere. The first successful cargo of refrigerated meat was on the shorter North Atlantic route and here the meat was not hard-frozen but chilled.

Mort and Harrison were not the only ones trying to send refrigerated meats to Europe; the rewards for doing so were judged to be large enough to encourage businessmen to invest in experimental cargoes from both North and South America. Experiments with small amounts of frozen beef were made in 1874, but the first really successful attempt was by Timothy C. Eastman in October 1875; who sent a cargo of chilled beef from New York to London. The carcases were not frozen before they were shipped, but hung on hooks in the hold and the temperature maintained at around freezing by blocks of ice and cold air was kept circulating around them by a system of fans.[71] This was not a particularly high technology technique but it was sufficient to keep the meat entirely fresh for the shorter North Atlantic crossing, and ensured it arrived in a better condition than any preserved by being frozen solid. As an advertisement, Eastman sent a baron of beef to Queen Victoria at Windsor Castle and she was reported to have found it 'very good'.[72] For some time Eastman was alone in this trade, but by 1878 seven other businessmen were doing the same, and very few steamers left the Hudson from New York without having several tons of beef and mutton on board. Some of them used the fanning process but others achieved and maintained the necessary temperature by mixing the ice with salt to produce low-temperature brine and then forcing this freezing mixture along pipes running between the rows of meat. After buying all the meat, the mutton could be carried almost free of cost as the shipper paid not for the amounts carried but for the refrigerated cargo space, and the smaller sheep carcases could be hung to take up the otherwise wasted space between the sides of beef.[73] The trade grew rapidly because the voyage was short, the refrigeration technology was easy, and the product was good. An annual average of 326,664 hundredweight of North American chilled beef reached Britain in 1875–79, but by 1900–04 this had grown to 2,685,550.[74]

Further attempts at sending refrigerated meat from countries further from Europe continued unabated through the late 1870s. These experiments had only partial success as the failure rates for the refrigeration machinery were still high and usually only some of the cargo arrived in saleable condition. But on 13 August 1877 the SS *Paraguay*, which had been financed in France and fitted out in Marseilles with an ammonia-compression refrigeration machine left Buenos Aires for Le Havre, carrying 5,500 carcases of mutton kept frozen on board at -17°F. In spite of the fact that that it had to put in to St Vincent for three months to undergo repairs caused by a collision, the ship finally arrived at Le Havre in May 1877 with all of the meat in tip-top condition. Following established tradition with earlier partial cargoes, the garrison of the port were among those supplied but some of it was also sent to the Grand Hotel in Paris. Both parties were apparently well satisfied with its freshness and palatability, but when some was also sent to a meat firm in London it described it as having 'extraordinarily good flavour' but remarked that the carcase size was 'very small'.[75] The latter comment is presumably an indication that at this time more work needed to be done on South American flock improvement. A frozen cargo of beef and mutton was finally successfully sent from Australia in 1880 on board the SS *Strathleven*. The ship was chartered from the Glasgow firm of Burrell and Son and fitted with a Bell-Coleman refrigeration machine. It left Melbourne on 6 December 1879 and arrived at the Port of London on 2 February 1880 with its cargo of 40 tons of meat in a state of perfect freshness. The success of the voyage was enthusiastically reported in the press along with the favourable comments of those who had tasted the meat. The quality was endorsed by a public testimonial from ten firms of meat traders at the London Central Markets, Smithfield and the *Daily Telegraph* claimed that in both appearance and eating quality it was indistinguishable from freshly killed English meat. [76]

After these initial successes the extension of the trade from Australia (and New Zealand), South America and the United States was accompanied by further refinement and improvement of the refrigeration machinery. But in addition to this one must not overlook the improvements in the shipbuilding and steam technology. The 1870s were the decade when steel and steam finally took over from iron, wood and sail as construction and power systems for ocean-going trade. The larger steel framed ships with more cargo space and greater carrying capacity were suited to the installation of the modern refrigeration systems required by the transport of meat over long distances. But in addition the merchant steamer was eventually able to greatly reduce the length of voyage and cost of ocean freight, further enhancing the price advantage of good quality imported meat over the European home produced item.

In addition, a further transport improvement was the introduction of better rail transport both for live animals on their way to slaughter yards, and for meat once it had left the processing establishment for another stage in its distribution to the final consumer. For example, until the 1870s the rail transport of cattle and other livestock, though enabling the animals to travel much further than on the hoof, was poor and still resulted in weight shrinkage through stress and poor care from the railway companies. In the United States cattle were losing between 10 and 15 per cent of their weight on the 500-mile rail journey from Chicago to Boston through the lack of care and basic comforts for them like regular food and watering and providing roofs to the railcars to save the animals from exposure to excessively cold or hot weather conditions. But in 1885 the Northern Pacific company led the way in good practice by allowing the animals off the train on very long journeys to feed and water in good pasture, and the force of competition forced other railway firms to follow. The first US patent for a refrigerator rail car to carry fresh meat was issued in 1867 to J.B. Sutherland of Detroit, and several more were issued for other systems between 1868 and 1874. The final and most efficient form to evolve had tanks of ice and salt at either end of the car with the meat suspended from the roof on hooks and a system of fans to circulate the cold air between the carcases.[77] In the United States the refrigerator helped expand the demand for better quality beef from better bred and fed animals, and this in turn led to the decline of the range industry. To meet the new demand production was expanded but it was not in the lower quality animals found on the cattle ranges, but in better quality highly bred animals fed on corn rather than the overcrowded, sparse and shrinking pastures of the Western cattle ranges.[78]

This aspect of railway technology, like all other technical developments in the industry had a global application. In South America the growth of the industry involved the extension of estates over vast distance and this meant that cattle destined for slaughter for freezing needed to be transported hundreds of miles. This made the use of comfortable air-conditioned railcars able to keep animals in good condition on long journeys in very hot weather an absolute necessity for the growth of its meat industry.[79]

As this trade grew it had profound effects on the structure of the meat industry everywhere. In Argentina as the export of frozen beef gathered pace after 1900 there was a reduced emphasis on sheep farming.[80] In Uruguay the export of frozen beef began with a modest 90 tons first exported by the Frigorica Uruguaya in 1905. In this country its growth reduced the former heavy reliance on *charqui*, which in the early 1900s utilised 550,000 head of cattle processed by the 21 *saladeros* around Montevideo or on the Uruguay. From then until 1914 an increasing number of improved cattle were sent instead to the factories packing frozen chilled beef. As late as 1900 the country's canning industry processed 100,000 animals, but these numbers also declined as more animals were sent to the fresh meat packers. Nevertheless, the persistence of a substantial number of unimproved animals meant that traditional users did not disappear entirely. Not all animals dressed into good beef, and the occasional droughts sent many animals to the packing plants in poor flesh. In 1914 600,000 cattle and 5 million sheep died of starvation and reduced resistance to disease from this cause.[81]

## Transport of Livestock by Sea

Although the sea transport of livestock had long been a reality, the limited size and speed of smaller wood and iron steam vessels had restricted this trade to short distances. The free trade measures of the 1840s saw the start of a steady traffic of European cattle boats between northern European ports and southern England, and before that in the 1830s there was a steady steamship trade in fat cattle and other livestock from Scotland and Ireland to England.[82] The steamship effectively opened the entire urban market for food of the west coast of England and Scotland to the Irish farmer and livestock dealer. But steamship developments in the 1870s had even wider repercussions on the movement of livestock by sea with the development of the transatlantic cattle trade. This required larger and faster ships than the Baltic and North Sea, but the first experiments began in 1868 when Nelson Morris shipped a few cattle from New York to Glasgow and London. Nothing further was done until the Glasgow firm of John Bell and Sons tried an experimental shipment of six animals in July 1873. This was successful as the animals only lost 50 lbs on average during the voyage but still left a good enough profit for the firm to arrange with the Anchor Line for regular shipments. Initially the animals were carried on the upper deck in open stalls and were cared for by one of the ship's stewards! But after losses when a number were washed overboard during a severe storm on one voyage they were carried between decks and this required hoisting. By the late 1870s a number of other dealers from Boston and New York had joined in and there was quite a brisk live export trade.[83]

Attempts at building up a trade in livestock from further away than America did not succeed at this time. Live animals required constant care and attention and the distances and climate stresses involved in voyages from Australia and New Zealand were just too great to make the journey worthwhile. There was also a trade in live cattle from Argentina, at its heaviest in the second half of the 1890s as more powerful marine engines cut journey times and increased the quality of livestock accommodation. Even so, the number of live Argentine cattle was only about 7 per cent of the transatlantic trade, while the United States made up over 70 per cent with the rest coming from Canada. As the general quality of Argentine cattle was lower, United States beef animals fetched highest prices in Britain. In addition, as the voyage from South America was still about a week longer than from the United States, there was a tendency for the South American cattle merchants to ship heavier animals to withstand the longer voyage, even though they were not always of the best quality.[84] The South American trade was only profitable because the initial price of animals was low enough to withstand the additional expenses of the longer journey time, higher weight losses *en route* of around 12 to 25 per cent compared with a maximum of 10 per cent from the United States, plus a general mortality rate that was ten times greater than for the north Atlantic journey.[85] But this trade had a short life, and after reaching around 70,000 head a year, it ended in 1900 when, as a precaution, the British government banned imports of live Argentine cattle because of the discovery of foot and mouth disease. Although cattle traders and the Argentine government complained, the ban probably helped the industry as a whole because it helped to boost exports of frozen and, later, chilled beef.[86]

**Table 2.2 Annual average prices of English, American chilled and American and Canadian port-killed beef, 1896–1910**

| Years | English Second quality per cwt | | English First quality Per cwt | | American chilled First quality per cwt | | American/Canadian port-killed First quality per cwt | |
|---|---|---|---|---|---|---|---|---|
| | s. | d. | s. | d. | s. | d. | s. | d. |
| 1896–1900 | 51 | 0 | 53 | 6 | 43 | 6 | 50 | 0 |
| 1901–1905 | 50 | 6 | 54 | 6 | 47 | 0 | 52 | 6 |
| 1906–1910 | 50 | 0 | 53 | 0 | 48 | 0 | 52 | 6 |

*Source:* Adapted from figures published annually by the Board of Agriculture in *Agricultural Statistics* (London, 1867–). For further details see R. Perren, 'The North American Beef and Cattle Trade with Great Britain, 1870–1914', *Economic History Review*, 24(3) (1971): 438.

The whole success of the North American trade depended on the positive difference in price between fresh and refrigerated meat that even the quality improvements in refrigeration technology were unable to eliminate entirely. Table 2.1 above shows the difference in price between chilled and port-killed meat from American and Canadian animals from the late 1890s, and although the price difference did narrow it did not entirely disappear. The port-killed meat commanded a price somewhere between first and second quality home-fed English beef. It is noticeable that the price of second-quality English beef fell slightly between 1896–1900 and 1906–10, whereas the price of the port-killed meat rose, confirming the assertions of contemporaries that American and Canadian port-killed beef competed very strongly with the sizeable proportion of second quality English beef.[87] When cut up and displayed by the English butcher it was very difficult, if not impossible, for the average customer to tell American and Canadian from the home-produced article. This was never so with chilled beef as chilling inevitably led to some discoloration, and as American butchers cut a carcass differently from English butchers its origins were always apparent to the experienced eye.

Although it grew steadily up to 1900, the North Atlantic cattle trade accounted for only a small proportion of the livestock carried by sea to Britain before 1914. In 1893, of the 2,656,000 cattle imported into Britain from all countries 2,253,000 came from Ireland; in comparison the North Atlantic trade, which numbered only 345,000 was a comparatively minor affair.[88] But, unlike the American trade, a large proportion of the trade with Ireland consisted of stores and dairy animals that were destined for further feeding in England. Although some Canadian stores were imported into England and Scotland, the majority of that country's store animals went across the border to the United States.

The transatlantic trade was also one that was subject to an increasing amount of restrictions. This was partly explained by a growing concern about the condition in which animals were carried over such long voyages. In the early years of the trade these were often fully justified. Cattle were carried in a variety of vessels, some of them regular liners built expressly for the purpose, other were liners specifically modified to carry livestock, and the rest were tramp steamers used only occasionally for the livestock trade and modified in a make-do fashion.[89] In this last group the accommodation was of a temporary nature and here conditions were worst. On these large numbers of animals were crowded below decks with neither adequate space nor proper care and attendance. By 1880 it cost between £10 and £12 to transport a beast by rail over two thousand miles of land from north eastern Colorado, Wyoming or Montana and then three thousand miles of ocean – amounting to 4d. per lb. on the cost of its beef after it was slaughtered in Britain. But when shippers used cheaper vessels that sailed with insufficient attendants, or insufficient fodder for their hungry cargo sometimes as many as 250 animals would have to be thrown overboard.[90] In response to public misgivings and lobbying when this was learned, and with government enquiries and inspections, shippers were ultimately forced to improve their conditions. Also from the shippers' point of view, with insurance and freight costs to be paid, it was ultimately in their interests that animals arrived in London or Liverpool in as good condition as possible free of bruises and having lost as little weight as possible.

In 1877 the trade was confined to the ports of Glasgow, Liverpool and Southampton, but by 1879 it was extended to Bristol, Cardiff, Hartlepool, Hull, London, Southampton and South Shields and in 1887 American cattle were landed at Aberdeen and at Dundee in 1889. Liverpool always took the largest number of animals, and that port had a large amount of capital invested in the trade. On the other side of the Atlantic, animals were dispatched from the northern ports of New York, Philadelphia, Baltimore, Boston, Newport, Norfolk and Charlestown. The animals themselves came from a number of places. Some were long-horned animals from the Rocky Mountains and Colorado, while others were stall fed beasts, including some Canadian animals between April and October that were always shipped from United States ports.[91] Until 1892 many of these Canadian cattle were not for direct consumption but were stores destined for final finishing in the United States or Britain before slaughter.[92]

## Notes

1  Grundy, J.E., 'The Hereford Bull: His Contribution to New World and Domestic Beef Supplies', *Agricultural History Review*, 50(1) (2002): 73–4.
2  Lynch, J., 'The River Plate Republics from Independence to the Paraguayan War', in L. Bethell (ed.), *The Cambridge History of Latin America, vol. III, From Independence to c.1870* (Cambridge, 1985), p. 618.
3  Clemen, R.A., *The American Livestock and Meat Industry* (New York, 1923), pp. 190–1.
4  Macdonald, J., *Food From the Far West* (London, 1878), pp. 267–8.
5  [C] 3747 (PP 1866, Vol. LXXI), *Report from Her Majesty's Diplomatic Agents in South America on Schemes for Curing Meat for the British Market*, p. 1.
6  Latham, W., *The States of the River Plate: Their Industries and Commerce* (London, 1866), pp. 5, 34–5, 36.
7  Koebel, W.H., *Argentina: Past and Present* (London, 1910), p. 138.
8. Latham, pp. 37–8, 151–2; Heiser, C. B., Jr., *Seed to Civilization: The Story of Man's Food* (San Francisco, 1973), pp. 117–19, 120.
9  Koebel, pp. 139–41.
10 Jones, C.F., *South America* (London, 1931), p. 378.
11 Brewster, J.A., 'The South American Trade', in F. Gerrard (ed.), *The Book of the Meat Trade* (London, 1949), vol. 1, pp. 203, 213.
12 Whetham, E.H., 'The Trade in Pedigree Livestock 1850–1910', *Agricultural History Review*, 27(1) (1979): 47, 48.
13 United States Department of Agriculture, *Reports of the Commissioner of the Operations of the Department for the Year1862* (Washington, 1863). See the illustration of the ox 'Constitution' at the front of this publication.
14 Clemen, pp. 481–4.
15 Walton, J.R., 'Pedigree and the National Cattle Herd circa 1750–1950', *Agricultural History Review*, 34(2) (1986): 149–170.
16 Lynch, 'The River Plate Republics from Independence to the Paraguayan War', p. 650.
17 Consulate-General of Uruguay, *The Republic of Uruguay; Its Geography, History, Rural Industries, Commerce, and General Statistics* (London, 1883), pp. 75–82.
18 Latham, pp. 22, 27–9, 33.
19 Davidson, B.R., *European Farming in Australia: An Economic History of Australian Farming* (Amsterdam, 1981), pp. 83–4, 120–122, 176–7.
20 Heiser, p. 120.
21 Rommel, G.H., 'Notes on the Animal Industry of Argentina', United States Department of Agriculture, *Twenty–Fifth Annual Report of the Bureau of Animal Industry for the Year 1908* (Washington, 1910), p. 319.
22 Davidson, B.R., *European Farming in Australia: An Economic History of Australian Farming* (Amsterdam, 1981), p. 251.
23 Brooking, T., 'Economic Transformation', in W.H. Oliver, with B.R. Williams (eds), *The Oxford History of New Zealand* (Oxford, 1981), p. 233–4.
24 Clemen, pp. 54–5, 63–4.
25 Critchell, J.T. and J. Raymond, *A History of the Frozen Meat Trade* (London, 1912), pp. 17, 93–9.
26 Macdonald, pp. 266–8; 291–7; *Meat and Provision Trades Review* (27 Oct. 1877): 397.

27 Grundy, 'The Hereford Bull', pp. 69–86; Irish Hereford Breed Society, http://www.irishhereford.com/aboutus.html.

28 Australian Hereford Society, http://www.hereford.com.au/index.html.

29 The Australian Poll Hereford Society Limited, www://pollhereford.com.au/html; Hereford Cattle Society, http://www.herefordwebpages.co.uk/herdsoc.shtml#.address.

30 (PP 1867–8, Vol. LV), *Return Relating to the Past and Present Supply of Dead Meat to the Country and the Metropolis*, pp. 3–5; *The Economist* (12 Jan 1850), p. 52; (23 Feb 1850), p. 220.

31 Herbert, R., 'Statistics of Live Stock and Dead Meat for Consumption in the Metropolis', *Journal of the Royal Agricultural Society of England*, 22 (1861): 131.

32 Lawrie, R.A., *Meat Science* (Oxford, 1974), p. 229.

33 Latham, p. 9; Lawrie, p. 229.

34 Hutchinson, T.J., *The Paraná; with incidents of the Paraguayan War and South American recollections from 1861 to 1868* (London, 1868), p. 222.

35 American Institute Foundation, *The Science of Meat and Meat Products* (San Francisco, 1960), p. 295.

36 Hutchinson, p. 222; J.A. Oddone, 'The Formation of Modern Uruguay. c.1870–1930', in L. Bethell (ed.), *The Cambridge History of Latin America, vol. V, c.1970 to 1930* (Cambridge, 1986), p. 453.

37 Keen, B., *A History of Latin America* (Boston, 1996), pp. 214, 218, 236–9; K.F. Kiple, *Blacks in Colonial Cuba* (Gainsville, 1976), pp. 79, 91, 94.

38 Smith, J.R., *The World's Food Resources* (London, 1919), p. 231.

39 [C] 3747 (PP 1866, Vol. LXXI), *Report from Her Majesty's Diplomatic Agents in South America on Schemes for Curing Meat for the British Market*, p. 2.

40 Hutchinson, pp. 226–7.

41 Clemen, pp. 114–15.

42 *Journal of the Society of Arts* (17 May 1867), 15(756): 414–15.

43 *Journal of the Society of Arts* (17 May 1867), 15(756): 416.

44 Wilcox, L.A., *Mr Pepy's Navy* (London, 1966), pp. 119–21.

45 Gradish, S.F., *The Manning of the British Navy During the Seven Years' War* (London, 1980), pp. 143–6.

46 Drummond, J.C., 'Historical Introduction', in J.C. Drummond (ed.), *Historic Tinned Foods* (Greenford, 1939), pp. 9–24; M. Lewis, *The Navy in Transition 1814–1864: A Social* History (London, 1965), pp. 166–7; C. Lloyd, *The British Seaman 1200–1800: A Social* Survey (London, 1968), pp. 257–8.

47 Wynter, A., 'Preserved Meats', in A. Wynter, *Our Social Bees: Or Pictures of Town and Country Life and Other Places* (London, 1865), p. 197.

48 Drummond, 'Historical Introduction', p. 27.

49 Wynter, 'Preserved Meats', pp. 195–8, 203; (PP 1866, Vol. XLVI), *Names of newspapers in which advertisements of May 1866, relating to contracts for ox beef and vegetables were inserted; letter on the subject by the Provincial Newspaper Society to the Admiralty; and reply*; Drummond, 'Historical Introduction', pp. 24–9.

50 Critchell and Raymond, p. 8; K.T.H. Farrer, *Australian Meat Exports to Britain in the Nineteenth Century: Technology Push and Market Pull* (London, 1988), pp. 2–3.

51 Linge, G.J.R., *Industrial Awakening: A Geography of Australian Manufacturing 1788 to 1890* (Canberra, 1979), pp. 102–3.

52 [C] (PP 1852, Vol. XXX), *Date and Terms of Contract for Preserved Meat for the Use of the Navy entered into with Goldner and others; the Quantities issued since the*

*commencement of the Contracts; Quantities returned into Store as unfit for use; Complaints made; also Contract Prices of Beef and Pork for the years 1848, 1849, 1850, and 1851.*

53  *Journal of the Society of Arts* (1867), Vol. 15, 4 January, p. 100.

54  Critchell and Raymond, p.9: K.T.H. Farrer, *Australian Meat Exports to Britain in the Nineteenth Century: Technology Push and Market Pull* (London, 1988).

55  Chaloner, W.H., *People and Industries* (London, 1963), p. 108.

56  Farrer, K.T.H., *A Settlement Amply Supplied: Food Technology in Nineteenth Century Australia* (Melbourne, 1980), pp. 94–5, 97, 99, 103.

57  Ibid., pp. 106–20.

58  Clemen, p. 464; Farrer, K.T.H., *A Settlement Amply Supplied: Food Technology in Nineteenth Century Australia* (Melbourne, 1980), pp. 125–8.

59  Perren, R., 'Food Manufacturing', in E.J.T. Collins (ed.), *The Agrarian History of England and Wales, Vol. VII, 1850–1914 Part II* (Cambridge, 2000), pp. 1094–5.

60  Clemen, pp. 464–6.

61  United States Department of Agriculture, *First Annual Report of the Bureau of Animal Industry* (Washington, 1884), p. 265.

62  Drummond, 'Historical Introduction', pp. 14–15.

63  Liebig, J. von, *Researches on the Chemistry of Food ... Edited from the manuscript of the author by W. Gregory* (London, 1847); Latham, p. 124; [C] 3747 (PP 1866, Vol. LXXI), *Report from Her Majesty's Diplomatic Agents in South America on Schemes for Curing Meat for the British Market*, pp. 3–4; Hutchinson, pp. 227–9.

64  *Pharmaceutical Journal*, Series 2, 8 (Nov. 1866): 287–8.

65  *The Times* (20 Jan. 1865), Supplement; Hutchinson, pp. 410–12.

66  *Pharmaceutical Journal*, Series 2, 8 (Nov. 1866): 349–50.

67  Ibid.: 198; A. Voelcker, 'On Australian Concentrated Mutton-soup as a Food for Pigs', *Journal of the Royal Agricultural Society of England*, Series 2, 9 (1873): 428–37.

68  Tibbles, W., *Foods: their Origin, Composition and Manufacture* (London, 1912), pp. 146–147.

69  Critchell and Raymond, pp. 18–21.

70  Ibid. p. 23.

71  Clemen, pp. 275–8.

72  Critchell, and Raymond, p. 26.

73  Macdonald, pp. 5–7.

74  Perren, R., 'The North American Beef and Cattle Trade with Great Britain, 1870–1914', *Economic History Review*, 24(3) (1971): 432.

75  Critchell and Raymond, pp. 28–30.

76  Ibid., pp. 30–32.

77  Clemen, pp. 195–9; 218–19; 233.

78  Osgood, E.S., *The Day of the Cattleman: The Legend of the Wild West viewed against the Truth of History* (Chicago, 1929), pp. 89–90, 176–7, 240–47; S.P. Hays, *Conservation and the Gospel of Efficiency: The Progressive Conservation Movement, 1890–1920* (Cambridge, Mass., 1959), pp. 49–51; M. Yeager, *Competition and Regulation: The Development of Oligopoly in the Meat Packing Industry* (Greenwich, 1981), pp. 171–2.

79  Richelet, J.E., 'The Argentine Trade', in R. Ramsay (ed.), *The Frozen and Chilled Meat Trade: A Practical Treatise by Specialists in the Trade* (London: The Gresham Publishing Company, 1929), vol. 1, p. 225.

80  Rock, D., 'The Argentine Economy, 1890–1914: Some Salient Features', in G. di Tella and D.C.M. Platt (eds), *The Political Economy of Argentina 1880–1946* (Basingstoke, 1986), p. 66.

81  Jones, pp. 403–5.

82  *Quarterly Journal of Agriculture*, 3 (Jun 1838–Mar 1839): 248; A.R.B. Haldane, *The Drove Roads of Scotland* (Newton Abbot, 1973), p. 49–54, 206–7.

83  Clemen, pp. 271–2.

84  Brewster, 'The South American Trade', pp. 204–5.

85  Platt, D.C.M., *Latin America and British Trade 1806–1914* (London, 1972), p. 260.

86  Rock, D. 'The Argentine Economy, 1890–1914: Some Salient Features', p. 67.

87  *Agricultural Gazette* (23 July 1877): 78; (PP 1897, Vol. VIII), *Select Committee on Agricultural Produce [Meat, &c.] Marks Bill*, QQ 3273–74, 3307, 3360, 3789–93, 3795, 3879–80.

88  Greg, I.M. and S.H. Towers, *Cattle Ships and our Meat Supply* (London, 1894), p. 5.

89  C. 6350 (PP 1890–91, Vol. LXXVIII) *Report of the Departmental Committee of the Board of Trade and the Board of Agriculture on the Transatlantic Cattle Trade*, p. 278.

90  *Meat and Provision Trades Review* (17 Apr. 1880): 57.

91  C. 6350 (PP 1890–91, Vol. LXXVIII) *Report of the Departmental Committee of the Board of Trade and the Board of Agriculture on the Transatlantic Cattle Trade*, pp. iv, viii.

92  MacLachlan, I., *Kill and Chill: Restructuring Canada's Beef Commodity Chain* (Toronto, 2001), pp. 69, 126.

# Chapter 3

# Capital and Markets

## Sources of Investment Before Refrigeration

The provision of capital for an industry that was to include a number of multinational businesses came from three sources between 1840 and 1914. In part, their growth was funded by domestic investment within the various countries that took part in supplying the global meat market, but in addition to this there was also foreign investment, as well as the use of reinvested profits by the industry itself.

As initially only small amounts of capital were needed for what were started off as butchering businesses to supply local markets in developing countries, local capital was often sufficient to finance this scale of operation. In Argentina the early meat-processing plants, or *saladeros*, were highly labour-intensive and needed little initial capital as they required hardly anything more in the way of equipment than a boiler to reduce the fat. Most were locally owned and only a few British merchant houses trading with South America invested in this type of industry before 1850.[1] The advantages of local ownership were a close knowledge of what was at that time a somewhat limited market.

But there is evidence of a little foreign capital being invested in the industry from early on, as some merchant houses trading with South America were involved with *saladeros* before 1850. This included the first meat curing plant opened in Ensenada, a few miles down the coast from Buenos Aires, by Staples, McNeile and Company in 1810. This pattern was continued in 1832 when a number of British capitalists and traders, led by Hodgson, Robinson and Company went into partnership with Francisco Agell, an Argentine merchant, to form a meat storage and meat drying business. And in 1850 two British import-export houses in Buenos Aires, Thomas Armstrong and Anderson, Maerae and Company, were named as one of the fifty merchant houses managing slaughtering and meat-salting establishments.[2] But South America took little part in canning meat in the 1860s and 1870s. Some of the local meat works did send small amounts to London in the early 1870s, but its reception was poor and there was no profit in the business. Until the development of the frozen meat trade in the 1880s Argentina was never an important source of supply; in the period 1860–80 its annual exports were less than a half of one per cent of all the United Kingdom's preserved meat imports and so there was limited British investment in the industry.[3]

In the United States the market for hog products was larger and the product was transported over longer distances, but here again the capital involved in the early days of the industry was from local mercantile sources. In some cases the early entrepreneurs were not fully committed to the industry as they found it a highly speculative business and they entered the pork trade as all-purpose rural merchants ready to switch their attention between a variety of competing activities, depending on which were currently the most profitable. City pork merchants had greater recourse to short-term bank loans, but they also used mercantile credit as well.[4] Both Australia and New Zealand in the 1840s and 1850s also had small meat industries supplying local markets and often relying on some local capital. For instance it seems that Australia's first commercial cannery, started in 1846 by the Sydney businessman Sizar Elliot, used local capital.[5]

The expansion of the industry, along with the first really serious experiments in new technology, required more than purely local finance. The industry also used techniques and inventions that were part of the general process of international development, most of them protected by some form of patent laws, so licensing and technical assistance could be one way to introduce foreign finance. But the amounts of overseas capital in the industry varied in each country, and such finance did not necessarily preclude local ownership and management. In Australia, New Zealand and Argentina foreign capital was more closely associated with their meat industries than in the United States, although it is impossible to assign precise percentages to each country. But even with the later use of foreign capital it seems that businesses owned by individuals, families and small partnerships continued to play a very significant role in the industry. When private companies were floated into public ones to aid enlargement a considerable block of the initial shares was often taken up by the previous owners. The remainder did not necessarily go abroad but could be quite widely spread among locals. In Australia, the Warrnambool Meat Preserving Company in Victoria was floated in March 1870 and the remaining 1449 shares not taken up by the company's original owners were distributed among 152 members of the public.[6]

At times it was difficult to define exactly what was local and what was foreign capital when the owner had residences in two countries. The main promoter of the Australian Meat Company Ltd in New South Wales was Charles Grant Tindall, who owned several pastoral properties in the Clarence River district of that colony, but as he was an absentee owner who lived permanently in England this firm needs to be counted as foreign owned. He set up the company in 1865 with a capital of £100,000 in 10,000 shares of £10 each. It was launched in England, but as its subscribers included old colonists and others connected with the colony we do not know just how much of the capital was from Britain and how much from local individuals.[7]

Another British financed meat preserving firm was Whitehead and Company, incorporated in London in 1874, with most of its shares held by H. M. Whitehead, a Limehouse provision merchant. However, this company seems to fit into the model where foreign capital arrives at a later stage as it was founded on a locally owned meat-preserving factory, also on the Clarence river, which Whitehead took over in 1865 but which was first established by a settler named Clarke Irving in 1858–59. This was perhaps typical of the Australian industry, which appears to have had no clearly distinguished pattern of ownership between colonial and British firms prior to 1890. In Queensland during this period at least eleven firms, four of them financed in Britain, one in Victoria and the remainder in Queensland

and New South Wales, operated at various times. But the fortunes of the industry were far from assured and many of them had a chequered existence. At times serious upward fluctuations in livestock prices brought about sometimes temporary, and sometimes permanent, closure of plants when they weakened the market for canned meat in Britain. But there were other hazards such as fire and cyclone damage that had an effect on the industry. And after the start of frozen meat export from 1880 there were attempts to develop the meat canning industry in Queensland, where early efforts suffered from the same discouraging disasters like fire in the processing plants, losses of cargo en route to Britain from storm damage and refrigeration equipment failure. There were also losses from competition from United States chilled beef as it was always a more commercially acceptable product than Australian frozen mutton.[8]

One problem faced by all the early Australian meat canning businesses was that they all seem to have been seriously under-capitalised. Farrer argues that men of substance were loath to put capital into canning as the product was aimed at those of limited means – the working-class public. This meant most of the firms could only raise a limited amount of paid-up capital and had to commit all of this to property and plant and then rely on current sales to run their business. When sales failed or were delayed they found the banks were generally unwilling to accommodate what they regarded as speculative and risky enterprises, making closure almost inevitable. Nor was it possible for shareholders to salvage much on liquidation, as the fixed capital of the company could not be adapted to other uses. Their losses then made original shareholders unwilling to undertake further advances to successor firms who had acquired their building and plant at knock down prices, but also found themselves just as short of working capital as their predecessors.[9] Although this argument ignores the possibility of cheap canned meat creating a dramatic expansion in demand, there is certainly some support for it as the boom in Australian canned meat exports only lasted so long as British meat prices were high and Australian livestock prices low. The British meat shortage and high prices occurred in the late 1860s when cattle plague reduced herd size and also disrupted the internal marketing system as British livestock markets were closed to prevent the disease from spreading. This only lasted from 1866 to 1871, but disappeared thereafter as plague was eliminated and livestock numbers rebuilt. Total Australian canned meat exports peaked in 1871 at 9,920 tons but had fallen by over 50 per cent to 4,476 tons by 1875; the decline in exports to Britain was even greater, falling from 9,383 tons in 1871 to 3,360 tons in 1875, and with it investment in Australian canning.[10]

At no time did this Australian canned meat make a significant contribution to British meat supplies. In 1871 H.S. Thompson showed that 87.5 per cent of Britain's meat came from home-bred animals, 5.6 per cent from live imports and only 6.9 per cent from imported preserved meat, which included not only Australian canned meat but also a quantity of fresh meat from Europe, as well as salted meat. Even though the stimulus of high prices showed there was very little elasticity in the import trade of live animals, the increase in preserved meats was more impressive, but still not enough to ensure that the Australian canneries could enjoy a continuously growing market in the early 1870s.[11] It seems that it was only after the initial teething problems of this branch of the meat industry were overcome with the development of a more palatable product by 1890, and it came to be established on a truly international scale in larger works with plant embodying greater amounts of invested capital, that there was greater stability in the patterns of ownership.

The position of New Zealand in early meat canning appears to have been almost non-existent, and all the early enterprise in its meat export industry was devoted to the frozen product. The smaller scale of the economy and its very late start of settlement seem to have been the reasons why no New Zealand companies took part in the export of canned meat in the 1860s and 1870s. At that time it was still largely at a stage of early settlement and pioneering; it was a pastoral economy unable to support industry of even limited complexity, such as meat canning. In the 1860s and 1870s most of its exports were wool, timber and gold, and that was where investment in the colony was concentrated. Local demand for the canned meat was very small in a country with such a European population in 1871 of only 256,000 and vast sheep pastures.[12] Wherever any demand for canned meat did arise, such as among gold diggers in the 1860s or loggers working in remote sites, it was easily satisfied by imports from the Australian colonies. Australian canned meat still continued to be received in Britain up to 1914 although, as we have seen in Chapter 2, it now faced stiff competition from the better packaged, cheaper and more palatable United States product, whose modern canning industry began in 1874.

In the United States, as with the entire meat packing industry, canning appears to have been entirely home financed, and there is less evidence of under capitalization. According to the *First Annual Report of the Bureau of Animal Industry*, 11 out of the 17 companies that entered the trade between 1874 and 1884 withdrew from it. Although some were unsuccessful, others left for reasons unknown to the writer, but a 'large number commanded ample means, and did not, therefore, discontinue the business from any lack of means'.[13] But by 1910 of the forty or so firms in the American meat canning industry, not all of these were particularly large establishments. Smaller firms could operate quite successfully because they produced a variety of specialised products with relatively small amounts of capital. They did not, like the Australian pioneers, need to invest in the sites and works to purchase and slaughter livestock themselves or even buy any animals. Instead they were able to purchase all their raw materials from the big American packers like Swift and Armour. Instead, they could devote all their capital to their packing plants and sales and marketing. After 1890 they achieved high output and low labour costs by automating their methods as much as possible with cans prepared, filled and sealed by machinery and employing mostly female labour on their production lines.[14]

## Sources of Investment After Refrigeration

When the refrigerated meat industry began operating in the late 1870s, it required much more integrated processing and distribution system than the canned product.

Canned meat effectively had an indefinite storage life and could at worst remain in the warehouse or the retail shop for as long as required, but frozen, and even more so chilled, meat had to reach the consumer much faster. Refrigerated shipping freight costs were naturally higher than the un-refrigerated cargo space required for canned meat, and refrigerated meat required extra care and handling at ports. When it arrived at its destination frozen meat had less urgency about its distribution and could remain in cold storage for several months, but to do this added to overheads. In the case of chilled meat it had to reach the consumer within a few days of arrival in Europe. This meant there was a greater need for specialist investment in the industry at the shipping, wholesaling and retailing stages, and this increased the capital requirements. Unlike canning, the refrigerated meat industry also required greater communication between producer, shipper, wholesaler and retailer. Canned meat could be treated as general cargo and required no special attention once it had left the processor, but refrigerated food required further investment in specialist equipment at every stage of distribution, and these stages were also opportunities for foreign capital to enter the industry.

In all four meat-producing regions foreign capital continued as the dominant constituent of capital formation after 1880. H. Schwartz's figures for Argentina, Uruguay, Australia and New Zealand show all of these dependent economies, relying even more heavily on Europe, and Britain in particular, to finance their development after 1880 than before that date. In 1913 the United Kingdom was the largest holder of private portfolio and direct debt and public debt in all four countries. As most of the United Kingdom's private investment was portfolio, in many cases local businessmen still controlled the management of these firms. The fall in agricultural prices from the 1880s provoked financial crises in all these countries in the early 1890s. These years were marked by failures of sheep stations in Australia and New Zealand resulting in them being taken over by local banks, to which most of them were already mortgaged.[15] In both countries the crisis also saw bank failures and presented governments with problems in debt servicing. In Australia the unprofitable railway system, owned by the state governments and financed by foreign borrowing, was a particularly heavy burden.

The Argentine financial crisis, which also affected Uruguay, began with the failure of an important local bank, together with Baring Brothers in 1890. These, and other associated business failures, also cast doubt on the ability of both governments to meet repayments on an increased level of foreign borrowing in the 1880s. But by the end of the decade all meat producers had recovered from their difficulties, first by government financial retrenchment and debt reorganisation, which in turn allowed the recovery of agricultural exports and the resumption of foreign lending. The part played in recovery by agricultural exports, through the intensification of production, though present in New Zealand and Australia, was particularly strong in Argentina and Uruguay where the renewal of foreign lending fuelled a rapid economic boom. Argentina's exports of beef (and wheat) doubled between 1890–94 and 1900–04, and tripled in 1910–14. By 1914 exports of chilled and frozen beef were second only to those of grain in value, and those of jerked beef had become insignificant.[16]

After 1870 South America always had the greatest foreign ownership of its meat export industry. Indeed here it was not so much a case of foreign penetration as one of foreign initiation and continued domination. In the early years there was in fact little participation of Argentine capital in this section of the meat industry, and it was predominantly British-owned until after 1900. We have already seen in Chapter 2 above how the first experiments with the voyage of the SS *Paraguay* were financed by the French, and soon after two French companies obtained a monopoly from the Argentine government to export frozen beef for the next five years. As with the *Paraguay*, their meat was not frozen onshore but in the holds of the ships before they left port. But once the trade was established the first Argentinian freezing plant, or *frigorifico*, was built in 1882 at San Nicholas on the Paraná. It was founded and managed by a local owner of a salting works, Eugenio Terrason. He shipped his first cargo in 1883 but only continued in business until 1894.

Also in 1882 a freezing works was built at Campana but by a British firm, the River Plate Fresh Meat Company. Its owner, G.W. Drabble, was British and originally intended only to freeze Argentine mutton and ship it to Britain, but after 1896 he also started to freeze and ship beef. In 1883 there was a serious indigenous challenge to the French and British domination of this trade when the wealthy Argentine Sansinena family financed the first locally owned freezing establishment on the Riachuelo in the suburbs of Buenos Aires with a business called La Negra. In 1891 this became a joint stock company under the name of *Compania Sansinena de Carnes Congeladas*, but always known in Britain as the Sansinena Co. It also extended its operations and built the Cuateros freezing plant at Bahia Blanca in 1903 and the *Frigorifico Uraguayo* in Montevideo. In 1886 the initiative once again passed to foreign capital when an English firm of livestock dealers, James Nelson & Sons, established a freezing works at Las Palmas and in 1893 this was incorporated as an Argentine company under the name of the Las Palmas Produce Company, Ltd. The last three companies, two of them British and one Argentine-owned, all extended their operations and continued to dominate the South American meat trade for twenty years or so, until after the Boer War.[17]

In the early 1880s the shipments from Argentina were almost entirely of mutton as most Argentine cattle were unimproved animals who produced low quality meat at a time when the United States meat companies were trying to build demand in Europe for their better quality chilled beef. Three of the four early plants, at San Nicholas, Las Palmas and Campana, were situated in what was a mutton-producing zone in the 1880s but, as the market situation changed and the local farmers responded to it, by 1914 that area was producing only beef.[18]

The ownership situation in South America was seriously disturbed in the early twentieth century for a number of reasons, and saw an increase in the proportion of local investment. After its initial growth spurt in the 1880s, the 1890s were a decade of relative stagnation for the whole international economy and this had a severe effect on the heavily export oriented Argentine economy.[19] But the period 1901 to 1903 has been described as a 'golden era' for the three existing meat companies. The first cause was the exceptionally high profits earned by all meat companies from Britain's involvement in the Boer War of 1901 to 1903. Prior to this, British imports of meat and livestock from all countries were at a low point, but the British market revived after the late 1890s. But labour troubles in the United States reduced its live cattle and chilled beef exports, and drought in Australia cut its frozen mutton exports, leaving the British beef and mutton market mainly to the three South American firms. As a result, the *frigorificos* found they were earning profits of between 50 and 100 per cent in the early twentieth century. In 1896–98 James Nelson and Sons' £1 ordinary shares paid no dividend at all, and just before the war stood at 16s; at their high point in 1902 they reached 84s and paid a dividend for that year of 10s per share.[20]

It was inevitable that returns of that order should attract new entrants to the industry, some of it financed by Argentine capital, and for the first time Argentine cattle and sheep owners decided to participate. In 1902 they founded *La Société Anonyme de Viande Congelées* with a capital of £300,000 and started operations in 1903 with a factory situated on the river Riachuelo in the port of Buenos Aires. In the same year the Sansinena Co. undertook more investment in partnership with the British firm of Thomas Borthwick & Sons and some Argentine *estancieros* and built a new works, the La Blanca, at Bahia Blanca. Also in 1903 a new foreign company, the La Plata Cold Storage Company, built an export works situated on deep water at Puerto La Plata. It was originally geared to export South American beef to South Africa, but as this trade declined it switched its outlets to London. The ownership of this company is somewhat ambiguous; its offices were in Cape Town but Critchell and Raymond regard it as a British company although it also included Australian and South African capital. Another of the new entrants to the industry, financed jointly by British and Argentine capitalists in 1903, was the Smithfield and Argentine Meat Company. This started operations in 1905 from a works near Zarate. The final company, the *Frigorifico Argentino*, was entirely Argentine owned and began its operations in June 1905. It was also built on the banks of the Riachuelo, a few miles up-river from the existing Sansinena plant, but it was later sold to the United States firm of Wilson. At the same time the Sansina Company established a Uruguayan plant on the northern side of the River Plate under the name of the *Frigorifico Uruguay*.[21]

The freezing firms in the Australian and New Zealand industry included more domestically owned and financed businesses, than in South America. Unlike the canning industry, the meat freezing began first in New Zealand and became more important to the country's economy than it did in Australia where the rising urban population absorbed more of the country's meat. New Zealand's economy was depressed in the early 1880s by low wool prices, and revived as its meat exports grew. To accommodate the change, sheep farmers undertook further livestock investment by concentrating less on the pure Merino breed purely for wool, but crossed this animal with various other breeds that still produced good wool with a heavier carcase. The industry could not become so large in Australia where large areas were unsuitable for sheep, and the whole country was also subject to periodic droughts, which interrupted the supply of animals to the freezing works. Sheep farmers in the Australian colonies continued to concentrate primarily on the wool crop for their income with meat production always regarded as a secondary output.

Here cattle were used for frozen beef exports as well, but again this industry was subject to periodic interruptions by drought.[22]

In New Zealand it was the large sheep owners who were the pioneers of the industry, with capital from New Zealand land, finance, and merchant companies. This was because the resources of the farmers alone, against the background of low wool and livestock prices in the early 1880s, were quite inadequate to undertake the amount of investment involved. In the 1880s there were five companies started and a further eight in the 1890s and 1900s. Although a number of these businesses were referred to as 'farmers' companies' they had in fact little control over sales and merely froze the sheep for the farmers and then consigned it to the various merchant houses and financial companies in England doing business in the colony.[23] As many of these firms were British owned, the actual amount of New Zealand control and capital involved in the industry was somewhat less than the foundation and ownership of the freezing works themselves might suggest. In Australia the ownership situation seems to have been very similar but here, as progress was slower there were only three freezing works in the 1880s, in Queensland, New South Wales, and Victoria. In the 1890s and 1900s the rate of expansion increased and these decades saw the construction of another 21.[24] Not all were directly concerned with the meat industry. Some were used intermittently and closed down when there were no surplus livestock available for slaughter. But as the use of refrigeration was applied to other food, and even non-food products, some freezing works might combine meat processing with a variety of other operations. In Melbourne in 1912 there were four freezing works occasionally available for meat export, including one owned by a butter-making co-operative, and another built for ice skating.[25]

These last four freezing works were partly geared to catering for the domestic meat market, and it is important to remember that the meat industries of all the meat-surplus countries also had to cater for their home demand as well. Australia was the most highly urbanized of the producers, and as it had the smallest surplus the domestic market absorbed almost all its meat output in drought years. The positions of New Zealand and South America were the reverse, each one having permanently large surpluses available for export. In Argentina only one of the three original firms in the industry, the domestically owned Sansinena Co. concerned itself much with that country's home market. Operating this branch of its operations under the old company name of La Negra it was the main meat supplier in Buenos Aires and had a number of shops throughout the city.[26]

The market pattern of the United States did not fit in neatly with the three others. Although it had a large and growing home demand, its meat companies built up a healthy export trade from the 1870s largely as a way of protecting their domestic profits in any years there was a meat surplus. As this surplus grew steadily up to the mid-1890s they had over twenty years in which to establish a remarkably efficient and permanent exporting branch of their industry. But by around the turn of the century the domestic market had grown sufficiently to absorb all of the United States meat output and the export had virtually disappeared by 1911. As prices rose and the world demand for meat increased, there were corresponding pressures on all sources of supply. This left the meat companies with two options. They could either dispose of their investments in the foreign meat trade or they could try and keep these assets profitably employed by finding alternative sources of meat. In fact they chose the latter option and switched their export operations to South America. As Argentina had now become the beef-producing centre of the world it was in the best position to provide an alternative supply for the American firms.[27] This decision marked the start of the final and most dramatic change in investment in and ownership of the Argentine meat industry. The American companies did not gain their first foothold in this industry by building their own freezing works, but by taking over two of the firms and plants from their existing owners. The decision to build fresh plants came after they were established.

As early as 1890 there had been overtures for amalgamation from Eastmans, the first exporter of chilled beef to Britain, with the British-owned River Plate Fresh Meat Co., but the River Plate owners declined this offer. Eastmans apparently made their move because they were impressed by the growth in the size of the trade.[28] The first effective action by United States firms was in 1907 when Swift & Co. purchased the La Plata slaughtering and cold storage plant in Buenos Aires for £350,000, from its British owners who were no longer interested in this trade. On learning of Swift's decision three of the other large American firms, Armour, Morris, and Schwarzchild and Sulzberger decided on the same strategy. After further negotiation Armour and Morris together with Swift bought the La Blanca plant from *La Société Anonyme de Viande Congelées*, through their jointly owned firm the National Packing Co. in 1908. From its foundation in 1903 the owners of the company had not found the meat trade as profitable as the golden years had promised and in some of their markets, particularly South Africa, they had like La Plata experienced losses. On hearing of the proposed sale to American interests the Argentine Government unsuccessfully tried to persuade the Argentine owners not to sell on patriotic grounds. It is not surprising that the government's appeal fell on deaf ears, as the Americans were offering 140 pesos for shares that had fallen to only 77 pesos before they arrived on the scene. Both of these plants were only a few years old and each was well suited to make a substantial contribution to Argentina's meat exports. This was particularly true of La Blanca; it was an ideally situated set of premises and was the third largest shipper of beef to Britain.[29]

## Business Methods and Organisation

In each of the four main meat-exporting regions the organisation and methods employed as the industry evolved in its period of high growth between 1870 and 1914 were quite distinctive. In the United States the meat companies' primary concern was to provide for the domestic market, whereas the New Zealand, South American, and to a lesser extent the Australian meat industries grew on the back of export demand. The United States had such a large and buoyant economy that here both the technical improvements and new management methods could be pioneered. The size of the United States internal market also meant that by 1914 the largest firms in the industry were located there. In various works since 1962 Alfred D. Chandler has identified the methods employed by United States meat firms, in common with other large businesses corporations, to reinforce their growth. Once they had attained sufficient size and efficiency they could enlarge their premises, set up branch houses, generate economies of scale, and eventually come to dominate the market. Large firms could benefit from economies of scale and scope in distribution through vertical integration, both backward into the lines of supply and forwards into the channels of distribution, as it allowed them to circumvent the networks of middlemen and wholesalers upon which smaller rivals were forced to rely.[30] The following section will outline the evolution of the most important of these features in the large American meat firms using them as a comparative model to see how they differed from those in other countries.

Chandler has paid particular attention to Swift & Co but it shared common features with the two other large meat firms that had come to dominate the industry in the United States by 1900, Armour and Co., and Morris and Co.[31] Meat packing did include other sizeable firms, like Cudhay and Co. and Messrs Schwarzchild and Sulzberger, but was dominated by the 'big three' who often worked together to reinforce their control. From an early stage in their history these firms had established close links with the large railroad companies, who shared several features in common with the meat companies. In 1865 the railroads opened the gigantic Union Stockyards in Chicago contributing $925,000 of the $1 million cost of these premises, and the city meat packers shared the rest. The railroad companies' size and importance in the internal transport system made them an essential part of the meat packers' supply and distribution chain. This was reinforced by the development of the refrigerated freight car by Gustavus Swift in the late-1870s. After the railroad companies refused to build them, the Chicago packing firms of Armour, Morris, Swift, and Hammond provided their own company-owned refrigerated cars for the year-round distribution of fresh meat to the cities of the east. These four firms also evolved very similar systems of large scale factory line processing, and by 1890 they handled 89 per cent of the cattle slaughtered in Chicago. Besides meat processing and distribution, they also paid attention to by-product manufacture with items like animal hair for upholstery, fats, fertilizer, gelatine, glue, industrial lubricants, and pharmaceutical products. They also absorbed a large number of their smaller competitors, further increasing their market power.[32]

In addition they took the lead in both the transatlantic trade in live cattle and meat.[33] Pressure on costs was also reduced when both the chilled beef and live cattle trade fell under the control of these large companies who conducted their businesses in a broadly similar manner on both sides of the Atlantic. By the 1890s exports of chilled beef were controlled by the five biggest Chicago meat packing firms of Armour, Morris, Swift, Hammond, and Schwarzchild and Sulzberger. Together they co-operated to regulate supplies, eliminate wasteful competition, and ensure stable prices. By 1900 this had become even more effective, and further concentration placed the British trade in the hands of only three firms, Armour, Morris, and Swift.[34] In the 1870s and early 1880s British salesmen such as Edward Pool who had dealt in livestock from Europe in the 1860s, and Thomas Bater who

imported Canadian cattle in the 1870s, controlled United States imports.[35] But by
the end of the 1890s American firms not only took control of shipping space, they
also established their own wholesale and retail distribution networks in Britain. Up
to the end of 1889 there were no advertisements for American firms in the chief
publication of the British meat trade, the *Meat Trades Journal*. But in the 1890s the
large American firms now installed their own managers. Some of them were from
America, such as L.J. Woodruff who worked for the Swift Beef Company and
Abraham Cohn who worked for Morris, but others, such as Isaac Hodgkinson, who
was the manager for Armour & Co., were British.[36] The United States firms were
partly forced to set up their own retail chains because most British butchers were
reluctant to stock American chilled beef, so the British housewife in search of
chilled beef was more likely to buy it from the specialist 'American meat store'.[37]

Within the United States itself the large companies operated very much as
cartels. They based their buying, processing and selling operations in several states,
and their oligopolistic practices such as their mutual co-operation over prices and
markets convinced many Americans that their government should take action to
prevent private economic power from destroying competition. This argument was
applied not only to the meat packers, but all industries and services where the large
corporation emerged. As early as 1888 large-scale refrigerated meat shipments had
evoked enough complaints from farmers, meat trade middlemen and butchers to
petition for the Senate 'to examine fully all questions touching on the meat product
of the United States'. This was the first of a number of investigations into the
packers prompted by cattlemen, butchers, and independent wholesalers who
believed their livelihoods were threatened by the big packers. The Senate
committee's report that followed was also the first of a number of reports and
investigations that were followed by government action.

In addition to coming under scrutiny at home for their oligopolistic trade
practices, it was perhaps inevitable that similar anxieties were expressed about
their behaviour in the international market. In Britain the question of trade
practices was quick to surface. It is surprising that Henry Macrosty made no
mention of the American meat firms in his 1907 study of trusts in Britain which
was published only two years before the British Parliament commissioned its
*Report of the Departmental Committee on Combinations in the Meat Trade*.[38] The
1909 Committee found that the companies in Britain were 'carrying on their
business in co-operation rather than in competition but it should be said that this
co-operation appears to be more for the purpose of advancing their own interests
than of acquiring the trade of others'. They concluded that the combination was not
yet sufficiently powerful to be a danger to the beef trade as a whole. They reached
that conclusion because the American companies did not control the home-
produced beef trade that made up 60 per cent of British consumption, nor did they
control all the imported beef trade. But the Committee expressed anxieties that the
position might change if the trust firms established large interests in other beef
exporting countries, particularly in South America.[39]

Criticism continued as the activities of the firms in the Meat Trust were also
called into question regarding public health.[40] The traditional interpretation used to
be that revelations about packing house conditions revealed by local journalists and

'factionalised' in Upton Sinclair's 1906 novel *The Jungle,* prompted the first serious government investigation of conditions inside the packing plants.[41] But the investigations had begun well before that date, and were initially prompted by complaints made by the smaller packing firms in the Chicago area and in the country at large, against what they regarded as unfair competition from their larger and technologically more advanced rivals. From 1880 onwards the small local slaughterhouses found they were the losers in the face of the advances made by the big Chicago packers, and were fighting a defensive battle. Unable to compete with the large firms technically, the small packers adopted a different strategy and accused the large packers of using diseased cattle and producing unwholesome beef. But the real reason for their grievances was they were losing control of their local markets, and many of them were being forced to close down. As far as the small packers were concerned, their complaints to local and federal authorities over the behaviour of the industry's giants were mainly attempts to manipulate government to bring in a regime of inspection and control. By doing this they hoped to reduce the economic advantages of the large packers by adding to their costs, rather than possessing any real desire to protect public health.[42] However, the investigations into both the system of inspection in those establishments and the moral and physical circumstances of the workers did result in the 1891 Meat Inspection Act.

The general verdict on all attempts to control trusts, like the Sherman Anti-Trust Act of 1890, the decisions of Federal courts, and President Theodore Roosevelt's attempts to impose Federal inspection of packing plants has to be that they left the large firms virtually unscathed.[43] The big packers were sufficiently flexible in their operations to be able to accommodate the government inspections and hygiene controls without raising their costs. They could do this because, unlike the trade in livestock,[44] there had never been any serious health problems associated with their plants in the first place. But once the regime of inspection was established the beef trust could use the fact they were inspected by the government as a further guarantee as to the quality of their meat.

In the last of its great attempts to regulate the industry, in 1910 the government finally brought a criminal prosecution against Swift and ten other packers, charging them with using the National Packing Company to fix prices, suppress competition, and control the industry for their own benefit. In reply the packers called no witnesses, claiming instead that the government's evidence supported their contention they were in active competition, and leaving it to the Federal jury to reach a verdict based on the government's witnesses and the judge's summing up. The jury agreed with the packers and returned a verdict of not guilty, based on how they judged the evidence and not as Judge Carpenter had warned them 'merely upon suspicion' and because they thought 'such a conviction might be popular'. Nevertheless in 1912 the National Packing Company was sold because it had not been profitable rather than in fear of the anti-Trust laws.[45] But other than that they did little in the fundamental way they organised and ran their businesses.[46] Part of the reason was that they were powerful enough to challenge legislation and legal verdicts in the courts, but they had also achieved this position by the logic of the free market and satisfying their customers, which was a fundamental principle of the United States economy.

**Table 3.1  Meat industry structure in the northern and southern hemispheres**

(A) Northern hemisphere in 1902

| Firm | Other companies owned | Number of US states in which they were owned | Number owned in the United Kingdom |
|------|------|------|------|
| Armour | 13 | 8 | – |
| Morris | 8 | 1 | 3 |
| Swift | 26 | 8 | 3 |
| TOTAL | 47 | – | 6 |

(B) Southern hemisphere in 1912

| Country | Number of freezing works | Number of owners | Number with owners in two countries* |
|------|------|------|------|
| Australia | 36 | 28 | 4 |
| New Zealand | 27 | 18 | 2 |
| South America | 13 | 11 | – |
| TOTAL | 76 | 57 | 6 |

*Birt & Co. Ltd and the British firm of Thomas Borthwick & Sons (Australasia), Ltd each owned two works in Australia and one in New Zealand.

*Sources:* Yeager, M., *Competition and Regulation: The Development of Oligopoly in the Meat Packing Industry* (Greenwich, Conn., 1981), pp. 162–4; J.T. Critchell and J. Raymond, *A History of the Frozen Meat Trade* (London, 1912), Appendix VII.

There are a number of reasons why the meat industries elsewhere could never achieve the same high degree of integration and control of their markets as the big North American firms. In South America the freezing firms became large, but they were not in the same class as those in the United States. Those in New Zealand were smaller and in Australia they were even smaller. It is possible, using information from two sources, to make an approximate comparison between the structures of the meat industry in the northern and southern hemispheres in Table 3.1 above. J.T. Critchell and J. Raymond's *A History of the Frozen Meat Trade* lists all the freezing works in the countries of the southern hemisphere in 1912, giving also the names of the companies who owned them. They all operated in smaller economies than the United States, but one is struck by the fact that there were 76 of them, owned by a total of 57 firms and that no firm owned more than three freezing works. In contrast, M. Yeager's study of United States meat packers presents a list of the stocks and properties of the firms and the states where they were located, owned by Armour, Morris, and Swift, which they initially agreed to merge into the National Packing Company in 1902. Although the two parts of the table do not measure the same things, they provide an accurate impression of the meat industry's north/south divide in terms of branch, interstate, and international structure.

Size was not entirely lacking in the meat industry of the southern hemisphere, though the most there was in the way of owning multiple businesses were two firms each with three freezing works, two of them in the country of the parent firm plus a further freezing works in another country. But in the United States, Armour, Swift and Morris owned at least 13, 26, and eight separate companies, respectively, and Morris and Swift each owned three other meat companies in the United Kingdom. The table in fact understates the extent of the northern hemisphere's diversification, as the plants counted in the southern hemisphere were only freezing works but those in the northern hemisphere reflected the vertically integrated structure of the industry that was largely absent in the south. The northern firms had rail transport, provisioning, leather, and rendering concerns, as well as one or two dealing with items that appear to have had little to do with meat such as fruit, cotton oil, and even a mining company. This diversification was a process that was to continue in the following years, although the amounts of all non-meat goods handled by the packers remained relatively small.[47]

Overall efficiency of the industry was greater in North America than the southern hemisphere, but there were also differences in efficiency between the three southern hemisphere countries. South America was probably closest to the North American model. All three specialised in the same product, frozen meat, but in early as 1899 when there were only 3 freezing works in South America, 25 in New Zealand and 17 in Australia, the South American plants worked at 70 per cent of their capacity while the New Zealand and Australian works could only achieve capacity utilisations of 40 and 25 per cent, respectively.[48] In New Zealand and Australia there were thus a large number of small plants, none of which were processing even half the number of animals they were capable of. With one major slaughtering centre at Buenos Aires and a more efficient system of railways with refrigerated livestock carriages to move beasts there in the summer months, the Argentine meat processing industry could become far more concentrated. But as New Zealand had freezing works in both islands, and each Australian colony eventually had freezing works, their industries were far more geographically and politically scattered, and railways in neither country were as efficient. Together these factors made the seasonal variations in slaughtering much more marked, giving Australian and New Zealand freezing works far more slack time each year.

Such differences were also present in the international trading pattern. In the nineteenth century the United Kingdom was always the main market for internationally traded meat, where both product quality and business organisation allowed United States firms to take the leading position before 1914. American chilled beef helped alter the whole balance of arrivals at London's main wholesale market, Smithfield, in favour of imported meats, and American firms also took a number of stalls there. In keeping with their increasing importance in the British market, they were prominent in their advertising. Both Swift and Armour used banner advertisements in the trade press and Swift in Britain stressed the link with its American parent, as well as the origin of its products. When they opened their own chains of retail shops this also gave them much greater control over the outlets for their own meat. Although this intrusion into the British wholesale and retail trade was viewed with alarm, their operations in Britain mirrored earlier changes in the United States. Because they were selling the same product in both countries they felt they needed to adopt the same broad methods in both, with whatever local adaptation the market required.

None of the Australian or New Zealand firms could match the United States firms in Britain for coordinated wholesaling and retailing operations. One reason was that the main product of their frozen meat industries was predominantly frozen mutton and lamb, which the consumer always found less desirable than chilled beef. But it also seems to have been a function of size of the trade, distance and the number of competing firms. Australian exports were the smallest, and the intermittent nature of some did not justify setting up retail outlets for meat from those colonies alone. The 28 Australian and 18 New Zealand freezing companies in Table 3.1 above did not co-operate with each other as did the three United States firms. They were more numerous and smaller and their atomistic structure, with less of the visible hand of corporate capitalism, militated against cooperation in the late nineteenth and early twentieth century.[49] As exporters they were also entering a market where the United States firms had greater experience. When they began in the 1880s Australia and New Zealand had no on-shore freezing; no direct steamer service to Britain; no preference of demand amongst British consumers for frozen meat; and no organization for storing the meat and controlling its release onto the market once it arrived in Britain.[50]

In overcoming these challenges the United States firms, and later the South American ones, would normally work together much more than colonial meat producers. With limits on the amounts of cold storage space available in British cities it was essential for shippers to act and arrange to stagger the arrival of chilled and frozen meat ships to prevent the British market from being glutted. The American firms were very effective at this, but the New Zealand and Australian freezing firms were never as good at coordinating their arrivals.[51] Meat on each ship was often despatched from a number of ports, which meant time lost in loading and expense added at each call. More damage was done to Australian and New Zealand cargoes by careless handling. Supplies, especially from Australia, were irregular which made it hard to establish a regular demand. In some years the heaviest quantities arrived at the wrong time, as in 1899 when large amounts of New Zealand mutton arrived in early autumn just when demand for that meat was falling off, and in the six weeks before Christmas when the London demand for beef was at its peak there was no beef from Queensland.[52]

They also had less close control over how their products were retailed. As late as 1901 H.C. Cameron, the New Zealand Produce Commissioner in London pointed to the 'slow growth of the field for the distribution of New Zealand mutton'. He attributed this to the keen competition from River Plate mutton in the Midlands, and the weak branding and advertising of the New Zealand product.[53] This could have ironic consequences. He (and others) complained that butchers often sold the best New Zealand frozen lamb as British, but sold inferior quality Australian and River Plate frozen lamb as New Zealand. The benefit to the retailer was that the wholesale price of frozen New Zealand lamb was lower than fresh British lamb but the retail price of the meat reflected the higher value of English lamb. In 1901–02 he successfully initiated prosecutions against three large butchers' firms in Liverpool for selling River Plate mutton as New Zealand mutton, and Australian lamb as New Zealand Canterbury lamb, and secured a conviction in each case. But the magistrates' fines of £10 with costs of £7 7s. seem small in relation to the overall size of the trade.[54]

Not only frozen New Zealand mutton and lamb was subjected to this treatment. It was also claimed that established traders circulated reports that all refrigerated meat was inferior in quality to the home-killed and that butchers endeavoured to excite a prejudice against Australian beef in order to obtain it cheaply and then sell it dear as English meat.[55] But as a counter Weddel & Co., a British firm who specialized in the frozen meat trade, argued that colonial and Argentine meat was the healthiest as it had the lowest percentage of carcases seized by inspectors checking for disease.[56] To improve its industry's sales the New Zealand government even appointed a panel of experts to investigate the possibility of opening its own chain of retail shops in Britain to sell the colony's meat, but eventually abandoned the idea.[57] But it was not only colonial frozen meat that was subject to misrepresentation. British farmers alleged that butchers from the Lancashire cotton towns travelled to Birkenhead where they bought the beef from port-killed American and Canadian cattle and sold it in their shops as good quality English beef, while passing off any poor quality English beef as port-killed.[58]

British producers were eventually saved from this situation by the fact that the trade in American beef was only temporary. By 1910 the United States cattle ranges had largely disappeared, and the absence of cheap land meant American beef was unable to compete in world markets with the products of South America and Australia and New Zealand – continents where conditions were still similar to those of the US in the early nineteenth century. British imports of North American chilled beef and cattle peaked in 1901 and 1905, respectively, but fell continuously thereafter.[59] The growth of the population fuelled by decades of immigration and supported by natural increase raised domestic demand to such a point that after 1910 meat production in the United States failed to keep pace with the demand, and the beef and bacon price differential between Britain and America disappeared.[60]

When, in response to these changes, the United States firms entered the South American industry they did so with a range of tried and tested business techniques that increased the competitive strength of the product. When supplies from the United States decreased, and South American beef came to dominate the export trade, the Trust companies saw a venture into the Argentine Republic as the only way of keeping their European organization afloat. They had built up a huge distributive organisation in Britain, and further investment in South America was the only way they could keep it supplied.[61] The prospect of selling a highly sophisticated wholesale and retail meat distribution system to their competitors was distinctly unattractive. But they needed to be able to bring in the same quantities of South American beef to keep it fully employed. They achieved this in two ways.

The first part of their strategy was the enlargement of their works. When they started none of the Argentine plants matched the great Chicago or Kansas City establishments. A River Plate plant with a daily capacity of 500 cattle and 3,000 sheep was a large one, but this was considered small by North American standards. Their small capacity meant there was not the same demand for labour-saving devices. Very little of the plant's work in moving carcases and loads was done by mechanical power, and processing times were considered as slow. Very few of the abattoir by-products were processed by the packers, unlike the United States, but usually sold in an unfinished state to local factories.[62] Investment and the introduction of new methods allowed the United States firms to handle more of the trade, but still not enough to keep their British retail chains fully supplied.

**Table 3.2  Percentage of South American meat exports held by British, Argentine, and American companies, 1910 to June 1914**

| Nationality | Normal competition 1910 | 1911 | First price war Jan. to Nov. 1911 | Period of agreement Dec. 1911 to Mar. 1913 | Second price war April 1913 to June 1914 | Agreed shares June 1914 |
|---|---|---|---|---|---|---|
| British | 37.0 | 33.9 | 30.2 | 32.5 | 24.4 | 26.4 |
| Argentine | 27.7 | 24.9 | 24.9 | 23.9 | 17.6 | 14.6 |
| American | 35.3 | 41.2 | 44.7 | 42.4 | 58.0 | 59.0 |

*Source:* Cmd 456 (PP 1919, Vol. XXV), *Inter-Departmental Committee on Meat Supplies. Report of the Committee appointed by the Board of Trade to Consider the Means of Securing Sufficient Meat Supplies for the United Kingdom*, p. 9.

To do this they also judged that they needed to take over an increased share from the established British and Argentine companies. This second part of their strategy involved two highly aggressive and successful price wars. The first was from the start of 1911 up to November 1911. This was followed by a period of agreement that lasted up to March 1913. It broke down in April 1913 and the second war lasted to June 1914. The first agreement in 1911 only applied to beef and included just the Argentine plants, as at that time the Uruguay works were small and produced no chilled beef, which was the new high-profit and high-profile product driving the contest to gain greater control of the trade.[63]

In the periods of these disputes the American firms bought from the *estancieros* as many animals as they could, forcing up the price of cattle in Argentina, but also forcing down prices in Britain when increased supplies of beef arrived. Even though by doing this they ensured all parties traded at a loss, they were large enough to bear these for longer than their competitors. The activities of the Trust firms aroused publicity and press comment and investigations in Britain and the United States as the question of public interest was held to be involved. In the event, the decisions of all parties after these conflicts became public knowledge when the results of the investigations were published. From Table 3.2 above it can be seen just how successful the Trust firms' price wars were, especially the second one. Plant extension during the 24-month period of normal competition only allowed the American firms to take an extra 5.9 per cent of the trade, but the two price wars earned them a further 17.8 percentage points in 25 months.

**Table 3.3  Percentage of South American meat exports held by individual British, Argentine, and American public companies in June 1914**

| Company | Ownership | Beef percentage five-sevenths | Mutton percentage two-sevenths | Total percentage overall |
|---|---|---|---|---|
| In Argentina | | | | |
| British & Argentine | UK | 20.034 | 24.180 | 19.500 |
| S. & A. M. Co | UK | 7.139 | 7.575 | 6.852 |
| F.A.C. (Wilson) | US | 8.156 | 7.575 | 7.819 |
| La Blanca | US | 16.313 | 9.960 | 14.571 |
| La Plata (Swift) | US | 31.922 | 27.010 | 29.611 |
| Sansinena | Argentine | 7.608 | 23.700 | 9.622 |
| | | | 100.000 | |
| In Uruguay | | | | |
| F.M (Swifts) | US | 5.862 | 47.690 | 7.064 |
| F.U. (Sansinena) | Argentine | 2.966 | 53.310 | 4.961 |
| | | 100.000 | 100.000 | 100.000 |

*Source:* Brewster, J.A., 'The South American Trade', in F. Gerrard, (ed), *The Book of the Meat Trade* (2 vols, London, 1949), vol. 1, p. 216.

As the agreement reached at the end of the second price war included mutton as well as beef, the distribution of the total trade among the different companies indicates the relative scale of their operations in both mutton and beef. Between the end of 1911 and April 1913 James Nelson & Sons, the Las Palmas Factory and the River Plate Fresh Meat Company had amalgamated to form the British and Argentine Meat Company. This United Kingdom firm was now a large player in the South American chilled and frozen meat trade, but although it controlled 20.034 per cent of the Argentine beef trade it also had control of 24.180 per cent of that country's exports of mutton.[64] The proportions of beef and mutton finally agreed upon by all eight firms can be seen in Table 3.3 above. The preoccupation with and concern of all the United States companies with their beef interests is clear from this table. Because beef was the major meat in the United States a good deal of their processing skills and marketing expertise were in this meat, rather than in mutton and lamb for which demand in the United States was much smaller. All four United States plants were processing a greater ratio of beef and a smaller ratio of mutton than either the British or Argentine firms who had entered the trade when exports of River Plate mutton were relatively more important than beef.

Whereas Table 3.2 above reveals the United States plants emerged from the second price war controlling 59 per cent of all South American meat, Table 3.3 above reveals their share of the beef trade on the eve of the First World War was even larger at 62.253 per cent of this meat.

Although the established firms protested strongly about the price-cutting, throughout the meat trade wars after 1910, there was very little that they could do to counter the United States firms. When they first entered the South American market, the American companies were far better equipped to pursue these tactics than the established British and Argentine firms. They had many years of successful experience in dealing with competitors in the United States in the same way, and there was no reason why they could not be effectively applied in South America.[65] In contrast, the British and Argentine firms seem to have established among themselves a rather steady and cosy working relationship which had not prepared them for the new situation in which they found themselves. Although the Anglo-Argentine firms met informally to agree prices and limit competition among themselves, they rarely included all firms and had never established a formal 'pool' on the model of the United States companies and along the lines they were to impose in South America after 1911. But the rise of the trade in chilled beef involved extra costs and risks for all firms. The life of chilled meat was only about forty days and the voyage to Europe took about a month, leaving only ten days for distribution and consumption. As R.C. Gebhardt has pointed out:[66]

> Price wars increased the cost burden of chilled beef because it could not be stored for long periods of time without being frozen down at an extortionate cost, especially due to the losses incurred in the price differences between higher value chilled beef and lower priced frozen meat. Within this context, the first pool was set up in December 1911, which was a joint agreement that divided total exports by *frigorifico*.

The American trust firms' success can be seen in their continued hold over the imported beef trade in Britain. By 1913 the United States meat companies operating in Britain contributed about 20 per cent of the beef supply, or about half the total beef imported; at Smithfield their influence was greater and they controlled over 45 per cent of the total beef and 57 per cent of the total supply of all meats. In 1914 the four American companies, and one British company in this trade, had 144 wholesale depots in 61 towns.[67]

In retaining this share of the British market the American firms also played their part in modifying the Argentine product to fill the place left by American beef. Prior to 1900 less attention was paid to livestock quality, as almost all the meat shipped from the River Plate was frozen and hence commanded a lower price than United States chilled.[68] But from 1901 British and South American companies sent increased quantities of chilled beef. At first this beef did not match the quality of United States chilled as the quality of Argentine cattle was lower, but *estancieros* undertook livestock improvements to bridge this gap and after 1907 the American firms encouraged them in this as well.[69] In any case, as United States chilled beef disappeared from the British market consumers lost this standard of quality against which to judge the substitute from Argentina. But the extent of the trade must not be exaggerated. Argentine chilled beef did not completely replace its frozen beef. In 1910 Britain imported 135,000 tons of South American chilled beef but imports of South American frozen beef were still over 250,000 tons.[70] By 1900 the River Plate meat producers had become the leading player in the meat export industry, providing a powerful stimulus to the country's growth. Between 1900 and 1914 its railway mileage doubled, and immigration and foreign borrowing resumed on a large scale following the relative stagnation of the 1890s.[71]

In addition, American firms were prompted to extend operations to South America by the fear that supplies of domestic beef alone might not be enough for the US market. By 1914 it was described as 'an open customer for meat' and there were anxieties that the Underwood Tariff Act, passed in 1913, which removed duties on meat shipped to the US, would see the long term diversion of Canadian, Australasian and South American meat from Europe. Considerable amounts were shipped from these countries to the US between the middle of 1913 and the outbreak of war.[72] By then the fear of all meat producing and consuming regions was that the US firms, driven by the need to supply their home market, would in future gain control of all meat producing regions in the way they had done for the River Plate. Their arrangements to share out the market were seen as evidence that this had already happened. But it is also possible to argue that by 1914 these shares were in fact fixed by the relative strengths of each firm. Meatpacking as a capital-intensive industry favoured the development of the large plant and the big firm. In the period before 1914 technical and organisational developments, both in the industry itself, and improvements in transport technology, had driven costs down as far as possible. Once this point was reached it was inevitable that the market shares of the leading firms would stabilise, as the only other alternative for a firm would be to drive prices below production costs to increase market share by driving one or more of its rivals out of business. But as in this situation all firms in the group would run similar risk of failure there was no incentive to carry this form of competition any further.

**Table 3.4 Meat Consumption in the United States, United Kingdom, Germany, and France, 1900–09**

| Country | Beef & Veal kg | % | Mutton & Lamb kg | % | Pork & Ham kg | % | Total Kg |
|---|---|---|---|---|---|---|---|
| USA | 35 | 45 | 5 | 6 | 38 | 49 | 78 |
| UK | 27 | 50 | 12 | 22 | 15 | 28 | 54 |
| Germany | 18 | 37 | 1 | 3 | 29 | 60 | 48 |
| France | 22 | 60 | 9 | 24 | 46 | 16 | 37 |

*Source:* USDA, *22nd Annual Report of the Bureau of Animal Industry for the Year 1905*, 1907, pp. 283–5; *26th Annual Report . . . for the Year 1909*, 1911, p. 315.

The anxiety about the Trust firms' control of the global meat trade was reinforced by the fact that besides beef, pig meat remained the other important

United States meat export. But it had negligible mutton to export, and Australia and New Zealand could supply greater quantities at lower prices. It can be seen in Table 3.4 above that although Britain was the largest consumer of mutton and lamb, it was the least important item in British meat consumption and even less important to the United States consumer. In fact even more pig meat was consumed than beef in the United States, and its exports of bacon and hams, were greater in volume, though lower in unit value, than those of beef.[73] Between 1870 and 1914 its exports of pork and hams remained as important as they had been between 1840 and 1870 and, unlike beef exports, did not disappear before the First War. But it is far harder to generalise about hog products than about beef because of their greater variety; even bacon is prepared in a number of ways.

The United States share of total imports of pig meat into Britain in 1888, when supplies reached their peak, was 92.2 per cent for hams and bacon, 88.1 per cent for salted pork, and 58.7 per cent for fresh, chilled and frozen meat. Thereafter, domestic demand in the United States began to increase, and the competition from third countries was more keenly felt. Imports of American salt pork declined in the face of imports of Dutch refrigerated pork, and American bacon experienced competition from Danish, so the United States lost its predominant position in the English import market. But substantial exports continued as Britain was a useful way of disposing of surpluses in years of overproduction, and for this reason American producers never bothered to cater specially for the tastes of the British market in the same way as Canadian and Danish manufacturers. The development of United States exports of lard also increased along with pig meat, but at the beginning of the twentieth century this trade received a check from increased production of artificial fats and margarine.[74]

**European Reactions to Imported Meat and Livestock**

By 1914 European attitudes were more or less fixed with most countries doing as much as they could to exclude it, but in Britain imports made up 42 per cent of the nation's meat consumption.[75] This situation was in contrast to the attitudes of the 1860s and 1870s when a number of Europeans enthusiastically helped pioneer further development of the industry and there were no difficulties about its entry into mainland Europe. In Chapter Two above it can be seen how the original Fray Bentos company that pioneered meat extract in Venezuela was Dutch owned, and the first shipment of frozen meat from South America was aboard the SS *Paraguay*, financed and fitted out in France where the meat was enthusiastically received and consumed. But by 1890 this open and receptive attitude towards augmenting Western Europe's food supply had hardened into a resolute determination to rely as much as possible on nationally produced foodstuffs.[76] This applied to cereals as much as to animal products, and the reasons behind it were the same in each case. Mainly it was because agriculture occupied larger shares of the economies of Europe than Britain and a higher proportion of the rural population owned and depended directly on the land for their livelihood. Peasant proprietorship was widespread and with such large numbers involved they formed their own political organisations to lobby on their behalf and governments depended on the agricultural interest for a large part of their support. In addition, those arguing the case for agricultural protection added the need for national self-sufficiency in food in case of war. This question was even considered in Britain but dropped because war was a temporary thing and Britain preferred to rely on imports of cheap food and invest in its naval strength to defend its international trade routes.[77]

The general depression in agricultural prices beginning in the late 1870s as a result of the growth of food production outside Europe and a fall in the cost of ocean transport added another powerful argument to the protectionist lobby. In France the first tariffs on agricultural products were introduced in 1881 and strengthened under the Méline Tariff of 1892 named after Jules Méline the protectionist Republican politician who was Minister of Agriculture from 1883 to 1885 and Prime Minister from 1896 to 1898. By 1887 there was a duty of 12 francs on every 100 kg of fresh beef and pork and 38 and 20 francs on every bullock and cow, respectively. In 1892 France, like Britain, stopped the import of cattle on the grounds of animal health and raised the duty on fresh beef to 25 francs. In 1903 the ban on cattle was removed but replaced by duties that were more or less prohibitive and a system of general and minimum duties was applied to meat and livestock. In 1897 the government was able to increase duties without reference to Parliament. The 1881 tariff checked the increase in imports of cattle and meat in the late 1870s and after 1900 under the new tariffs France became self-sufficient in cattle and beef and the number of pigs was also increased. [78]

The first tariffs on German agricultural products, including meat and livestock, were introduced in 1879, raised in the 1880s, before being lowered but not abolished in 1891, only to be raised again in 1902 and then lowered in March 1906. Imports of live animals were held approximately level from 1880 but meat imports rose to 1900 but then reduced by legislation in that year by stringent restrictions on some types of meat, the ports where meat could be landed and high inspection fees.[79] Germany and France had the most restrictive attitudes towards agricultural imports, and as they were the two largest markets of Western Europe, their protectionism had the greatest effect on the international meat industry

Although Britain was always the main market for American meat, US firms made some attempts to develop a trade with the rest of Europe, but with limited success. The size of the European market for meat from the United States was determined by income level, national patterns of meat consumption, and the extent of agricultural protection. The United Kingdom's adherence to free trade and its high income made the United Kingdom the largest market. Lower incomes, less urbanisation, and a larger rural population who demanded protectionist policies, limited the market in other countries. In addition, their consumption patterns were rather different from Britain's. A reasonably complete picture of consumption per head for the United States, Britain, France and Germany is presented in Table 3.4 above, which was prepared by the United States Bureau of Animal Industry to familiarise its producers with the nature of the European market. France had the greatest veal consumption and Germany the largest amount of pork. Britain's pattern of consumption with its higher percentage of beef was closest in character to the American. All three countries were potential markets as per capita meat consumption was lower than the United States, but if we take per capita consumption as an indicator of relative income levels and effective demand, then Britain, followed by France and Germany, offered the best opportunities. The American market was northern Europe and very little went to lower income southern Europe.

Germany was the next largest importer of United States meat products in Europe but lagged a long way behind the United Kingdom. In 1901 the US exported $M186 worth of meat products, of which $M118 went to Britain, $M21 to Germany and $M13 to Holland.[80] The high per capita consumption of pig meat in Germany suggests that here was the largest unexploited potential market for American meat. The largest item of meat products exported to Germany was lard, which in 1903–04 comprised over two-thirds of its US meat products.[81] Like other European countries, Germany used both tariff and non-tariff barriers against the import of American meat. For example, Germany placed an absolute ban on all imports of pig meat from 1883 to 1891 based on the fear of infection from trichinosis. Even after this was removed there is evidence that municipalities exercised their duties of inspection in a burdensome and even arbitrary way.[82]

The United States government actually provided assistance to ease the way for American meat firms and products into the European and British markets, but its efforts were more effective in Britain. For example, in June 1897 the US Bureau of Animal Industry representative for the United Kingdom successfully lobbied the chairman of the London and South Western Railway to establish a foreign animals wharf at Southampton to provide outlets for US beef to more markets along the south coast.[83] But despite the hindrances European governments placed on American meat imports, the industry still attempted to advertise itself there. In July 1900 the Bureau of Animal Industry organised the packing firms to provide a comprehensive range of fresh meats for the food section of an international exhibition held in Paris. These were displayed in large glass-fronted refrigerated display cases that had to be periodically replenished with fresh supplies throughout the two weeks of the event. Although the exhibit excited much interest on the part of merchants and approval from the general public, it encountered opposition from government officials, acting on behalf of French farmers. Ignoring a government dispensation given to the American exhibitors for the duration of the exhibition, freeing them from current restrictions on meat imports, they obstructed the movement of fresh supplies of meat from the port to the exhibition site as well as hindering the sale of the replaced meat at the Paris markets. As a result harassed American officials spent a considerable amount of time arguing with the local Paris meat inspectors, the result of which was that the local population had no opportunity to taste the imported meat.[84] But there is a suspicion of hypocrisy in this, as then the United States itself imposed tariffs on meat imports to shelter the American livestock producer.

However, there was a similar attitude to imports of livestock in all countries. Even the United Kingdom imposed restrictions, and sometimes complete bans, on imports of live animals.[85] But elsewhere in Europe they became more strict and permanent over time. In some cases there were legitimate reasons for restrictions on the international trade in livestock other than protecting the home market for a nation's farmers. This was when they were imposed because of fears of the diseases carried by foreign livestock, as in the case of the German ban on United States hogs referred to above. But they could also be used as a disguised form of protection to complement a ban on the import of meat. Very often the distinction between the two reasons became unclear as governments retained livestock embargos even after the immediate danger of transmitting any human or animal disease to the native population and herds had disappeared. Such reactions always aroused protests from the farmers and traders in the countries denied access to a market, but they were rarely successful, and as knowledge of human and animal disease advanced it became increasingly easy to justify a ban, even if it was only a pretext for disguised protection.

The first serious ban imposed by Britain was in the 1860s because of the outbreak of cattle plague, or rinderpest, caused by infected cattle imported from Europe.[86] This disease was endemic in central Europe, but without adequate veterinary inspections at national frontiers it was spread westwards by the livestock trade. When it arrived in Britain in June 1865 it rapidly spread through the national herd and the delay in measures taken to control this process in Britain disrupted the meat and livestock trade and helped to increase the price of meat.[87] The other set of measures to control the disease were bans on the imports of live animals from countries where the disease was present, which in this case meant those of northern Europe, as it was from the port of Revel in Estonia that the first infected animal was imported.

Although the first arrival of the disease in the nineteenth century was in 1865, some had warned of this possibility once the veterinary and animal control conditions in Europe had become more widely known after the introduction of free trade in livestock in the 1840s. In 1857 Joseph Sampson Gamgee had addressed letters to the Home Secretary for the need of efficient inspection of foreign cattle arriving in Britain from Europe.[88] The most vocal of them was his son, John Gamgee, founder of the New Veterinary College in Edinburgh. In 1863 he followed his father, arguing that other animal diseases had already been imported besides rinderpest, and it was only a matter of time before that disease would emulate both animal and human diseases and cross into the United Kingdom from Europe.[89] That year bills were put forward in Parliament for some measure of livestock inspection at the ports, but were stifled by opposition from graziers, dealers and butchers who feared such measures would damage their businesses.[90] Following the appearance of cattle plague two years later matters became far more serious and the import of livestock from parts of Holland where the disease was known to be present was forbidden in 1866.[91]

But there was some reluctance over such measures. The British government wanted to protect domestic agriculture from imported epizootics, but not from the price effects of free trade in livestock. Greater control did come about in 1869 with the introduction of the Contagious Diseases (Animals) Act. It also added two other diseases, the lung infection of pleuro-pneumonia and foot-and-mouth disease, to rinderpest as ones which if reported justified a prohibition on the entry of livestock from a country or area of country. At various points in the nineteenth century imports were excluded from most European countries, though re-allowed after they were declared free of infection. There were further outbreaks of cattle plague in Europe in 1869, 1872 and 1877. In 1872 and 1877 the disease spread into Britain again, but on both occasions was effectively halted. In 1869 the Cattle Diseases Prevention Act had introduced the practice of compelling the slaughter of animals at the port where they landed within ten days, and not allowing them to be moved inland alive. This had been advocated in Britain in 1866 by the Chambers of Agriculture as a way of reducing the threat of imported disease from places where the authorities did not think it so serious as to entirely exclude livestock, but where there were doubts about just how strong the threat was.[92] The system of slaughtering at the ports was strongly opposed by all connected with the livestock trade who argued it would cause it to move to other markets in Europe where it was not subject to these restrictions. In the event this practice, called 'scheduling', did not have that effect. British demand for imported meat was sufficiently high, and the profits of the trade large enough, to allow it to cope with the scheduling of livestock from certain countries at certain times, or just from certain foreign ports, and eventually on a permanent basis.

It also led to the development of a livestock industry at certain ports receiving foreign animals. The London market was the most prosperous one in Britain and prior to any restrictions all animals were sold at the Metropolitan Cattle Market in Islington. But as the trade was subject to closer control and more foreign livestock were handled at the Deptford Market by the Thames, close to where the cattle ships unloaded. In 1871 45 per cent of cattle and 39 per cent of foreign sheep went inland alive to the Islington market, but by 1880 only 22 per cent of imported cattle and nine per cent of sheep were handled at Islington; the majority were slaughtered at the foreign cattle lairages at Deptford.[93]

In addition to Deptford in London, the other main centre for landing cattle from America for slaughter was Woodside at Birkenhead on the River Mersey and by 1889 it was receiving more than London. The bulk of the animals landed at these places by the 1890s were from the United States, but there was some trade in South American cattle and also in European cattle, sheep and pigs. The whole of the livestock import trade was protected by the fact that the public continued to have a stronger preference for fresh meat than any other kind. The concentration of slaughter at a few lairages did cause some problems of distribution, with complaints of gluts at the central markets but a relative scarcity in outlying districts.[94] By the 1890s the size of the European livestock trade was generally smaller than the transatlantic one, and most livestock from Europe was landed at different ports. After Birkenhead the next provincial port for the trade was Newcastle, which received the majority of its animals from Scandinavia. Hull took animals from Holland and north Germany. But the general decline of the European livestock trade worked against British east coast ports, whereas the rise of the transatlantic trade made the west coast, in particular Birkenhead, more important.[95]

Before 1878 free entry was the norm and restricted entry for slaughter only was seen as the chief methods of control. But after the Contagious Diseases Animals Act of 1878 came into force from 1 January 1879, restricted entry was the norm. In the 1880s scheduling became much more common as disease was detected abroad or detected in a foreign livestock cargo.[96] The transatlantic livestock trade was affected by the Act from the start, as from the beginning of 1879 all cattle from Argentina and the United States had to be slaughtered at the port of debarkation. Here the main fear was of pleuro-pneumonia, but Canadian cattle could still be taken inland alive, which led to a small trade in store stock for fattening. This stopped in 1892 when they were also scheduled because there was an alleged case of pleuro-pneumonia in one animal. Although this was later found to be a false diagnosis the ban remained in place up to 1914, which led to the strong suspicion that it was a non-tariff barrier put there to protect British livestock farmers, but not all of them as it evoked protests from farmers who had been fattening Canadian animals.[97] But not all Canadian cattle were fattened, as from enquiries at the time it was judged that only 60 per cent, or around 50,000 of these animals, were stores. They were no loss to the British livestock feeders as there was a compensating increase in home stores; in the 5 years from 1887 to 1891 an average of 353,000 stores were imported from Ireland, and this had risen to 471,000 between 1900 and 1904.[98]

## Notes

1  Reber, V.B., *British Mercantile Houses in Buenos Aires 1810–1880* (Cambridge, Mass., 1979), p. 129.

2  Ibid.

3  Hanson, S. G., *Argentine Meat and the British Market: Chapters in the History of the Argentine Meat Industry* (Stanford, 1938), p. 35.

4  Walsh, M., *The Rise of the Midwestern Meat Packing Industry* (Lexington, Ky., 1982), pp. 30–32.

5  Linge, G.J.R., *Industrial Awakening: A Geography of Australian Manufacturing 1788 to 1890* (Canberra, 1979), p. 102.

6  Ibid., pp. 276–77.

7  Farrer, K.T.H., *A Settlement Amply Supplied: Food Technology in Nineteenth Century Australia* (Melbourne, 1980), p. 97.

8  Linge, pp. 451, 687–8.

9  Farrer, K.T.H., pp. 128–30.

10  Ibid., p. 248.

11  Thompson, H.S., 'On the Management of Grass Land, with Especial Reference to the Production of Meat', *Journal of the Royal Agricultural Society of England*, Series 2, 8 (1872): 162

12  Graham, J., 'Settler Society' in W.H. Oliver, with B.R. Williams (eds), *The Oxford History of New Zealand* (Oxford, 1981), p. 117.

13  United States Department of Agriculture, *First Annual Reports of the Bureau of Animal Industry* (Washington, 1884): 262–3.

14  Clemen, R.A., *The American Livestock and Meat Industry* (New York, 1923), pp. 466–7.

15  Schwartz, H., *In the Dominions of Debt: Historical Perspectives on Dependent Development* (Ithaca, 1989), pp. pp. 35–6, 64–7, 174–7.

16  Finch, M.H.J., *A Political Economy of Uruguay Since 1870* (London, 1981), pp. 8, 135–6; H. Schwartz, *In the Dominions of Debt*, pp. 84, 88–9, 214–17; H. Schwartz, 'Foreign Creditors and the Politics of Development in Australia and Argentina 1880–1913', *International Studies Quarterly*, 33(3) (1989): 292–6.

17  Critchell, J.T. and J. Raymond, *A History of the Frozen Meat Trade* (London, 1912), pp. 77, 80–81, 308; The Times, *The Times Book on Argentina* (London, 1927), p. 229; J.E. Richelet, 'The Argentine Trade', in R. Ramsay (ed.), *The Frozen and Chilled Meat Trade: A Practical Treatise by Specialists in the Trade* (London, 1929), vol. 1, p. 164.

18  Brewster, J.A., 'The South American Trade', in F. Gerrard (ed.), *The Book of the Meat Trade* (London, 1949), vol. 1, p. 204.

19  Ford, A. G., 'British Investment in Argentina and Long Swings, 1880–1914', *Journal of Economic History*, 31(3) (1971): 650–63.

20  *The Economist* (13 Sept. 1902), pp. 1420; (25 Oct. 1902), p. 1643–4; (25 Apr. 1903), p. 737; (10 Oct. 1903), p. 1719.

21  Critchell and Raymond, pp. 76, 83–4; Richelet, 'The Argentine Trade', p. 197; Brewster, 'The South American Trade', p. 207.

22  Harrison, G., *Borthwicks: A Century in the Meat Trade, 1863–1963* (London, 1963), p. 25.

23  Critchell and Raymond, pp. 60–71.

24  Ibid., pp. 24, 47–59.

25  Ibid., p. 58.

26  The Times, p. 228.

27  Yeager, M., *Competition and Regulation: The Development of Oligopoly in the Meat Packing Industry* (Greenwich, Conn. (1981), pp. 158–9.

28  *Meat Trades' Journal and Cattle Salesman's Gazette* (31 May 1890): 10.

29  Richelet, 'The Argentine Trade', pp. 207–8; Yeager, p. 159.

30  All the features of the large multi-divisional, multi-national firm are comprehensively detailed and analysed in Chandler's three seminal works, viz., A.D. Chandler, Jr., *Strategy and Structure: Chapters in the History of the Industrial Enterprise* (Cambridge, Mass., 1962); idem, *The Visible Hand: The Managerial Revolution in American Business* (Cambridge, Mass., 1977); idem, *Scale and Scope: The Dynamics of Industrial Capitalism* (Cambridge, Mass., 1990).

31  Clemen, pp. 146–69.

32  Yeager, pp. 14, 49–51, 58–68, 72–7.

33  Perren, R. (1971), 'The North American Beef and Cattle Trade with Great Britain, 1870–1914', *Economic History Review*, XXIV, 3, pp. 430–44.

34  M. Yeager, p. 158; A. D. Chandler, Jr., *Strategy and Structure: Chapters in the History of the Industrial Enterprise* (Cambridge, Mass., 1962), pp. 25–6.

35  *Meat Trades' Journal* (13 Oct. 1910): 432; (27 Oct. 1910); 488.

36  Cd 4643 (PP 1909, Vol. XV), *Report of the Departmental Committee on Combinations in the Meat Trade*, pp. 43, 213; *Meat Trades' Journal* (6 Oct 1910): 385.

37  Whitechurch, V.L., 'The London and North Western Railway and American Meat', *Railway Magazine*, 5 (1899): 358.

38  Macrosty, H.W., *The Trust Movement in British Industry* (London 1907); Cd 4643 (PP 1909, Vol. XV), *Report of the Departmental Committee on Combinations in the Meat Trade*.

39  Cd 4643 (PP 1909, Vol. XV), *Report of the Departmental Committee on Combinations in the Meat Trade*, pp. 9, 15.

40  Sinclair, U., *The Jungle* (New York, 1906).

41  McCoy, J.H. and Sarhan M.E., *Livestock and Meat Marketing*, 3$^{rd}$ ed. (3$^{rd}$ edn, New York, 1988), p. 513.

42  Libecap, G.D., 'The Rise of the Chicago Packers and the Origin of Meat Inspection and Antitrust', *Economic Inquiry*, 30 (1992): 242–162.

43  Yeager, M., pp. 174–95.

44  Olmstead, A.M. and P.W. Rhode, 'An Impossible Undertaking: The Eradication of Bovine Tuberculosis in the United States', *Journal of Economic History*, 64(3) (2004): 734–72; idem, 'The "Tuberculous Cattle Trust": Disease Contagion in an Era of Regulatory Uncertainty', *Journal of Economic History*, 64(4) (2004): 929–63.

45  Clemen, pp. 763–7.

46  Cmd 456 (PP 1919, Vol. XXV), *Inter–Departmental Committee on Meat Supplies. Report of the Committee appointed by the Board of Trade to Consider the Means of Securing Sufficient Meat Supplies for the United Kingdom*, p. 9.

47  McFall, R.J., *The World's Meat*, (New York, 1927), pp. 556–7.

48  *Cold Storage and Ice Trades Review Supplement* (15 Jan. 1900): ii.

49  On this point see W., 'An Institutional Perspective on British Decline', in B. Elbaum and W. Lazonick (eds), *The Decline of the British Economy* (Oxford, 1986), pp. 4–11.

50  Beattie, D., 'The Opening of the Totara Estate Industrial Park' in R.A. Barton (ed.), *A Century of Achievement: A Commemoration of the First 100 Years of the New Zealand Meat Industry* (Palmerston North, 1984), p. 16.

51  Anderson, G., *The Frozen Meat Industry: A Paper Read before the Otago Agricultural and Pastoral Society, Dunedin, 15 June 1905* (Dunedin, 1905), p. 9.

52  *Cold Storage and Ice Trades Review Supplement* (15 Jan 1900): ii–iii.

53  New Zealand Department of Agriculture, *Ninth Report of the Department of Agriculture* (Wellington, 1901): 304.

54  New Zealand Department of Agriculture, *Tenth Report of the Department of Agriculture* (Wellington, 1902): 102–3.

55  Duncan, R., 'The Demand for Frozen Beef in the United Kingdom, 1880–1940', *Journal of Agricultural Economics*, 12(1) (1956): 83.

56  *Annual Review of the (Chilled and) Frozen Meat Trade* (London, 1906): 4.

57  *The Economist* (20 Sept. 1903), p. 9.

58  (PP 1893–94, Vol. XII), *Report from the Select Committee House of Lords on the Marking of Foreign Meat*, pp. 16–18, 20.

59  Wrenn, J.E., *International Trade in Meats and Animal Fats* (Trade Promotion Series 26, Washington: United States Bureau of Foreign and Domestic Commerce, 1925): 10; Perren, pp. 164, 170.

60  Pearse, A.W., *The World's Meat Future* (London, 1920), p. 6.; E.G. Nourse, *American Agriculture and the European Market* (New York, 1924), pp. 297–8, 300–1.

61  Anthony, D.J. and W.G.T. Blois, *The Meat Industry* (London, 1931), p. 48.

62  Rommel, G.H., 'Notes on the Animal Industry of Argentina', United States Department of Agriculture, *Twenty–Fifth Annual Report of the Bureau of Animal Industry for the Year 1908* (Washington, 1910): 329–31.

63  Brewster, 'The South American Trade', p. 216.

64  Ibid.

65  Gebhardt, R.C., *The River Plate Meat Industry since c.1900: Technology, Ownership, International Trade Regimes and Domestic Policy* (London School of Economics Unpublished PhD Thesis, 2000), pp. 138–42.

66  Ibid., p. 144.
67  Bergman, A.M., *A Review of the Frozen and Chilled Trans-Oceanic Meat Industry* (Uppsala: Swedish Government, 1916), pp. 25–6; Cmd 456 (PP 1919, Vol. XXV), *Inter-Departmental Committee on Meat Supplies. Report of the Committee appointed by the Board of Trade to Consider the Means of Securing Sufficient Meat Supplies for the United Kingdom*, p. 444 paragraph 19.
68  Gibson, H. (1896), 'The Foreign Meat Supply', *Journal of the Royal Agricultural Society of England*, Series 3, 2 (1896): 207–11.
69  Rommel, 'Notes on the Animal Industry of Argentina': 331–3.
70  Ibid., 315–16; Critchell and Raymond, p. 423.
71  Harley, C.K., 'The World Food Economy and Pre-World War I Argentina', in S.N. Broadberry and N.F.R. Crafts (eds), *Britain in the International Economy 1870–1914* (Cambridge, 1992), p. 265.
72  *Meat Trades' Journal and Cattle Salesman's Gazette* (1 Jan. 1914): 12; (15 Jan. 1914): 68; R. Ramsay, 'The World's Frozen and Chilled Meat Trade', in R. Ramsay (ed.), *The Frozen and Chilled Meat Trade: A Practical Treatise by Specialists in the Trade* (vol. 1, London, 1929), p. 18.
73  Perren, p. 170.
74  United States Department of Agriculture, *Yearbook of the Department of Agriculture 1897* (Washington, 1898): 271–2; Ministry of Agriculture and Fisheries Economic Series, *Report on the Marketing of Pigs in England and Wales* (London, 1926), pp. 4, 6; International Institute of Agriculture, *International Trade in Meat* (Rome, 1936), pp. 92, 94.
75  Perren, p. 3.
76  Gibson, 'The Foreign Meat Supply': 216; R.F. Crawford, 'The Food Supply of the United Kingdom', *Journal of the Royal Agricultural Society of England*, Series 3, 11 (1900): 28–30.
77  Cd 2643 (PP 1905, LXXIX), *Report of the Royal Commission on Supply of Food and Raw Materials in Time of War*.
78  Tracy, M., *Government and Agriculture in Western Europe 1880–1988* (London, 1989), pp. 66, 68–9, 75.
79  Tracy, pp. 88, 92, 101.
80  United States Department of Agriculture: Section of Foreign Markets, *Distribution of the Agricultural Exports of the United States, 1897–1901* (Bulletin 29, Washington, 1903): 21.
81  United States Department of Agriculture, *Twenty–First Annual Report of the Bureau of Animal Industry*, Government Printing Office (Washington, 1905): 481.
82  United States Department of Agriculture, *Fifteenth Annual Report of the Bureau of Animal Industry for the Year 1898* (Washington, 1899): 516–19.
83  United States Department of Agriculture, *Fifteenth Annual Report of the Bureau of Animal Industry for the Year 1898* (Washington 1899): 440.
84  United States Department of Agriculture, *Seventeenth Annual Report of the Bureau of Animal Industry for the Year 1900* (Washington, 1901): 223–34.
85  Duckham, T. and G.T. Brown, 'The Progress of Legislation Against Contagious Diseases of Livestock', *Journal of the Royal Agricultural Society of England*, Series 3, 4 (1893): 262–86.

86  Hall, S.A., 'The Cattle Plague of 1865', *Medical History*, 6 (1962): 45–58; Ministry of Agriculture, Fisheries, and Food, *Animal Health, 1865–1965* (London: HMSO, 1965), pp. 125–34.

87  Erickson, A.B., 'The Cattle Plague in England, 1865–1867', *Agricultural History*, 35(2) (1961): 94–103.

88  Gamgee, J.S., *The Cattle Plague and Diseased Meat, in their Relations with the Public Health and the Interests of Agriculture*, (London, 1857), p. 25.

89  *The Times* (10 and 13 Nov. 1863); J. Gamgee, The System of Inspection in Relation to the Traffic in Diseased Animals or their Produce', *Edinburgh Veterinary Review*, 5 (Nov. 1863): 665–6.

90  Hall, 'The Cattle Plague of 1865': 49–50.

91  Herbert, R. 'Statistics of Live Stock and Dead Meat for Consumption in the Metropolis', *Journal of the Royal Agricultural Society of England*, Series 2, 3 (1867): 91, 93.

92  Duckham and Brown, 'The Progress of Legislation Against Contagious Diseases of Livestock': 271.

93  Board of Agriculture, *Agricultural Statistics* (London, 1887), Table XXVI.

94. Gibson, 'The Foreign Meat Supply': 206–10, 215–16.

95  *Meat Trades' Journal and Cattle Salesman's Gazette* (22 Feb. 1890): 12; (28 Sept. 1889): 6.

96  Cd 4643 (PP 1909, Vol. XV), *Report of the Departmental Committee on Combinations in the Meat Trade*, Appendix IV, p. 286.

97  MacLachlan, I., *Kill and Chill: Restructuring Canada's Beef Commodity Chain* (Toronto, 2001), p. 126.

98  Anon, 'The Economic Effects of Cattle Disease Legislation', *Economic Journal*, 15 (1905): 160–1.

# PART 2
## 1914 to 1945

# Chapter 4

# War and Depression

In both World Wars the global meat industry was subjected to a number of radical changes, some of which lasted only for the duration of the conflict, but there were others that had a permanent effect on the industry in the return to peacetime conditions. War itself, as in all industries, disrupted both the normal channels of supply and the pattern of demand. It also led to a much more marked government intervention in the industry, some of which remained after the war.

## Wartime Supplies

In both world wars the broad pattern of international trade among the allies became much more a bilateral affair, with the United Kingdom emerging as the largest buyer and the United States as the major exporter for many items. There were of course some exceptions to this pattern like middle-eastern oil and some Empire and Dominion food products, but for many strategic goods – and food came into this category – the United States was a pivotal source of supply. But for all the food surplus countries each war was a severe source of strain on all stages of their product supply chains. The most important food requirement was to ensure for all parties an adequate supply of cereals, but after cereals, meat was the next most important item and with its own special transport requirements. Like cereals, it was a vital internationally traded food in wartime and by 1914 its monetary value was higher than that of cereals.

At the start of each war British government policy was somewhat ambiguous with regard to imported meat. It was immediately conscious that a ton of shipping space devoted to meat would feed fewer people that a ton of shipping space devoted to cereals. However, both New Zealand and Australia had important livestock sectors and New Zealand in particular was a regular supplier of the United Kingdom with mutton and lamb. In addition, they were both part of the British war effort and suppliers of manpower and other items required for the conflict. If imports from their meat industries, or any other sector of their economies, were openly restricted there might be a question as to how enthusiastic their support might be in other respects. To some extent the problem of shipping space could be overcome by guaranteeing them War Office contracts for military supplies, as such items had overriding priority. In the short term this was a welcome arrangement for both parties. The British army's decision to feed its troops in France very largely on frozen meat fitted with both the Dominions whose meat exports consisted largely of this. The storage life of Australian and New Zealand frozen meat was much longer than that of chilled meat that made up the bulk of South American beef and mutton from Argentina and Uruguay by 1914 and 1939. It was not practical to import chilled meat and freeze that in Britain because the British cold storage industry itself had comparatively little freezing capacity; most of its cold storage was designed for storing meat and other foods that had already been chilled or frozen abroad. But in the longer term the shortage of shipping space meant that it was more economical for the South American meat firms to expand their freezing capacity. Eventually the South American firms were persuaded to do this but it could not be done overnight.

The view put forward by the Americans that 'in the early stages of the war there was no serious disturbance of the food supply' was certainly not true for meat.[1] In the first place the immediate breakdown of the international system of payments in the late summer of 1914 made it very difficult for British traders to make payments abroad, so they were more than willing to work to firm government orders. Producers themselves, particularly those in South America, were also immediately affected by the rise in freight rates and the breakdown of the multilateral system of trade payments. The insulated meat ships carrying chilled meat from the River Plate were run under contracts between the ship owners and the meat companies and these contracts had a war clause.[2] Immediately after its outbreak, the war clause was invoked to raise freight rates up to four times their peacetime level to cover the increased risk. The meat companies refused to pay these levels as they were uncertain what price the meat would sell for in London, and it was only after the British Government had persuaded the (largely British) shipping lines to reduce the rates to a more moderate level that the meat companies agreed to resume the trade. In addition, the confusion over the financial arrangements with Argentina meant it was frequently impossible to get money over there and the Argentine packers were unable to pay wages or buy cattle. Some firms were actually forced to suspend business and the threat of the loss of a vital source of supply alarmed the War Office who wanted to make contracts with the Argentine meat companies. To secure these supplies the Board of Trade came to an agreement with the Argentine firms on 28 August 1914 to supply the British army with 15,000 tons of meat a month. The uncertainty about what price to ask was removed for the packers by the British government guaranteeing payment to them of the average price during the week the contract meat arrived. In addition, they could continue using the rest of their capacity to supply the British civilian market on the old scale, as far as circumstances allowed. Uncertainties over payment were removed by paying them 75 per cent of the value of each cargo in Argentina the week it left.[3]

For the United States the war represented an unexpected (though temporary) revival of its domestic meat exporting business as well as a chance for US meat firms to enlarge their market power in the international meat industry. These changes, and others can, be seen in Table 4.1 below. The increased dependence on the United States and reduced reliance on South America and Australia and New

Zealand shown in this table was mainly a consequence of the shorter voyage, which reduced the cost and use of scarce shipping space. But in addition, the United States loans made to Britain to fight the war probably reinforced the tendency to buy American wherever possible.[4] However, the decline in both American and Argentine supplies in 1916 and 1917 was a reflection of the increased shipping losses on Atlantic routes due to enemy submarine attack. And as shipping operation became more difficult increasing amounts of insulated shipping was diverted from the Australian and New Zealand routes to the shorter Atlantic voyage

**Table 4.1 Sources of British chilled and frozen beef imports in the First World War (thousand hundredweight)**

|  | 1908–13 | 1914 | 1915 | 1916 | 1917 | 1918 |
|---|---|---|---|---|---|---|
| US | 494 | 88 | 1,001 | 930 | 938 | 2,584 |
| Argentina | 5,426 | 5,993 | 5,096 | 4,038 | 2,671 | 1,977 |
| Australasia | 760 | 2,028 | 1,972 | 1,641 | 1,968 | 936 |
| TOTAL | 8,601 | 10,023 | 9,984 | 8,525 | 7,494 | 7,415 |

*Source: Annual Statement of Trade of the United Kingdom.*

The immediate effect of war on Australian and New Zealand livestock farmers was equally disruptive, as the main uncertainties about their market began in 1914. Shortage of shipping space was the major problem from the very beginning. The normal market mechanism was distorted further from 1915 by the decision by the colonial governments to become the sole purchasers of all meat exported. This effectively meant that farmers' profits were now determined by the prices agreed between the government in London and individual Australian state governments, and the government in Wellington for New Zealand farmers. Faced with this monopoly purchaser who had also taken control of shipping space with the United Kingdom government, they sought reassurance of their own position. This was certainly necessary, as there was to be a marked reduction in British imports from both countries after 1916. In 1915 Australia sent over 3.5 million carcases of mutton and lamb to Britain, and New Zealand 6.5 million: from 1916 to 1918 Australia averaged only 636 thousand and New Zealand 3.7 million.[5]

The United States has been represented as the great saviour of the allied food supply in all histories of the war, and it supplied 80 per cent of Britain's meat and fats in 1917 and 1918.[6] However, its position in the earlier part when it was officially neutral was more ambiguous. In the case of meat it probably added to Britain's difficulties. The 1913 Underwood Act, by removing the duties on meat shipped to the United States, meant that considerable amounts of Australian, New Zealand and Argentine meat were shipped from these countries to the United States from mid-1913 to the outbreak of war and continued into the early part of the war.[7] In January 1915 the Australian *Pastoral Review* carried comments from its correspondent, sent from London in November 1914, that 'Argentine supplies of chilled beef are being diverted to the States in growing quantities, and will increase when the existing shipping facilities are augmented'.[8] The same thing was also noted in the 1915 *Report* on the Australian meat export trade.[9]

The slow realisation of the seriousness of the situation in Europe, and the time taken by the British government to implement a comprehensive system of controls, allowed United States firms to concentrate on supplying the American market and profiting from the war, with little regard for anything else. In the early stages of the war it was alleged South American meat was imported by the United States and stored there rather than in the United Kingdom in order to avoid it being commandeered by the British authorities.[10] American firms also attempted to make purchases for the American market in Australia and New Zealand. As far as Commonwealth and South American farmers were concerned it made little difference to the price they received, as the overall level of demand was the same. But the ability of the American firms to hold back supplies out of the immediate control of British military requisitioning officers did increase prices for the United Kingdom and helped fuel the rapid rise in consumer prices in the early part of the war. It was also claimed that the use of extra ships to take Argentine meat to cold stores in New York, hold it there and then re-ship it to England when the firms had negotiated a sufficiently high price with the British authorities, tied up shipping space and added further to freight charges, which were then passed back to the New Zealand, Australian and South American farmers.[11]

The shortages in Europe and increased prices did eventually have a positive effect on United States farmers, stimulating them to increase meat output as well. The gradual fall in cattle numbers in progress for some years before the war changed to a slow increase after 1914, rising from 56.6 million in 1914 to 66.8 million in 1918 and the prices of all meat animals rose steadily, the greatest increase being for hogs whose price almost doubled.[12] In the early stages of the war the government took no measures to impose any form of control over meat prices or measures to encourage farmers to raise production. Indeed, most of the wartime increases in United States livestock numbers were simply the normal responses of farmers to rising prices. Even with the establishment of the Federal Food Administration under Herbert Hoover after the United States entered the war in 1917, there was no attempt to control meat in the same manner as wheat.

Although most British trans-oceanic supplies of meat were from long distances, the exception was the Danish pork and bacon trade, and this was diverted to Germany during the war. Denmark underwent impressive growth of all its agricultural exports after Germany used the excuse of disease control to ban imports of live Danish pigs in 1887, forcing Danish farmers to look for new markets. Germany had been an important export market for them, so instead they concentrated on supplying Britain with bacon. Exports of Danish live pigs were 279 thousand and pig meat only eight thousand tons in 1881–85, but by 1896–1900 the export of live animals had ceased, while bacon and ham exports had increased to 65 thousand tons and 95 thousand by 1906–10.[13] In the 1880s the United States provided almost 80 per cent of British bacon imports and Denmark just 5 per cent. By 1910 48 per cent of British bacon imports were from Denmark, while those from the United States were only 37 per cent.[14] The loss of Danish supplies of British breakfast bacon were keenly felt, particularly in the final stages of the war.

In all European countries at war, livestock production was given a lower priority than arable production. Although no one food supplies all the requirements of good nutrition, grain production was given the most assistance and encouragement as cereals were seen as being the most efficient use of resources under wartime conditions. In terms of immediate energy requirements 100 g of white bread supplies 1030 kJ, while beef only supplies 735 kJ and milk 280 kJ.[15] The chief constraints operating on domestic livestock and meat production were shortages of land, shortages of labour and shortages of livestock feed. For Britain, all of these restrictions were severe. Some of these difficulties were recognised even before the war when home supplies were practically stationary and imports were relied upon for 40 per cent of consumption.[16] Writing in 1922, Thomas Middleton argued that some of the estimates of British meat production made before the war were over-optimistic and that in the 5 years from 1909–10 to 1913–14 the production of beef and mutton alone in Britain was only 1 million tons per annum.[17] However, he gave no figures for pork and bacon, and never fully explained his reasons for downgrading cottage production of food – where pig keeping played a significant part.[18] But speaking before the British Association two years before the war, Henry Rew estimated the domestic output of all meat in Britain at 1.45 million tons for 1911, making up 55 per cent of total consumption, and this figure is generally accepted.[19]

Although their effects on British meat consumption were severe, each conflict had even more severe effects in mainland Europe. The first was an overall reduction in local output and the second was a diversion of many exports by the smaller European countries, such as bacon from Denmark or beef from Holland away from the British market to other European countries. When this occurred their new main export market was often Germany. For Germany the First World War caused just as dramatic a reduction in livestock than in Britain. The number of pigs, a more important source of that country's meat, fell by 40 per cent and the number of cattle fell by 20 per cent.[20] But although Britain's pig herd fell even more by 64 per cent of its pre-war level by 1918, cattle numbers only declined by 2 per cent, and she was better able to supplement these losses by imports, whereas Germany was largely cut off from most major overseas suppliers.[21]

During both conflicts the general economic degradation within Germany and the rest of Europe seriously reduced the intra-European trade in meat. This was one part of the general reduction in European food supplies and was reflected in a deterioration of civilian diets. Food rationing and production controls, though imposed earlier in the Second World War than the First War, were never able to provide the urban population with sufficient protection from this process. The only possibility of supplementing inadequate rations was by going outside the normal channels of exchange and using the black market. When this happened, as it frequently did, the rural population were not as vulnerable to shortages as being nearer the point of production they had greater access to supply arrangements that bypassed the official food rationing channels.

The overall meat supply situation at the outset of both wars was very similar. Although in a number of respects the actual mechanics and military circumstances of each conflict differed, the food supply situation of the main European belligerents was still remarkably unchanged between 1914 and 1939. As in 1914, Britain in 1939 was heavily committed to the whole international food industry as its main customer, and in 1939 the rest of Europe still followed a food policy perfected in the nineteenth century that was geared very largely to home production and a minimal dependence on imports. There had been some minimal erosion of Britain's adherence to the principles of free trade following the World depression of the 1930s, but the legacy of free trade remained with the policy of imperial preference which gave Australia, New Zealand and Canada first access to the British food market. In 1939 Britain imported 43 per cent of its meat.[22] But Germany and France, as in the years before 1914, for a variety of economic, political and strategic reasons, had both remained fiercely committed to the reduction of grain and meat imports and the protection of their farmers.[23] They also still had larger agricultural sectors than Britain, though somewhat reduced from the levels of 1914.

**Table 4.2  Cattle numbers in the Western world 1939–45 (million)**

| Country | 1939 | 1940 | 1941 | 1942 | 1943 | 1944 | 1945 |
|---|---|---|---|---|---|---|---|
| Belgium[b] | 1.6[c] | 1.5 | 1.9 | 1.8 | 1.5 | 1.5 | 1.6 |
| Denmark[b] | 3.3 | 3.2 | 3.0 | 2.9 | 3.0 | 3.1 | 3.2 |
| France[b] | 14.2[c] | 14.4 | 15.5 | 15.8 | 14.5 | 13.5 | 14.3 |
| Germany[a] | 19.9[c] | 19.6 | 19.4 | 19.1 | 19.6 | 20.3 | – |
| Holland[b] | 2.8 | 2.7 | 2.7 | 2.4 | 2.1 | 2.2 | 2.3 |
| UK[a] | 8.9 | 9.0 | 8.9 | 9.0 | 9.3 | 9.5 | 9.6 |
| Canada[b] | 8.4 | 8.3 | 8.5 | 8.9 | 9.7 | 10.4 | 10.8 |
| USA[a] | 68.2 | 71.5 | 75.2 | 79.1 | 82.4 | 81.9 | 79.8 |
| Argentina[b] | 34.3 | – | – | 31.5 | – | – | 34.0 |
| Uruguay[b] | 8.3 | – | – | – | 6.3 | – | – |
| Australia[b] | 12.8 | 13.0 | 13.3 | 13.6 | 14.0 | 14.2 | 14.1 |
| New Zealand[b] | 4.6 | 4.5 | 4.6 | 4.6 | 4.5 | 4.5 | 4.6 |

[a] Importing countries; [b] Exporting countries, [c] The territory of these countries changed after the outbreak of war.

*Source:* International Institute of Agriculture, *International Yearbook of Agricultural Statistics 1940–41, vol. II, Numbers of the Principal Species of Livestock and Poultry* (Rome, 1941), pp. 189–93.

After 1939 the supply situation for both Britain and Europe became worse than it had been after 1914. Domestic production in both Britain and the rest of Europe relied very heavily on imported fodder grains and oilcake, so domestic production was equally vulnerable to their reduction. Production in Britain held up well and meat output in 1941 was only 2 per cent below its pre-war level, the largest reduction being in pork. [24] Over the war as a whole this meat experienced the greatest fall in output as pig numbers were cut back from an average of 3.18 million in 1929–38 to 1.38 million in 1943. Sheep and poultry numbers were also reduced, but it can be seen from Table 4.2 above that the number of British cattle actually increased after 1942, though most of this was to raise milk output, which was always given a higher priority than beef production. As in the First War, pig, poultry and sheep numbers were reduced most because the first two were heavy consumers of grain and other items which could be better used for feeding humans, and sheep were the least efficient converters of calories and protein equivalents into human food. [25] The worst year was 1941, when total meat moving into Britain's civilian consumption, calculated on edible weight, was only 78 per cent of its level before the war. There was some recovery over the following years, and by 1944 it was back to 88 per cent of the pre-war level. [26]

The European situation was far worse. Pre-war domestic meat output of all Europe, excluding the USSR, was 11,130,000 metric tons but for 1945 it was only 6,850,000 metric tons, a fall to 62 per cent of the pre-war level. [27] This is not strongly evident in the figures for cattle numbers in Table 4.2 above, though it has to be remembered that the cattle slaughtered for meat after 1940 were being killed at lighter weights than before 1939. But whereas some of the increased beef and other meat outputs of the United States, Canada, Australia and New Zealand were available to United Kingdom consumers, the European blockade and restrictions on trade with the enemy meant there was no chance of the Axis Powers being able to tap this source. Nor were they able to draw on these extraneous sources of pig meat or lamb and mutton; as in Britain it was these smaller animals that felt the worst effects of wartime reductions in European livestock numbers.

In addition to quantities, the actual types of meat available to consumers underwent change in both wars. The scarcity of international shipping space led the British government to raise the tonnage of edible meat by encouraging exporters to send less carcase meat and more canned and boned meat. There was also a preference for frozen rather than chilled, as frozen meat had a longer storage life, though this is not apparent in Table 4.1 above as it makes no distinction between chilled and frozen meat. Both these changes reduced the quality of meat during wartime in an attempt to maintain quantity as far as possible, but in doing so they put back some of the progress that had been made in the overall quality of meat imports before 1914, and once again between the wars. In the Second War the largest falls were in beef with bone in, and pork and bacon, but the consumption of both boneless and canned meats increased. [28]

The European situation was somewhat different in the two wars. In the First World War Germany only occupied Belgium, northern France, Poland and the

Baltic States and Rumania and the Ukraine, but in the Second World War the area was far greater. The occupation of much of the Soviet Union and Eastern Europe, the Danube countries and Greece, Denmark, Norway, Finland, Holland, Belgium, France and parts of Italy gave Germany effective control over most Continental food and other resources. As far as foodstuffs were concerned, the plan of the Agricultural Group of the Economic Staff East in May 1941 was to entirely feed the occupying Wehrmacht from conquered enemy territory in the East of Europe by the third year of the war – at any price. The amounts to be used for this purpose were fixed, as were those that were to be diverted to support the German economy. It was only after these two aims were met that the local population were allowed to be fed, a policy generally applied to its other territories.[29] They were able to achieve these objectives to varying extents. The main surplus of the Soviet Union was grain but surprisingly large amounts of meat were sent to Germany from the other countries of Eastern Europe in 1941–42 and 1943–44, in spite of large shipments of feed grain also going to Germany. France was also a large meat supplier, but over the whole duration of the war they were both surpassed by Denmark. Imports from Denmark were 768,000 tons, those from France were 758,000 tons and imports from the occupied Soviet areas were 731,000 tons. In normal pre-war years Germany had imported just under 8 per cent of its meat supply, but in 1939–40 and 1944–45, the two lowest war years, imports accounted for 13 per cent of consumption and for 1942–43, the year of highest imports, they rose to 29 per cent.[30]

But although the old German Reich on balance took meat, mostly in the form of livestock for slaughter, and other foodstuffs from the territories it controlled, there was still a need to supply the deficit areas within its conquered territories and some of this was done from the old Reich itself. Thus the Polish territories of Eastern Silesia between 1939 and 1944 received 95,000 tons of meat from Germany, although the whole of Poland sent 330,000 tons over the same period. The high point of all German food, and meat imports was in 1940–41, and its greatest decline was after 1942–43 as territory was re-taken by the Allies and the German transport system was subject to increasing damage from military action. In addition, overall food output fell throughout Europe because of a lack of adequate investment. In 1940–41 Holland exported 49,000 tons of meat, principally as hogs and cattle for slaughter, but in 1943–44 it was only able send the equivalent of 12,000 tons.[31]

The meat problems facing the European consumer in both wars were the result of a number of causes. In the first place there was an absolute shortage from reduced home output and a fall in imports. The reduction in domestic production was probably not so much because pasture was converted to arable, but more likely to have been caused by the reduction of animal feed. This was particularly apparent in the case of pig meat as they compete directly with humans for food. While greater emphasis on arable crops certainly reduced sheep and cattle pasture, the concentration on bread corn and any increase in flour milling ratios were important factors in reducing the availability of livestock feed from domestic sources. There were also serious reductions on any imports of cheap animal feed, on which pre-war livestock industries were based. For Britain in the First World War Dewey estimates that by 1918 there was an overall reduction in imported and domestic feedstuffs of approximately 60 per cent.[32] But the meat question was not only one of availability: it was one of choice, along with palatability and variety. Offer quotes an American physiologist living in Germany in 1916, when meat and fat shortages then were far more severe than they ever became in Britain, who said: 'Had the Germans been vegetarians, there would have been no problem.'[33] The main problem for all wartime economies is that once the initial patriotic appeals have died away, consumers soon become demoralised by food queues and restricted choice. In Britain this was acutely noticeable for meat, where reduced domestic output and a heavy reliance on canned and frozen imports, along with substitutes of unpalatable United States and Canadian bacon, represented for many in both wars a noticeable deterioration of dietary standards. There are very real limits to the extent which nations can suffer a reduction in their levels of consumption and also avoid a serious deterioration in morale.

**Wartime Demand**

Although all governments recognised that it was essential to secure adequate supplies of cereals, they understood how a balanced diet was also essential to preserve good health and physical efficiency. This made meat and animal fats generally second in their order of priorities, followed by fresh vegetables, as the other vital components of good nutrition.[34] But in some respects the First World War actually raised the military demand for meat, in addition to restricting supplies available to the civilian markets. In their April 1917 survey the British meat importers W. Weddel & Co. recorded the existence but were unable give actual amounts of the 'large quantities' of New Zealand and Australian frozen beef and mutton 'diverted from the UK to the Continent for British Army purposes'.[35] The extra demands on supplies of imported meat from its European allies were a serious cause of the shortages that developed in the United Kingdom towards the end of the war. Extra pressure was placed on meat supplies as the British Army's recruitment rose, by its policy of feeding its troops to a higher standard than the civilian average in peacetime.[36] This was British army policy from the outset of the war, and the French army were so impressed by the way in which British troops had fought the previous autumn, that from the start of 1915 they raised their meat rations above those allotted to British soldiers.[37] This view of diet was not simply a matter of calories. The emphasis on meat and fats as an important component of both civilian and military rations, and as essential items of a balanced diet, was in evidence in both wars.[38] But at the same time the other features of war were conspiring to reduce global supplies.

In his survey of British livestock numbers and meat production, J.B. Guild, who was one of the statisticians at the Ministry of Food, concluded that overall cattle numbers had been maintained from 1914 to 1918, but that sheep and pig numbers (excluding pigs kept by cottagers) had declined by 3 and 29 per cent, respectively. The ploughing up campaign from 1917, whereby livestock pasture was converted to producing arable crops, did not have a great impact on overall cattle and sheep numbers. The most serious decline was in pigs, but the largest fall in their numbers was in Ireland from 1917 onwards. As this animal is most seriously a rival for potential sources of human food than the other two the shortages of imported and home grown fodder crops from that year onward had a greater impact on their numbers. But the most serious strain on all meat supplies came from feeding the growing Allied armies in Europe, who were absorbing an increasing proportion of imports of refrigerated meat, which was also reduced by the stringency in the shipping position, in spite of attempts to save space by sending US refrigerated meat boneless.[39] These losses left only 375,000 tons of refrigerated meat, or around half the pre-war supply, available for the civilian population and troops stationed in the United Kingdom in 1917. In addition, the shortage of feeding stuffs meant a reduction in the slaughter weights of cattle.[40] The general picture to emerge from Guild and other authors' analysis is that it was from the second half of 1917 that the reduction in the home-produced supplies of meat became significant.

A large part of the total allied deficit was the effect of the increased demand from France. Although no figures were kept of French meat production before the war, cattle numbers were increasing but the numbers of sheep declining, requiring imports of over a million a year to maintain the supply of wool and mutton. The export of 50,000 cattle a year indicates that France was self-sufficient for beef, and net imports of all meats were very small at around 6,500 tons. But although, as with all food products, France was largely self-supporting for its meat requirements it must be recognised that the immediate impact of war imposed a greater strain on the French economy than the British. This was because French mobilisation placed millions of men under arms, whereas the initial British target was only in the tens of thousands. In the early stages of the war the French Commissariat, unlike the British, held the archaic belief that armies should still be followed by everything necessary for their subsistence, including enormous herds of cattle. Besides being an encumbrance to armies in the field, large numbers of livestock fell into German hands during the initial allied retreats until the front was stabilized after November 1914. As with Britain, mobilization also brought about a large increase in meat consumption. In civilian life meat eaten was estimated at about 4 ounces a day but for its soldiers the French army budgeted at over 16 ounces down to 11 ounces, depending on whether a man was in the front line, in positions to the rear, or in barracks.[41]

Throughout the war one effect of the military operations of all sides in Belgium and northern France was to drastically reduce both fodder and pasture for all farm livestock.[42] The French army's early heavy requisitions of cattle, which amounted to 735,000 animals in the last five months of 1914, aroused protests from the farming community, and the government sought to remedy the situation by allowing the import of cattle from Canada and sheep from Algeria. As these sources alone could never satisfy the growing military requirement the only alternative was to remove the embargo on the import of fresh meat in October 1914; by January 1915 the whole of the French front, including what remained of the Belgian Army, was receiving frozen meat. During the whole of the war nearly 60 per cent of the meat consumed by the French Army was frozen meat. As the war progressed, one can see from Table 4.3 below that the total amounts of meat imported into France from the United States and Argentina rose from approximately 25,000 tons in 1914 to 231,000 tons in 1918. These imports, of which 93 per cent were beef, were vital to preserve the French cattle industry; from 1915 to 1918 the numbers of cattle annually requisitioned averaged only 540,000.[43]

**Table 4.3  French meat imports 1914–18 (tons)**

| Year | Beef | Mutton | Pork | Total |
|------|------|--------|------|-------|
| 1914 | 22,000 | 3,000 | – | 25,000 |
| 1915 | 213,000 | 9,000 | – | 222,000 |
| 1916 | 203,000 | 13,000 | 1,000 | 217,000 |
| 1917 | 166,000 | 13,000 | 1,000 | 180,000 |
| 1918 | 214,000 | 15,000 | 2,000 | 231,000 |
| TOTAL | 818,000 | 58,000 | 4,000 | 875,000 |

Source: Augé-Laribé, M. and P. Pinot, *Agriculture and Food Supply in France During the War* (New Haven, 1927), p. 75.

Up to 1916 French civilian meat supplies were not a problem. Although the military took all imported meat, domestic supplies remained sufficient until losses of merchant shipping in that year reduced imports and consequently raised military demands. One way of limiting civilian demand, resorted to by all European governments in both wars, was the largely pointless imposition of meatless days. French civilian demand became a problem as the reduced domestic herd was less cared for and well fed under wartime conditions, and forced the government to impose two meatless days a week from May 1917. In 1918 meat imports and the domestic supply both fell, so from May 1918 the number of meatless days was increased to three until July. The situation eased in 1919 when demobilisation reduced meat consumption and large quantities of imported frozen meat could be released for civilian consumption.[44]  British meatless days were not introduced until very late in the war and were very limited in scope, though voluntary ones were proposed as early as 1916. The compulsory measure, announced in November 1917, intended to forbid sales of meat on one day a week from January 1918 but was reduced to apply only to hotels, clubs and restaurants for two days a week and was not enforced until April 1918.[45] But even this order was seen as too much and was revoked in May because it was said to have reduced the consumption of home-produced meat but increased that of imported cereals.[46]

Between 1939 and 1945 measures to control demand were much more in evidence. In Britain meat was not rationed in London and the Home Counties until February 1918 and this was extended to the rest of the country in May. But in the Second World War there was the mechanism for a fully articulated system of British rationing from the outset with ration books and coupons, with similar schemes in Germany and followed in most of occupied Europe not long after. British bacon rationing, along with butter and sugar, began in January 1940 and was soon extended to cover other forms of meat, and all the important foods. As in the First World War, the consumer had to register with a particular retailer who could only supply meat to the customer registered to him. In addition, as in the First War, the customer's weekly meat ration was limited by value, and not by weight, in theory thus preventing discrimination between rich and poor as to quality.[47] Scarcity of meat became apparent from early on and the meat ration was reduced, by reducing the weekly value consumers were allowed to purchase. The control of catering required more elaborate measures. In the First War customers had to surrender coupons for meals containing meat purchased in public places, but this had involved these businesses in extra bureaucracy accounting for the coupons. In the Second War various schemes were tried but proved unworkable and so the coupon-free meal out was adopted. [48]

One might have expected there would have been greater problems meeting the demand for meat in the United Kingdom as it relied far more heavily than either France or Germany on overseas food imports.[49] It also had a larger percentage of urban population than the rest of Europe and these people were wholly reliant on the official controlled market, whereas the rural populations were able to seek alternative sources. In addition the British consumption of all meat was higher. Germany produced 4.25 tons of meat per 100 acres of cultivated land while Britain produced only 4 tons and could only do so by using 2.8 tons of imported oilcake and feed grain more than the German farmer.[50] In all these respects, therefore, one would have expected that the fall in wartime over peacetime standards would have been most keenly felt in Britain. Between July 1914 and September 1916 the cost of working-class food expenditure rose by 68 per cent in British towns of over 50,000 but by only 62 per cent in small towns ands villages. For meat the differential increase was greater at 83 per cent in the large towns and 73 per cent elsewhere.[51] But although the shortages were reflected in higher urban prices, by the end of the war the levels of meat consumption in Britain, though depleted, held up better than in Germany or France or almost anywhere else in Europe. In Germany by 1916 it was reported that there was almost no meat to be had in Berlin, and by 1918 there were local shortages lasting for weeks at a time.[52] In both wars no one actually starved but the same picture of progressive European protein deprivation emerged over the course of the Second World War, and was accompanied by deterioration in the general health of those who experienced it.

In the Second World War the British system of rationing was different from that of Continental Europe. In Britain there was a standard allowance of all foods to all consumers. Where it was thought that certain groups had higher needs there were special communal feeding schemes like industrial canteens in workplaces, school canteens, and local authority and Ministry of Food-sponsored 'British Restaurants' where cheap nutritious meals were available. In these establishments extra meat and other foods were made available to groups entitled to use them. There were also special distribution schemes for children of pre-school age and nursing and expectant mothers who did not generally benefit from communal feeding.[53] But as far as the basic ration of meat for people to prepare and consume in their own homes was concerned, a distinction was made between fresh meat and meat products and bacon and ham. The same amount of fresh meat was made available to all consumers on a price basis per week, but children under six were allocated only half the value of meat allowed for adults. Bacon and ham for all consumers was rationed to a fixed weight of either, or a combination of the two, each week. As official prices were also controlled, though not stationary, the fall in the monetary and weight allowances of all meats meant that there was a decline in the amounts moving into civilian consumption over the war as a whole. Table 4.4 below gives the actual rations of meat allowed but, like all figures for official rations, it takes no account of individuals' failures to secure them because of absolute shortages, distribution difficulties, or attempts to supplement them from black market and other sources.

**Table 4.4  United Kingdom meat rations 1940–45**

|                                            | 1940   | 1941   | 1942 | 1943 | 1944 | 1945 [a] |
|--------------------------------------------|--------|--------|------|------|------|----------|
| Meat for normal consumers [b]              | 1/11   | 1/1½   | 1/2  | 1/2  | 1/2  | 1/2      |
| Meat for all children under 6 years        | 11/½   | 7/¾    | /7   | /7   | /7   | /7       |
| Bacon and ham for all consumers [c]        | 143    | 115    | 115  | 115  | 129  | 105      |

[a] for first three quarters only; [b] shillings and pence per week; [c] grams per week

*Source*: Lindberg, J., *Food, Famine and Relief 1940–1946* (Geneva: Economic, Financial and Transit Department League of Nations, 1946), pp. 158–9.

Britain basically had an egalitarian points system, not only for meat but for all other foods, but after 1939 in Germany and its occupied areas a much more precise system of specific rationing was applied to almost all foods, and consumers were classified into different categories each based on occupation. The largest rations were allocated to those with the arduous manual jobs, and the smallest to those whose occupations were largely sedentary and did not involve heavy labour. Manual workers received extra meat, bread and fats to provide the additional calories necessary to cope with the severity of their work. There were further differences according to age, sex and health with nursing mothers receiving larger rations. In Belgium and Northern France, for instance, the standard daily meat ration was 50 grams per day falling, to 20 grams by 1944. In addition, ordinary manual workers received an extra 12 grams, those in very heavy manual work an extra 35 grams and miners an extra 47 grams; and these supplementary rations remained constant over the whole of the war.[54] Britain experienced a fall in pre-war civilian meat consumption of 19 per cent and 26 per cent for poultry by 1944.[55] In Europe the decline in consumption was far more severe. For example the basic Dutch meat ration for adults was 22.4 kgs in 1940 but had fallen to only 22 per cent of this level and was 5.0 kgs by 1944.[56]

The relative European meat situations are shown in Table 4.5 below, but here estimates of workers' family consumption have been used, rather than rations allowed just referred to, because it is thought that they convey a more accurate impression of the real meat situation facing the average consumer, although official ration figures are available.[57] Table 4.5 is meant to represent a family that consists of a husband and wife and three children aged 3, 6 and 9 years. J. Lindberg explains that the rations of the members of the family have been added together and divided by the number of consumption units contained in the family. The scale used to convert family members into consumption units was the League of Nations scale, under which the five persons of the family correspond to 3.32 adult male equivalents.[58]

**Table 4.5  Comparison of the daily calorie consumption of meat and meat products per consumption unit of a typical family in various countries of Europe during the inter-war period and 1940–1944**

|                | Pre-war | 1940 | 1941 | 1942 | 1943 | 1944 |
|----------------|---------|------|------|------|------|------|
| Baltic States  | 535     | –    | –    | 145  | 115  | 115  |
| Belgium        | 355     | –    | –    | 105  | 100  | 90   |
| Bulgaria       | 240     |      | –    | 195  | 240  | 225  |
| Czechoslovakia | 285     | –    | 210  | 160  | 140  | 110  |
| Finland        | 250     | –    | 160  | 75   | 75   | 195  |
| France         | –       | –    | 160  | 100  | 75   | 100  |
| Germany        | 350     | 225  | 200  | 160  | 140  | 110  |
| Italy          | 90      | –    | 130  | 100  | 60   | 40   |
| Netherlands    | 235     | –    | 140  | 135  | 75   | 70   |
| Poland         | 335     | –    | 60   | 45   | 55   | 55   |

*Source:* J. Lindberg, *Food, Famine and Relief 1940–1946* (Geneva: Economic, Financial and Transit Department League of Nations, 1946), pp. 31–3.

The table confirms the impression of the serious shortages of meat over most of Europe. In addition to quantity, quality also deteriorated and, as in Britain, the quantities purchased contained more bone and waste and less fat. Moreover, the legal rations of meat were often unobtainable in the shops of occupied countries. In some countries, particularly in east and southern Europe, meat practically disappeared from the normal diet.

In each conflict the British strategy of protecting its overseas source of meat supply ultimately paid off. The decision to concentrate domestic agricultural production on the bulky foodstuffs like cereals, and even reduce home output of meat in order to produce more cereals, provided the best outcome for the consumer. By producing more of the cheap carbohydrates in Britain some of the scarce ocean shipping space saved was used to carry high value meat, but also allowing the rest to be used for other essential items. In both wars this option was denied to Germany, its allies, and occupied territories.

**Interwar Depression**

The years before 1914 and those after 1945 both saw a general overall growth in the industry. Although these were never times of completely uninterrupted advance, and periodic fluctuations and downturns could still be severe, there was a general optimism that the industry would be able to satisfy a generally rising demand for its product. This was reinforced by a general progress of product diversification that reinforced this view and made producers confident they would be able to exploit fresh areas of demand and supply new markets. In contrast the interwar years were ones of two very sharp downturns – after 1920 and again between 1930 and 1933 – with a recovery in 1939 only to about the point reached in 1914.[59] In addition, the industry in some regions and situations underwent a definite contraction, and output was reduced in response to a stagnant demand and political circumstances. Before 1914 Europe had been largely protective, but the British government's adherence to free trade made this vital market open to foreign supplies. But after 1930 even Britain introduced some protective measures that favoured certain Commonwealth countries at the expense of South American meat producers. The overall result of all these changes was to reduce the previous confidence the industry had that it would be able to sell its products in a growing market. It also caused producers themselves to examine more positive ways in which they could protect their own interests, and to do this they looked to government assistance.

In addition, the growth of demand in Britain as the largest market for internationally traded meat was affected by a slowing down in the rate of population growth as the demographic transition took full effect. In the nineteenth century with high birth rates and falling death rates population had grown rapidly. But from the late nineteenth century family size began to fall and population growth slowed. This phenomenon was most noticeable in most Western industrial countries, especially in Britain, where population growth rates fell to less than half what they had been between 1860 and 1914. The interwar rates of population growth were regarded by some as so low that anxieties were even expressed about the consequences of population decline. As Britain was the largest market for internationally traded meat the slow aggregate growth of this market in the interwar years had serious implications for the whole industry, especially at a time when similar constraints were not operating on the supply side.

These are themes that will be explored in greater detail in the two following chapters, but in the rest of this section the extent and the main features of the industry's global stagnation will be outlined.

**Table 4.6 Cattle numbers in the Western world for selected years from 1913 to 1938 (million)**

| Country | 1913 | 1925 | 1928 | 1930 | 1932 | 1936 | 1938 |
|---|---|---|---|---|---|---|---|
| Belgium[a] | 1.8 | 1.6 | 1.7 | 1.8 | 1.8 | 1.8 | 1.7 |
| Denmark[b] | 2.3 | 2.8 | 3.0 | 3.1 | 3.2 | 3.0 | 3.2 |
| France[a] | 15.3 | 14.4 | 15.0 | 15.5 | 15.6 | 15.8 | 15.6 |
| Germany[a] | 18.5 | 17.3 | 18.5 | 18.5 | 19.2 | 20.1 | 19.9 |
| Ireland | 4.1 | 4.0 | 4.1 | 4.0 | 4.0 | 4.0 | 4.1 |
| Holland | 2.1 | 2.1 | 2.2 | 2.4 | 2.9 | 2.6 | 2.8 |
| Western Europe[c] | 44.1 | 42.2 | 44.5 | 45.3 | 46.7 | 47.3 | 47.3 |
| UK[a] | 7.8 | 8.0 | 8.0 | 7.8 | 8.3 | 8.6 | 8.9 |
| Canada[b] | 6.7 | 9.3 | 8.8 | 8.0 | 8.5 | 8.8 | 8.5 |
| USA[a] | 58.7 | 60.6 | 58.9 | 63.0 | 70.2 | 66.5 | 66.8 |
| Argentina[b] | 25.8 | 37.1 | – | 32.2 | – | 30.8[d] | 33.2[e] |
| Uruguay[b] | 8.2 | 8.4 | – | 7.1 | 7.4 | – | 8.3[e] |
| Australia[b] | 11.5 | 13.3 | 11.3 | 11.7 | 12.8 | 13.9 | 12.9 |
| New Zealand[b] | 2.0 | 3.5 | 3.3 | 3.8 | 4.1 | 4.3 | 4.5 |

[a] Importing countries; [b] Exporting countries; [c] i.e., Belgium, Denmark, France, Germany, Ireland, Holland, above; [d] 1934; [e] 1937

*Sources:* International Institute of Agriculture, *World Production in Meat* (Rome, 1938), pp. 92–3, 109, 121, 298–301.
International Institute of Agriculture, *International Yearbook of Agricultural Statistics 1940–41, vol. II, Numbers of the Principal Species of Livestock and Poultry* (Rome, 1941), pp. 152–5.

The paths that interwar production of livestock took can be seen in Tables 4.6 to 4.8. Table 4.6 above shows the increase in Western cattle numbers, which, though not the only determinant, were at that time the most important indicator of livestock production and the internationally traded output of the global meat industry over the interwar period. It also provides a comparison between the changes in the 1920s and 1930s, with the situation in 1913. This table is not a comprehensive one as it excludes Russia, Eastern and Southern Europe, Africa and Asia. Estimates of world cattle number for 1936 were 650.3 million, whereas those included here are about 149.4 million. Another omission that deserves mention is Russia, which had 60.6 million head of cattle in 1913, rising to 70.5 million in 1928 under the New Economic Policy that lasted from 1921 to 1928. But after the introduction of collectivisation to increase exports of grain, a great reduction in cattle and all livestock numbers set in as farmers, especially the more prosperous ones, tried to prevent the collectivisation of their animals by slaughtering and consuming them. This caused the cattle herd to decline by an astonishing 45 per cent to 38.4 million in 1933, and was only slowly reversed by allowing people to keep some livestock. The same happened with sheep and pig numbers. In the single years 1929 to 1930 sheep decreased from 67.2 to 52.9 million and pigs from 20.5 to 13.3 million.[60] But although this had a severe effect on meat consumption within the USSR, it had comparatively little impact on other countries, as the Soviet system was very effective in limiting the demand for imported meat.

So although those included in Table 4.6 represent a minor part of world output, all the countries selected used substantial numbers of animals for beef production of various sorts and, unlike large parts of Asia, especially India, did not have substantial numbers that did not enter into meat production. Nor were they used for draught purposes before they were converted into meat, as in Africa, Asia, and Eastern and Southern Europe, or as in parts of Africa were aged animals kept as symbols of power and status long after their economic value as food sources had passed. Those included in Table 4.6 were almost all of the improved type discussed on pages 30 to 34 of Chapter 2 above. Even the Western European cattle that are included, although not improved by predominantly English bloodlines like those in the New World and Australia and New Zealand, underwent a similar process of improvement using Continental breeds with characteristics close to those of British breeds. They were also managed and traded by very broadly the same Western form of businesses involving private ownership and protection of property rights that have been discussed in Part 1 above. Africa, Asia and the USSR have been excluded because, for the most part, they were subject to fundamentally different commercial systems.

The meat industry shared the same overall features as the rest of agriculture and benefited from the artificially high prices of the First War. But the reductions in soil fertility and losses of livestock in Continental Europe were soon made up by 1925 and the growth of European output thereafter was maintained up to 1930. Overseas livestock production had also expanded during the war and continued to rise in the 1920s so that by 1930 all, with the exception of Argentina and Uruguay, were producing more cattle than in 1913. During the 1920s there had been some fluctuations. For example, in 1921 the increase in all food supplies, combined with the effects of general post-war depression after the end of the economic boom during the months immediately after the war, caused a sharp fall in prices. The downturn was accompanied by high unemployment, falling wages for many still in work and a general fall in consumption. The difficulties experienced after 1920 caused people to reduce their personal spending and so prices of all goods, especially food, fell. There was some recovery to 1924 but once again in 1926 depression set in. But throughout the rest of the 1920s agricultural output continued to rise as the revival of industry lifted demand and provided some cushioning of the price effects of agricultural overproduction.

**Table 4.7 Sheep numbers in the Western world for selected years from 1913 to 1938 (million)**

| Country | 1913 | 1925 | 1928 | 1930 | 1932 | 1936 | 1939 |
|---|---|---|---|---|---|---|---|
| France [a] | 16.2 | 10.5 | 10.4 | 10.2 | 9.8 | 9.8 | 9.9 |
| Germany | 5.0 | 4.7 | 3.6 | 3.5 | 3.4 | 4.3 | 4.7 |
| Ireland [b] | 3.3 | 2.8 | 3.3 | 3.5 | 3.5 | 3.0 | 3.2 |
| UK [a] | 27.5 | 23.6 | 24.6 | 24.7 | 27.2 | 25.0 | 26.8 |
| Canada | 2.1 | 2.8 | 3.4 | 3.7 | 3.6 | 3.3 | 3.4 |
| USA | 37.8 | 40.4 | 48.4 | 53.2 | 53.0 | 52.6 | 53.8 |
| Argentina [b] | 43.2 | 36.2 | – | 44.4 | – | 39.3[e] | 43.9[f] |
| Uruguay [b] | 26.3 | 14.4[c] | 22.5[d] | 20.6 | 15.4 | – | 17.9[f] |
| Australia [b] | 85.0 | 103.6 | 103.4 | 110.6 | 113.0 | 112.2 | 113.4 |
| New Zealand [b] | 24.2 | 24.5 | 27.1 | 30.8 | 28.7 | 30.1 | 32.4 |

[a] Importing countries; [b] Exporting countries; [c] 1924; [d] 1927; [e] 1934; [f] 1937

_Sources:_ International Institute of Agriculture, _World Production in Meat_ (Rome, 1938), pp. 135, 140–1, 302–5.
International Institute of Agriculture, _International Yearbook of Agricultural Statistics 1940–41, vol. II, Numbers of the Principal Species of Livestock and Poultry_ (Rome, 1941), pp. 156–9.

In the case of the meat and dairy industry the extent of overproduction was not as serious as it was with cereals and this meant the downturn in prices was not so severe as demand fell when the world economic depression set in from 1930 onwards.[61] But at this point all governments were prepared to offer assistance to their farmers in the form of protective duties and other measures and this allowed overall cattle numbers, with the exception of the United States, Argentina and Uruguay, to increase in the 1930s. Part of this increase, as in the 1920s, can be explained by the growth of the dairy industry, rather than directly for beef production. Much of the German increase in numbers was for dairy cattle to supply home demand, and countries expanding their dairy output for export were New Zealand and Denmark.[62] But these animals would ultimately enter the meat chain and add to surplus output. The overall growth in Europe is particularly noticeable and in addition to government measures to protect the livestock industry, it is also an indication of rising living standards for the bulk of urban consumers who were in work and experienced some increase in real wages. In the case of Germany, France and Italy there also seems to have been an increased desire for greater self-sufficiency when the international situation grew more unsettled from 1933 onwards.[63]

Although the United Kingdom remained the world's largest importer of mutton and lamb, followed by France, it also had the largest sheep population in Europe outside the USSR. It can be seen from Table 4.7 above that France had more sheep than Germany and that it was also a net importer as well. But it took second place to the United Kingdom, which was the only really large importer of internationally traded supplies of mutton and lamb. Numbers of sheep in Britain itself had declined since the 1870s in the face of cheaper imports of lamb and mutton from the Southern Hemisphere, and during the war they declined further from 27.5 million in 1913 to 20.2 million in 1920. They then recovered up to 1927 but fell up to 1929 before recovering again and reaching 27.2 million in 1932 before declining to around 25.0 million in the later 1930s.[64]

These same broad changes of a sharp upturn in demand which producers struggled to satisfy in the months after the war, a sharp depression in 1920 and slow recovery to the mid-1920s, by which time most of the damage to European farming and food production in general was made good, affected both sheep and pig numbers as well. Supplying no other output, pigs are far more important sources of meat than sheep, but for the rest of the 1920s and 1930s both these inputs into the Western meat industry suffered a series of fluctuations that depended, like cattle farming, on the general prosperity of the economy, which determined the demand for pork and bacon, lamb and mutton, changes in the costs of feeding stuffs and the actions of government.

As Table 4.7 also shows, the big producers of mutton and lamb were Argentina, New Zealand and Australia, the same big exporters and suppliers of the United Kingdom market as before 1914. Other exporters of these animals were Ireland and Uruguay. Ireland was in the strongest market position, being the only one that could export fresh mutton and lamb to Britain and France, but its industry stagnated. Exports to Britain became more difficult after Irish independence in 1922 and the worsening relations between the two countries in the interwar years. This led the Irish sheep population to stagnate at around 3.2 million for the whole period, with small rises to 3.5 million in 1930 and then falling back to 3.0 million in 1937. Although Australia had a larger sheep population, New Zealand retained its nineteenth century position as chief mutton exporter and saw its numbers rise from 23.3 million in 1921 to 31.3 million in 1937. When the United Kingdom introduced tariffs on meat imports during the depression of the 1930s, all Commonwealth countries were favoured over Ireland and South America under the Ottawa agreement, and this had the effect of holding back sheep numbers in South America, as well as Ireland.[65]

As pigs are even shorter-lived animals than sheep, their numbers can be rapidly restored once restrictions on their feeding stuffs are removed, and for the same reasons their numbers are also liable to very sharp fluctuations, depending on movements of fodder and pig prices.[66] As Table 4.8 below indicates, a number of Western European countries were importers of pork and bacon. The United Kingdom was the largest, followed by Germany and France. But also Austria, Czechoslovakia, France, Belgium and Switzerland took smaller amounts. The largest producer, and sometimes exporter, was the United States. As exporters, Canada, Ireland, Holland and Denmark followed.[67] After not fully recovering after the war in Western Europe, Table 4.8 also shows how in all regions, with the exception of North and possibly South America, pig numbers rose between 1925 and 1938.[68] The United States differed as pig production and profitability there depended far more on the ratio between pig and fodder prices (or the 'hog-corn ratio') than anywhere else.[69] By the 1930s that country had large surpluses of cereals that could not be transformed into livestock in any other way than by feeding to pigs. But the resultant increase in pig output pushed prices down to such un-remunerative levels by 1936 that when European governments placed controls on imports to protect their own farmers, the American industry had no alternative but to cut back production. This was a forced reduction as the United States government put controls on its own farmers to limit output.[70] But as the United States pig industry was mainly dependent on the home market, its chief difficulties were mainly caused by the severe depression of the 1930s, and cannot simply be blamed on problems in European export markets.

**Table 4.8 Pig numbers in the Western world for selected years from 1913 to 1938 (million)**

| Country | 1913 | 1925 | 1928 | 1930 | 1932 | 1936 | 1938 |
|---|---|---|---|---|---|---|---|
| Belgium [a] | 1.4 | 1.2 | 1.1 | 1.3 | 1.2 | 1.0 | 1.0 |
| Denmark [b] | 1.5 | 2.5 | 3.4 | 4.9 | 4.9 | 3.5 | 2.8 |
| France [a] | 7.5 | 5.8 | 6.0 | 6.3 | 6.5 | 7.0 | 7.1 |
| Germany [a] | 22.5 | 16.3 | 20.2 | 23.6 | 23.0 | 22.3 | 23.5 |
| Ireland [b] | 0.9 | 0.7 | 1.2 | 1.1 | 1.1 | 1.0 | 1.0 |
| Holland [b] | 1.3 | – | – | 2.0 | 2.7 | 1.7 | 1.5 |
| Western Europe [c] | 35.1 | 26.5 | 31.9 | 39.2 | 39.4 | 36.5 | 36.9 |
| UK [a] | 3.3 | 2.9 | 3.4 | 2.8 | 3.6 | 4.6 | 4.7 |
| Canada [b] | 3.4 | 4.4 | 4.5 | 4.0 | 4.6 | 4.1 | 4.3 |
| USA [b] | 51.8 | 52.1 | 59.0 | 54.8 | 62.1 | 42.9 | 49.3 |
| Argentina [b] | 2.9 | – | – | 3.8 | – | – | 4.0[e] |
| Australia [b] | 0.8 | 1.1 | 0.9 | 1.0 | 1.2 | 1.3[d] | 1.1 |
| New Zealand [b] | – | 0.4 | 0.6 | 0.5 | 0.5 | 0.8 | 0.8 |

[a] Importing countries, [b] Exporting countries, [c] i.e., Belgium, Denmark, France, Germany, Ireland, Holland, above; [d] 1935; [e] 1937

*Sources:* International Institute of Agriculture, *World Production in Meat* (Rome, 1938), pp. 154–5, 166–7.
International Institute of Agriculture, *International Yearbook of Agricultural Statistics 1940–41, vol. II, Numbers of the Principal Species of Livestock and Poultry* (Rome, 1941), pp. 164–7.

At this point it is worth noting that most pigs in the United States were chiefly fed corn, whereas elsewhere they were fed on the liquid by-products of butter and cheese factories. The worldwide expansion of the dairy industry in the interwar years thus put a constant upwards pressure on pig output almost everywhere, as pork pigs of good quality could easily be fattened on the fresh milk from centrifugal creamers. This encouraged most dairy companies to take advantage of this by adding modern scientifically managed pig units to their businesses. But all countries heavily dependent on the British market faced changes after 1932 when the British government started to impose import duties on pigs and pig meat in an attempt to protect its own pig industry. Denmark and Ireland were affected particularly adversely. Table 4.8 above shows that in the case of Denmark these restrictions caused pig output to fall from 4.9 million in 1932 to 2.8 million by 1938. Britain's new trade policies also affected output in Sweden, Holland, and Poland who were small exporters of pork and bacon. But Commonwealth exports from Canada, Australia and New Zealand were given a strong boost, as the last group were favoured by the preference given to Commonwealth producers, although the last two had by no means large pig industries. But Canada was allowed such a substantial bacon quota that by 1935 she was exporting three times as much to the UK as in 1932.[71]

## Notes

1  Hibbard, B.H., *Effects of the Great War upon Agriculture in the United States and Great Britain* (New York, 1919), pp. 171–2.

2  Greenhill, R.G., 'Shipping and the Refrigerated Meat Trade from the River Plate 1900–1930', in K. Friedland (ed.), *Maritime Food Transport* (Köln, 1994), pp. 426–8.

3  Macrosty, H.W., 'Army Meat Supplies', *The Board of Trade Journal*, New Series 99(1357) (30 Nov. 1922): 603.

4  Nourse, E.G., *American Agriculture and the European Market* (New York, 1924), p. 50.

5  Pearse, A.W., *The World's Meat Future* (London, 1920), p. 17.

6.  Offer, A., *The First World War: An Agrarian Interpretation* (Oxford, 1989), pp. 376.

7  *Meat Trades Journal* (1 Jan. 1914): 12; (15 Jan. 1914): 68; R. Ramsay, 'The World's Frozen and Chilled Meat Trade', in R. Ramsay (ed.), *The Frozen and Chilled Meat Trade: A Practical Treatise by Specialists in the Trade* (2 vols, London: The Gresham Publishing Company, 1929), vol. 1, p. 18; R. Perren, 'Big business and its customers: the European market for American meat from 1840 to 1939', *Journal European Economic History*, 32(3) (2003): 602.

8  *Pastoral Review* (16 Jan. 1915): 71.

9  Cd 7896 (PP 1914–16, vol. XLVI), *Report of the Royal Commission on the Meat Export Trade of Australia.*, pp. 24–5, 27, 40.

10  W.D. Lysnar, *Meat and shipping problems* (Wellington, 1917), pp. 10–12.

11  Ibid., pp. 14–16.

12  Hibbard, *Effects of the Great War upon Agriculture*, pp. 56–7.

13  Tracy, M., *Government and Agriculture in Western Europe 1880–1988* (London, 1989), pp. 112–13.

14  Putnam, G.E., *Supplying Britain's Meat* (London, 1923), p. 159.

15  Mottram, R. F., *Human Nutrition* (3rd edn, London, 1979), p. 8.

16  Leighton, G.R. and L.M. Douglas, *The Meat Industry and Meat Inspection* (5 vols, London, 1911), vol. 2, p. 432.

17  Middleton, T. H., *Food Production in War* (London, 1923), pp. 37–68.

18  Dewey, P. E., *British Agriculture in the First World War* (London, 1989), pp. 15–16.

19  Rew, R.H., 'The Nation's Food Supply', *Journal of the Royal Statistical Society*, 76(1) (1912): 101.

20  Cecil, R. (1979), *The Development of Agriculture in Germany and the UK: 1. German Agriculture 1870–1970* (Ashford, 1979), p. 17.

21  Dewey, *British Agriculture in the First World War*, p. 244.

22  Perren, R., 'The Retail and Wholesale Meat Trade, 1880–1939', in D. Oddy and D. Miller (eds), *Diet and Health in Modern Britain* (London, 1985), pp. 48–9.

23  Tracy, *Government and Agriculture in Western Europe 1880–1988*, pp. 164–73, 188–99.

24  Murray, K. A.H., *Agriculture* (London, 1955), p. 103.

25  Russell, E. J., *World Population and Food Supplies* (London, 1954), pp. 31–2.

26  Cmd. 7203 (PP 1946–47, Vol. XI), *Food Consumption Levels in the United Kingdom*, p. 10.

27  Cmd. 6879 (PP 1945–46, Vol. XX), *Second Review of the World Food Shortage July 1946*, p. 32.

28  Cmd. 7203 (PP 1946–47, Vol. XI), *Food Consumption Levels in the United Kingdom*, pp. 5, 10.

29  Brandt, K. et al., *Management of Agriculture and Food in the German-Occupied and Other Areas of Fortress Europe: A Study in Military Government* (Stanford, 1953), Appendix A, pp. 621–40.

30  Ibid., pp. 611–13.

31  Ibid., pp. 50–51, 421.

32  Dewey, *British Agriculture*, pp. 167–69, 252.

33  Offer, *The First World War*, p. 25.

34  Murray, *Agriculture*, pp. 40–3.

35  Weddel, W., *Memorandum on the Imported Meat Trade of the United Kingdom (Frozen and Refrigerated) of the United Kingdom With suggestions for fostering production within the Empire* (London, April 1917), Appendices II and III.

36  PRO, MUN 4/6541 (SGS/2295) War Office. Comparative Army rations, 31 July 1915 to 31 May 1917.

37  Macrosty, 'Army Meat Supplies', p. 603.

38  Offer, *The First World War*, pp. 41–3: Murray, *Agriculture*, p. 41.

39  Guild, J.B., 'Variations in the Numbers of Live Stock and in the Production of Meat in the United Kingdom During the War', *Journal of the Royal Statistical Society*, 88(4) (1920): 534–45; J.R. Smith, *The World's Food Resources* (London, 1919), p. 224.

40  Guild, 'Variations in the Numbers of Live Stock and in the Production of Meat in the United Kingdom During the War': 534, 551–2.

41  Augé-Laribé, M. and P. Pinot, *Agriculture and Food Supply in France During the War* (New Haven, 1927), pp. 17, 19, 73–4.

42  Gibson, C., 'The British Army, French Farmers and the War on the Western Front 1914–1918', *Past & Present*, 180 (2003): 180–4, 192–4, 201, 214–15.

43  Augé-Laribé and Pinot, *Agriculture and Food Supply in France During the War*, pp. 71, 74–5, 196.

44  Ibid., pp. 194–6.

45  Perren, R., 'Farmers and Consumers Under Strain: Allied Meat Supplies in the First World War', *Agricultural History Review*, 53(2) (2005): 214–16.

46  Beveridge, W.H., *British Food Control* (London, 1928), pp. 21, 36, 140, 145.

47 Curtis–Bennet, N., *The Food of the People: The History of Industrial Feeding* (London, 1949), pp. 234, 237.
48 Hammond, R.J., *Food and Agriculture in Britain 1939–1945: Aspects of Wartime Control* (Stanford, 1954), pp. 208–12.
49 Hendrick, J., 'The Growth of International Trade in Manures and Foods', *Transactions of the Highland and Agricultural Society*, Series 5, 29 (1917): 30–6.
50 Middleton, T.H., *The Recent Development of German Agriculture* (London, 1917), pp. 6, 10, 11, 73.
51 Cd 8358 (PP 1916, Vol. XIV), *Departmental Committee on Increase of Prices of Commodities since the Beginning of the War, Interim Report, Meat Milk and Bacon*, p. 4.
52 Offer, *The First World War*, pp. 28, 53, 76.
53 Lindberg, J., *Food, Famine and Relief 1940–1946* (Geneva, 1946), pp. 57–60.
54 Fenelon, K.G., *Britain's Food Supplies* (London, 1952), pp. 77–8. Brandt, *Management of Agriculture and Food in the German-Occupied and Other Areas of Fortress Europe*, pp. 470–1.
55 Lindberg, *Food, Famine and Relief 1940–1946*, p. 61.
56 Brandt, *Management of Agriculture and Food in the German-Occupied and Other Areas of Fortress Europe*, p. 419.
57 For the meat rations in grams per week of the individual countries of Europe see Lindberg, *Food, Famine and Relief 1940–1946*, pp. 123–57.
58 Ibid., p. 30.
59 Harberler, G., *Prosperity and Depression: A Theoretical Analysis of Cyclical Movements*, 3rd edn (New York, 1943), pp. 266–7.
60 Royal Institute of International Affairs, *World Agriculture: An International Survey. A Report by a Study Group* (London, 1932), pp. 154–5; International Institute of Agriculture, *World Production in Meat* (Rome, 1938), pp. 88, 242, 298–9.
61 Royal Institute of International Affairs, *World Agriculture*, pp. 94, 96.
62 International Institute of Agriculture, *World Production in Meat*, pp. 96, 110, 120.
63 Intelligence Branch of the Imperial Economic Committee, *Cattle and Beef Survey: A Summary of Production and Trade in British Empire and Commonwealth Countries* (London: 1934). p. 337; Tracy, *Government and Agriculture in Western Europe 1880–1988*, pp. 173, 199–201.
64 International Institute of Agriculture, *World Production in Meat*, pp. 136–7.
65 Ibid., pp. 140–6.
66 Ibid., pp. 147–8.
67 Ibid., pp. 154–5.
68 Ibid., p. 148.
69 McCoy, J.H., *Livestock and Meat Marketing* (Westport, 1972), pp. 74–6.
70 International Institute of Agriculture, *World Production in Meat*, pp. 168–71.
71. Ibid., pp. 172–6.

# Chapter 5

# Production and Output

This chapter deals with the part also played by the international application of improved methods of production and business organisation. As a result of these changes the large multinationals increased their influence on the industry. The further application of scientific management and technical improvement to livestock farming and meat processing improved quality, cut costs and extended the range of products. These technical changes were worked out and had their greatest application in the regions producing large meat surpluses. They were first tried by the large United States meat Trust firms, which is not altogether surprising as they had been the leading pioneers of factory production methods in the nineteenth century. But they were also applied to a lesser extent and on a smaller scale in the non-American parts of the industry elsewhere. They also contributed to an increase in the amount of meat domestically produced within Europe itself, although it was not the only factor behind that increase. In mainland Europe there was a continuing search for national self-sufficiency in food production. As this applied both to cereals and animal protein, the attempts by European governments to restrict competing imports of cheap meat reduced the size of the potential market for all the major meat surplus producers. When this happened, especially in the world depression of the 1930s, it reduced the incentive for livestock farmers to invest in both land and livestock improvements.

In addition, price fluctuations had effects on all meat producers. They experienced a sharp reduction in prices following the First World War as the accumulated stocks were consumed and the pent-up demand that generated the post-war boom of 1919 and 1920 were exhausted. Meat companies in the export trade were particularly badly affected by the fall in demand. In 1921 Argentine exporters were producing rather less than half of what they had in 1918. The canned meat trade was particularly badly affected as the inflated wartime demand disappeared once supplies of fresh meat were fully restored. The experience of the meat packers was of course not unique, as they shared experiences similar to those of many other producers once the immediate post-war boom ended.

## Farm and Livestock Improvements

In all countries there were continued efforts at improvement, but the constraining factors were the restrictions of wartime conditions and the fluctuations in prices, that determined the profitability of such expenditures. In all the other meat producing countries there was a similar wartime hiatus and then a post-war revival of livestock improvement. In addition to the lack of demand for prime meat during the war itself, other factors holding back the pedigree livestock trade were high wartime ocean freight rates and insurance costs for valuable pedigree animals, as well as a shortage of ships still equipped for this trade. It took some months to re-establish the links between breeders and beef and mutton farmers, but once this was done meat prices were once again the controlling influence on the demand for pedigree animals and that particular part of the livestock trade. However, just as important were the complementary farm improvements that were required to get the best return from improved livestock. As before 1914, better quality animals required better shelter and better feeding than the unimproved cattle and sheep that could survive better on the sparse pastures of poor quality land.

**Argentina**

In Argentina alfalfa was already widely grown in 1914 and its acreage seems to have increased during the war in response to the demand for meat. In 1915–16 it occupied 16.5 million acres, out of 32 million acres of arable crops. Its acreage was almost 20 million by 1924, at that time, or one third of the land under arable crops and the largest acreage of any crop grown. However it does not seem to have increased after that date, as in 1926–27 it covered 12 million acres out of a total arable acreage of 39 million.[1] Its decline seems to be explained by the fall in meat prices after 1920 and a decision by some farmers from the mid-1920s to switch from livestock to cereals.

But alfalfa, still occupied almost a third of the arable acreage and its importance for livestock farming continued. Combined with year round grazing, it made it possible to send an animal to market a year earlier than if it were kept on native pastures alone. As the effect of all measures that produce earlier maturity is to increase the feeding capacity of the land, the benefits of alfalfa tended to vary with the demand for meat. During times of buoyant demand and rising consumption the farmers gained because it allowed them to supply the market better, but during times of depression it just added to the surplus livestock production. In the early 1920s the general trend was a rising demand, but the sharp fluctuations experienced after the mid-1920s certainly reduced the incentive to increase the acreage of alfalfa.

Livestock improvement continued in the years after the war and saw an extension of the number of introduced breeds, but the war itself slowed the process in most countries. This was because once the armies of Europe were mobilized the military demand was for tinned and frozen meat, and the export of chilled beef was almost entirely suspended. Soldiers' ration tins of tinned meat required flesh from animals with muscle and tendons and little fat, and this is what came from unimproved cattle. In Argentina between 1916 better prices were paid for native beef of poor quality than for the more refined kind used for chilling; the demand for old and ordinary animals was so high that their price rose to as much as 18 pence a pound, while those of the chilled type were only five or six pence a pound. The fall in the general quality of beef exported encouraged the transport of animals over very long distances to canning and freezing plants, from the Andes, Paraguay, Bolivia, and even the heart of the Brazilian rainforests. But after the war the process of livestock improvement took off again with the demand for chilled beef from Germany and Italy.[2]

The herd book kept by the *Sociedad Rural Argentina* listed 24 separate pedigree breed types by 1926, and the flock book 17. We do not know the status of the cattle population in the 1920s, but according to the 1922 livestock census 81 per cent of the 36 million sheep were either pure or crossbred, and unimproved native animals were only 19 per cent.[3] By the 1940s there were about 34 million cattle of which approximately 20 million were shorthorns, three million were Herefords and one and three-quarter million Aberdeen Angus, leaving less than 30 per cent partly improved native and crossbred animals. At the same time the number of sheep was approximately 56 million, including 14 million Lincolns, 13 million Merinos, seven million Romney Marsh, and three million Corriedales.[4]

**Uruguay**

In Uruguay the process of increased investment can be dated from the decade before 1914, and had a great deal to do with the introduction of the frozen meat trade after 1905. The value of the country's exports had doubled between 1900 and the outbreak of the First World War following the introduction of this trade. Throughout the 1920s and 1930s the livestock sector of farming enjoyed a greater popularity than cereal production. Unlike neighbouring Argentina, the expansion of livestock farming had not been accompanied by a boom in cereal production in the decades before the War. In 1920 it was reported that still 'Landowners prefer to rent for pasture rather than for cultivation because of their distaste for arable farming on their lands'. Their preference for livestock over arable seems to be explained partly by tradition. As cattle and sheep farming were long established in the country, both farmers and workers regarded the manual labour associated with the use of the plough and hoe of arable farming with distaste. But it was also a rational preference as price trends continued to favour livestock production, while further investment was required for crop disease control and the development of high yielding crop strains, and finally only about 20 per cent of the available land was suitable for cereal farming.[5]

Against this background, investment in the livestock sector, which provided 54 per cent of agricultural exports in 1935–40, continued to grow in the inter-war period, as shown in Table 5.1 below which is based on figures provided by Finch in his 1979 study of the Uruguayan economy. However, the growth of this investment was lower than it had been before 1914. The only variable to show a continuous positive trend in the inter-war years was the number of registered pedigree beef cattle. But these are total numbers and include both imported and Uruguayan breed stock. The ratio of imported breed stock to the numbers bred in Uruguay seems to have declined rapidly. Censuses of breeding farms showed the proportion of imported beef cattle dropped from 10 per cent in 1920 to 2.1 per cent in 1928 and to 0.5 per cent in 1936. For sheep the percentage of imported breeding stock was higher but still fell from 13.8 per cent in 1920 to 9.7 per cent in 1928, and to 4.7 per cent in 1936. There were large fluctuations in the imports of pedigree breeding cattle before the First World War, with pronounced peaks in 1905–07 and 1912–14. The last great surge in cattle imports was in 1917–20, taking advantage of the post-war revival of animal exports, but thereafter the imports of pedigree cattle remained low, although imports of pedigree sheep did see small peaks in the late 1920s and mid-1930s.[6]

**Table 5.1 Number of pedigree animals registered in Uruguay and indexes of import volumes of fencing materials 1901–40 (five-year averages) and annual rates of growth between groups of years**

|           | Beef cattle | | Sheep | | Wire | | Fence posts | |
|-----------|------|-------|------|-------|-----|--------|------|--------|
|           | No.  | %     | No   | %     |     | %      |      | %      |
| 1901–05   | 471  | –     | 134  | –     | 100 | –      | 100  | –      |
| 1906–10   | 1388 | 24.13 | 1672 | 65.66 | 119 | 3.54   | 103  | 0.59   |
| 1911–15   | 1961 | 7.16  | 2076 | 4.42  | –   | –      | –    | –      |
| 1916–20   | 3353 | 11.32 | 1406 | -7.50 | 68  | -5.44  | 104  | 0.10   |
| 1921–25   | 5164 | 9.03  | 1580 | 2.36  | 90  | 5.77   | 80   | -5.11  |
| 1926–30   | 7809 | 8.62  | 2946 | 13.27 | 98  | 1.72   | 83   | 0.74   |
| 1931–35   | 10,980 | 7.05 | 2268 | -5.10 | 48  | -13.30 | 25   | -21.34 |
| 1936–40   | –    | –     | –    | –     | 66  | 6.58   | 41   | 10.40  |

*Source:* Finch, M.H.J., *A Political Economy of Uruguay Since 1870* (London, 1981), p. 78.

The traditional *criollo* cattle had disappeared by the late 1920s through a process of piecemeal improvement using for the most part Uruguayan breed animals plus better feeding. But investment in land improvement seems to have lagged somewhat behind livestock improvement. The big period of investment in better fencing seems to have been before the First War, as can be seen from Table 5.1 above. But a law of 1913 intended to bring in a standard seven-strand wire fence for all boundaries by 1923, to reduce the spread of animal disease, seems to have been a dead letter. The time period for its enforcement was extended by a further ten years to 1933 but as late as 1928 only about 30 per cent of fences were thought to comply with the legal requirement. Little progress was made either in raising the feeding capacity of the pastures. Instead, there was a heavy reliance on the natural fertility of the land rather than attempts to raise it further by sufficient investment in watercourses, planned crop rotations, and artificial pastures to support more animals and ensure they were kept supplied in times of shortage.[7]

In 1920 one writer pointed out that 'The success of cattle-breeding and the lack of adequate means of transport has greatly retarded the development of [other forms of] agriculture'.[8] This situation did not change very much thereafter. As a result there was always a seasonal inadequacy of feed during the periods of excessive heat, strong winds and sharp changes in temperature between July and September. Although annual rainfall averaged about forty inches it was sporadic, and annual drought could last from twenty to forty days. In the interwar years ranch owners did little to protect themselves against these by constructing farm ponds, or producing hay or silage, or practising rotational grazing[9]. One survey in 1930 showed that 75.2 per cent of the capital in livestock production was accounted for by the cost of land, 16.4 per cent by the cost of livestock, and only the remaining 8.4 per cent by investment in machinery, housing, fences, other buildings and pasture and woodland. The main way in which farmers expanded their livestock numbers was simply by allowing more land per animal.[10]

Against this background of low levels of farm investment, it is not surprising that farming methods remained little changed and overall productivity remained low, although output did experience a modest expansion as farmers enclosed more land. The *frigorificos* slaughtered a peak number of 663,500 cattle in 1919 to supply the European market but this number was not reached again until 1926. There was a further increase in beef production in the late 1920s, and in 1930 1.1 million cattle were slaughtered for export. In that year the price of cattle for slaughter was the highest since 1920, and the slaughter of calves was also exceptionally high at 400,000 head. But over the whole period the slaughter weights of fat cattle showed very little change and remained at around 470 kilos per head between 1905 and 1929. As Uruguayan beef was generally lighter than Argentine there was a tendency to ship most of it to Europe where it suited the requirements of that market, rather than to Britain where the heavier animals produced further south were more in demand.[11] There was a small increase in the 1930s, so that by 1939 it was around 490 kilos. From the early 1920s, following something of a substitution of mutton for beef in the First World War, the numbers of sheep slaughtered for the *frigorificos* grew. This led to something of a substitution of the dual purpose Lincoln and Romney Marsh breeds to replace the wool Merino which fell from favour in the face of low and stagnating wool prices, no doubt explaining the small peaks in pedigree sheep imports in the late 1920s and mid-1930s.[12]

## Australia and New Zealand

In Australia, because that country's export trade in mutton and lamb ceased to grow very much in the inter-war years, the country continued to concentrate on wool production. This meant that improvements in livestock continued to concentrate on the Merino type of sheep that made up 90 per cent, or more, of the country's animals. More attention was given to pasture improvement, but here the extent of this was limited by climatic feasibility. In drought-prone western New South Wales and in equally dry western Queensland most sheep runs continued to be huge properties of up to 5,000 acres. Here, intensive pasture improvement or the introduction of fodder crops was an economic impossibility. And even in those regions where climate offered more prospect of profit, its effectiveness was still limited by the inability to effectively control many of the livestock pests.[13] In New Zealand, because the production of meat was far more important, flocks had a greater breed diversification before 1914, and this characteristic continued into the inter-war years and beyond. The proportion of wool Merinos had been in decline since the late nineteenth century and by the 1940s the main breeds became Cheviot, Romney Marsh, Southdown, Border Leicester and Corriedale. All of them gained popularity because they were suited to New Zealand's wetter climate and could produce either prime lamb or good mutton carcases, or a combination of both.[14]

New Zealand has sometimes been known as 'Britain's outlying farm' and its concentration on this branch of economic life was confirmed after 1914. The proportion of people employed in primary production fell as towns developed, but the towns themselves were processing and servicing centres catering for the needs of farming, rather than manufacturing centres in their own right. Butter and cheese factories and freezing works were more in evidence than heavy industry, or footwear and clothing factories. The inter-war years saw an increase in dairying activities, and this biased a lot of the interwar farm improvement work towards dairying rather than sheep farming. There was more mechanisation of farm tasks, and a lot of this was electrical milking machines and cream separators for the dairy farms. But farmers did also invest in the machinery necessary for improved grassland farming, such as fertilizer distributors, harrows, mowers, hay collectors, and silage hoists. Although these were more directly applied to dairying rather than sheep farming, there was still a certain amount of overlap between the two branches, and the same was true with the use of better fertilizers. Some of the grassland research that was undertaken after it became apparent around 1925 that increasing acreage of land would become less important as a factor in adding to the numbers of animals kept and raising product, was also applied to sheep pasturing.[15]

The high dependence on agriculture in both countries made them particularly vulnerable to the steep drop in primary commodity world prices in 1929 and 1930, which had a marked effect on all sectors of farming. In New Zealand the universal fall in export prices reacted back on farm incomes and inevitably reduced levels of all forms of farm, and other, investment. The depression of the 1930s caused farmers' income to continue to fall, despite their spectacular increase in production.[16] Gross farm income at current prices was £65 million in 1928/29, but fell to a low point of £37.9 million in 1931/32 and only passed its 1928/29 level in 1936/37 when it reached £74.6 million. Against this the total real value of capital on New Zealand farms, that is livestock, plant and machinery and improvements, did not fall, but continued to grow in the 1930s as farmers reacted to falling prices by fresh investment to raise productivity. However, it is impossible to separate out how much of this was accounted for by meat production, and how much was attributable to other branches of farming.[17]

In Australia the effect of the depression seems to have been even more severe than in New Zealand, because meat and dairy prices held up far better than wool. In the 1920s an unknown proportion of small farmers' incomes had come from doing fencing, shearing and rabbit control for the larger farmers, as well as contract work for small gangs working on roads and other types of government construction. As the depression deepened many large farmers ceased to make improvements in their holding so some of their work disappeared and state governments halted road and other construction. At the same time official policy was to encourage the city unemployed to look for work in the countryside, so on all sides the Australian small farmer's income was squeezed and worsened the severity of the depression. The worst year for wool farmers was 1931, when prices reached their lowest point, though they did revive by 1934. Technical change, though not entirely absent, was certainly held back by financial pressures. As wages were low, this discouraged farm mechanization and most land improvement investment was devoted to arable cultivation. Up to 1939 almost all the artificial fertilizer (mostly superphosphate) applied as topdressing was devoted to cereal crops, even though it was discovered in the 1920s that this practice was the only way to achieve high yields of clover.[18]

Exports of meat to Britain from both countries did undergo some changes after 1932 as a result of developments in refrigeration technology and the start of chilled beef exports. The first shipments of beef from Australia on board the *SS Mooltan* were not a success and 70 per cent of the meat was condemned on arrival. The first company to try exports from New Zealand was Thomas Borthwick & Sons on board the *SS Port Fairy*. Close temperature control was necessary to keep the meat within the close limits required, and carbon dioxide was pumped into the compartments where the meat was carried to limit the growth of mould. More shipments were made from both countries by other companies and by 1939, when the trade was halted at the outbreak of war, New Zealand shipped 18,000 tons and Australia 27,000 tons. One reason that encouraged Borthwicks to take part in the early development of this trade was because they had no refrigeration plant in South America.[19]

## The Fortunes of the Multinationals

The struggle for the control of production in the River Plate meat industry that began before the First World War continued during the war itself and into the 1930s. The first price agreement in 1911, detailed in Chapter 3 above, applied only to the plants in Argentina and not to those in Uruguay, which were comparatively small and at that time produced no chilled beef. This agreement broke up in April 1913 because output from the Uruguayan plants had since increased. The agreement that led to the second pool in June 1914 was modified throughout the war and into the mid-1920s to take account of the increased capacity brought about by wartime investment and the entry of new firms into the trade. However, there was no return to the 'great fight' of 1912–13, although it was suggested that the memory of the fierce price-cutting then, and the possibility that they could revive hostilities at any time was sufficient to give a dominating influence in the trade to the companies with the largest financial resources.[20]

The war itself provoked worries that world supplies of meat would be insufficient on the return to peace. The United States was a source of particular anxiety. In 1893 it imported 3,293 head of cattle, most of which were breeding animals, and exported over 287,000 cattle for beef. By 1915 the import and export figures were practically reversed and it only exported 5,484 head of cattle but imported 538,000, most of them for slaughter. Although production and exports were revived during the war there were doubts about whether this would be permanent. It was against this background that South America was looked upon as a source of extra production. Argentina and Uruguay were already substantial exporters and the British and United States meat firms believed that their output could be expanded. But they also had ideas of bringing Brazil, Paraguay, Columbia, and Venezuela into the world beef economy as well. By 1917 there was some expansion in Brazil with four freezing works in operation and it shipped 66,450 tons of beef in that year, mostly to Europe for the Italian and French armies. But although that country had about 30 million cattle most of them were of poor quality, and that limited its potential for expansion.[21]

In the event these anxieties turned out not to be the major concern after 1918 as herds and flocks had been built up sufficiently during the war in those countries that were capable of expansion to ensure that exports were well maintained in the early 1920s. What did worry many livestock farmers and other members of the industry, and also governments on behalf of the consumer, was that the further growth of giant meat businesses threatened to become a monopoly. In the war the British government took over the management of the Las Palmas plant from which it shipped meat to supply the British army. This meant that it had to be added into the shares agreed by the meat-exporting firms in June 1914, reducing those of existing participants accordingly. Then in 1916 Armours, who had remained outside the agreement in 1914, added their plant to the scheme, causing the share of the others to be adjusted accordingly, and in 1921 Wilson returned.

In addition to the powerful American firms present well before 1914, the war had strengthened the position of the British owned Union Cold Storage Company, started in 1897 by the Vestey family who began as food merchants in Liverpool, and entered the meat business in Argentina in 1890. They also had interests in China and Russia, but the major part of their trade was in South America. The First World War did not make the Vesteys' fortune but it was responsible for its rapid growth in a few years. During the war the Vestey's business had made enormous profits from its meat contracts with the British Army. Their ownership of the Blue Star Line of refrigerated cargo ships placed them in a powerful position from the start. This company, registered in London and Liverpool in 1911 with a capital of

£100,000, had seven meat ships by 1914. From its start in the 1890s with a capital of around £50,000 and one cold store, by 1925 Union Cold Storage was a major player in the meat trade with a paid-up share capital of nearly £9 million and a dozen subsidiary meat companies operating in Argentina, New Zealand and Australia, and it was also building up a large retail trade in Britain where it owned a third of the cold storage capacity.[22]

Like the American companies, such as Swift and Armour, Union Cold Storage had a totally integrated business operation where it owned every link in the food chain between producer and consumer, enabling it to compete with them on equal terms. But, unlike the American companies whose interests were first and foremost concentrated on supplying the United States, the Vesteys were geared to supply the British market. During the war they built cold storage facilities at Boulogne, Le Havre and Dunkirk to supply the British troops in France as well as building more cold stores in Liverpool and Glasgow. By 1919 the Blue Star Line had acquired seven more ships and Union Cold Storage had ranches, plants and cold stores in Australia, New Zealand, South Africa, Madagascar, France, Spain and Portugal. In 1915 they established a powerful presence in Argentina when they acquired the Las Palmas Cold Store and began a substantial extension of its capacity.[23] In 1922 they bought the British and Argentine Meat Company and joined the meat conference, taking over its share of meat exports. By this time the Vesteys' Argentine operations had grown sufficiently for them to command a larger share of the beef export trade, and by this time Union Cold Storage was large and powerful enough to engage in a price war with the Trust members with good prospects of success.

From April 1925 until June 1927 a second price war was fought, but this time, unlike the first one from April 1913 to June 1914, it was not initiated by the American firms to gain a larger share from the British and Argentine companies.[24] This time it was a firm owned by two British nationals, Baron William Vestey who had been made a peer in 1922 and his brother Sir Edmund Hoyle Vestey who had received his knighthood in 1921. The strategy followed in the 1920s was similar to that in the 1910s. Like the Americans before the First War, the Vesteys cut wholesale prices and also reduced them in their British retail shops. In order to cope with the increase in sales this brought about, they also expanded the scale of their livestock purchases in Argentina driving up prices paid to the cattle feeders. When the Americans responded by doing the same thing it further reduced the price of meat in Britain and raised cattle prices in Argentina. But in two important respects the situation was different in the 1920s.

In the first place the Vestey family's group of companies had come to occupy a much more powerful position in the United Kingdom retail meat business than any of the British companies before 1914. By 1925 they were the owners of 2,356 retail shops, scattered over the whole country. They were acquired when the Vestey brothers took over five firms who had already built up chains of retail meat shops selling American meat, some of them beginning in the 1880s. All the shops' former owners, the British and Argentine Meat Company, Eastmans, W. and R.

Fletcher, the Argenta Meat Company and J.H. Dewhurst were taken over by Union Cold Storage at various dates since 1911. By the mid-1920s it was estimated that together they handled about 9 per cent of the country's retail trade, although William and Edmund put it at no more than 5 or 6 per cent. Whatever the precise share might have been, there is no doubt the growth of their importance in the British retail meat business was at the expense of some of the American Trust firms who had reduced their presence in Britain since 1914. The total employment of the Union Cold Storage Company was 30,000 worldwide and it was responsible for some 20 per cent of Britain's imports of chilled beef. Given the fact that their company had such extensive ownership interests in all parts of the meat food chain, the brothers argued it was essential for it to be able to control the retail outlets for a very large proportion of it.[25]

During the First World War imports of chilled meat for civilian consumption had fallen off as the British government had increased its army orders for frozen meat. This had encouraged the meat firms, sometimes with government assistance, to undertake a substantial expansion of cold storage space in all the major British cities. The wartime uncertainty about shipping losses, and the regularity of arrivals, made it a common practice to hold large stocks of frozen beef and mutton in these stores for some time, to guard against interruptions in supply. But much of this space became surplus to requirements on the return to peace and the growth of imports of chilled beef was resumed. Part of the excess was also caused by the improved organization of the lamb and mutton trade. Before the war arrivals could be irregular, but after 1920 increased amounts of frozen lamb and mutton were held in store in Argentina, Australia, and New Zealand and shipped to Britain in regular amounts each month. In January 1925 the owners of around twenty of the largest cold stores in Britain estimated that about 80 per cent of the space was unoccupied, in spite of several stores closing down since the war.[26] These developments, which meant meat was often going straight from the ship to shop, made the Vesteys' possession of sufficient retail outlets to handle it even more important than before 1914.

The second feature of the industry that had changed by the 1920s was that though the demand for meat was not declining, it was no longer growing at the rate it had before the mid-1900s. Indeed, aggregate demand had almost stagnated. Table 5.2 below indicates that by 1925 the average weekly consumption of fresh meat was around 2 lbs per head, which was much the same as it had been in the years immediately before the First War. Over the 34 years from 1880–89 to 1910–14 total meat consumption had risen by 1.13 per cent a year, whereas over the 18 years from 1910–14 to 1924–28 the rate of increase was only 0.09 per cent a year. There was also more difficulty in disposing of cheaper cuts in the 1920s. Besides the near stagnation of the whole industry in the 1920s, the rise of the multiple firms, including the Cooperative Society, made things harder for the small retail butcher operating a single shop, as in large parts of the country there were complaints that the big firms operated 'buying rings'.[27] From the early 1920s the National Federation of Meat Traders' Associations, representing the small independent retail butcher, had noticed that the meat importers were opening an increasing number of their own retail shops.[28] In Jefferys' study, which concentrates on the development of the multiple retail shop business, he estimates that the proportion of meat sales handled by single shop firms shrank from approximately 84 per cent in 1920 to 78 per cent in 1939.[29]

### Table 5.2  United Kingdom meat consumption, c.1880–1939

|         | Beef and veal 000 tons | Mutton and lamb 000 tons | Pork and bacon 000 tons | All meats 000 tons | All meats per head lbs |
|---------|------------------------|--------------------------|-------------------------|--------------------|------------------------|
| 1880–89 | 852  | 417 | 475 | 1744 | 110.8 |
| 1890–95 | 1068 | 536 | 583 | 2187 | 126.6 |
| 1900–09 | 1178 | 515 | 772 | 2465 | 130.3 |
| 1910–14 | 1265 | 580 | 710 | 2555 | 126.9 |
| 1915–19 | 1202 | 452 | 756 | 2410 | 122.6 |
| 1920–23 | 1287 | 531 | 774 | 2592 | 123.2 |
| 1924–28 | 1297 | 491 | 808 | 2596 | 128.6 |
| 1929–32 | 1321 | 545 | 905 | 2771 | 135.3 |
| 1933–36 | 1298 | 562 | 898 | 2758 | 132.4 |
| 1936–39 | 1408 | 588 | 909 | 2905 | 137.2 |

*Source:* Perren, R., 'The Retail and Wholesale Meat Trade, 1880–1939', in D. Oddy and D. Miller (eds), *Diet and Health in Modern Britain* (London, 1985), pp. 48–9.

But at the same time that the Vesteys were extending their influence in the British market, there seems to be evidence of some decline in the relative importance of the American firms. Part of this development seems to have been driven by the change in the internal meat supply situation of the United States. After its decline as an exporting country between 1900 and 1913, detailed in Chapter 3 above, its wartime transformation into an exporting country did not last much beyond 1920.[30] From then on its exports were negligible and in the face of competition in the British market, the American firms had to increase their efforts to retain their share of the trade in South American meat. They were already secure in their domination of the United States market, the world's most valuable and where they faced no external competition, and where their position was already so strong that they were unchallengeable. But a different set of circumstances applied to the British market, which still absorbed over 90 per cent of River Plate meat exports in the 1930s.[31]

The position of the Trust firms within the United States market started to change after the war and they began to lose some of their power in the face of new entrants to the industry and pressure from the Federal Government forcing them to abandon some of their restrictive practices.[32] Whatever the changes in the United States supply situation, the United States firms certainly could not abandon their operations in the United Kingdom. They had an established position as importers and wholesalers with a strong and elaborate marketing network of salesmen to supply the retail business. And though they do seem to have reduced these over time, sometimes by disposing of them to the other large meat companies like the Vesteys, their interest in the largest meat importing market was too important to disappear before 1939. They remained significant players in the whole international meat business up to 1939, trading with all the major meat exporting regions in their searches to supply both the United Kingdom and United States markets. In what still remained the most important of these, the River Plate, they found their share was slightly reduced in the 1920s by the competition from the Vestey group, though they still retained over half of this trade.

**Table 5.3  Percentage of South American meat exports held by British, Argentine, and United States public companies in 1918**

| Company | Ownership | Beef percentage five-sevenths | Mutton percentage two-sevenths | Total percentage overall |
|---|---|---|---|---|
| In Argentina | | | | |
| British & Argentine | UK | 16.962 | 20.472 | 16.294 |
| S. & A. M. Co | UK | 6.044 | 6.414 | 5.706 |
| Armour | US | 15.333 | 15.333 | 14.235 |
| F.A.C. (Wilson) | US | 6.906 | 6.414 | 6.518 |
| La Blanca | US | 13.812 | 8.433 | 11.647 |
| La Plata (Swift) | US | 27.027 | 22.868 | 24.212 |
| Sansinena | Argentine | 6.442 | 20.066 | 9.894 |
| | | | 100.000 | |
| In Uruguay | | | | |
| Armour | US | — | 15.333 | 1.094 |
| F.M (Swift) | US | 4.963 | 40.378 | 5.847 |
| F.U. (Sansinena) | Argentine | 2.511 | 44.289 | 5.553 |
| | | 100.000 | 100.000 | 100.000 |

*Source:* Brewster, J.A., 'The South American Trade', in F. Gerrard (ed.), *The Book of the Meat Trade* (2 vols, London, 1949), vol. 1, p. 217.

During the latter stages of the war there were slight changes in the allocations of shipping space that were allotted to each firm in June 1914 as, in response to the increased wartime demand, new freezing plants were opened in Argentina and Uruguay. In addition, the United States firm of Armour joined the conference in 1916. As a result, at the end of the war the allocation of shares between the different firms and countries was as set out in Table 5. 3 above.

There were further changes in 1920 when Wilson left the agreement and their shares of beef and mutton were reallocated among the remaining plants and firms. However, in 1921 Wilson thought better of their decision and decided the benefits of returning outweighed those of having the freedom to export as much as it wanted to, but no doubt coping with the difficulties involved in trying to obtain and fill the necessary shipping space for it outside the conference. Securing enough insulated shipping space could be a serious problem, as was demonstrated in the war when special conditions applied. But in normal times contracts usually ran for a long time, normally four or five years ahead, and after the war the space had to be paid for whether meat was carried or not. It was always possible for the *frigorificos* to resell the space, but there were limited opportunities there and the only purchasers were competing firms.[33] This did not apply to the Vesteys with their Blue Star shipping line, but it left them under an equally strong compulsion to utilise this heavy fixed investment.

**Table 5.4  Percentage of South American meat exports held by British, Argentine, and American public companies from 1924 to 1932**

| Company | Ownership | Total percentage overall |
| --- | --- | --- |
| Vestey (Anglo) | UK | 22.599 |
| River Plate British & Continental | UK | 6.000 |
| S. & A. M. Co | UK | 6.500 |
| Armour | US | 23.954 |
| Wilson | US | 6.500 |
| Swift | US | 24.447 |
| Sansinena | Argentine | 10.000 |
| | | 100.000 |

*Source:* Brewster, J.A., 'The South American Trade', in F. Gerrard (ed.), *The Book of the Meat Trade* (2 vols, London, 1949), vol. 1, p. 219.

In 1920 Armour also brought the beef production from its new Montevideo plant at Artigas into the agreement, as well as transferring part of their mutton quota for this plant across the river to Argentina. Then in 1922 the Vesteys were powerful enough to be admitted to the agreement, and were allocated 11.25 per cent of the total percentage overall. After this there were minor adjustments before the next major set of changes in 1924. These involved considerable competition and losses on the part of the meat companies as they battled for increased shares as well as trying to retain their existing quotas. Vesteys sold their Las Palmas works to an English and Dutch firm called Meta Company and purchased the Liebig plant at Fray Bentos in Uruguay. They also sold their Zarate plant to the River Plate British and Continental Meat Company, and opened a new plant on the mouth of the Riachuelo in Buenos Aires. The Smithfield and Argentine Meat Company increased their processing capacity and Swifts decided to withdraw any meat they shipped from their plant at Rosario from the agreement.[34] As a result of this, the final allocations in 1924 can be seen in Table 5.4 above.

These changes brought the Argentine share of the trade to its lowest point at 10 per cent, which contrasts with the 27.7 per cent held in 1910 and before the first of the price wars were started in 1911, though most of the subsequent loss was made by 1914. The North American firms also experienced a small reduction in their share from 56.612 per cent in 1918 to the 54.901 per cent in 1924. After 1924 the only major change was the closure of the River Plate British and Continental Company's plant, and their share was taken over by the remaining six firms. The trade continued pretty much unaltered until the depression after 1929 when further major changes were made in the way the trade was controlled, by the Ottawa agreements of 1932. The implications of the sets of quotas and allowances involved in the agreements with Commonwealth meat producers are explained in greater detail in Chapter 6 below, but under these the British Board of Trade granted licences for River Plate imports of frozen and chilled meat into Britain. They were formalized later on in the 1930s in treaties with both countries. The broad outlines of the shares finally allocated to each exporting company are shown

**Table 5.5  Percentage of South American meat exports held by British, Argentine, and American public companies from 1932 to 1939**

| Company | Ownership | Total percentage overall |
| --- | --- | --- |
| Vestey (Anglo) | UK | 24.4607 |
| S. & A. M. Co | UK | 6.9149 |
| Armour | US | 25.8157 |
| Wilson | US | 6.5000 |
| Swift | US | 26.3087 |
| Sansinena & F.N. Uruguay* | Argentine and Uruguayan | 10.0000 |
| | | 100.0000 |

* The Sansinena Company sold their plant in Uruguay to Frigorifico National Uruguay. The shares of the trade were Sansinena 7.5 and F.N. Uruguay 2.5.

*Source:* Brewster, J.A., 'The South American Trade', in F. Gerrard (ed.), *The Book of the Meat Trade*, Vol. I (London, 1949), p. 219.

in Table 5.5 above. Under this arrangement, the share of the North American companies rose to 58.6244 per cent on the disappearance of the River Plate British and Continental Company. This was at the expense of the overall British share, but the Vestey businesses did see their share edge up to just under a quarter of the trade, although it was still less than that of both Armour and Swift. The South American 10 per cent share held steady but was now divided between two Argentine and Uruguayan firms. But Table 5.5 does not include the whole of the trade. An additional 15 per cent of overall Argentine shipments were granted to two privately owned businesses and the Argentine Meat Producers Corporation, which was controlled by the Argentine government. This division lasted until the outbreak of war, when the governments of both countries, together with the United Kingdom government, exercised much more control over how River Plate meat exports were allocated to each shipper.

## Notes

1 Figures for 1915–16 and 1926–27 from C.E. Solberg, 'Land Tenure and Land Settlement: Policy and Patterns in the Canadian Prairies and the Argentine Pampas, 1880–1930', in D.C.M. Platt and G. Di Tella, (eds) *Argentina, Australia and Canada: Studies in Comparative Development, 1870–1965* (Oxford, 1985), p.57; Figure for 1924 from C.F. Jones, *South America* (London, 1931), pp. 378–9.
2 Richelet, J.E., 'The Argentine Trade', in R. Ramsay (ed), *The Frozen and Chilled Meat Trade: A Practical Treatise by Specialists in the Trade* (2 vols, London, 1929), vol. 1, pp. 230–31.
3 The Times, *The Times Book on Argentina* (London, 1927), pp. 231–2.
4 Brewster, J.A., 'The South American Trade', in F. Gerrard, (ed.), *The Book of the Meat Trade* (2 vols, London, 1949), vol. 1, p. 215.
5 Finch, M.H.J., *A Political Economy of Uruguay Since 1870* (London, 1981), pp. 9, 74.
6 Ibid., p. 78.
7 Ibid., pp. 79–80.
8 Domville-Fife, C., *The States of South America: The Land of Opportunity* (London, 1920), p. 222.
9 Brannon, R.H., *The Agricultural Development of Uruguay* (New York, 1967), p. 86.
10 Finch, *A Political Economy of Uruguay Since 1870*, p. 80.
11 Ramsay, R., 'The World's Frozen and Chilled Meat Trade', in R. Ramsay (ed.), *The Frozen and Chilled Meat Trade: A Practical Treatise by Specialists in the Trade* (2 vols, London, 1929), vol. 1, p. 16.
12 Finch, *A Political Economy of Uruguay Since 1870*, pp. 86–8.
13 Grattan, C.H., *The Southwest Pacific Since 1900* (Ann Arbor, 1963), p. 79.
14 McLintock, A.H. (ed.), *An Encyclopaedia of New Zealand* (Wellington, 1966), vol. 3, pp. 236–8.
15 Grattan, The Southwest Pacific Since 1900, pp. 242, 264–6.
16 Brooking, T., 'Economic Transformation', in W.H. Oliver, with B.R. Williams (eds), *The Oxford History of New Zealand* (Oxford, 1981), p. 228; G.R. Hawke, *The Making of New Zealand* (Cambridge, 1985), pp.142–3.
17 Philpott, B.P. and Stewart, J.D., 'Capital, Income and Output in New Zealand Agriculture 1922–1956', *Economic Record*, 34 (1958): 224, 226–7.
18 Davidson, B.R., *European Farming in Australia: An Economic History of Australian Farming* (Amsterdam, 1981), pp. 308–9, 318–20, 321–2.
19 Harrison, G., *Borthwicks: A Century in the Meat Trade, 1863–1963* (London, 1963), pp. 122–23.
20 Cmd 2390 (PP 1924–25, Vol. XIII), *First Report of the Royal Commission on Food Prices, Volume I*, pp. 117–18.
21 Pearse, A.W., *The World's Meat Future* (London, 1920), pp. 6–7, 14.
22 *Royal Commission on Food Prices, Volume II, Minutes of Evidence* (London: HMSO, 1925), p. 213; P. Knightley, *The Vestey Affair* (London, 1981), pp. 17, 21.
23 Knightley, *The Vestey Affair*, pp. 25–6.

24 Cmd 5839 (PP 1937–38, Vol. VIII), *Report of Joint Committee of Enquiry into the Anglo-Argentine Meat Trade*, p. 117.
25 Jefferys, J.B., *Retail Trading in Britain 1850–1950* (Cambridge, 1954), p. 187, 191, 193; *Royal Commission on Food Prices, Volume II, Minutes of Evidence* (London, 1925), pp. 213, 217, 220–21.
26 Cmd 2390 (PP 1924–25, Vol. XIII), *First Report of the Royal Commission on Food Prices, Volume I*, p. 107.
27 Cmd 2390 (PP 1924–25, Vol. XIII), *First Report of the Royal Commission on Food Prices, Volume I*, p. 150.
28 Jackson, A.J., *Official History of the National Association of Meat Traders* (Plymouth, 1956), p. 111.
29 Jefferys, *Retail Trading in Britain 1850–1950*, pp. 187, 191, 193. *Royal Commission on Food Prices, Volume II, Minutes of Evidence* (London, 1925), p. 201.
30 Ramsay, 'The World's Frozen and Chilled Meat Trade', p. 18.
31 Cmd 5839 (PP 1937–38, Vol. VIII), *Report of Joint Committee of Enquiry into the Anglo-Argentine Meat Trade*, p. 6.
32 Arnould, R.J., 'Changing Patterns of Concentration in American Meat Packing, 1880–1963', *Business History Review*, 45(1) (1971): 26–7.
33. Greenhill, R.G., 'Shipping and the Refrigerated Meat Trade from the River Plate 1900–1930', in K. Friedland (ed.), *Maritime Food Transport* (Köln: Böhlau Verlag, 1994), pp. 428–31.
34 Brewster, 'The South American Trade', pp. 218–19.

# Chapter 6

# Government and Business

This chapter considers how the industry experienced an increasing amount of official control over the first half of the twentieth century, including the various ways the attitudes of different governments towards the industry changed. These also involved shifts in enforcement mechanisms, in the form of new health and veterinary regulations, commercial marketing methods, the abandonment of free trade and introduction of tariff controls and quotas.

Both wars and the depressed economy in the years between them forced all governments to intervene in most aspects of the meat industry. This rule applied to farmers, processing and packing firms, as well as ocean shipping lines. Because the situations facing North American, South American, Australian and New Zealand farmers and processors differed only slightly, they responded by adopting broadly the same combination of measures. For example, all meat producers experienced a sharp reduction in prices following the First World War and both farmers and meat exporting companies were particularly badly affected by the fall in demand. In 1921 Argentine exporters were producing rather less than half of what they had in 1918.[1] The canned meat trade in all countries was particularly badly affected as the inflated wartime demand – much of it for military rations – disappeared once supplies of fresh meat were fully restored. Although there was a recovery by 1924, principally because the reduction of meat prices once depleted wartime stock levels had been restored helped stimulate demand, the severe economic fluctuations of the 1930s introduced such instability into all aspects of economic life that governments had to offer some assistance. Farmers were in a strong position to ask for help and sympathy, partly because of the effective lobby groups built up over the nineteenth and early twentieth centuries and also the way in which they had raised output in a time of national emergency. But the meat firms were in a rather weaker position and were not so well regarded: they were known to have made very heavy profits during the war, to which was attached the suspicion of wartime profiteering.

## The Trust Threat

In Chapters 4 and 5 above there has already been some reference to how much the growth of the large United States and British meat exporting companies, both before and after 1914, was a source of anxiety and comment among other nations. In the interwar years some meat-exporting countries tried to place restrictions on their further expansion, to protect livestock farmers and native-owned meat companies from unfair competition. As the trade in all agricultural products contracted after 1929 controls were reinforced, and at times used rather indiscriminately, as the calls for government help from farmers and domestic meat exporters became stronger.

Uruguay and Argentina had the longest experience of complaints and grievances against the predominantly foreign-owned meat companies, going back to pre-1914. Their unpopularity there was even greater and certainly more long-standing than in the Dominions where more serious complaints only started to emerge after 1918. In South America, there were fewer companies and as they were more powerful their domination of the trade was obvious. On numerous occasions protests were made about their activities, and although governments after 1918 took firmer action to control them, they do not appear to have been any more effective than in other countries. In Argentina laws passed in 1922 and 1933 tried to compel *frigorificos* to give farmers selling cattle to them better information about their pricing practices. There were also attempts by the state to set up non-profit making *frigorificos* to increase general competition and so force up cattle prices paid by the commercial packing firms. However, government control measures had little success. The meat processing companies were powerful and they acted as an oligopoly in normal times when market shares remained settled in the periods of agreement between any price wars. They always held large amounts of meat in their cold stores, which had been extended during the War, and it was a simple matter for them to put pressure on governments by ceasing to purchase cattle when they were under attack.

There is certainly evidence that they attempted to operate more or less independently of any attempts by governments, either to control them or enquire into their business methods. In 1933 the British and Argentine governments agreed to set up a joint committee to investigate the industry and in 1934 the Argentine Senate started their own enquiry. They wanted to find out the reasons for the great differences between the prices for cattle in the Argentine and the price of beef abroad. When state accountants were sent to examine the books of the large *frigorificos*, they were obstructed, particularly by the Vestey group, Armour, La Blanca and Wilson. When the Vesteys denied them any access to their accounts, telling them they had been sent abroad, the Senate regarded this as contempt and ordered the arrest of the firm's chief in Argentina, Richard Tootell. It subsequently turned out that the accounts were still in Argentina, on board a ship in disguised corn beef boxes, and waiting to be shipped either to London or the firm's Fray Bentos plant in Uruguay where even more of the firm's documents were found.[2] Episodes such as these further worsened the packers' relations with cattle farmers and the government.

In the Dominions there had been little criticism of the freezing firms before the First World War, but anxieties were starting to surface even then. In Australia the whole question of foreign firms was first examined seriously by the 1914 Royal Commission on its meat export trade.[3] The underlying reason was to investigate if there was any likelihood of the American trust firms becoming so powerful that they could do what they had done in South America before 1914 and control the prices they paid to the Australian livestock farmers, as well as seize a larger share of the export trade from the existing freezing companies. But as with all these investigations, there was some doubt about the extent of foreign firms' activities. The very nature of the enquiries made them reluctant to reveal too much about the way in which they conducted their businesses to a government that might place restrictions on them, or reveal their methods to commercial rivals. The trust firms had already been subject to lawsuits in the United States before 1914, and the British firms were also nervous about the way in which the Inland Revenue were making their overseas operations liable to tax. The Vestey brothers, in particular became obsessed about business secrecy after they set up a series of offshore trusts to reduce the United Kingdom tax liability, despite still being anxious to acquire honorific titles. One British firm who were prepared to comment more frankly on their overseas operations in these years was Borthwicks, although theirs was a much smaller business than the other two.[4]

The Royal Commission found that among the 47 companies exporting meat from Australia, American companies in the United Kingdom had been purchasing Australian meat, through distribution agencies, for some time. The Swift Beef Company of London, under the guise of the Australian Meat Exporting Company registered in Queensland, had works in that state and they were also exporters. The Morris Beef Company of London had a site on the Brisbane River in Queensland with a view to establishing a freezing works there. And Armour and Company of London was purchasing frozen and canned meat through the agency of the British registered firm, Birt and Company. But in addition to these American controlled firms, the English firms controlled by the Vestey brothers and Thomas Borthwick also controlled firms or had subsidiary branches in Australia, but the commissioners expressed no anxieties about them.[5] The reasons for this seem to have been that they had been present in building up Australian meat exports since the 1880s and 1890s and so were part of the institutional structure of the industry, whereas the American firms as new entrants had brought with them their unwelcome popular reputation for commercial ruthlessness, exposed by United States government enquiries.

In fact the 1914 investigation found that the influence of the American companies did not at that time amount to a threat either to the Australian livestock farmer or the other freezing works and exporters. Nevertheless, the fear was expressed that if they extended their operations they might bring increased efficiency to the trade and eliminate weaker competition, but they would ultimately suppress competition, with a consequent reduction in prices paid to the farmer and an increase to the consumer. At the time the Australian livestock producer viewed the increased activity of the American firms with approval, while the exporters were not so approving, as they feared the effects of competition from the well organised and wealthy American meat giants. The Australian government was concerned, partly for the farmer and for the existing meat exporters, but also because it was afraid American control would see a rise in domestic meat prices.[6]

It was only after the boom conditions and prosperity of the wartime years slipped into post-war depression that British owned meat firms were regarded in a similar way to the American ones. The experience of Borthwicks, as a London firm who concentrated in the colonial trade and had freezing works and livestock farms in both Australia and New Zealand, illustrates some of the changes in attitude that took place after 1918. The Borthwick family had developed the New Zealand and Australian parts of their business since the 1890s, largely free from control in the pre-1914 era, and did not find it easy to adjust to the controlled climate of the 1920s and 1930s. They in fact found conditions easier in Australia than in New Zealand, but in both countries the constant possibility of further restrictions being placed on foreign-owned firms made them nervous and, according to Harrison, reduced their overall investments in both countries.[7]

Some degree of control in New Zealand had already been present since the passing of the Slaughtering and Inspection Amendment Act of December 1918.[8] This legislation gave the Minister of Agriculture the power to refuse a license to any exporting or freezing works if he believed it was operating in a manner contrary to public interest. This measure made no immediate difference in wartime because all meat was still disposed of by the New Zealand Government acting for the Imperial Government. But in 1920, when prices started to fall the American firm of Armour were refused a meat exporting license, because it was feared they would use their power to force down New Zealand meat prices in London. Armours protested as they had meat deteriorating in freezing plants in New Zealand but the government refused to weaken, saying the meat could be exported to America but could not be used to upset the prices in the vital English market that absorbed over 90 per cent of the country's meat exports. But at the same time the New Zealand Farmers Union was also blaming Vesteys and Borthwicks for the recent slump in British prices.[9]

New Zealand's reaction to the price fall and slump after the war was the formation of the New Zealand Meat Producers' Export Board in 1922.[10] This was the first export control board, and was established to supervise the grading of meat for export and regulate shipments. It operated by granting export licences and prohibiting the export from New Zealand of any meat not controlled by the Board. It comprised eight members, two of them government representatives from the Ministry of Agriculture, and the other six were effectively farmers' representatives with five of them elected by farmers producing meat for export, and the other was a representative of stock and station agents. As there were no representatives from the freezing and exporting firms, in theory this gave farmers complete power to control exports.[11] Borthwicks found this development alarming, as they believed it would grow into an instrument of discrimination against foreign-owned companies. As a condition of their licenses the Board required freezing works to kill stock on request from any farmer, and hand it back to the farmer on request after charging the appropriate rate for the service. This measure took away from the meat companies their former ability to control the amount of stock being killed and also gave the farmers the ability to export the meat themselves if they thought they could obtain a higher price than the freezing plant offered.[12]

As things turned out the firm found life under the Export Board not so difficult as it had imagined. Although the Board was an export monopoly board, it made no attempt to restrict the numbers of animals exported in order to raise the prices the freezing companies paid the farmer for them. What it did do was to try and reduce the costs of distribution by putting pressure on the shipping companies. It may have had some success here as New Zealand refrigerated lamb and mutton rates fell faster than world tramp rates and New Zealand wool rates between 1922 and 1936. It used its influence to reduce slaughtering and freezing costs, but as it did not operate the plants itself there was a limited amount that it could do there. In addition, there were other factors driving down these costs like the introduction of chain killing and improvements in refrigeration technology. But its main work was in improving the quality of meat exported, rationalising and simplifying grading and marking, and enthusiastically advertising New Zealand meat in Britain. In addition, it arranged the allocation of quotas among the freezing companies that were imposed by the Ottawa Agreements in 1932.[13]

As in New Zealand, in Australia there was a similar lack of any regulation in 1914. There was nothing to prevent any person with the necessary capital and enterprise to set up and start exporting meat. The only thing that the government did was to satisfy itself that the meat was free from disease and fit for human consumption. Three American firms, through their branches in London had begun to purchase meat in Australia, sometimes setting up new companies and sometimes by entering into contracts with established ones. The American firm of Swift seems to have been behind a new freezing and exporting firm registered in Queensland, the Australian Meat Export Co. Ltd. Armour and Company bought frozen and canned beef through the agency of an established firm, Birt and Co., and was in further negotiations with other firms. The Morris Beef Co. looked poised to start operations there as well, as it had purchased a site on the Brisbane River in Queensland with a view to building a meat works there. However, there was no evidence of combined or concerted action by these companies in Australia, as there were more than 50 meat firms in total, including Vesteys and Borthwicks as well as Australian companies. Also as in New Zealand, there was no sign that they wanted to enter the local trade in the country, but were only interested in supplying their London and American beef operations.[14]

The Australian position regarding government intervention was somewhat different as its most important agricultural export commodities were wool and wheat. As meat provided a smaller proportion of farmers' incomes both federal and state governments paid less attention to control and support measures in the 1920s, and presumably to any threat from the multinational bogeyman. In response to the crisis facing the industry from the disastrous price fall of 1922, the Australian Meat Council was set up in that year but unlike the New Zealand Meat Board, it was just an advisory body. The compulsory pooling of meat in Australia was much more difficult because the country was much larger, it had a federal structure and a variety of producing conditions. Although there seems to have been some further consolidation of the American and British firms' position in the 1920s, there seems to be no suggestion that they were ever regarded as seriously as in New Zealand. Borthwicks found that they were 'quite wrong' to be anxious about any threat of discriminatory treatment in Australia. They already had one Queensland cattle fattening station and felt secure enough to buy another in 1924 and lease a third in 1932.[15] After the Ottawa Agreements, from 1935 onwards the Australian government added a powerful Export Monopoly Board to the Australian Meat Council, but Capie concludes that over the 1920s and 1930s little was achieved by either of these bodies.[16]

## International Trade

In the 1920s and 1930s increased state intervention and support was given to the meat industry in two stages. The first was in the crisis of the early 1920s to hit the industry on the collapse of the immediate post-war boom. Here the remedy was heavily centred on the provision of state assistance to farmers. By and large, these measures were national in character and had a limited effect on international trade. But with the depression of 1930–32 the whole question of international trade came under consideration in all countries. Importing countries wanted, as far as possible to protect domestic farm incomes from foreign competition, and exporting countries did as much as they could to stimulate exports and maintain farm incomes.

Throughout the 1920s, not just meat but all types of agricultural output had increased steadily. British imports of meat rapidly recovered their pre-war levels after 1918. Once more the pre-war trends reasserted themselves as total meat imports increased and those of chilled beef and veal rose particularly strongly at the expense of frozen beef. In 1909–13 imports of frozen and chilled beef together totalled 7.52 million cwt.; by 1932 they had risen to 13.23 million. The pressure of imports on the British market was also increased as other importing countries reduced their imports by embargoes, customs duties and other means in the 1920s.[17] France reintroduced its pre-war tariff in 1929 and raised tariffs again in 1928. In 1925 Germany regained the right (suspended by the Treaty of Versailles) to determine its own tariffs. In September of that year the government, representing the big landowners, also re-established the pre-war tariffs on grains and livestock.[18] As the world financial crisis deepened after the American stock market crash of October 1929 all European governments increased their tariff levels on both industrial and agricultural goods, and this further increased the farm imports, including meat and livestock, flooding into Britain.

The more the prices of meat and livestock fell under this pressure, the more strenuous were the efforts made by United Kingdom farmers to obtain protection for the home production of meat. The British market was of pivotal importance for the international meat industry. As the world's largest importer of many types of temperate farm produce, its attitude toward its own farmers and any measures it adopted for their protection would always have severe effects on the level of international demand. In the past governments had always refused farmers' demands for protection because it would mean an increase in the price of food. This argument had a particularly strong appeal at the time, as high unemployment in manufacturing was exerting a strong downward pressure on incomes in general, and the minority Labour government was very reluctant to do anything that would help push up the cost of living. At the Imperial Conference in London in October and November 1930 Britain rejected a Canadian proposal for a preferential tariff to help Dominion wheat. But in August 1931 the Labour Government was replaced by a National government, attitudes had changed in the face of overwhelming pressure and in February 1932 an Import Duties Act introduced a general 10 per cent tariff on all goods, except basic foodstuffs. Thus British agriculture, and livestock farmers, did not obtain any advantages from initial measures of protection.

The first changes to benefit them came about as an indirect result of a dispute between the British government and the Irish Free State's refusal to pay certain sums agreed in the 1922 treaty between the two countries. In order to partially recover this money, Britain imposed a 20 per cent *ad valorem* duty on imports of live animals and meat of any kind from the Irish Free State from 15 July 1932. In November this was raised to 40 per cent for live animals and 30 per cent for meat. As the dispute between the countries continued, the duties were revised in 1933 and restrictions were placed on the number of animals that could be imported. These arrangements were subject to further changes in subsequent years and were closely connected with the general regulation of imports of livestock that arose out of the Ottawa Conference.[19]

The prime reason for the Ottawa Imperial Conference, called in July and August 1932, was to settle the whole question of Commonwealth foodstuffs, among them meat. Although Britain was the main market for Australian and New Zealand meat, they were only the major suppliers of mutton and lamb as Britain obtained most of its beef from Argentina. The British delegation arrived in Ottawa with no clear idea of what arrangements to make about meat. The whole atmosphere of this meeting of former wartime allies, each determined to protect their own industry and agriculture, was charged with suspicion and less than friendly. At one point a member of the British delegation, J.H. Thomas, believed his transatlantic telephone conversations with Ramsey Macdonald were being tapped.[20]

Lamb and mutton prices in Britain were unsatisfactorily low for British farmers and the only way that they could be raised was to restrict the entry of Dominion sheep meat into Britain, something that would be unsatisfactory for both Australia and New Zealand. What they, especially New Zealand, who was the major supplier, wanted was some element of imperial preference and quotas for British lamb and mutton imports from foreign countries. They also made similar demands for the treatment of foreign beef. Although mutton and lamb was their main export earner, both countries also exported some low quality frozen beef and they wanted similar help for this meat, particularly Australia. They felt their industries had been hurt by Argentine chilled beef whose price had fallen so low it was now competing with their frozen beef, a product which could never hope to compete in quality with South American chilled beef, but had formerly found a sale with institutions and the poor, for whom cost was an important consideration. Indeed, by the 1930s the retail trade in frozen beef had already practically disappeared and almost all was sold to institutions and public bodies.[21]   The Australian delegation believed this could only be stopped if Britain restricted the entry of Argentine and Uruguayan chilled beef.[22]   But there was never any hope that Australia and New Zealand would ever be able to produce enough beef to replace what Britain drew from the River Plate.

In the compromises eventually arrived at neither side could be entirely satisfied. The British objective was to secure development of home production and allow the Commonwealth an increased share of British meat imports. However, it did not want Commonwealth imports to rise to such a level that they replaced home produced meat. For mutton, lamb and beef, Britain adopted a system of tariffs and quotas for foreign meat, which principally meant River Plate beef, but Dominion meat was left free of tariffs and was allowed more generous quotas. The Ottawa agreements officially ended on 30 June 1934, and after this the United Kingdom was not precluded from imposing further quantitative restrictions (quotas) on imports of Dominion meat. However, as far as tariffs were concerned Britain could not impose these until August 1937 without the agreement of the government concerned. Thus the broad arrangements remained the same for the rest of the decade, though there were periodic meetings and discussions that tinkered with the quotas allowed based on Britain's imports in the twelve months ending 30 June 1932, which became known as 'the basic Ottawa year'.[23]

The introduction of quotas for Commonwealth beef lamb and mutton was justified on the grounds that all sides believed prices of frozen meat had fallen so low they had caused grave depression in the livestock industries of the United Kingdom and the Dominions. If the depression continued, they feared it would bring about a serious decline in production and this would ultimately harm the consumer. They argued it was essential to take whatever steps appeared feasible to raise the wholesale prices of frozen meat in the United Kingdom market to such a level as would maintain efficient production. But in fixing quotas the first priority would be the protection of the British livestock industry, and only secondly to give the Dominions an expanding part of the British market.[24]   Australia was particularly concerned to protect its exports of chilled beef to the United Kingdom, which started in 1932. Although of poorer quality and more expensive to transport, this product was directly targeted to compete with South American chilled beef. New Zealand on the other hand, although it did export some chilled beef could never produce as much beef as Australia, but its main concern as the major supplier of frozen mutton and lamb was River Plate mutton and lamb. Therefore, when Commonwealth quotas were introduced they were applied only to *frozen* beef.[25]

**Table 6.1 Maximum quantities of South American meat allowed into the United Kingdom from 30 January 1933 to 30 June 1934, as a percentage of quantities imported in the corresponding quarters of the twelve months ending 30 June 1932**

| Meat | 1933 | | | | 1934 | |
|---|---|---|---|---|---|---|
| | Jan. – March | April – June | July – Sept. | Oct. – Dec. | Jan. – March | April – June |
| Chilled beef | 100 | 100 | 100 | 100 | 100 | 100 |
| Frozen beef | 90 | 85 | 80 | 75 | 70 | 65 |
| Frozen mutton and lamb | 90 | 85 | 80 | 75 | 70 | 65 |

*Source:* Cmd 4174 (PP 1931–32, Vol. X), *Imperial Economic Conference at Ottawa, 1932. Summary of Proceedings and copies of Trade Agreements*, p. 55.

The meat quotas agreed at Ottawa for Argentina and Uruguay are shown in Table 6.1 above, and although the volume of chilled beef was to be maintained at the level imported in the basic Ottawa year, serious restrictions were placed on the volumes of frozen beef and frozen lamb and mutton. But even the quantities of chilled beef actually admitted into the United Kingdom were subject to some further revision, as after the Ottawa meeting it was also necessary for the United Kingdom to meet with South American governments and meat shippers to discuss tariffs and proportions of the British market they would be allowed to supply with meat — mostly beef. The discussions that finally settled this matter were held in London and conducted, on behalf of Uruguay as well, by an Argentine delegation led by Vice-President Julio A. Roca and a British team led by Walter Runciman, President of the Board of Trade.

Roca's first priority was to maintain, as far as possible, the position of chilled beef and secondly, to ensure that restrictions in excess of those specified at Ottawa were not applied. He also wanted to reduce the control the foreign meat firms held over the Argentine trade. On their side the British had a number of priorities, some of them being matters more directly related to manufacturing and finance than farming or meat, something that is not always made completely clear in all accounts that mention these negotiations.[26] There was an urgent need to unblock balances amounting to around £11 million for British manufactured exports and dividend payments due to British investors in Argentina, which were blocked by stringent exchange controls. It also wanted to preserve the market for British manufactures, which would certainly be harmed if Argentina's severe balance of payments problems forced the country to default on its large foreign debt, much of which was held in London.[27] It also needed to protect and help, as far as possible, the position of the British farmer within the constraints of the Ottawa agreements. It is hard to say in exactly what order the British priorities were placed, but it seems highly likely that any further disruption of the international financial system that would occur from an Argentine default would have been regarded as more serious than the difficulties currently facing British livestock farmers.[28]

In May 1933 the Trade Agreement with the Argentine Republic, also known as the Roca-Runciman Treaty, was concluded. In this it was agreed, except so far as necessary to maintain the price of home-killed beef in Britain, not to restrict imports of chilled beef from Argentina below the levels of the basic Ottawa year. However, although the chilled beef quota was maintained at the Ottawa base year volume, Britain reserved the right to reduce this quota by a further 10 per cent according to article 1, clause 2 of the treaty, but this was subject to various restrictions. If it were done the amounts of River Plate beef so excluded could not be effectively replaced by chilled beef from other sources, except in the case of the Dominions by experimental shipments only. And if there were any reductions of more than 10 per cent, it would be applied proportionately to all other meat-supplying countries, including the Dominions.[29]  But frozen meat restrictions would not be any more than those specified in the Ottawa agreements. [30]  In the event British cattle prices failed to improve sufficiently, and so the 10 per cent reduction of the chilled beef quota agreed at Ottawa was applied. The resulting fall in British imports of Argentine chilled beef that this brought about can be seen in the first column of Table 6.1 above.

In the protocol of the treaty, the British government also agreed to permit 15 per cent of the quota to be allotted to domestic non-profit meat packing houses. But two existing Argentine meat packing plants (the *Frigorifico Gualeguaychu* and the Buenos Aires Municipal Frigorifico) were already incorporated in this quota.[31] This meant that only 11 per cent of the quota remained to be allotted to any new non-profit making plants that the Argentine government chose to establish in order to help maintain domestic cattle prices. In a separate agreement concluded in October 1933 the British government granted Argentina what was known as the Roca Funding Loan of £10 million at 4 per cent. The money granted allowed the Argentine government to stabilise national finances, reduce interest rates and halt the slide in exchange rates.[32]

From the whole South American point of view, 1931–32 was not a good year on which to base quotas. Meat production in both Argentina and Uruguay had declined since the late 1920s. The highpoint of the 1920s was in 1924 when 840,000 tons of chilled and frozen beef were exported, but this had declined to 465,000 tons by 1932. At the same time the region's dependence on the British market had increased, as in 1924 it absorbed 66 per cent of River Plate beef exports but 85 per cent in 1932.[33]  Livestock had been lost to drought, and low prices caused by the increasing world meat surplus had encouraged some ranchers to switch to corn growing. Argentine meat exports had already declined 25 per cent between 1929 and 1932 and Uruguay's exports of chilled beef declined 40 per cent between 1929 and 1932.[34]  But both Australia and New Zealand's meat output and exports had risen since the late 1920s. Subsequent restrictions of exports to Britain therefore held back any recovery of Argentina and Uruguay's beef production up to 1939.

The effects on the industry were indeed severe; for the first time since the introduction of refrigeration in the 1880s market access had become the River Plate meat industry's major problem. The quota, by limiting supplies, artificially raised the price of beef in Britain, to the benefit of the British farmer. But it also drastically lowered the price of cattle in South America. In March 1933 complaints were made in the British House of Commons that within three weeks of the introduction of the meat restrictions of November 1932 the price of cattle in the Argentine fell by 25 per cent, while meat prices at London's Smithfield, the main wholesale market for the south of England, increased by 25 to 60 per cent. In addition, increased profits to meat importers (according to Lord Beaverbrook) were supposed to be running at £800,000 a year.[35] During the war its proximity to the United Kingdom had given it a relative advantage over the Dominion industry, but this was greatly reduced by the imposition of tariffs and quotas, and after Ottawa all River Plate meat exports to Britain were controlled at levels determined by the British government. Table 6.2 below shows just how much, in the absence of any other comparable outlets, all of Argentina's meat exports to the United Kingdom fell – particularly those of frozen beef.

**Table 6.2  Metric tons of beef, mutton and lamb exported from Argentina, and the percentages exported to the United Kingdom, 1925–36**

| Period | Chilled beef | | Frozen beef | | Mutton and lamb | |
|---|---|---|---|---|---|---|
| | Total exports | % exported to the UK | Total exports | % exported to the UK | Total exports | % exported to the UK |
| Average 1925–29 | 402,182 | 99.1 | 201,238 | 41.4 | 80,081 | 92.1 |
| Year | | | | | | |
| 1930 | 345,525 | 99.7 | 98,748 | 51.2 | 80,601 | 89.2 |
| 1931 | 352,227 | 99.7 | 83,681 | 64.1 | 83,510 | 91.1 |
| 1932 | 370,634 | 99.9 | 36,660 | 61.1 | 70,985 | 94.6 |
| 1933 | 350,046 | 100.0 | 31,549 | 45.5 | 62.649 | 91.4 |
| 1934 | 349,644 | 99.9 | 31,584 | 26.4 | 48,658 | 87.6 |
| 1935 | 348,531 | 99.9 | 30,651 | 30.4 | 49,881 | 92.4 |
| 1936 | 357,473 | 99.9 | 39,651 | 21.9 | 50,035 | 92.8 |

*Source:* Cmd 5839 (PP 1937–38, Vol. VIII), *Report of Joint Committee of Enquiry into the Anglo-Argentine Meat Trade*, p. 10.

The arrangement under the Roca-Runciman Treaty to permit the Dominions to send unrestricted 'experimental' shipments of chilled beef to Britain proved something of a Trojan horse, as it allowed chilled beef from the Dominions to grow at the expense of Argentina's. It seems that the solution of the technical problems gave Australia, but also New Zealand, South Africa and Southern Rhodesia the ability to supply the British market with chilled beef. In 1932 only 0.1 per cent of Britain's chilled beef came from Dominion sources, but by 1939 this had risen to 12.4 per cent. But although the rate of growth was fast, it was still only a small amount in comparison with South American chilled beef. It is also doubtful if much of the Dominion chilled could compete in quality with Argentine beef. Ottawa, and its quotas was also a great benefit for the Dominion lamb and mutton trade. They were already Britain's prime suppliers of sheep meat but the South American share of mutton and lamb imports also suffered further from Dominion substitution. In 1929 Argentina supplied 27.3 per cent of Britain's imports of mutton and lamb, while New Zealand and Australia supplied 59.4 per cent. By 1937 the Argentine share had more than halved to 13.1 per cent and Australia's and New Zealand's had risen to 80.5 per cent.[36]

All the revisions of the Ottawa arrangements that took place from 1933 to 1939 benefited the Dominions. Faced by falling prices and meat import embargoes elsewhere, Dominion producers were constantly trying to secure a larger share of the British market. The Australians in particular always believed they had a divine right to foist onto the British consumer their mostly frozen low-grade beef and lamb, in preference to the distinctly higher quality Argentine chilled versions of these meats. New Zealand may have produced higher quality lamb and mutton but it still faced competition from the Argentine versions of these meats. But while granting Australia and New Zealand preferential terms, Britain wished to provide some measure of protection for its own farmers, although this plainly could not be the entire monopoly of the home market granted to French and German farmers by their governments.

The situation became serious on 13 February 1935 when the British government cabled its long-term meat policy proposal to the Dominions and Argentine governments. Because of the low prices still facing its livestock industry it proposed that a levy be collected on all meat imports (with preferential rates for the Dominions) and the proceeds be applied to supporting the home industry, leaving overseas producers free to regulate their exports to Britain themselves. Both Dominions were strongly opposed to the plan, arguing that the levy would destroy the mutually beneficial solution arrived at by the Ottawa agreements. New Zealand argued that as the low prices were essentially a beef problem it was an unfair solution for her as predominantly a producer of mutton and lamb.[37] The whole matter was discussed with the Dominions, including South Africa and Canada, at a Meat Conference in London that year, and Argentina was also consulted about proposals. Australia pressed for unregulated entry to the British market with the levy but New Zealand felt a levy would totally nullify the concessions won at Ottawa. The process of discussion dragged on, with many adjournments and modified drafts of proposals, into July 1936 before a long-term meat policy could finally be devised. At the final outcome the situation worsened for the Argentine when, after 1937, an import duty of 0.75d per lb was levied on Argentine chilled beef, but all Dominions beef was to remain untaxed.[38]

The net effect of the combination of quotas and Commonwealth preferences and later tariffs on Argentine beef was certainly to raise the price and restrict the choice of meat for the British consumer. This seems an extraordinary thing to do in a decade of high unemployment and uncertainty for many of those working in important sectors of manufacturing industry affected most by the general downturn in demand. It seems likely that tariffs on all meat, but without quotas, would not have raised their price to the British consumer, as the meat companies would have shifted the cost of the tariff onto the producer, in the form of lower prices paid to the Dominion and Argentine farmer. In any struggle for the British market that followed it is likely the Argentine beef and mutton and lamb would have increased their market share at the expense of the Dominion products as they had the advantages of lower transport costs and, certainly in the case of beef, far better quality. However, by guaranteeing as far as possible a reasonable level of the home market to Commonwealth farmers the British government hoped to prevent them from seriously discriminating against British imports of manufactures. But it was also anxious not to alienate or destabilise Argentina, as it was also a profitable market for British goods. It was also sensitive to the threats from both sets of governments that if Britain pushed the earnings from their primary products any lower, it would worsen their balance of payments, and threaten their ability to maintain international payments.

## Assistance for Farmers

Besides the use of tariffs and quotas, governments in all countries, whether exporters or importers, eventually found it necessary to undertake at least some measures and set up schemes to provide direct assistance to their livestock farmers. The 1920s and 1930s did see something of a shift in emphasis in various governments' thinking about the meat industry. Up to then talk of combinations had been directed at meat packers, shipping lines, and exporters, but measures to control them had placed little emphasis on positive counter-measures to help farmers. But the 1930s saw the farmer being listened to more closely and allowed a greater say about any steps taken to regulate the industry. This section will look at the stronger action adopted, from both governments' and farmers' points of view, to see what success it had.

The first example of this type of help, already referred to above, was the New Zealand Meat Producer's Export Board, established in 1922 in response to the sharp fall in meat prices. The call from farmers for this type of assistance, that is a body set up specifically to safeguard their interests against the packers, became increasingly strong in the 1920s and more so after 1930. This is because whenever meat, or almost any other farm product price falls, it is very easy for the processing and exporting companies to pass most, or even all, of the price reduction back to the farmer. Farmers found themselves in a very weak bargaining position, as they were price takers. That is, there were many of them, and even the largest concerns produced only a small amount of a packer's total throughput of animals, and they did so in competition with each other. When livestock prices fell their natural reaction was to try and send more animals for slaughter in order to maximise their incomes. As the meat firms were large concerns, small in number and able to act in concert to protect their interests, they reduced the prices they paid farmers whenever there was a surplus of animals for slaughter. But as they could always control numbers of animals being processed there was less need for them to reduce the price for which they sold their meat. There is little doubt that once again, as in the war, at times when farmers faced difficulties the meat processors were making large profits.

The ability of farmers to persuade their governments to take any action depended very much on their political and economic importance. In Britain they were small in number and agriculture was only a minor part of the economy, although livestock was the most important part of agriculture. As a result much less was done on their behalf than for South American and Dominion farmers, where agriculture was more important and where, for historical reasons, they still retained more political muscle. But even in these countries, the position of the farmer was under at least some challenge from the meat packers. The meat companies were often foreign owned and could appeal to their own governments, which were either Britain or America, when facing pressure from overseas governments. In addition, although there were Dominion and South American owned meat companies they were often smaller in size and less powerful than the foreign owned ones and they always had a poorer marketing network in Britain.

It has already been noted above that New Zealand was the first to place direct pressure on foreign owned meatpacking firms in response to farmers' requests. In Australia there was less anxiety about regulating foreign firms, possibly because they had a smaller presence there. About 1925 there were 54 separate freezing works, a larger number than New Zealand where there were only 39 and South America which had 25.[39] Their capacity was lower and they often operated on a seasonal basis. For instance, the majority of Queensland works concentrated on cattle and completed their killing in five to six months, although a few around Brisbane did work on a year round basis. In the southern states the emphasis was on sheep and there the majority of the lambs for export were killed between September and November.[40]

The Australian Board was not set up in response to the fall in meat prices after 1920, but only after the Ottawa Conference in 1932 forced Dominion governments into regulating output and allocating production quotas. In Australia the record of joint farmer and government direction of its pastoral industry was less impressive than New Zealand. The Australian Meat Council established in 1922 was less powerful than its New Zealand equivalent. It is difficult to say exactly why this was so, but the different circumstances of the two countries and their livestock industries offer a number of reasons.

In New Zealand pastoral farming and pastoral industry had a greater relative importance, and meat was a far larger export earner than in Australia. This meant the pastoral lobby wielded a greater political influence in New Zealand. The Zealand Meat Board had to regulate a single product – mutton and lamb – and it was one for which the country produced no substitute at similar prices. Because it had only one commodity with a single group of producers to satisfy, it was easier for it to obtain support and cooperation from the whole industry. But Australia was producing both cattle and sheep by the 1920s, and not only were each set of producers complaining, their meats were also substitutes for each other. Australian beef producers argued that it was they who needed most assistance, because beef prices had fallen more than those of lamb and mutton.[41] The shorter distances involved made it easier for the New Zealand Board to allocate production quotas after Ottawa, as it was possible to estimate the likely output from various regions. But droughts in Australia made it difficult to predict and agree on how to allocate regional shares of output from year to year. In addition, the rivalries inherent in Australia's federal structure probably encouraged jealous state governments to defend their own interests, and made it difficult for the Meat Council to persuade them to cooperate in any closer measures of control.

Nevertheless, an Australian Meat Board was finally set up in 1935 under the Meat Export Control Act of that year, to supervise the issue of export licences and regulate shipments of meat. Unlike the New Zealand board, which was composed of eight farmers' representatives and two government officials, the Australian Board comprised representatives of farmers, processors, exporters and the Australian government. It was empowered to purchase or sell any meat, meat products or edible offal and to manage and control the handling, storage and treatment of any meat purchased by the Australian government. It could also slaughter and treat stock and submit for inspection on the owner's behalf.[42] Unlike the 1922 Meat Council it had powers of compulsion, but for the reasons already given for the Council, it never exerted a great deal of control over the industry before the Second War.

For New Zealand, meat was a more important export commodity than for Australia, and so its government was more responsive to the complaints from its farmers, and prepared to grant them greater assistance. In 1926–30, mutton, and lamb accounted for 17.3 per cent of the total value of New Zealand's commodity exports, but only 1.5 per cent of Australia and Argentina's. Beef did not figure as an important export commodity in either New Zealand or Australia where its value was only 1.5 per cent and 1.8 per cent of exports, respectively. But mutton and lamb was even more important for New Zealand than beef was for Argentina, where beef exports only accounted for 10.8 per cent of that country's exports in 1926–30.[43] Against this background it is not so hard to see why the New Zealand government made its Meat Producers' Export Board potentially so powerful when it was established in 1922. It saw the whole industry as an important export earner and its sheep farmers as a valuable part of the economy and was anxious to do as much as possible to protect them from the meat firms. The original idea behind the board was to let sheep farmers provide their own assistance through the collective management and regulation of the industry, including marketing. It hoped by denying the meat freezing and exporting firms any of the seats on the board that this would remove the feelings of exploitation on the part of the farmers, following the price fall after the collapse of the immediate post-war boom.

The view in Britain was that the board had been set up under the misapprehension that the freezing and exporting firms were largely to blame for the low prices facing the New Zealand sheep farmer.[44] During the price collapse in 1921 the meat firms already had enormous quantities of meat lying in store and aboard ship en route to Europe, and traders in Britain were not inclined to buy forward. Whether or not their information was entirely correct, they had no way of knowing the precise situation regarding quantities of meat in cold stores. They also had no way of knowing exactly how much meat was already aboard ship and how future arrivals might be affected by factors like the weather. Hence there was a great deal of caution in the trade in the last half of 1921. In addition, the merchant always had more control over the situation than the producer and could always delay any purchases until the very last moment.

As a result the New Zealand farmer found that his beef was being sold in Britain below cost, and he was only making a very small return on his best lamb. In December 1921 and early January 1922 the first bids for forward delivery were very low, even for first grade North Island lambs. But then in January 1922 the situation began to ease and prices for New Zealand meat started to rise. Those dealers who had bought during December were able to re-sell in January making a good profit, whereas many farmers who had produced the meat made a loss in supplying their dealers. With their produce sold at a loss, it was difficult to convince the farmers, at a great distance from the final market, that they had received a fair price for their meat. The lesson that the New Zealand farmers drew from these events was that if they wanted a better deal, they needed to strengthen their position as sellers in the market.

The constitution of the Meat Export (Control) Board gave it full powers to regulate exports and shipments, including the right to take over the whole meat-marketing organisation for New Zealand meat in any importing country. Its expenses were met by a levy of 1d. a carcase on mutton and lamb and 1d. a quarter on any beef exported. But as the Board was being established, prices in Britain improved and as they were satisfactory for the New Zealand producer, there was no reason for the Board to start to exercise its wider powers and take control of the marketing of New Zealand's meat in Britain. In the 1920s it confined its attention to other matters. It appointed expert graders and rationalised the whole grading system by reducing the number of grades and marks under which meat was shipped. By making contracts with the shipping companies on behalf of meat producers as a whole it obtained reductions in shipping freights, as well as a reduction in marine insurance rates and railway rates in New Zealand. It also had an office in London and appointed a representative to safeguard the British interests of New Zealand producers, as well as providing daily information about trends in the British market. It took charge of publicity and interested itself closely in proper advertising. The Board thought it important to monitor the state of other markets as well, even to the extent of having a representative in Argentina. It provided the market with as much information about its product as possible, with regular publication of meat shipments and quantities held in Dominion cold stores.

In many respects the Board was an active player in the whole marketing process. Probably the feature that raised most comment and criticism was its attempts to give farmers better prices by regulating and controlling shipments. In the 1920s the normal Australian mutton and lamb season lasted up to around March and in New Zealand it finished about June or July. This meant that if Dominion mutton and lamb were shipped as they were killed and frozen all supplies would arrive in the first eight months of the year and there would be none for the last four months. This had never happened as the cold stores were also filled during the first eight months and gradually emptied in the last part of the year before the next season began. But the existence of some weak sellers on the market, with an urgent need for ready cash, meant that sometimes day-to-day deliveries could be more than were necessary to meet current demand. When this happened the effect on the market could be disastrous. Several weak sellers rushing forward supplies in the early part of the year would drive down spot prices and also reduce forward prices. After 1922, the Board's intervention to regulate supplies was an effective way of stopping unnecessarily large shipments and gluts in the early part of the year; it also prevented excessively high prices after August when supplies were scarce. Overall the producer was not compensated by these high prices as they were spread over only a small part of his total output and obtained at the cost of a low price for all the rest. As the Board had no control over output it could never regulate it to raise overall prices, but its operations did help to iron out any damaging short-term fluctuations and reduce the amount of speculation.

It might be argued that because there was never any really serious crisis in the industry after 1922 the effectiveness of the Board was never really tested in the 1920s. The reforms it did undertake certainly helped farmers, but they were relatively minor matters. One thing that had increased freight costs and journey time to London was that New Zealand had a large number of small ports, close to widely scattered freezing works, at which meat was loaded. The Board cut both by reducing the ports of call where refrigerated shipping took on small parcels of meat, as well as getting the New Zealand railways to improve terms and conditions for moving it to the ports still used, and where it was combined with others into larger quantities. But as there was never any serious slump in prices, it never needed to have recourse to its major power of taking over the sale of New Zealand meat in world markets. To do so would have been a daunting prospect. It had no wholesale or retail distribution networks, and although it did have some knowledge of regional differences in demand and marketing conditions in Britain, this type of information had always been publicly available in the trade press and elsewhere.[45]

In the serious price fall after 1930 the limitations of the Board soon became apparent. Its ability to take over the distribution of New Zealand meat in Britain was largely irrelevant in the face of powerful quantitative controls on consumption such as quotas, and further price discouragements like tariffs. In the face of threats from privately owned meat processing and trading firms, it had been comparatively easy to implement national measures of control and regulation. But the restrictions on New Zealand meat imports imposed by foreign governments involved complex and difficult international negotiations where the outcome was uncertain and not always what the New Zealand farmer wanted.

Although in the 1920s meat was slightly less important as an export earner in Argentina, the agricultural lobby still had a great deal of political power and the meat producers, as extensive landholders, held a larger share than the wheat farmers, who were predominantly their tenants. As Solberg explains:[46]

> The few thousand large landowners who owned most of the pampas had enormous political power. Well organized in the elite cattlemen's association, the Sociedad Rural, the landowners were a powerful voice in both the Radical and the Conservative Party. Strongly opposed to any plan to redistribute pampa rural property or to alter the main features of the tenant farming system, the ranching elite subordinated agricultural development to cattle raising. Deprived of the vote by restrictive citizenship laws and, in many cases, not intending to remain permanently in Argentina, the pampa [wheat] farming population was totally unable to mount a political challenge against the landed elite.

But although they were in a powerful position with their own government, their ability to influence it to safeguard their interests regarding the meat exporters in the 1920s and the British import restrictions in the 1930s was less strong than one might expect. Their immediate adversary was the meat packing firms, but unlike New Zealand and Australia, there were only a few of them and they were all very large and powerful. And although they had long competed with each other, sometimes fiercely, at times when they felt threatened by the *estancieros* or government they had always been able to co-operate and protect their common interests. But sometimes it was even not necessary for them to do that, as market factors could come to their rescue.

The first cattle producers' agitation came after the First World War during the 1922–23 crisis caused by the decline of cattle prices. During this, grievances over monopoly grading and other unfair practices by the packers surfaced. The dissatisfaction of the cattlemen produced talks of a strike in which they would withhold their cattle from the packers, and threats from Congress of the expropriation of the foreign owned meat firms, and the establishment of government-sponsored factories. In the early 1920s sales of animals were generally made by the farmers arranging for the packer's representatives, called revisers, to visit farms and decide on the quality of the animals and how many cattle they wanted and fix a price with the seller. Relatively few sales were at markets, as prices there were usually lower. If a rancher did not like what the reviser offered he could always try another packing firm but there was little point as they all offered more or less the same range of prices.

This system lasted, more or less without any official intervention, until 1924 when an attempt was made to improve the selling arrangements for the farmer by Law No. 11,228. This stated that *every* cattle sale had to be on a live-weight basis and that *frigorificos* and cattle markets had to be furnished with the necessary scales. Prices were to be determined on the basis of live-weight according to the grading of meat after slaughter.[47] The expectation was that both would improve the position of the cattle farmer, who would be furnished with more information when making a sale. But Law No. 11,228 also included a number of provisions intended to reduce the power of the meat companies, such as setting minimum cattle prices, and a plan to set up state-owned national factories. The *friorificos* retaliated by suspending cattle buying. Faced with the enormous expense of financing the cattle owners itself, as well as setting up its own packing plants and no doubt replicating their European and United Kingdom distribution networks, the Congress was forced to shelve this legislation.[48] It had to accept, even if the ranchers would not, that government had no real answer to the low prices, which were not the fault of the meat firms but the result of world oversupply of beef. As in New Zealand, the pressure and urgency for reform was removed by the revival in prices of the late 1920s and bargaining strength was still left with the packers.

The next ranchers' struggle came in the depression of the 1930s, when once again they blamed their problems on the packers, and ignored the effects of the British government's import restrictions after 1932. The drastic fall in cattle prices severely reduced, even if it did not obliterate, most feeders' profits, while the *frigorificos* largely maintained theirs. Once again the Argentine Rural Society lobbied the government for help and this resulted in the passing of Law 11,747 in 1933. Once again the existing companies resorted to their old technique of closing their plants in protest, again delaying but this time not stopping any of its operation. Law 11,747 became known as the meat law (*ley des carnes*). It unsuccessfully attempted to strengthen the cattle sales provisions of the 1924 law, but introduced other measures as well. For cattle sales the new law provided, among other things, the establishment of official standards for the grading and classification of cattle and meat. Prices were to be determined on the basis of live-weight according to the grading of meat after slaughter.[49] But it did not work because the packers failed, or refused, to agree a uniform system of grades. The expectation was that both laws would improve the position of the cattle farmer, who would be furnished with more information when making a sale, but in the end neither made much difference.

In addition, the 1933 law set up a National Meat Board to regulate the market to safeguard producers from the low margins imposed by the packers, and a state run cooperative packing works, the *Corporacion Argentina de Productores de Carnes* (*CAP*) to compete with the privately owned firms. It also established the National *frigorifico* for Buenos Aires, and only it was allowed to supply the city with meat. This last organisation was based on the Uruguayan *Frigorifico*

*Nacional*, in operation since 1929 with the monopoly of supplying meat to Montevideo. Once again the foreign owned firms tried to sabotage the plan by closing their own plants, but although they succeeded for a while, the whole scheme was finally brought into operation, financed by a compulsory 1.5 per cent levy on cattle producers' sales, of which 80 per cent went to setting up the *CAP* and 20 per cent to the National Meat Board. The meat companies complained that the non profit-making cooperative packing plants given a 15 per cent share of the UK quota under the Roca-Runciman Agreement, would reduce their throughput, and with it the efficiency of their processing and distribution arrangements. In fact the *CAP* did not operate until 1936, so in the meantime the portion of the quota reserved for it was shared among the foreign firms.[50]

**Table 6.3  Trading results of a number of cattle companies and *frigorificos*, 1929–36**

| Year | Limited liability cattle breeding, raising and feeding companies | | | Frigorificos | | |
|------|------------------|----------------|-------------------|------------------|----------------|-------------------|
|      | No. of companies | Capital 000$   | Profits per cent  | No. of companies | Capital 000$   | Profits per cent  |
| 1929 | 38 | 193.56 | 8.49 | 9  | 166.94 | 10.96 |
| 1930 | 38 | 176.70 | 4.91 | 9  | 166.94 | 13.22 |
| 1931 | 41 | 209.46 | 2.29 | 10 | 167.96 | 12.97 |
| 1932 | 34 | 191.08 | 0.65 | 10 | 171.86 | 11.86 |
| 1933 | 33 | 188.54 | 1.15 | 10 | 171.88 | 11.83 |
| 1934 | 32 | 184.69 | 1.91 | 10 | 165.28 | 14.73 |
| 1935 | 32 | 190.34 | 3.15 | 10 | 165.13 | 5.78  |
| 1936 | 32 | 188.77 | 3.61 | 10 | 165.02 | 7.58  |

*Source:* Cmd 5839 (PP 1937–38, Vol. VIII), *Report of Joint Committee of Enquiry into the Anglo-Argentine Meat Trade*, pp. 136, 137.

In paragraph 2 of the Protocol to the Roca-Runciman agreement, and reiterated in the Anglo-Argentine Agreement of 1936, the two governments agreed to set up a Joint Committee of Enquiry into the Anglo-Argentine Meat Trade. It was to thoroughly investigate the meat trade with particular reference to the means to be adopted to ensure a reasonable return to the cattle producers. By the time it finally reported in 1937, it was against a history of earlier unsuccessful measures already taken by the Argentine government. According to the figures collected by the Joint Committee of Enquiry, reproduced in Table 6.3 above, the published financial results of over thirty limited liability cattle breeding and fattening companies showed a continuous decline in profits from 8.49 per cent in 1929 to 0.65 per cent in 1932. At the same time figures collected with some difficulty from the packers showed their profits rose in 1930 and were still higher than their 1929 level in 1932. The packers' high point came in 1934 with an average profit of

14.73 per cent, while the *estancieros'* profits even in 1936 were lower than those of the meat packing firms. At the same time there was a writing-down of the cattle companies' capital, while the capital of the meat companies was largely maintained.

Anselmo M. Viacava, who reported these results to the rest of the Joint Committee, found that cattle producers strongly believed the meat companies had taken advantage of the conditions created by the world economic crisis, to make profits at their expense.[51]

> In brief, the cattle industry has been for several years a poorly paying business. ... this is largely due to the world economic crisis which started in 1929; however, careful observation and analysis of different facts connected with the industry have brought about the conviction that it is principally due to an understanding between the Frigorificos covering the purchase of cattle in Argentina and the distribution and sale of meat in the foreign market.

But whatever they may have thought, the farmers were really in no position to alter their position as price takers. There were many of them, and as can be seen from Table 6.3 above, and if we take the publicly owned cattle companies as being representative of the larger producers, their average capital resources did not nearly match those of the average *frigorifico*.

It is here that the real strength of the *frigorificos* resided. Although the meat companies always vehemently protested each time the *Sociedad Rural* pressured the government to pass a law in the interests of the cattlemen, and challenged the legislation in the Supreme Court, they lost each time. They argued that Law 11,226, allowing the governmental inspection of packinghouse books and accounts, violated guarantees to private industry contained in the Argentine Constitution. But the Court said although the beef industry had started as a private industry, it had become one that affected the public interest and therefore justified state legislation. The *Sociedad Rural* represented only about 10 per cent of stockmen, but because its membership included individuals with key positions in the government and Congress it was able to obtain legislative protection in the 1920s and 1930s and defend it in the Supreme Court. The meat companies, as predominantly representatives of United States and British capital, were excluded from the special position of influence enjoyed by the Argentine cattlemen.[52] But although the cattlemen secured special state protection, just as the livestock farmers in New Zealand, Australia, and even in Britain did, it was never enough to redress the mismatch in real economic power between them and the meat companies.

One other outcome of the Ottawa Agreements and the Roca-Runciman Treaty that disadvantaged the cattle farmer, and benefited the packers, was that they eliminated any further price wars between the packers. Because both governments agreed that the British government should administer the beef quotas, there was no longer any point in the packers competing for a larger share of the meat pool than had been agreed at the start of the quota in 1932. The American trust firms realised that neither the Argentine nor British government would let them increase their share of exports at the expense of their own country's meat packing firms. The quotas institutionalised each firm's existing shares of the pool and discouraged further meat wars in the 1930s. This meant that Charles and Edmund Vestey, who owned Union Cold Storage and the *Frigorifico* Anglo, the largest meat processing works in South America, were left undisturbed by the expense of any more competition with the American trust companies. They had the largest British share of the South American trade with their own chain of retail shops in Britain, and were left in a strong position by the international meat agreements. The cattle farmers, on the other hand, liked meat wars. They looked back nostalgically to the struggles between the *frigorificos* before the First World War when the American firms were increasing their share of the pool, and again in the 1920s as the Vesteys established themselves as major players in the trade, as both had raised cattle prices. But meat wars required growing markets and non-interventionist governments to thrive, and both of these were absent by the 1930s.

## Notes

1 Brewster, J.A., 'The South American Trade', in F. Gerrard (ed.), *The Book of the Meat Trade* (2 vols, London, 1949), vol. 1, p. 210.

2 Gebhardt, R.C., *The River Plate Meat Industry since c.1900: Technology, Ownership, International Trade Regimes and Domestic Policy* (Unpublished PhD Thesis, London School of Economics, 2000), pp. 186–8; P. Knightley, *The Vestey Affair* (London, 1981), pp. 65–7.

3 Cd 7896 (PP 1914–16, Vol. XLVI), *Report of the Royal Commission on the Meat Export Trade of Australia*.

4 Yeager, M., *Competition and Regulation: The Development of Oligopoly in the Meat Packing Industry* (Greenwich, Conn., 1981), pp. 171–95, 219–32; Knightley, *The Vestey Affair*, pp. 33–53; G. Harrison, *Borthwicks: A Century in the Meat Trade, 1863–1963* (London, 1963), pp. 105–33.

5 Cd 7896 (PP 1914–16, Vol. XLVI), *Report of the Royal Commission on the Meat Export Trade of Australia*, pp. 8–10, 13, 40.

6 Ibid., pp. 32–5.

7 Harrison, *Borthwicks: A Century in the Meat Trade, 1863–1963*, pp. 105–6, 131.

8 Cmd 456 (PP 1919, Vol. XXV), *Inter-Departmental Committee on Meat Supplies. Report of the Committee appointed by the Board of Trade to Consider the Means of Securing Sufficient Meat Supplies for the United Kingdom*, Appendix, pp. 29–30.

9 O'Connor, P.S., *Mr Massey and the American Meat Trust: Some sidelights on the Origins of the Meat Board* (Palmerston North, 1973), pp. 9, 14.

10 Hawke, G.R., *The Making of New Zealand* (Cambridge, 1985), pp. 99–100.

11 Capie, F., 'The First Export Monopoly Control Board', *Journal of Agricultural Economics*, 29 (1978): 133–6.

12 Harrison, *Borthwicks: A Century in the Meat Trade, 1863–1963*, p. 106.

13 Ibid., pp. 106, 126; Capie, 'The First Export Monopoly Control Board': 136–40.

14 Cd 7896 (PP 1914–16, Vol. XLVI), *Report of the Royal Commission on the Meat Export Trade of Australia*, pp. 4–5, 40–41, 44–6.
15 Harrison, *Borthwicks: A Century in the Meat Trade, 1863–1963*, pp. 106–8.
16 Capie, F., 'Australian and New Zealand Competition in the British Market 1920–39', *Australian Economic History Review*, 18(1) (1978): 48.
17 International Institute of Agriculture, *International Trade in Meat* (Rome, 1936), p. 23.
18 Tracy, M., *Government and Agriculture in Western Europe 1880–1988* (London, 1989), pp. 163–4, 182.
19 International Institute of Agriculture, *International Trade in Meat*, pp. 23–5.
20 Drummond, I.M., *Imperial Economic Policy 1917–1939: Studies in Expansion and Protection* (London, 1974), p. 261.
21 Duncan, R., 'The Demand for Frozen Beef in the United Kingdom, 1880–1940', *Journal of Agricultural Economics*, 12(1) (1956): 87.
22 Drummond, *Imperial Economic Policy 1917–1939*, pp. 253–5, 257.
23 Capie, 'Australian and New Zealand Competition in the British Market 1920–39': 59; International Institute of Agriculture, *International Trade in Meat*, p. 25.
24 Cmd 4174–4175 (PP. 1931–32, Vol. X), *Imperial Economic Conference at Ottawa, 1932. Summary of Proceedings of Trade Agreements with Appendices*, pp. 54–5.
25 Drummond, I.M., *British Economic Policy and the Empire, 1919–1939* (London, 1972), pp. 106–7.
26 No mention is made of Britain's concern about the fortunes of its financial and manufacturing industries in, for example: International Institute of Agriculture, *International Trade in Meat*, p. 27, or in Tracy, *Government and Agriculture in Western Europe 1880–1988*, p. 154.
27 A good summary of both the meat and financial issues is found in Gebhardt, pp. 260–62.
28 There is excellent coverage of the financial issues in R. Gravil, *The Anglo-Argentine Connection, 1900–1939* (Boulder, 1975), pp. 188–203.
29 Cmd 4492 (PP. 1933–34, Vol. XXVII), *Convention between the Government of the United Kingdom and the Government of the Argentine Republic Relating to Trade and Commerce, with Protocol*, pp. 2–5.
30 International Institute of Agriculture, *International Trade in Meat*, p. 27.
31 Cmd 4492 (PP. 1933–34, Vol. XXVII), *Convention between the Government of the United Kingdom and the Government of the Argentine Republic Relating to Trade and Commerce, with Protocol*, p. 10.
32 Alhadeff, P., 'Public Finance and the Economy in Argentina, Australia and Canada during the Depression of the 1930s', in D.C.M. Platt and G. Di Tella (eds), *Argentina, Australia and Canada: Studies in Comparative Development, 1870–1965* (Oxford, 1985), pp. 71, 73.
33 Intelligence Branch of the Imperial Economic Committee, *Cattle and Beef Survey: A Summary of Production and Trade in British Empire and Commonwealth Countries* (London, 1934), pp. 112, 126.
34 Gebhardt, p. 256.
35 Belshaw, H. (ed.), *Agricultural Organization in New Zealand* (Melbourne, 1936), p. 802.
36 Gravil, pp. 185–6.
37 Belshaw, p. 803.

38  Drummond, *Imperial Economic Policy 1917–1939*, pp. 339–54.
39  Jones, D., 'New Zealand Trade', in R. Ramsay (ed.), *The Frozen and Chilled Meat Trade: A Practical Treatise by Specialists in the Trade* (2 vols, London, 1929), vol. 1, p. 142; J.E. Richelet, 'The Argentine Trade', in R. Ramsay (ed.), *The Frozen and Chilled Meat Trade: A Practical Treatise by Specialists in the Trade* (2 vols, London, 1929), vol. 1, p. 210.
40  Grant, R., 'The Australian Meat Industry', in R. Ramsay (ed.), *The Frozen and Chilled Meat Trade: A Practical Treatise by Specialists in the Trade* (2 vols, London, 1929), vol. 1, p. 48.
41  Ministry of Agriculture and Fisheries Economic Series, *Report on the Trade in Refrigerated Beef, Mutton and Lamb* (London, 1925), p. 50.
42  Commonwealth Economic Committee [Compiler] (1948), *Meat*, HMSO, London, p. 67.
43  Empire Marketing Board, [Compiler] *Meat*, (London: HMSO, July 1932), pp. 11, 22.
44  Ministry of Agriculture and Fisheries Economic Series, *Report on the Trade in Refrigerated Beef, Mutton and Lamb*, pp. 48–50.
45  See *Meat Trades Journal*, 1920s, passim.
46  Solberg, C.E., *The Prairies and the Pampas: Agrarian Policy in Canada and Argentina, 1880–1930* (Stanford, 1987), p. 229.
47  Cmd 5839 (PP 1937–38, Vol. VIII), *Report of Joint Committee of Enquiry into the Anglo-Argentine Meat Trade*, p. 13.
48  Crossley, C. and R. Greenhill, 'The River Plate Beef Trade', in D.C.M. Platt (ed.), *Business Imperialism 1840–1930, An Inquiry Based on British Experience in Latin America* (Oxford, 1977), p. 317.
49  Cmd 5839 (PP 1937–38, Vol. VIII), *Report of Joint Committee of Enquiry into the Anglo-Argentine Meat Trade*, p. 13.
50  Gebhardt, pp. 183–5.
51  Cmd 5839 (PP 1937–38, Vol. VIII), *Report of Joint Committee of Enquiry into the Anglo-Argentine Meat Trade*, p. 95.
52  Berensztein, A. and H. Spector, 'Business, Government and Law' in G.D. Paolera and A.M. Taylor (eds), *A New Economic History of Argentina* (Cambridge, 2003), pp. 345–7.

# PART 3
## 1945 to the Present

# Chapter 7

# Shortages and Plenty

The wartime years were followed by a continued distortion of the whole structure of international trade that was somewhat more profound than immediately after the First War. The cost and extent of the conflict, and the damage to agriculture, meant that a much larger part of Europe was unable to produce enough food for immediate survival. The United Kingdom had always depended on food imports, but now France, Germany, and Italy who had all been more self-sufficient also needed food aid for their immediate survival. As in 1918, the production potentials of the great food exporters of the southern hemisphere, Argentina, Uruguay, Australia and New Zealand were largely untouched by the conflict, and there seemed little in the way of them restoring their trade with Europe. However, there was a problem of how food aid was to be paid for, as European industrial capacity was severely reduced. For a number of years purchasing power remained below the level of 1938 and restricted the demand for meat and other food imports. Also, as in the 1930s, most countries in Western Europe, including Britain, took a political decision to develop and protect agriculture after 1945. This long-term decision to invest in domestic farming meant that access to markets was in many cases no easier once initial supplies of foodstuffs had been paid for, largely by United States grants of aid. Thus, in the long-term traditional meat exporters had eventually to search for new markets, in Southern Europe, the Middle East and Far East.

## Scarcity and Rationing, 1945–55

Although world meat output probably regained their pre-war levels after 1950 per capita meat consumption did not, as population grew at a faster rate than output in the post-war years. Post-war disruption in a number of states, meant that estimates of overall food output were not made for the late 1940s. However, cattle numbers in the United Kingdom, New Zealand, Australia, Canada and the United States were higher than their 1937–39 levels by 1946–48, but sheep numbers had fallen everywhere, except New Zealand. Over the same years pig numbers were higher in the United States and Canada, but lower in the United Kingdom, Australia and New Zealand.[1]

It can be seen from Table 7.1 below that the British meat consumption in the first half of the 1950s was 30 per cent less than it was before the war. As the United Kingdom remained the largest market for internationally traded meat, food policy objectives had to be framed in terms of what was desirable and also what was possible. With the passing of the Agriculture Act of 1947 the country took the decision to stimulate British agriculture, an objective that seemed very reasonable at the time, as there was still a shortage of all foodstuffs on world markets.

**Table 7.1  United Kingdom meat consumption per head in 1938 and 1950–54 (lbs)**

|                   | 1938 | 1950 | 1951 | 1952 | 1953 | 1954 |
|-------------------|------|------|------|------|------|------|
| Beef and Veal     | 55   | 47   | 34   | 32   | 37   | 43   |
| Mutton and lamb   | 25   | 25   | 15   | 21   | 24   | 23   |
| Pig-meat          | 39   | 26   | 24   | 31   | 37   | 42   |
| Total consumption | 119  | 98   | 73   | 84   | 98   | 108  |

*Source:* Commonwealth Economic Committee, *Meat: A Summary of Figures of Production, Trade and Consumption* (London, 1955), pp. 17, 33, 48

With regard to domestic meat, Britain's pre-war marketing system was seen as being particularly inefficient and acting as a constraint on home production. It was alleged that marketing costs were excessive, partly because most animals passed through more than one wholesale market and travelled long distances before reaching an abattoir, and also because of the wastage of hides and offal at many of the 16,000 slaughterhouses existing in 1939. There was no systematic quality grading and almost no advertising of home-produced meat, with the result that the higher price the consumer was prepared to pay for good quality fresh-killed home-produced meat was never fully realised. Among its proposals for distribution and marketing reforms, the Ministry of Agriculture attempted to mimic many of the features of the imported meat business. It wanted to introduce a proper livestock quality-grading scheme, greater control over markets and regulating the deliveries by farmers to these markets. It also sought to rationalise the slaughtering system, and reorganise it along factory lines so that by-products could be fully utilised.[2] These may have been grand ideas for an ideal world, but in practice were impossible to implement in the short term.

The plans for regulated marketing did not meet with any enthusiasm from any part of the meat industry. British farmers certainly did not want to be directed from above in these matters. They preferred to sell when prices seemed at their best for them, not when some local official said that they should in order to ensure continuity of supplies to local markets. The apathy of British farmers, their lack of capital and the post-war shortage of materials, combined with the small size of many holdings, made extensive immediate investment in quality livestock production unattractive for most. Output of cereals had risen during the war but not meat (see Chapter 4). In pre-war years the country supplied around 45 per cent of its meat, but this had dropped to 35 per cent by 1944. Even on the cereals front the outlook in 1945 was not promising and ominous signs of over-cropping were beginning to appear. The increase in cereal acreage had produced large amounts of straw, but there were insufficient livestock numbers to produce the dung to mix it with and convert it to good farmyard manure and maintain soil fertility. Shortage of foreign exchange meant that imports of feeding stuffs had to be reduced, and by 1950 output of beef, as can be seen in Table 7.2 below, was less than 5 per cent above its pre-war level.[3]

**Table 7.2  Estimated United Kingdom meat consumption, selected years between 1938 and 1953 (thousand tons)**

|  | 1938 | 1947 | 1949 | 1950 | 1953 |
|---|---|---|---|---|---|
| Home production |  |  |  |  |  |
| Beef and veal | 605 | 509 | 528 | 634 | 632 |
| Mutton and lamb | 211 | 117 | 140 | 149 | 170 |
| Pig meat | 393 | 102 | 232 | 279 | 279 |
| Total home production | 1,209 | 728 | 900 | 1,073 | 1,079 |
| Imported meat |  |  |  |  |  |
| Beef and veal | 585 | 506 | 361 | 329 | 286 |
| Mutton and lamb | 342 | 424 | 359 | 391 | 348 |
| Pig meat | 409 | 135 | 159 | 273 | 335 |
| Total imports | 1,336 | 1,065 | 879 | 993 | 969 |
| Total consumption | 2,545 | 1,793 | 1,779 | 2,066 | 2,048 |

*Sources:* 1938, 1947 and 1949, Commonwealth Economic Committee, *Meat: A Summary of Figures of Production, Trade and Consumption*, (London 1952), pp. 11, 27, 35; 1950 and 1953, ————, *Meat: A Summary of Figures of Production, Trade and Consumption*, (London 1955), pp. pp. 21, 37, 46.

There was also a powerful anti-reform lobby among wholesale and retail butchers, of whom many wished to restore the pre-war system of slaughter largely unchanged. Although there were large publicly owned abattoirs in the major towns, there was still quite a large number of small privately owned slaughterhouses that supplied the local meat retailers. Although not particularly efficient, they often suited the needs of the local meat retailer being close at hand and often able to supply small traders with what they wanted more or less on demand. In other respects, however, the retail trade did want to see improvements, particularly in the quality of what they had to sell. They complained that enterprise had been sapped under the wartime Meat Control Scheme. They alleged it had established a 'complete stranglehold over the retail meat trade and sapped the energy of private enterprise'. Shopkeepers could no longer choose what they sold and had to accept what was allocated 'whether it was too fat or too lean, too tough or too soft, telescoped or frozen like a brick, soiled or slashed'. They also said that it was no use complaining, as the officials of the Ministry of Food told them they had to accept it because there was no other meat to take in its place.[4] The experience of the wartime conditions and official intervention therefore made them very hostile to anything that bore the mark of central direction.

Although the Ministry of Agriculture made the above criticisms of the domestic meat supply system with a view to stimulating domestic output, it was not able to achieve it in this way. As we will see later in this chapter, it had to provide long-term incentives for the livestock farmer rather than central directives that encompassed all stages of the meat production, processing, and supply chain. In the meantime it relied heavily on imports to make up any deficit and in the immediate post-war years the United Kingdom remained the largest customer in the international meat market. Meat imports were actually higher than home production in 1947, as can be seen from Table 7.2 above, and although they declined somewhat after 1948, they still accounted for 47 per cent of consumption in 1953.

But both the international and domestic markets remained subject to severe distortions. International trade in meat was still largely governed by contracts and agreements between governments and quasi-official organisations that had been set up in wartime. They may not all have been strictly necessary by the late 1940s, but in the immediate post-war years the whole apparatus of control showed a remarkable capacity to survive. Britain continued its wartime practice of bulk purchases of meat from Australia, New Zealand and the River Plate, and actually re-negotiated most of these agreements at different times, before ending them in 1954. They allowed the United Kingdom to continue to regulate its trade (and conserve foreign exchange) through a series of long-term contracts with its most important suppliers that covered all types of meat. It also concluded similar arrangements with Denmark, the Netherlands and Poland for bacon. The Ministry of Food remained the sole importer for meat after 1947 until the first slight relaxation of controls on imported meat in June 1950.[5] But these arrangements also had advantages for most of the suppliers as the bulk purchase agreements provided a guaranteed market for the major proportion of their output.

Rationing of all foodstuffs continued in the United Kingdom, but most of its suppliers were able to free domestic consumption by the end of 1949. But the overall growth of the meat trade in these years, when compared with the post-1955 era, was not spectacular. Consumer demand was kept low because resources were diverted to the process of reconstruction and recovery, a process that applied to all of Western Europe. Among policy instruments used to achieve these aims were restrictions on personal consumption. United Kingdom meat rationing was particularly severe, where the lowest level of meat consumption was reached in 1948 at only two-thirds the pre-war level.[6] Although some part of this fall was balanced by substantial increase in fish and poultry and a much higher consumption of milk, the impact of this restriction of the biggest market was still strongly felt by established suppliers. Table 7.2 above shows that British meat supplies from all sources declined steadily from 1946 and only began to improve in 1950, but this was followed by a further setback in supplies at the end of 1950 and the beginning of 1951 owing to the cessation of imports from the Argentine. Home production did begin to recover after 1947, but even in 1953 consumption was still 18 per cent below what it had been before the war (see Table 7.1). This reduction in meat was severely felt by all classes of the community, and was regarded as the main reason for the impoverishment of the national diet as compared with pre-war standards.[7]

Against this background of interrupted supplies and overall decline on an annual basis, the British meat ration was periodically re-adjusted in the immediate post-war years, sometimes on a weekly basis, principally because Britain was unable to obtain, or to afford, the necessary overseas supplies to keep it at wartime levels. Before the war imported and home-produced supplies were distributed equally throughout the year and seasonal supply matched seasonal demand. But in the post-war years, lack of imported oilcake and other concentrates meant winter production of British meat was severely reduced. As imported meat contracts often provided a flat-rate price throughout the season, they give overseas suppliers little incentive to ship more in December to May when the output of British meat was low.[8] For the long-suffering British public the uncertainty that seasonal, monthly and weekly re-adjustments of the meat ration gave to their lives – against a general background of shortage – caused particular annoyance. It was a situation for which most sections of the press berated the Labour government, accusing it of waste and mismanagement, and even among sympathetic observers willing to acknowledge the severe constraints under which government was forced to operate there were still reservations about the ways policy was implemented. In April 1950, after eight and a half years, the points rationing scheme was abolished, and rations were for fixed monetary amounts of commodities.[9]

In July 1951 Britain's meat ration was 10d a week, which amounted to 10 oz. at current prices.[10] This was at such a low level (it was roughly equivalent to 1 lb a week during the war) that the government progressively raised it over the following weeks until September, when it had reached the level of 2s. 2d. Meat prices at the same time were also raised by 3d per lb, so that at the new prices a ration of 2s. 2d would purchase around 1 lb 6 oz. But in mid-September butchers reported that, as the increased ration was not fully taken up, they objected to paying the Ministry of Food a surcharge of 10d in the £. The surcharge was part of the system by which the butchers paid the Ministry when the ration rose above 1s 8d, and the Ministry paid the butchers when the ration was below that amount – the general aim being to give the trade a fair profit in the light of what it earned before the war. With the ration fixed at 2s. 2d, traders said their shop assistants needed to work overtime and this, with the higher surcharge, was said to reduce the butchers' gross profits. As *The Economist* caustically observed:[11]

It would be hard to imagine a combination of more absurdities than the system which gives the butchers a vested interest in selling less meat, pays them for not selling it, freezes the trade at its pre-war size, although the quantity of meat to be handled is much less, and leaves meat piling up at some butchers while others, in wealthier districts, could sell twice as much. ... Never was scarcity organised with such intricate care.

Complaints such as these were commonplace and applied to other things besides the meat ration. They reflected the general feeling of disillusion and weariness engendered by the restricted choice and inconvenience associated with six years of rationing, managed in its latter stages with a complete absence of imagination.

In addition to physical shortages, the quality of both home-killed and imported meat was also a matter of complaint in these years. Here the root of the problem was the failure to restore and make good the wartime decline in the distribution network. Home-killed meat was available in quantity at only two seasons – between March and May, when about 20 per cent of the total came to market, and in August to October, when 40 per cent was provided. Because of the wartime run down of plant and equipment in the domestic meat trade there was insufficient chilling plant and storage space to handle home supplies, so meat was sold as soon as it was slaughtered and not hung a sufficient time to improve its quality. This meant it was generally sold before it lost its 'bloom' – the luscious blood-red colour that gives meat an attractive appearance but often leaves it tough. Thus the meat ration varied directly with home killings, and the basic reserves and supplies depended entirely on imports. This meant the weekly ration was raised in spring and autumn when the consumer was presented with tough home-killed meat that needed to be disposed of quickly, but fell back at other times of the year. The only solution was to pay higher prices to attract more imports or increase supplies of home produced meat. However, the first would further unbalance Britain's external payments and the latter require more investment in storage space.

These were problems that resided in Britain and can be attributed to the wartime run-down of plant and equipment in the domestic meat trade, but similar situations also existed overseas. The wartime demand for frozen meat had meant that freezing capacity and frozen cold storage space had been expanded at the expense of chilling capacity and chilled storage space. After the war the continuing shortage of chilling capacity and the necessary distributive system meant that all imported beef and lamb still remained either canned or frozen. Before the war over 75 per cent of Britain's beef imports had been chilled, and besides South America, the chilling process had also made significant inroads into the Australian and New Zealand beef trade.[12] In New Zealand the immediate obstacles to a revival of the trade were the shortage of refrigerated railway wagons sufficiently well insulated to carry chilled beef, and difficulties in the way of prompt loading and despatch of vessels from the New Zealand ports. Even when only frozen meat was handled there was serious congestion and delays in despatching meat ships from both Auckland and Wellington. With chilled meat the timetable was much more strict; the period between killing the animal and the distribution of its meat in Britain could not exceed fifty days, of which thirty to thirty-five were taken up by the voyage. If the meat were not distributed within this period it had to be frozen and sold at a lower price than chilled meat, which carried a premium of £23 a ton over frozen beef, or else be condemned.[13]

Although faults in the distribution and rationing system were an obvious target for critics, the rest of the problem lay in the inability to restore either home production or imports to their pre-war level in the short term. In this respect the situation was more serious than it had been after the First World War. The over-expansion of cereal farming in Britain has already been mentioned, but with the exception of milk production the rest of the livestock sector was comparatively neglected. There was little investment in buildings and with meat prices closely controlled there was little incentive to concentrate on quality beef production. The result was that a high proportion of what was forthcoming from home production was from lower quality beef animals, and cow beef. Before the war the major source of beef imports was South America, but even here, the livestock farmers and meat packers were not in a position to supply the amounts they had done in 1938.

In the 1940s and 1950s a process, which had begun after 1914, brought about a decline in the proportion of Argentine meat exported. As domestic real incomes increased so too did local demand for meat, and this had an adverse effect on the exportable surplus. As can be seen from Table 7.3 below, already in the 1920s over half the cattle slaughtered in Argentina were sold for domestic consumption.

**Table 7.3  Production, exports and domestic consumption of beef and veal in Argentina, 1914–59 (thousand tons)**

|  | Total production | For export | % | For domestic consumption | % |
|---|---|---|---|---|---|
| 1914–19 | 1068 | 597 | 56 | 471 | 44 |
| 1920–24 | 1342 | 628 | 47 | 714 | 53 |
| 1925–29 | 1669 | 758 | 45 | 911 | 55 |
| 1930–34 | 1459 | 547 | 37 | 912 | 63 |
| 1935–39 | 1695 | 626 | 37 | 1069 | 63 |
| 1940–44 | 1724 | 670 | 39 | 1054 | 61 |
| 1945–49 | 1854 | 488 | 26 | 1366 | 74 |
| 1950–54 | 1888 | 289 | 15 | 1599 | 85 |
| 1955–59 | 2350 | 562 | 24 | 1788 | 76 |

*Source:* Grunwald, J. and P. Musgrove, *Natural Resources in Latin American Development* (Baltimore, 1970), p. 423.

In the 1930s this rose to 63 per cent, and fell only slightly to 61 per cent in the Second World War. But after 1945 the pace of the trend towards increased local consumption accelerated so that in the late 1940s over 70 per cent of animals went for domestic consumption, with exports reaching their low point in 1950–54 when they accounted for only 15 per cent of total production. There would have been no reason why this should have had an adverse effect on the export market if the growth of total output had been continuously maintained. Faced with an adverse export market in the 1930s output growth was not maintained, so that in 1940–44 total beef and veal output was only slightly higher than it had been in 1930–34. Although total output picked up again after the war, the volume and value of exports continued to decline. Meat exports in 1940–44 averaged 1,295 million pesos and declined to a little over 1,000 million pesos in 1945–49, but for 1950–54 they were down to 566 million pesos.[14]

On 18 July 1948 Britain and Argentina signed a meat agreement which was due to last for five years, but which could be terminated by either party on 1 July of any year. Argentina undertook to supply Britain with 300,000 tons of meat in the first year, and if possible, 400,000 tons subsequently. In 1948 total Argentine meat exports to all countries were 509,000 tons (684,000 tons if exports of live animals are included). The following year meat exports stood at approximately 497,000 tons; total exports, including exports on the hoof, had however fallen to 550,000 tons. For 1950 the reduction in the exportable surplus was even more spectacular. Total exports, both slaughtered and live, amounted to only 422,000 tons – barely the amount that Argentina had promised to send to the British market alone. In July 1950, shipments to Britain were suspended when the two governments failed to agree over prices. The agreement was amended in August 1951, and shipments resumed but at the reduced rate of 200,000 tons per annum. The total exportable surpluses for 1951 and 1952 were 369,000 and 294,000 tons respectively. But meat exports were not alone in experiencing a decline in these years. Partly as a result of the Argentine government's policy with regard to agriculture, the effects of industrialization, and natural disaster, virtually every other sector of the country's agriculture experienced some decline in production.[15]

In these years part of the reason for Argentina's failure to raise exports to the levels required by Britain was the result of the policies that dated from the era of military government after 1943, associated with Juan Perón. The establishment in these years of a state selling agency, the Argentine Trade Promotion Institute (*Instituto Argentino para la Promoción del Intercambio*) or I.A.P.I. was supposed to give the Argentine government the means of protecting its agricultural sector from existing world conditions.[16] But instead it was used as an instrument to give low prices to farmers, while selling agricultural output at world prices with the government using the difference to finance a policy of rapid industrialisation. This policy was an attempt to end the country's dependence upon Britain and the United States for industrial goods, which were in short supply during the war years. However, import substitution industrialisation (ISI) failed for a number of reasons. Part of the money abstracted from the rural sector was swallowed up in the expensive and wasteful bureaucracy common to many South American regimes, and more was used to support industrial wages and finance social reform, both of which raised industrial costs leaving shortages for investment.[17] The effects of the forced taxation of the rural sector was felt by all farmers, but worst of all by livestock farmers between 1946 and 1949, when cattle prices fell relative to those of grain.[18]

Although after the war Argentina appeared to be in a strong position to negotiate with Britain, who still depended on her for some 30 to 35 per cent of its meat, Britain was not in an entirely weak position either. The British market absorbed about 80 per cent of the country's meat surplus, and British ships carried 90 per cent of Argentina's meat exports. In addition, post-war inflation eroded the purchasing power of the blocked sterling balances that Britain had paid for wartime meat, and were still being used to pay for Argentine meat, every day that they remained unused in London.[19] As in these years Argentina had no other customer for its meat, she had to accept this rather unsatisfactory payment arrangement.

Argentina's vulnerability became apparent with the interruption of meat shipments from Argentina (and also Uruguay) in July 1950 as a result of a dispute over prices, a situation that was no doubt worsened by the British decision to devalue sterling by 30 per cent in 1949.[20] At first the effects were not severe because meat shipments had been heavier than usual in the first half of 1950, owing to a severe summer drought in Argentina which had led producers to send large amounts of cattle to the packing stations. The dispute with both countries was not finally resolved until April 1951 and meant the United Kingdom absorbed a far smaller proportion of both countries' beef exports than in previous years. The amounts from Uruguay were insignificant and not noticed, but Argentina exported 163,000 tons to Britain, which amounted to 78 per cent of her beef exports, in 1950 but sent only 56,000 tons, which was 28 per cent of its beef exports, to Britain in 1951. After the dispute was resolved Britain imported smaller quantities of Argentine beef, and the average for 1952–54 was only 72,000 tons. This was partly because the total beef exports of Argentina were lower after 1951, averaging only 106,000 tons per annum in 1952–54 compared with 171,000 tons in 1950 and 117,000 in 1951. Poor output performance in these years forced Argentina to consume more of its beef at home, and in 1953 there were domestic beef shortages. But by this time it did not leave Britain seriously short of supplies, as it bought more from Canada, Australia and New Zealand, as well as managing to increase in domestic output.[21]

It was against this background of interrupted supplies and overall decline on an annual basis, that the British meat ration was re-adjusted with bewildering rapidity in the immediate post-war years, sometimes on a weekly basis. Principally it was because Britain was unable to obtain, or to afford, the necessary overseas supplies to keep it at wartime levels. The pressure came from a number of directions. During the war meat exporting governments had been forced to accept a rigidly controlled structure of prices, but the return of peace found them less inclined, or able, to do so. In the case of New Zealand there was still a great deal of goodwill towards Britain, and the wish to do as much as possible to increase the British meat ration was by no means confined to its politicians. In 1947 New Zealand exported 375,000 tons, or 67 per cent of its meat production to Great Britain.[22] But for any increase in output, its farmers needed to rear more cattle, sheep and lambs as well as expand the facilities for the preparation and shipment of extra meat; and all of this required capital investment. New Zealand formerly had large wartime meat account balances in Britain in the Meat Pool Account and the Meat Industry Stabilisation Account. But as the British government treated this account like Argentina's and kept it frozen immediately after the war, it could not be used to import machinery from the United States to expand the industry's processing and storage capacity. From the late 1940s the Stabilisation Account ceased to grow as the New Zealand farmer was granted the full proceeds from the sale of meat, but the British Prime Minister, Clement Atlee, still requested New Zealand not to draw on its sterling balances, which meant it had to continue its import restrictions.[23]

In April 1951 the two meat accounts were merged into the Meat Industry Reserve Account. Early in 1952 the British government agreed to raise the scale of prices established the previous October by 15 per cent, and guaranteed to accept for the next fifteen years all the meat New Zealand could send.[24] Uncertainty over markets was the main disadvantage of the pre-war system, so this reversal was a dramatic change of British policy. But there were still difficulties in translating the immediate price improvement into a form that New Zealand farmers could take advantage of to ensure they could supply this guaranteed market.

With the agreement the New Zealand government was faced with the uninviting prospect of making retrospective payments to thousands of farmers who had sold their stock for the coming season at the prices ruling before the new prices had been fixed. It found this unattractive because of concern over the effect of a 15 per cent rise in export prices upon retail meat prices in New Zealand, especially as the New Zealand Federation of Labour was about to renew demands for a general rise in wages based upon an increase in the cost of living. The government placed the undistributed balance of the price increase for 1952 that was expected to be anything from £1¾ million to £2½ million in the Meat Industry Reserve Account, which already amounted to £37 million. Like its predecessors, the money in this account was frozen in long-term stocks in London and not distributed to farmers, as sterling was still not fully convertible, and it was also feared the increase in purchasing power from this account might cause inflation in New Zealand. In the meantime the New Zealand Federated Farmers Organisation, representing most of the producing organisations, was urging that effective control, as well as titular ownership of this asset and also the Dairy Industry Reserve Account which amounted to over £23 million, be placed in the hands of the producers. As any increase in meat output would require that some of the Meat Industry Reserve Account as well as part of the Dairy Industry Reserve Account be used for investment, both British exchange control policy and New Zealand government policy had already precluded such an outcome.[25]

It was only after the mid-1950s that the post-war world food-shortage started to give way to an incipient surplus in Western markets. The general freeing of exchange controls permitted higher levels of investment, and this permitted striking improvements in agricultural productivity and reductions in real costs, not only in Europe, but also in most of the developed world. The gains were not only made in the traditional primary producing regions, but also Europe. They were most spectacular in the United Kingdom, assisted by the Agriculture Act of 1957, which provided positive incentives for farmers to improve the technical efficiency of the industry. For instance, the Pig Industry Development Authority set up with considerable funds at its disposal by the Act operated a national recording scheme, supervised progeny testing, developed a national artificial insemination service and introduced an accredited herds scheme.[26] But in the rest of Western Europe the Common Agricultural Policy with its greater reliance on subsidies and protected markets presented less incentive for increased efficiency.[27]

But by the end of 1954 post-war recovery of the meat industry everywhere was largely complete; world output was 37 per cent greater than in 1938, and exports had resumed their pre-war level. Incomes had grown and overall demand was restored to its pre-war level, making the prospects for future expansion encouraging. The ending of rationing and other controls in the United Kingdom in July 1954 freed the largest international market, while government restrictions on consumption and trade in meat remained in only a few countries. Throughout the late 1940s price controls and domestic subsidies had held the price of meat below the general level of wholesale prices, but after 1952 lamb and beef subsidies were reduced allowing their price to rise, but pig meat supplies increased and so masked the effect of similar measure for that meat.[28] Against this background of rising incomes and technical advance all meat industries in the Western world responded with an increased output, but for some countries the industry's growth was particularly spectacular.

## Prosperity and Growth, 1955–99

From the mid-1950s the overall food supply situation became much easier for the whole of the developed world. Also, international agencies paid more attention to measuring world output as part of the concern over food shortages in the underdeveloped world. But the collection of accurate data was far easier for the developed world, with its efficient government services to carry out the task. As a result we know more about the production of meat for the developed countries, which remained the main producers. But even there measurement was not entirely straightforward, as the number of countries defined as 'main producers' changed over time. In the first half of the 1950s according to figures collected by the Intelligence Branch of the Commonwealth Economic Committee in Table 7.4 below there were 16 major beef producers, 10 major sheep meat producers and 16 major producers of pig meat. But by the early 1970s this had grown to 34 main producers of beef and veal, 15 producers of mutton and lamb, and 26 pig meat producers. This increase was partly an effect of decolonisation in the 1960s, and partly the inclusion of some of the communist countries, like China, for which the collection of data was difficult in the 1950s. This does impart something of an upward bias to the figures but, more importantly, the increase in the number of countries considered important enough to be defined as main producers reflects the very real growth in world output.

This is shown in Table 7.4 below, showing the output of the major producers increased rapidly after 1954, reaching 9.8 per cent per annum between 1954–55 and 1955–59, but slowing considerably thereafter, its next highest growth rate being 3.5 per cent per annum between 1960–64 and 1965–69. Output of all three main meats seem to have grown at roughly the same rates with an approximate distribution of 52 per cent beef, 6 per cent mutton and lamb and 42 per cent pig meat. The growth of output was also a reflection of a continued increase in consumer prosperity. As in the nineteenth century, increases in incomes were accompanied by a more rapid rise in expenditure on meat than on most other foods. Another estimate, for 1959–61, put the volume of world meat production from all countries, not just the main producers, at 63 million tons or 46 per cent above the average for 1948–52. The whole industry remained a high cost enterprise, requiring expensive inputs with costly overheads. As it continued to rely on the use of grass and grain for animal feed it remained concentrated predominantly in the developed temperate countries, particularly Western Europe and North America. Among the developing countries the only two substantial producers continued to be Argentina and Uruguay, although Brazil and Mexico did develop smaller beef cattle industries after 1950.[29]

In these years greater meat production did little to solve global world food problems, as their solution remained a matter of raising grain output in the developing nations. Only something under 10 per cent of world meat output entered international trade at the beginning of the 1960s, and it remained a trade between the richer nations. In the case of the developing world, production was held back by problems of investment, pasture and fodder management, marketing and disease control. For the developed world, production for export was also held back, but here it was mainly problems of uncertainty over access to markets. This was because even in those regions that had always been importers there was a tendency to support prices and markets for domestic producers, to reconsider previous open door policies and impose policy measures like tariffs and quotas at frontiers. All of these had the effect of reducing growth of output and exports in those countries that possessed a comparative advantage in the production of meat.

One effect of this was Britain's decision to provide a much stronger system of support for its own farmers than it had done in the 1930s, and its eventual decision to join the European Economic Community (EEC) in 1973. The outcome of these two radical changes was a progressive weakening and eventually a sharp reduction in its former reliance on the Commonwealth for a substantial proportion of food imports, including meat. A further casualty of this change was that it eventually led to the cessation of the collection of commodity reviews giving output and trade data on a Commonwealth basis. Up to then the Commonwealth's annual reviews of *Meat: A Summary of Figures of Production, Trade and Consumption* provided a very convenient source of the overall trends in the international meat industry.

After Britain joined the EC this publication stopped in 1976 and it is necessary to use the Food and Agriculture Organization's three series of annual *Commodity Reviews*, beginning in 1961, to follow the general progress of the industry and the international trade in meat.

**Table 7.4  Estimates of meat output from the main producing countries between 1950–54 and 1970–72 (thousand tons)**

|                              | 1950–54[a] | 1955–59[bc] | 1960–64[cd] | 1965–69[e] | 1970–72[e] |
|------------------------------|-----------|------------|------------|-----------|-----------|
| Beef and veal                | 13,432    | 20,009     | 24,016     | 28,996    | 31,791    |
| Mutton and lamb              | 1,584     | 2,712      | 3,487      | 3,670     | 3,930     |
| Pig meat                     | 9,424     | 16,247     | 19,042     | 22,595    | 26,175    |
| Total output                 | 24,440    | 38,968     | 46,545     | 55,261    | 61,896    |
| Growth of output (% per annum) |         | 5.3        | 2.0        | 1.9       | 1.7       |

[a] 1950–54, beef and veal 16 countries; mutton and lamb 10 countries; pig-meat 16 countries
[b] 1955–58, beef and veal 22 countries; mutton and lamb 11 countries; pig-meat 23 countries
[c] 1959–61, beef and veal 27 countries; mutton and lamb 13 countries; pig-meat 25 countries
[d] 1962–64, beef and veal 29 countries; mutton and lamb 15 countries; pig-meat 26 countries
[e] 1965–72, beef and veal 34 countries; mutton and lamb 15 countries; pig-meat 26 countries

*Sources:* 1950–54, Commonwealth Economic Committee, *Meat: A Summary of Figures of Production, Trade and Consumption* (London, 1955), p. 2; 1955–58, ———, *Meat: A Summary of Figures of Production, Trade and Consumption* (London, 1960), p. 2; 1959–61, ———, *Meat: A Summary of Figures of Production, Trade and Consumption* (London, 1963), p. 4; 1962–64, Commonwealth Secretariat, *Meat: A Summary of Figures of Production, Trade and Consumption* (London, 1967), p. 9; 1965–72, ———, *Meat: A Summary of Figures of Production, Trade and Consumption* (London, 1973), p. 8.

This source, reflecting the FAO's continuing preoccupation with world food supplies and agricultural development, divides production of the main varieties of meat into various groups of countries. The weakness of these potentially very helpful volumes is that the details of the classifications of the data change constantly over time, although the basic information remains the same. There is little point in going into any detail over the problems in using the data in the printed volumes, as their shortcomings for the purposes of long-term comparisons can be overcome by using figures from the FAO's web based series. Data from this source has the advantage that it has been updated on what seems a comparable basis from 1961, thus making it possible to follow long-term trends in meat and other food output. This series, and the printed volumes, have been used in Table 7.5 below to follow the long-term trends in the industry from 1970–74 to 1995–99. However, the printed volumes are still very useful because they contain annual surveys that help to explain some of the changes in Table 7.5.

**Table 7.5  Global meat output 1975–99 (million tons)**

|                | 1970–74 | 1975–79 | 1980–84 | 1985–89 | 1990–84 | 1995–89 |
|----------------|---------|---------|---------|---------|---------|---------|
| Bovine meat    | 40.1    | 47.4    | 47.5    | 52.2    | 54.4    | 56.8    |
| Sheep and goat | 6.6     | 7.3     | 7.5     | 8.5     | 9.6     | 10.3    |
| Pig meat       | 39.4    | 49.0    | 53.7    | 63.2    | 72.4    | 82.7    |
| Poultry        | 16.8    | 26.0    | 27.6    | 34.6    | 44.7    | 58.1    |
| Other meats    | 3.2     | 3.9     | 3.4     | 3.5     | 3.8     | 4.3     |
| Total output   | 106.1   | 133.6   | 139.7   | 162.0   | 184.9   | 212.2   |
| Growth of output (% per annum) |  | 2.6 | 0.5 | 1.6 | 1.5 | 1.5 |

*Source:* FAOSTAT August 2004

We can see from the Table that output growth at 2.6 per cent per annum was rapid in the second half of the 1970s, but slowed markedly in the first half of the 1980s. Although it revived after 1985, at just over 1.5 per cent per annum it was never above the level of the 1960s. In these years the meats that showed the most spectacular increases were pig and poultry. As production times for pork and poultry are short, just a few weeks for chickens and a few months for pigs, they allowed easy responses to increased demand. Beef and mutton, however, are more expensive to produce and have a longer production time. But also long-term changes in the demand for meat, and the development of mass production pig units and poultry units were other factors behind the dramatic expansion of output of these meats. Between 1970–74 and 1995–99 annual growth of beef and veal output was 1.2 per cent, mutton and lamb (and goat) was a little higher at 1.5 per cent, but pig meat grew by 2.6 per cent a year, and poultry meat by 4.4 per cent.

Overall growth in these years was partly a function of increased herd and flock sizes as well as increases in slaughter weights. The general trend of availability of feedstuffs for all meats was one of increase although, as ever, short-term weather conditions were responsible for local fluctuations in output. In most importing countries feed grains and concentrates were an increasingly important input item, especially for beef production and they made an important contribution to rising slaughter weights. In the United States, for example, the system of grain feeding cattle in feedlots had, by the early 1970s reached a stage where 95 per cent of all steers and heifers slaughtered for beef were fed on grain prior to killing. This change was brought about by the development of heavy yielding varieties of hybrid corn in the 1950s, which remained abundant and cheap throughout the 1950s and 1960s. There was far less reliance on lot feeding in the EC, but here there was more reliance on improved pasture supplemented with forage crops and conserved fodders, and the use of feed grains for over-wintering cattle. Japan, who started to increase its meat production in the 1960s, always had limited grazing land and so relied heavily on imported feed grains. In contrast, the livestock industries in the exporting countries of the southern hemisphere could rely on pasture to provide year-round grazing animals. But as the scope for pasture improvement has always been more limited than for raising the yield of field crops, here increases were confined mainly to herd and flock sizes, rather than higher slaughter weights. [30]

One result of this was that a relatively slow growth of beef output was a feature common to some of the traditional beef producing and exporting countries. It was particularly noticeable for the River Plate economies where, even after the removal of Perón in September 1955, much of the Argentine economy failed to recover rapidly after the unsuccessful rapid industrialization programme. The country remained politically divided between loosely organized anti-Perón groups and a strong Perónist following. Struggles between opposing factions, with frequent interventions from right wing military elements continued, and little attempt was made to reverse the underlying economic weaknesses that remained a persistent legacy of the Perón years. As a result, the meat output of the River Plate region in the 1950s grew far more slowly than in the rest of the world. In the USSR and Western Europe it grew by 78 and 69 per cent respectively and in North America and Oceania (Australia and New Zealand) it was 37 and 35 per cent. Also in these regions output rose faster than population, but for Argentina and Uruguay total output increased by only 3 per cent and output per head fell by 15 per cent.[31]

In addition to the modest growth of all River Plate farm output from 1955 to 1965, the United Kingdom became a less important destination for its meat exports as Western Europe became a more important market. In 1950–54 the United Kingdom took 73 per cent of Argentina's exports of chilled beef and Western Europe 16 per cent, but by 1964–66 the United Kingdom's share was down to 32 per cent and Western Europe's had risen to 66 per cent.[32] The failure of Argentina to raise its beef export levels was partly caused by a steep rise in domestic demand, which outstripped the increase in total output. Until 1970 Argentine home prices were high enough to reduce the incentive to increase its export volumes. But while supplies from Argentina and Uruguay ceased to grow, Australia and Brazil took advantage of the buoyant market conditions and raised their beef exports. By 1971 and 1972 Australia had replaced Argentina as the world's leading exporter. Australia could also take advantage of the United States market for fresh beef that was closed to Argentina because of foot-and-mouth disease.[33]

## Fluctuations in the International Meat Trade

Although the international trade in meats grew after 1955, it did so very unevenly. Measurement of this is not entirely perfect, as some changes were made to the classifications used in the FAO *Commodity Reviews* over time. For example, it can be seen in Table 7.6 that internationally traded canned meat was classified as a separate item up to 1975, but is included with other meats thereafter, as the trade in both classes of meat become less important. Nevertheless, the data presented are

*Taste, Trade and Technology*

sufficiently comprehensive to give a broad indication of long-term trends. Growth between the groups of years after 1953–55 was rapid until 1980, but there was a

**Table 7.6  Annual average world meat exports for various groups of years between 1953–55 and 1993–95 (thousand tons)**

| | 1953–55 | 1956–60 | 1963–65 | 1966–70 | 1973–75 | 1978–80 | 1983–85 | 1988–90 | 1993–95 |
|---|---|---|---|---|---|---|---|---|---|
| Bovine meat | 569 | 929 | 1,504 | 1872 | 2,623 | 6,237 | 4,219 | 4,710 | 4,750 |
| Sheep and goat | 407 | 420 | 522 | 647 | 738 | 1,061 | 1,042 | 800 | 660 |
| Pig meat | 516 | 547 | 787 | 1034 | 1,116 | 3,066 | 1,804 | 1,730 | 2,180 |
| Poultry | 52 | 144 | 325 | 420 | 821 | 1,396 | 1,331 | 1,800 | 3,740 |
| Canned meats | 363 | 431 | 516 | 672 | 1,327 | | | | |
| | | | | | | 1,166 | 1,136 | 1,730 | 240 |
| Other meats | 229 | 397 | 613 | 640 | 2,526 | | | | |
| Total exports | 2,136 | 2,868 | 4,267 | 5,285 | 9,151 | 12,926 | 9,532 | 10,770 | 11,570 |
| Growth of exports (% per annum) | | 4.3 | 4.5 | 3.1 | 6.3 | 5.1 | -4.3 | 1.8 | 1.0 |

*Sources:* 1953–55, Food and Agriculture Organization, *FAO Commodity Review 1966* (Rome, 1966), p. 80; 1956–60, ———, *FAO Commodity Review 1965* (1965), p. 58; 1963–65, ———, *FAO Commodity Review and Outlook 1968–69* (1969), p. 45; 1966–70, ———, *FAO Commodity Review and Outlook 1973–74* (1974), p. 82; 1973–75, ———, *FAO Commodity Review and Outlook 1977–79* (1979), p. 61; 1978–80, ———, *FAO Commodity Review and Outlook 1983–84* (1984), p. 64; 1983–85, ———, *FAO Commodity Review and Outlook 1988–89* (1989), p. 62; 1988–90, ———, *FAO Commodity Review and Outlook 1993–94* (1994), p. 110; 1993–95, *FAO Commodity Market Review 1998–99* (1999), p. 65.

marked decline in the international meat trade in the early 80s and this had not been entirely restored even by the mid-90s. The picture to emerge from the producer's point of view from 1955 onwards is that the whole of the international market, even including the supply of the United Kingdom, was an extremely unstable one. There were a number of reasons for this, but first and foremost was that whenever they experienced a shortage of meat, most major importing countries adopted measures to attract imports, but when beef and other meat surpluses appeared they always tried to protect as much of the home market as possible for their own livestock farmers. These periodic short-term fluctuations in the international demand for all meats made exporters very cautious at times about undertaking long-term investment.

This happened despite the General Agreement on Tariffs and Trade (GATT) signed by 22 countries in 1947 that was designed to promote freer trade and avoid a return to the protectionism of the 1930s. GATT was based on the twin principles of reciprocity in liberalising trade and non-discrimination. These laudable aims were to be achieved by eliminating import quotas and reducing tariffs. Attempts were made at reducing tariffs during the various negotiating 'rounds' that have been conducted in different countries over the years, but progress in this direction has mainly applied to industrial goods. In the early years Britain was concerned lest liberalization adversely affect the special arrangements it had with Commonwealth food exporters. United States liberals were always strongly against imperial preference and had lobbied against Britain retaining any special relationship with its former colonies throughout the war, even though the United States has never been in favour of any international restriction on its power to legislate assistance for its own farmers at any time since. So although substantial progress was made on reducing quotas during the 1950s and 1960s, the effect was limited by escape clauses allowing countries to impose 'temporary' quotas either to reduce balance of payments difficulties or because domestic producers were being injured by imports. The overall weakness of the GATT negotiations was that its freer trade agreements were voluntary: they depended on the principle of reciprocity and there was no mechanism for enforcement. As most other industrial countries after 1945 also had national agricultural policies to help their farmers, the assistance granted under national policies took precedence over any attempts under GATT to bring about freer international trade. As all farm assistance policies always embodied very strong elements of trade protection, and as they were extended from the early 1970s, they were also largely responsible for slowing down the growth of international trade in almost all agricultural products, including meat.

Food importing countries used two main types of measures to discriminate against and restrict imports. Firstly, they separated the foreign producer from the domestic market by placing tariffs, levies and quotas on imports. They would also cushion the effect of market forces on their own producers by price guarantees, subsidies and grants. The first group of measures directly restricted imports, but the second had the effect of raising domestic output above what it would have been if market forces had been left to operate freely. But they both raised home production by making farming more profitable in the importing country than it would have been without discrimination. Table 7.7 below gives a summary of the great variety of non-tariff measures adopted in 1960 or 1961 in 33 countries and covering between 87 and 93 per cent of world imports. In some cases the percentages add up to more than 100 because several countries employed measures that fell into more than one category. The table does not include any tariff measures, and gives no indication of the intensity of protection afforded by the various non-tariff measures. In all cases the measures in the table were aimed at improving domestic producers' incomes, but each country adopted its own particular combination of measures.

**Table 7.7  Percentage of world meat imports, divided according to the various non-tariff measures applied in importing countries in 1960–61**

|  | Quantitative restrictions | Import levies | Deficiency payments | No non-tariff measures |
|---|---|---|---|---|
| Beef and veal | 25 | 2 | 49 | 24 |
| Pig-meat | 28 | 2 | 69 | 3 |
| Mutton and lamb | 2 | – | 93 | 5 |
| Total meat | 21 | 2 | 65 | 13 |

*Source:* Food and Agriculture Organization, *The World Meat Economy* (Rome, 1965), p. 51.

For example, the high percentage of deficiency payments in the table is explained by the large share of the United Kingdom in world meat imports and its heavy reliance on this form of support for its farmers. The deficiency payment was given to farmers when world prices were not enough to allow British farmers a reasonable income. By 1960–61 more or less all aspects of British livestock farming were receiving an impressive list of payments. For the meat producer they included £5.8m of hill cattle and hill sheep subsidies, £17.6m of calf subsidies, £12.3m in price guarantees for fat cattle, £13.9m for fat sheep guarantees, and £20.0m in guarantees for fat pigs.[34] Up until 1963 the United Kingdom maintained an open door policy and low or zero tariffs for most of its meat imports, while at the same time the above deficiency payments maintained relatively high prices for domestic producers but still allowed imports to come in freely and thus keep prices low for consumers. But in May 1963 it announced that home output would have a 'proper share' of future growth in home demand. As a result Argentina and Yugoslavia 'agreed' to keep their beef exports to the United Kingdom within certain limits, and an 'understanding' on bacon was reached with the most important overseas suppliers, limiting their shares of the British market from 1 April 1964. From then on home production had good prospects, and the controls were designed to prevent any major expansion in total meat imports, especially beef.[35]

The deficiency payments made up the difference between the higher costs of domestic producers and the lower world prices. In the short-term, both farmers and consumers gained from the system, but its cost had to be met by the British taxpayer. In the long run, however, had greater dependence been placed on imports, meat price trends would have followed costs of production in the exporting countries and these might well have been lower if overseas producers had been confident of a more rapidly growing market for the products in the United Kingdom and had thus been encouraged to expand production more efficiently.[36] It has also been doubted whether the cattle pig or sheep farmers obtained the full benefit of the subsidy payments as higher meat prices encouraged landlords to extract higher farm rents, and feed, fencing, fertilizer and other suppliers of agricultural goods to raise their prices as well. Not having to pay rent the owner farmer capitalized this benefit, possibly borrowing more to expand his livestock enterprise, but tenant farmers were worst hit. At the end of the day the real cost of higher meat, and other food prices where the same system operated, was borne by British food buyers as taxpayers.

In Western Europe, other governments provided their own combinations of controls on imports and assistance to their livestock industries in the 1950s, even before the Six began to act together once the Treaty of Rome was ratified, and the European Economic Community came into operation from 1 January 1959. In West Germany the 1952 Livestock and Meat Law set up an Import and Storage Agency (ISA) to control imports and operate a stockpiling scheme. When supplies were heavy excess quantities were stored at government expense and released when supplies were reduced. Prices were not supported but the West German livestock farmer gained some protection from fairly high import duties and quantitative controls on the import of meat and livestock. Individual importers were required to sign a contract with the ISA under which it bought and re-sold the meat to the importer, thus allowing it to control the rate at which it was released onto the German market. West German measures were aimed at raising producer's incomes, but France was even more ambitious throughout the 1950s. France's Second Plan for Modernisation and Equipment lasted from 1952 to 1957 and aimed at raising agricultural production by 20 per cent, principally by increased output of livestock products. The Third Plan, which covered the years up to 1961, saw a shift to improving net farm income. Under this it was envisaged that increased production would be necessary to provision growing internal and external markets. Under it the output targets for all meat were raised; beef was set to rise from 955,000 tons in 1956 to 1.3 million tons in 1961, veal from 360,000 to 450,000 tons, mutton and lamb from 110,0000 to 150,000 tons and pig meat from 1,075,000, to 1,200,000 tons. But the plan did not stop at increased production for the home market, as exports in 1961 were estimated to include 125,000 tons of beef and 50,000 tons of pig meat.[37]

The market situation for the traditional meat exporting regions grew worse as the European Community, along with the amount of agricultural protection it extended to its farmers, was enlarged and turned what had formerly been a deficit producing food area into a high-cost surplus producer. In order to encourage its farmers as much as possible the Community used the Common Agricultural Policy (CAP) to actively expand almost all forms of agricultural output. It is argued by some mainland European commentators that there was a basic strategic necessity to stimulate the industry in the aftermath of the war when food was in short supply.[38] But this is unconvincing, as the severe food shortages of the immediate post-war years had been eliminated well before the European Community implemented the policy in 1964. However the CAP had political overtones because agriculture was still economically important, at least as an employer, in much of the community, and the farming lobby remained an effective pressure group. In

1955 France had 25 per cent of its working population in agriculture, Germany had 18.5 per cent and Italy 36.1 per cent.[39] In the 1950s most of the European countryside consisted of tiny peasant farms worked as small and uneconomic family holdings that were only capable of generating low levels of income, but efficient farmers' political organisations in both France and Germany had considerable influence on government policy.[40] On one level the policy talked about encouraging the enlargement and modernisation of farmers by assisting farmers to leave the land and move into higher earning occupations.

This aim was successful and the number of people engaged in agriculture halved in just over twenty years. But further problems arose as the output of the farmers remaining continued to increase and more than compensated for that lost from those that left. As a result, a minority of farm businesses came to account for a major part of farm output. A good example of this is dairy farming; the largest contributor to EC beef output is dairy cattle, and by the 1980s over 60 per cent of dairy animals was owned by the largest 20 per cent of dairy producers.[41] Because CAP assistance was given to all farm output, it preserved the status quo by supporting farm incomes with its combination of levies, quotas and other restrictions on food imports from foreign low-cost producers, and paid a series of subsidies and allowances to high cost European farmers. As a result output rose and European food prices were maintained at levels significantly higher than world prices and often above the level required for equilibrium between supply and demand within the Community. One study carried out in 1988, concluded that, taking the effect of the CAP on world food prices into account, its probable net effect was to raise consumer prices between 5 and 10 per cent overall.[42] As the Community imposed few restrictions on the quantities produced, European agricultural output continued to rise dramatically, increasing, among other things, the demand for agricultural land.[43] In the case of meat the whole policy transformed the EC from a net importer in the 1950s to a net exporter by the 1970s.

The earlier European farm support policies started to take effect from 1958. As they became more comprehensive from the mid-1960s high-cost European agricultural exporters increased their share of world exports, while the exports of the low-cost producing countries remained static or fell. It was a trend that was fully evident by the early 1970s and applied not only to meat but all the main temperate-zone agricultural products, and affected all of the low-cost exporting countries.[44]

As early as the 1960s the agricultural support policies of the EC, and other nations, were causing problems in world markets. Once the broad principles of the CAP were settled in January 1962, all agricultural exporters complained they were bound to affect them adversely. Under the GATT negotiations Cereals and Meat Groups were formed in that year to try and establish practicable ways of creating acceptable conditions of access to world markets for agricultural commodities. The Meat Group concerned itself with better access for Australian, New Zealand and Argentine beef shipments to Europe and Japan. But as the United States was not interested in opening its borders to beef exporters international negotiations on better market access got nowhere, and the work of the Meat Group was suspended early in 1967.[45] The effect of the CAP restrictions was felt most by non-EC members, whereas the removal of tariff barriers among members, which was an integral part of the Treaty of Rome, increased intra-EC trade in all meats. But even this was not achieved without some setbacks, and the first reaction of each member state was to protect its agricultural sector against what it saw as unfair competition from lower cost fellow members. Nevertheless, intra-EC trade in live cattle rose almost seven times between 1961 and 1970, and trade in beef rose threefold. But the imports of live cattle from non-members rose by 28 per cent, and beef imports only doubled.[46]

**Table 7.8 Net imports of beef and veal of selected major importing countries, 1973–76 (thousand tons)[a]**

|  | 1973 | 1974 | 1975 | 1976[b] |
|---|---|---|---|---|
| North America[c] | 937.0 | 776.0 | 852.3 | 933 |
| EC (9 members)[d] | 720.0 | 88.0 | 77.0 | 290 |
| Others[e] | 367.6 | 162.6 | 170.5 | 251 |
| Total of above countries | 2,024.6 | 1,026.6 | 1,099.8 | 1,474 |

[a] In carcase weight, excluding meat equivalent of live animals; [b] Estimate; [c] United States and Canada; [d] France, Germany, Italy, Benelux Countries, United Kingdom, Ireland, and Denmark; [e] Greece, Israel, Japan, Portugal, Spain, Sweden and Switzerland.

*Source:* Food and Agriculture Organization, *Commodity Review and Outlook 1975–76* (Rome, 1976), p. 54.

Throughout these years Europe's levels of demand for meat imports were strongly influenced by the controls imposed on them by the EC. As a result of the shortage of beef and veal within the EC import levies were suspended in 1965, 1966 and 1967. In 1966 there was limited expansion in the world trade in beef and veal, helped by the relaxation of these controls, which normally restricted imports from third countries. To some extent the generally restraining tendencies of EC restrictions were counterbalanced by strong import demand in the EC for frozen meat for manufacturing purposes. As this was mainly a help to countries who exported mostly frozen beef Argentina, who also exported a large amount of high quality chilled beef, got less assistance. But she was helped by the United Kingdom's open market policy, which remained in place in the 1960s and allowed most of the world's meat exporters to increase their sales by diverting their surpluses there. Higher Common Market tariff barriers in 1966 led to a small fall of Argentine exports from 137,100 tons to 133,000 tons to that area, but those to the United Kingdom were 22 per cent higher in 1966.[47]

Towards the end of the 1960s the growth of Argentine beef exports started to slow, partly as a result of increased output in the EC but also because of a set of independently operating production difficulties in Argentina, still the world's largest beef exporter. In 1967, following an outbreak of foot-and-mouth disease (FMD), the United Kingdom introduced a ban on Argentine chilled and frozen beef that lasted to April 1968.[48] In response to high prices record numbers of Argentine cattle were slaughtered in 1969, but this so severely reduced cattle stocks that by 1970 numbers were 3 million down on their level of 1968. Progress in the usual cyclical rebuilding of herd numbers was slowed by drought in 1970, so that in the early 1970s Argentina had serious shortages in the amounts of beef available for export.[49]

Whereas the expansion of beef production in Argentina was largely a matter of increasing the numbers of beef animals, in Europe where it depended much more on dairy herds, declining dairy cow numbers in the late 1960s also held back the growth of EC beef output. In addition, European demand for veal was always high and reduced the calves available for beef production. Shortages of beef actually led the EC countries to suspend their tariffs for part of 1972, but duties were re-imposed in September 1973 following a fall in wholesale beef prices.[50]

Probably the largest disturbance to Argentine meat exports came after the extension of EC membership in 1973, bringing the United Kingdom, Irish Republic, and Denmark into the Community. The entry of Britain meant that the world's greatest open market for food exports would in time be largely closed to outsiders. But even by 1974 the combined effect of EC tariffs, etc. and its increased domestic production was having a serious effect on Europe's imports. The drastic fall in EC imports of beef and veal from 720,000 tons to 77,000 by 1975 can be seen in Table 7.8 above. The virtual closing of the Community market to beef imports by 1975 created major difficulties for a number of countries, particularly Australia and Argentina.[51] In these years the cause was falling producer prices and producer incomes in the EC. These provoked such severe import controls that they caused serious difficulties for producers in the exporting countries. As a result it became necessary for governments in the exporting countries to assist their own producers with a series of special measures. In Argentina and Uruguay domestic prices were strengthened by the removal of constraints on domestic consumption, the reduction of export taxes and rebates on exports of meat and meat products. New Zealand beef producers continued to receive guarantees on prices of exported beef in the 1975–76 marketing season, and emergency carry-on loans were made available to rescue hard-pressed cattlemen in Australia.[52]

The problems in the beef export market of these years were mainly because the current beef production cycles in most of the major producing countries were approaching their peak at the same time. Record cattle inventories, together with continuing high feed costs, weak consumer demand and limited pasture and forage availabilities caused high slaughter rates throughout 1975 and 1976. This was just part of the normal cyclical pattern of all meat production cycles and, apart from its current severity there was little unusual about it. But what was of greater long-term significance was the permanent strengthening of EC beef and other meat surpluses under the CAP. After 1973 total EC beef output rose from 87 per cent to its becoming more or less self-sufficient in beef by 1979, as well as an exporter of pig and poultry meat.[53] The growing EC beef surpluses were also exported, and grew steadily from 0.5 million tons in 1982 and 0.6 million tons in 1983. By then it had become the largest exporter of beef, with its surpluses still growing. Throughout that decade beef output continued to remain above the level of domestic demand and the Community was expected to remain as the world's largest exporter in 1992, with exports of beef and veal of over 1.2 million tons.[54]

This basic instability of the EC as an export market, along with increased levels of import restrictions and rising levels of production within the Community, applied in varying degrees to other meats as well as beef. Throughout the 1960s there was uninterrupted expansion of the world trade in mutton and lamb, but this came to a halt in 1971. Of the three largest exporters, New Zealand, Australia and Argentina, only New Zealand was able to expand its exports in that year. The volume of Argentina's exports at 17,100 tons was only half of what it had been in 1970. A new development affecting world trade in sheep meat in July 1971 was the United Kingdom's introduction of import levies. Freight rates on the New Zealand/United Kingdom route also rose substantially, adding further to the cost of imports. To protect their farmers from losses at this time the New Zealand Meat Producers' Board introduced a scheme to support lamb prices.[55]

By the late 1970s the extent of protection afforded to different types of meat varied. Both beef (and dairying) had high levels of protection from imports and considerable internal support measures as well. But poultry producers had no internal support and the measures available for pig meat were seldom used. For beef imports there were not only permanent customs duties, but also variable levies. The Community set guide prices for its own producers and if world prices were so low that the import prices plus the customs duty was below the guide price, the levy was added to make the price of beef imported from third countries up to, or sometimes above, European prices. If European prices were particularly high, indicating an internal beef shortage as in 1965–67, then the full levy was not imposed and this encouraged imports of cheap beef from third countries by keeping import prices below European prices.[56]

By the late 1970s sheep meat was one of the few commodities for which there was no price or market regime, but this changed in 1980 with the extension of the CAP to cover sheep meat. As with beef, this entailed negotiations with the major suppliers to 'voluntarily' restrict their shipments of this meat into the EC at past levels in return for a reduction in EC import duties from 20 to 10 per cent.[57] There were two overall effects of these changes. The first can be seen from Table 7.6 above as the amount of internationally traded sheep (and goat) meat fell from 1,061,000 tons per annum in 1978–80 to 660,000 tons per annum in 1993–95. The second, assisted by the introduction of EC milk quotas in 1984 and the consequent reduction of dairy herds, was an increase in Western Europe's sheep numbers, as well as the number of sheep farmers.[58] The only new 'exporter' who was aided by this change appears to have been the United Kingdom. Under the new arrangement it became easier for her to send sheep and lamb to France and other parts of the

EC, after the European Court of Justice found that some of France's previous import regulations discriminated against British imports. However the gradual closing of the British market to New Zealand lamb and mutton caused serious difficulties there, as well as raising lamb and mutton prices for the British consumer.

However, it is misleading to see the European Community as the only body distorting the whole international trade in meat after 1955, as almost every country at some time had resort to a similar range of measures aimed at assisting its own farm sector. What has been different is that the EC has spent more on farm support than many other countries. This can be measured by what is called the Producer Subsidy Equivalent (PSE). It can be expressed either as a total money amount spent on agriculture, or as the share of farm income that is accounted for by subsidies. As a percentage of farm income EC policies have been less generous than Japan or Switzerland, but more generous than Australia, New Zealand, and the United States. Throughout the 1980s the EC distributed the largest amount of money to its farmers; in 1990 they received a total of 86.3 US$ bn, whereas the next largest, the United States, paid a total farm support bill of 35.2 US$ bn. It is argued that such large amounts of support have been large enough to distort world food markets.[59] But to these must also be added the other features of the CAP, and the restrictive measures of other nations, such as tariffs and quotas, that directly interfered with world trade flows. Although it is a combination that has affected all farm products, as can be seen from the fluctuations in global trade shown in Tables 7.6 and 7.8 above, meat has been no exception and examples of such interruptions can be found for every important meat exporting and meat consuming country.

The United States beef industry, though different in nature from the EC, faced many of the same problems. Although agriculture made a much lower contribution to GNP, as the country was the largest producer and consumer of beef the beef sector was of major importance, accounting for a fifth of agricultural output in 1985. But unlike the EC where in the 1980s only 20 per cent of cows were in the beef herd and beef output was a direct by-product of the dairy sector, over 75 per cent of cows in the United States were beef herd. It was therefore a matter of concern to United States legislators that this sector was not injured by imports. Aid to American farming went back as far as the 1920s and the Agricultural Adjustment Act of 1933 was the first of a long line of legislation to help support agricultural incomes. Although most of the measures adopted were designed to help cereal farmers, either by the government lending money to farmers against harvested crops and then allowing them to pay off the loan by turning the crop over to the government, or deficiency payments to farmers if the market price of a commodity fell below a guide price set by the government, these measures had repercussions for livestock farmers. When government grain stocks rose too high it would reduce them by releasing them to farmers either to sell or feed to livestock.[60] As the great majority of beef cattle were fed not on grass, but on grain in feedlots, such releases had a direct effect on the availability and price of purchased feed and were of crucial importance to the United States beef industry.

When grain was abundantly available and feed prices were low more animals were retained and fed by livestock farmers, and this would eventually cause beef prices to increase in response to a restricted supply. But when the government had released most of its surplus cereal stocks, feed costs rose to a point when it became more profitable to slaughter more animals, taking advantage of improved cattle prices as well as reducing the outlay on rising feed costs. All of this led to periods of accumulation as the cattle herd was built up, and then liquidation as more cattle were slaughtered and total numbers declined. These movements amounted to production cycles, and the tendency was for them to become shorter, possibly because livestock farmers adopted faster fattening techniques producing earlier maturing animals. The accumulation phase was remarkably constant, lasting between six and eight years, but after 1950 the liquidation phases became shorter, dropping from around ten years to just two or three years. Also the extent of the liquidation in terms of numbers and percentages of the herd fell as well, thus reducing the amplitude of fluctuations in herd size.[61] In addition, there were also measures of more direct relevance to beef. After the war the United States had retained its position of being a meat importer in most years, only exporting meat at times when home production was particularly high. But in 1979 the Meat Import Law was passed and this set quotas on the amount of beef that could be imported in any one year. When domestic production was high quotas were maintained but they were reduced as domestic production fell. In this way beef imports were used as a counter-cyclical stabilising force. In addition countervailing duties could be applied on imports of commodities from any countries if it was felt that they were being excessively subsidised.[62] But although these changes in the import regulations were meant to bring greater stability to the domestic beef market, and appear to have achieved this, they increased market instability for countries exporting to the United States by restricting its demand for imports.

The Meat Import Law was not immediately enforced, but the United States took advantage of its counter-cyclical formula for the first time in 1982 and negotiated 'voluntary' restraint agreements with its major beef suppliers for the first time. Nevertheless imports of beef and slaughter cattle were still slightly higher for that year.[63] In the 1980s EC beef surpluses grew steadily so that in 1984 the Community exported over a million tons of heavily subsidised meat. As this increase exceeded the decrease in exports from Australia, New Zealand, Argentina and Uruguay, the United States again used the Meat Law to reduce import levels.[64] Throughout the rest of the decade EC beef stocks remained high because of sluggish demand in both domestic and overseas markets, heavier slaughter weights, and the extra slaughter of dairy cows that resulted from reductions in milk quotas.[65] EC beef exports remained at over a million tons a year until 1995, falling to 0.9 million in 1998, and the United States also maintained its imports at a steady level of around or a little below a million tons in the 1990s.[66]

One consequence of its traditional policy of protecting its own farmers was to turn the United States into a net exporter of beef (and poultry and pork) once again after 1985. Although a net importer for many of the years between 1945 and then, the United States had in some years been a net exporter, depending on the levels of domestic and foreign demand, and the stages of the production cycles of the various types of meat. But in the 1990s the export trade in beef and other meats was determined partly by international cost differences and partly by international differences in consumer preference. For example, in 1998 the United States was the world second largest exporter beef after Australia. Part of the trade in beef was because the lower labour costs of the large United States packing plants gave it a competitive advantage in processing cattle over Australia. In addition, in some of the Asian markets various parts of an animal were valued more highly than in the United States. In the Far East the internal organs and other offal made up 15 to 20 per cent of the value of a slaughtered steer or hog, but only 5 per cent in the United States. It therefore became profitable to transport only certain parts of carcases to those markets where they earned the highest return, and the United States was ideally suited to exploiting this trade in beef and other meats. But the United States still had a demand for beef and did not turn away imports. Much of Australia and New Zealand's beef was grass-fed, and in 1998 the United States imported $800 million worth of frozen beef from those countries for grinding into hamburgers, while it exported some of its own grain-fed beef to Japan and Korea.[67]

Against its background as a pioneer in technical developments in the meat industry and with extensive feed resources, the use of trade policies by the United States to help its meat producers was perhaps understandable. But it was less so in the case of Japan, a country where there has been a large and increasing demand for beef since 1945, but with only a small meat production industry. As Japan had no great surplus of cheap subsidised cereals that it could easily convert into meat, it had always been a net importer of meat products. But even it made extensive use of farm support and trade restriction policy to assist all branches of agriculture, including its domestic meat producers. A major turning point for the Japanese meat industry was the Agricultural Basic Law of 1961. This was aimed at reducing the farm sector's dependence on rice, which was already highly protected but suffering from overproduction as incomes rose and food preferences changed, by developing the livestock industry. Up to that time Japanese beef output depended largely on traditional Wagyu steers that were originally used mainly for draught purposes and some beef production. These are horned cattle, derived from native Asian cattle and crossed with British and European breeds in the late 1800s. Although the breed was closed to outside bloodlines in 1910, regional isolation produced a number of different lines with varying colour and other characteristics. But as farm mechanisation proceeded in the 1950s and 1960s the number of these cattle fell until 1967, though they recovered thereafter until the mid-1980s. But the biggest increase under the Agricultural Basic Law was in the number of dairy cattle, with the surplus steers fattened on grain in feedlots to provide dairy beef. To maintain and encourage this growth, import quotas were used and the construction of modern capital-intensive feedlots was encouraged by government grants and low interest loans.[68]

As Japan imported almost all its grain, the first oil shock of 1973, accompanied by large increases in grain prices, severely reduced the margins of feedlot owners. Japan responded by temporarily suspending imports on 25 per cent of its import quota of 160,000 tons of beef for 1973–74. Japanese (and EC) import quotas were reduced further and their markets virtually closed in 1974–75 to try and maintain wholesale beef prices, although prices in both Japan and the EC did recover in 1976 and both relaxed the pressure on imports.[69] During this time Japan introduced its Beef Wholesale Price Stabilisation Scheme. This allowed a government body, the Livestock Industry Promotion Corporation (LIPC) to remove stocks from the market to maintain both Wagyu and dairy steer beef prices. The LIPC also determined import quotas and awarded import licences, thus virtually controlling Japanese beef prices and supplies. Under this regime dairy production expanded dramatically, though after 1985 growth slowed and imports once again began to displace domestic production. In 1970 imports were only seven per cent of total supplies, but in 1990 imports, mainly frozen beef from the United States and fresh/chilled beef from Australia, comprised 49 per cent.[70]

Both countries complained the Japanese quota system was unfair, lobbying the Japanese government directly and applying indirect pressure through GATT. As a result there was some liberalisation of the beef import regulations, in progressive stages from 1988 onwards. The logic behind this relaxation of attitude was the Japanese government's cognition that domestic beef production had reached a plateau and was unlikely to expand sufficiently to satisfy forecast increases in demand. But in addition, Japanese investment in overseas beef production increased. By 1991 Japanese investment in United States agriculture was worth $6bn. In the beef industry Japanese corporations purchased cattle ranches in several states and had feedlots and processing plants in California and Washington State. The same occurred in Australia where Mitsubishi, Marubeni, Itoh Ham and Nippon Meat had large shares in farms, feedlots and processing plants in New South Wales and Queensland. As a result, in 1990 Japanese firms accounted for 15 to 20 per cent of US beef exports to Japan and 23 per cent of Australian beef exports. In addition Japanese shipping lines also carried a significant amount of Japan's beef imports.[71] This development was very similar to British and United States firms operating in Australia, New Zealand and South America in the second half of the nineteenth and first half of the twentieth centuries, referred to in earlier chapters. All three countries have at different times accepted that domestic supplies were unlikely to increase in the medium term, and that overseas investment was the only way to increase supply and provide consumers with the product they demand. However, the very fact that such meat is produced abroad, albeit with Japanese capital, may possibly make it vulnerable if ever beef farmers in Japan come under pressure.

Against the basically incompatible objectives of all the nations participating in the international meat market, there were at times attempts to discuss difficulties and possibly arrive at some sort of accommodation between competing interests. But they were, without exception unable to make any more real progress than similar attempts made in the inter-war period. Market instability was considered in intergovernmental consultation on meat under the auspices of the FAO. In 1970 an Ad Hoc Consultation on Meat discussed beef, but was unable to recommend any way of reducing fluctuations in the world beef market. It did, however, suggest an Intergovernmental Group on Meat that met to exchange information about monitoring national marketing and expansion plans, as well as keeping a record of changes in national meat and livestock import regulations.[72] Although this body held periodic meetings, it operated as a source of information rather than a body to bring about reform. Further attempts to dismantle the obstacles and restrictions to world trade in bovine meat and live animals were made by the Tokyo round of GATT negotiations (1973–79). They resulted in the International Arrangement Regarding Bovine Meat that came into force from January 1980. By January 1988 the Arrangement had 27 signatories and included all the major beef exporting and importing nations.[73] Under the Arrangement, an International Meat Council (IMC) was established to provide an international forum on all matters regarding trade in beef and veal. But, like all the other outcomes of the GATT and all the other negotiations mentioned in this section, the IMC was never a major step forward in reforming agricultural policies and trade practices for beef, or any other meat.[74]

For most of the time since 1947, discussions between meat importers and meat exporters foundered whenever importing countries have considered their own meat industries. It has only been after the Uruguay round (1986–94) of negotiations that there seems to have been some change of heart by the agricultural superpowers with some moves towards the reduction of spending on farm assistance. One feature, which affected meat along with a range of other agricultural products, has been the increase in the amounts covered by minimum access agreements that set the physical quantities allowed into world markets before extra restrictions were imposed. From 1986–88 up to the late 1990s this included an extra 186,000 metric tons of beef and veal, an extra 133,000 tons of pig meat, and an extra 94,000 tons of poultry. However, these amounts were not large relative to the total world meat trade. Perhaps the best way to view the concessions is that they had the potential for a possible future freeing up of market access, and the expansion of world trade in meat, if the spirit of the Uruguay round were to be maintained.[75]

## Notes

1 Commonwealth Economic Committee, *Meat: A Summary of Figures of Production, Trade and Consumption* (London, 1948), pp. 2, 23, 37; ———, *Meat* (London, 1950), pp. 2, 22, 36.
2 Ministry of Agriculture and Fisheries Economic Series, *Report on the Committee Appointed to Review the Working of the Agricultural Marketing Acts* (London, 1947), pp. 64–6.
3 Russell, E.J., *World Population and Food Supplies* (London, 1954), pp. 35, 36, 38.

4  Jackson, A.J., *Official History of the National Association of Meat Traders* (Plymouth, 1956), p. 218.

5  Commonwealth Economic Committee, *Meat* (London, 1952), pp. 91–2.

6  Cairncross, A. K., *Years of Recovery: British Economic Policy 1945–51* (London, 1985), pp. 31–2.

7  Fenelon, K.G., *Britain's Food Supplies During the War* (London, 1952), p. 114.

8  Hunt, K.E., 'Notes on the Shortage of Meat in the United Kingdom and on Costs of Overcoming it', *The Farm Economist*, 6 (1949): 84–5.

9  Hammond, R.J., *Food and Agriculture in Great Britain: Aspects of Wartime Control*, (Stanford, 1954), p. 125.

10  *The Economist* (14 July 1951), p. 79.

11  *The Economist* (22 Sept. 1951), p. 670.

12  Imperial Economic Committee, *Meat: A Summary of Figures of Production and Trade* (London, 1938), p. 29; G. Harrison, *Borthwicks: A Century in the Meat Trade, 1863–1963* (London, 1963), p. 123.

13  *The Economist* (22 Mar. 1952), p. 738.

14  Lewis, C., 'Anglo–Argentine Trade, 1945–1965', in D. Rock (ed.), *Argentina in the Twentieth Century* (London, 1975), pp. 121–2.

15  Ibid., pp. 122–3.

16  Fodor, J., 'Perón's Policies for Agricultural Exports 1946–48: Dogma or Commonsense?' in D. Rock, *Argentina in the Twentieth Century* (London, 1975), pp. 155–6.

17  Crassweller, R.D., *Perón and the Enigmas of Argentina* (New York, 1987), pp. 217–19.

18  Díaz Alejandro, C.F., *Essays on the Economic History of the Argentine Republic* (New Haven, 1970), p. 172.

19  Wright, W.R., *British-Owned Railways in Argentina: Their Effect on Economic Nationalism 1854–1948* (Austin, 1974), p. 246.

20  Cairncross, *Years of Recovery*, pp. 186–8.

21  Commonwealth Economic Committee, *Meat: A Summary of Figures of Production, Trade and Consumption* (London, 1952), pp. 7–8; ———, *Meat* (London, 1955), pp. 16, 18, 22.

22  *New Zealand Journal of Agriculture*, 77(6) (15 Dec. 1948): 548.

23  *New Zealand Journal of Agriculture*, 77(5) (15 Nov. 1948): 517.

24  Commonwealth Economic Committee, *Meat* (London, 1952), p. 76.

25  *The Economist* (22 Mar. 1952), pp. 736, 738.

26  Commonwealth Economic Committee, *Meat* (London, 1960), p. 91.

27  Pollard, S., *The Development of the British Economy 1914–90* (London, 1992), pp. 232–3.

28  Commonwealth Economic Committee, *Meat* (London, 1955), pp. 1–2, 9, 10.

29  Food and Agriculture Organization, *The World Meat Economy* (Rome, 1965), pp. 1–2.

30  Reeves, G.W. and A.H. Hayman, 'Demand and Supply Forces in the World Beef Market', *Quarterly Review of Agricultural Economics*, 18(3) (1975): 130, 134.

31  Food and Agriculture Organization, *The World Meat Economy*, p. 15.

32  Grunwald, J. and P. Musgrove, *Natural Resources in Latin American Development* (Baltimore, 1970), pp. 422, 427.

33  Commonwealth Secretariat, *Meat: A Review of Figures of Production, Trade and Consumption* (London, 1973), pp. 18–19.

34  Commonwealth Economic Committee, *Meat* (London, 1965), pp. 109–18.

35  Food and Agriculture Organization, *Trade in Agricultural Commodities in the United Nations Development Decade* (Part 1, Rome, 1964), p. 18.

36  Food and Agriculture Organization *The World Meat Economy*, p. 49.

37  Commonwealth Economic Committee, *Meat* (London, 1960), pp. 106–10.

38  Lintner, V., 'The European Community 1958 to the 1990s', in M. Schultz (ed.) *Western Europe: Economic and Social Change Since 1945* (London, 1998), pp. 146–8.

39  Knox, F., *The Common Market and World Agriculture: Trade-Patterns in Temperate Zone Foodstuffs* (New York, 1972), p. 130.

40  Atkin, M., *Snouts in the Trough: European Farmers, the Common Agricultural Policy and the Public Purse* (Abington, 1993), pp. 49–53.

41  Wagstaff, H., 'EEC Food Surpluses: Controlling Production by Two–Tier Prices, *National Westminster Bank Quarterly Review* (Nov. 1982): 30–31.

42  National Consumer Council, *Consumers and the Common Agricultural Policy* (London, 1988): 43–4, 147.

43  Martin, J., *The Development of Modern Agriculture: British Farming since 1931* (Basingstoke, 2000), pp. 150–57.

44  Knox, p. 125.

45  Josling, T.E., Tangerman, S. and Warley, T.K., *Agriculture in the GATT* (Basingstoke, 1996), pp. 41, 56, 69.

46  Knox, p. 38.

47  Commonwealth Economic Committee, *Meat* (London, 1967), p. 45.

48  Food and Agriculture Organization, *Commodity Review and Outlook* (Rome, 1968–69), p. 44.

49  Commonwealth Secretariat, *Meat: A Summary of Figures of Production, Trade and Consumption* (London, 1973), p. 16.

50  Ibid., pp. 19–20.

51  Allen, G., 'Agricultural Policies in the Shadow of Malthus', *Lloyds Bank Review*, 117 (July 1975): 28.

52  Food and Agriculture Organization, *Commodity Review and Outlook* (Rome, 1974–75), p. 97.

53  Meat and Livestock Commission, *MLC International Market Survey 2* (Bletchley, 1979), p. 7; Wagstaff, 'EEC Food Surpluses': 31.

54  Food and Agriculture Organization, *Commodity Review and Outlook* (Rome, 1984–85) pp. 74, 75; ———, *Commodity Review and Outlook* (Rome, 1988–89), p. 63; ———, *Commodity Review and Outlook* (Rome, 1992–93), p. 98.

55  ———, *Commodity Review and Outlook* (Rome, 1971–72), p. 64.

56  Fennell, R., *The Common Agricultural Policy of the Agricultural Community: Its Institutional and Administrative Organization* (London, 1979), pp. 136, 141–5.

57  Food and Agriculture Organization, *Commodity Review and Outlook* (Rome, 1984–85), p. 58.

58  Meat and Livestock Commission, *Meat Market Review, 9*, (Bletchley, June 1991), p. 5.

59  Atkin, pp. 152–3.

60  Meat and Livestock Commission, *International Market Review 3* (Bletchley, 1986), pp. 2–3, 6.

61  McCoy, J.H., *Livestock and Meat Marketing* (Westport, 1972), pp. 61–3.

62  Meat and Livestock Commission, *International Market Review, 3* (Bletchley, 1986), p. 4.

63 Food and Agriculture Organization, *Commodity Review and Outlook* (Rome, 1982–83), p. 69.
64 ———, *Commodity Review and Outlook* (Rome, 1984–85), p. 74.
65 ———, *Commodity Review and Outlook* (Rome, 1988–89), p. 61.
66 ———, *Commodity Review and Outlook* (Rome, 1996–97), pp. 62, 63; ———, *Commodity Review and Outlook* (Rome, 1988–89), pp. 65, 66.
67 Dyck, J and K. Nelson, 'World Meat Trade Shaped by Regional Preferences and Reduced Barriers', *Agricultural Outlook* (Mar. 2000): 7–10.
68 Meat and Livestock Commission, *International Meat Market Review 10* (Bletchley, 1991), pp. 2–3.
69 Food and Agriculture Organization, *Commodity Review and Outlook* (Rome, 1973–74), p. 91; ———, *Commodity Review and Outlook* (Rome, 1974–75), p. 98; ———, *Commodity Review and Outlook* (Rome, 1975–76), p. 59; Reeves and Hayman, 'Demand and Supply Forces in the World Beef Market': 136.
70 Meat and Livestock Commission, *International Meat Market Review 10* (Bletchley, 1991), pp. 3–4.
71 Ibid., p. 5.
72 Food and Agriculture Organization, *Commodity Review and Outlook* (Rome, 1973–74), pp. 93–4.
73 General Agreement on Tariffs and Trade, *The International Markets for Meat, 1987/88*, (Geneva, 1988), p. 1.
74 Josling, Tangerman and Warley, pp. 92–3, 97.
75 Ibid., pp. 188–90.

# Chapter 8

# Tastes and Incomes

An important feature of the post-1945 era has been relative changes in the consumption of different types of meat. Up until the 1940s any increase in Western meat consumption was seen very much in terms of eating more red meat, but after the war patterns of consumption started to shift as more poultry was consumed. This did not mean that there was a decline in the absolute amount of red meat produced and consumed, but for a number of reasons the poultry sector of the industry now grew at a much faster rate in the second half of the twentieth century than at any time before. The changes in meat tastes were also accompanied by radical changes in the structure of the meat processing and retailing sector itself. Up to 1945 the small firm had a much stronger position within the retailing section of the industry. But after then the large concern took a stronger hold on the retailing of meat and meat products, partly assisted in this process by the changes in taste.

## Meat Substitutes – Vegetarianism

Although it never had a serious impact on overall consumption there was a growing interest in meat substitutes during the nineteenth and first half of the twentieth century. Most of the interest in meat substitutes prior to 1950 came from two groups of people:

- firstly, those who were searching for alternatives to meat protein for ethical reasons, particularly vegetarian groups;
- and secondly, from those who were regular meat-eaters, but were confronted by shortages, particularly during the two World Wars.

At various times, dating back at least to the ancient Greeks, there have been Western philosophers and thinkers who have advocated a non-meat diet, but the numbers who have been persuaded to follow such a course has always been too few to offer a serious alternative to the diet of the majority. The arguments in favour of a non-meat diet have ranged from those who adopt a moral and ethical stance, respecting all forms of life, to those who see non-meat eating as less destructive to the natural world, and others who have advocated it as a healthier diet. Often the justification for a vegetarian lifestyle has been mixed, sometimes with elements of religious ritual expressed by some adherents, whereas other vegetarians have followed a secular way of life.[1] Atkins and Bowler have also pointed out that vegetarianism is an umbrella term for a wide range of food practices. Some who see themselves as vegetarians do not eat red meat, but do occasionally eat other sorts of meat – usually poultry or fish. But there are also far more strict vegetarians who consume and use no animal products at all. In this group are the vegans, who eat no dairy products and wear no items of clothing or footwear made of leather, as all of these products involve some degree of animal exploitation.[2]

It is significant that modern vegetarianism really started its development in the mid-nineteenth century at more or less the same time as the modern capitalist meat industry began its rapid growth and meat was generally regarded as an essential item of diet. The first European vegetarians developed from an English nonconformist working-class Christian sect that preached temperance in food and drink to its followers. The ironically named Reverend William Cowherd (1763–1816) who in 1809 established the Bible Christian Church in Salford, urged his congregation to abstain from meat as well as alcohol. In the middle of the nineteenth century members of this sect gained positions of civic power as well as a parliamentary platform when Cowherd's successor in 1816, Joseph Brotherton (1817–57) became the first Member of Parliament for Salford after the Reform Act of 1832. From these beginnings the modern vegetarian movement began when the Vegetarian Society was founded in 1847, chaired by Brotherton.[3]

In the first half of the nineteenth century Brotherton and his Nonconformist circle of friends and family members took over the reins of local power in Salford. Among this group were William Harvey (1787–1870), Mayor of Salford and president of the Vegetarian Society, his sister Martha (1783–1861) who married Brotherton and wrote the first vegetarian cookery book, and James Simpson (1812–59), Harvey's son-in-law, who was the Society's first President. Brotherton as a Liberal, free trade and reform-minded MP, had strong links between his religious vegetarian views and his political philosophy. He was a pacifist who respected all forms of life, and gave the first House of Commons speech against capital punishment. In addition to the reverence for life argument, Brotherton's group also claimed a vegetarian diet was the best way to promote health and prolong life. From the Northwest of England, Bible Christian emigrants spread the vegetarian message across the Atlantic to the United States. The first American Vegetarian Convention was held in New York in 1850, and the following year the Vegetarian Society of America was established, with strong personal links between the American and British societies.[4]

In the United States the vegetarian movement, as in Britain, became linked with other reformist movements that rejected parts of the lifestyles of nineteenth century industrial society. Among these the various branches of the health reform lobby were prominent, and the blossoming medical sciences of nutrition and bacteriology were called in to support the other arguments against eating meat. While some of these have been ultimately rejected as quackery, elements of some of them are currently accepted by modern medicine. This was the case with the brothers John Harvey Kellogg and Will Kellogg, who built a vegetarian health sanatorium at the family's home of Battle Creek in Michigan in the 1880s. They quickly turned it into a thriving business, producing an assortment of cereal-based meat substitutes for the patients that also developed into a thriving business and has preserved the family name in the range of breakfast cereals named after them. John Harvey Kellogg, who was trained as a doctor, wrote a number of books on the subject of diet and health that attacked the high protein diet of flesh eaters and played on the fear that undigested protein could produce toxic compounds that were absorbed into the human bloodstream and cause 'autointoxication'. In addition, he embarked on extensive lecturing tours extolling the low protein and high fibre content of the purely vegetarian diet. Presumably hoping that the latter would also contain a high proportion of the family's products, to provide beneficial bowel stimulation! But the family was also able to use negative publicity against the meat companies to further their dietary and commercial crusade. In one of his books, appearing a year before Upton Sinclair's *The Jungle*, Kellogg regaled his readers with nauseating descriptions of the Augean nastiness of the typical abattoir, with meat infested with every known harmful micro-organism.[5]

Neither of these societies made any notable impact on the diets of the overwhelming majority of their countrymen. The London Food Reform Society was formed in 1877 and merged with the Vegetarian society in 1885, only to break away again in 1888 to form the London Vegetarian Society as a rival national organisation in 1888. There was some increase in the number of commercial outlets that marketed vegetarianism in Britain in the 1880s, and the first vegetarian restaurant opened in Manchester in 1885. But by 1914, *The Times* observed that: 'The vegetarian movement makes very slow progress, but has had some useful side results.' Some Soho restaurants did now provide an alternative course of a special vegetable dish, or of chicken and salad. But general returns of food sales demonstrated the whole subject was noted vastly more in the press than in the home. In fact, the general effect of the Vegetarian Society's pamphlets and meetings on national food demand was scarcely perceptible. One area where the vegetarians had failed to tempt the general public was in the sale and preparation of new and palatable vegetables. Martha Brotherton's book had done little to tempt people in this direction. Main courses consisted of savoury pies, bread and parsley fritters, mushroom pies and rice fritters. Deserts were mainly moulded milk-based preparations such as ground rice, sage blancmange or cheesecakes.[6]

Nineteenth century vegetarianism never had much of a general popular appeal. At the first annual general meeting of the society in Manchester, the membership was only 476, and the failure of the Manchester group to combine with the London Vegetarian Society in the 1880s must have reduced the effectiveness of both in any national campaigning. The London society was in favour of becoming a vigorous national reforming society but Manchester wanted it to just be a branch of the older Manchester society. Even the adherence in the early twentieth century of certain minor members of the great and the good, such as George Bernard Shaw, to the general principles of vegetarianism did little to wean the general public from their fondness for the traditional meat dishes. For the most part vegetarianism continued to have a rather ascetic middle-class image throughout the late nineteenth and first half of the twentieth centuries. Mahatma Gandhi joined the London society but George Bernard Shaw was a member of the original Manchester one. Other moderately well known vegetarians included Bramwell Booth of the Salvation Army, the birth control campaigner and member of the Theosophical Society Annie Besant, the antivivisectionist and women's rights campaigner Anna Kingsford, and the novelist Count Leo Tolstoy.[7]

It was plainly impossible for a movement whose membership numbers were dwarfed by the number of meat retailers to have a measurable effect on meat consumption. According to the 1911 census there were 135,000 persons in England and Wales working as butchers and meat salesmen and over 155,000 in the whole of the United Kingdom, whereas *The Vegetarian News*, the newspaper of the London society had a circulation of 4,500. Both the London and Manchester societies were somewhat coy about publishing membership figures but it is doubtful if at the beginning of the twentieth century both together could have amounted to more than a few thousand.

Meat substitution for regular meat eaters during the World Wars was seen initially in terms of substituting alternative sources of either fish or animal protein. For example, in 1918 a correspondent wrote to the American magazine *The Outlook* complaining that even these were in short supply:[8]

> Great pressure is being put upon the country to save food. There is restriction in the use of meat. We are urged to eat fish. But a little investigation will, I believe, convince you that fish and also poultry, are inexcusably and unreasonably high in price and not by any means reasonably abundant in supply.

At first sight the expansion of sea fishing seemed an attractive proposition as it did not place any strain on scarce supplies of feeding stuffs, but in wartime there are other constraints on increasing the amount of fish landed. There was little prospect of expanding the fishing fleet as shipyards were converted to war production, and in the United States and Britain existing fishing vessels were taken over in both wars by the military authorities for war work. When this happened they were usually converted to minesweeping and other coastal protection duties. Fishing crews were also reduced when men either volunteered for, or were drafted into, the navy. There were even shortages of materials necessary for the manufacture and repair of nets as the army and navy took control of increasing supplies of yarn and thread. Attempts to increase poultry numbers ran up against the same shortages of feeding stuffs that were one of the major constraints on red meat supplies. In Britain shortages of feeding stuffs became particularly severe in the First World War and purchased feeding stuffs in 1917 and 1918 were 32 per cent and 61 per cent below their level in 1909–13.[9] In the United States the heavy slaughter of poultry early in 1918 placed pressure on egg supplies and led the

Federal Food Administration to place rigid controls on the sale of hens during the hatching season.[10]

During the rationing in the Second World War the dietary alternatives for non-meat eaters were again seen in terms of fish, poultry and dairy products. In Britain those who registered as vegetarians were allocated extra rations of cheese. The size of the meat ration was so small that this inevitably caused an increase in those who registered to claim vegetarian status, in the hope of obtaining extra cheese, which aroused complaints from lifelong vegetarians. But the overall shortage of meat meant an increasing amount of non-meat meals were also eaten by the general meat-eating public. The government's 'Dig for Victory' campaign encouraged everyone to grow vegetables as much as possible, and as a result more vegetarian meals were eaten but this was out of necessity and not by choice. By 1944 the British Restaurants, run by the government and started during the Blitz to feed the homeless, were serving half a million meals a day, many of them employing vegetarian recipes.[11] Much of the enforced dietary switch put pressure on the limited amount of high-calorie meat substitutes – principally cheese and nuts – used by vegetarians and they were so concerned to protect their position and argue their case that a Committee of Vegetarian Interests with representatives from the two vegetarian societies, health food retailers and manufacturers was formed to negotiate with the Ministry of Food. As rationing continued after the war, the committee continued to represent both the individual vegetarian and the commercial manufacturers of vegetarian products. In 1969 the two British societies decided to amalgamate and become the Vegetarian Society of the United Kingdom.

Since 1945 their numbers both in Britain and the United States have certainly increased. By 1985 the Vegetarian Society was claiming there were more than a million vegetarians in Britain, although Keith Roberts, the Chairman of the Meat and Livestock Commission, strongly denied that there had been any public swing towards vegetarianism.[12] But all the evidence since seems to support the case for an increase, although the extent is still uncertain. In 1989 the Vegetarian Society was claiming there were one and a half million complete vegetarians who ate no meat, poultry or fish, plus a further four million 'semi-vegetarians' who were avoiding red meat only, mainly because of red meat food scares.[13] By 1997 the numbers of complete vegetarians had risen to an estimated 3 million, or 5.4 per cent of the population, whilst almost a further 8 million, or 14.3 per cent of the population claimed to eat no red meat.[14] Although these are only estimates based on market surveys conducted by Realeat, creators of the 'vegeburger' in 1983, the case for an increase in non-meat and restricted meat-eaters is also supported by the increase in the number and variety of non-meat products becoming available.[15] But absolute numbers were not the whole story; the continued existence of the movement did mean that throughout the twentieth century there has always been a group challenging and publicising the dietary alternatives to the consumption of all types of meat.

The forces behind their publicity were an increased emphasis on 'healthy eating', a growing movement that protested about animal cruelty associated with post-war factory farming, various meat scares associated with fears about disease, and a long-term shift in the preferences of some consumers, away from red meat and towards an increased consumption of poultry. Twentieth-century medicine also became more sympathetic to certain aspects of the vegetarian diet. The consumption of fibre has been recognised as an essential dietary component as high fibre diets have been linked with a lower incidences of various diseases of 'modern living' such as colon cancer, gallstones, and obesity. Medical studies have linked the cholesterol and saturated fats present in meat with cardiovascular disease, and studies of the disease in some vegetarian groups have tended to show a somewhat lower incidence. The Vegetarian Society had always been ready to use medical and other reports to support its message. Over 150 years it built up a reputation for confrontational campaigning, with a number of peaceful and not so peaceful demonstrations against the butchery business. But sometimes it has been rebuked for making exaggerated and unfair claims. A campaign in 1996, with a poster showing the rear end of a bull with the copy line 'if you eat hamburgers here are a couple of quarter-pounders you will be familiar with' was described by the Advertising Standards Authority as 'provocative'. And a year later the Authority again warned the Society about the accuracy of its claims, as well as causing needless distress, in a national press campaign that exaggerated the connection between red meat and cancer.[16]

While there has been a strong public debate over the human welfare benefits of vegetarianism as an alternative to meat eating, there has been less doubt about the effects of modern farming methods on animal welfare. Numerous exposés of the excesses of factory farming with its reported examples of animal cruelty, including calves kept in crates in darkness to produce white veal and intensively fed chickens confined in tiny spaces for their short unpleasant lives, have made it easy to represent vegetarianism as the ethical alternative. Further disillusionment with agribusiness was also linked to a growing emphasis on animal rights and concerns for the environment.[17]

## Meat Substitutes – Simulated Meats

Although the traditional vegetarian diet had substituted various preparations for meat, and sometimes even given them names that mimic meat products such as 'nut cutlets' and 'cheese and vegetable pies', the attempt to substitute animal products never went much further than this before 1945. The vegetarian movement was an alternative to meat eating, not as an attempt to produce non-animal products that looked and tasted like meat. But after 1960 commercial food technologists paid more attention to producing products that closely mimicked meat in terms of texture and taste.

The most popular, and probably the best, raw material for meat substitutes is the soya bean. Containing 38 per cent protein and 18 per cent oils and fats, it is one of the richest of vegetables. It was originally a plant of the Far East where it was eaten as pastes and curds and fermented sauces. After the 1920s it was grown extensively in the United States, initially mostly for livestock feed, but later as a vegetable oil and additive to margarines and other manufactured foods. In addition it was used in industry.[18] Its high protein content provided an ideal base material for spinning into threads and then adding flavouring and colouring materials to simulate a meat structure. The initial development of this industry was in the United States and Japan. Isolated soya protein was used in the United States food industry as early as 1936, but high quality grades for food use were unavailable before the 1960s.[19] In Japan the growing popularity of meat, particularly beef, meant there was a ready market for meat substitutes, but in the United States the ready availability of large amounts of cheap raw material also stimulated the development of this industry. Other sources of protein have also been used in this branch of food manufacture. In Japan the protein from wheat has been commercially extracted to produce simulated meats. An alternative to soya and wheat, which was developed from the 1960s, was the biochemical synthesis of protein by a fermentation process, where the most popular technique involved the use of yeast.[20]

Once the protein was obtained a variety of different techniques were developed to impart the required tastes and textures. In some cases meat essences were added to give it the flavour of beef, pork, or chicken. In these cases the use of animal extracts would exclude its use by strict vegetarians, but not by some of those simply requiring a healthier alternative to meat. The final simulated product can take a wide variety of forms. Sometimes it is ready cooked (or smoked) by the manufacturer for direct consumption, but it can also be produced in a number of forms that leave the final preparation for eating to the customer. It can be comminuted (or ground) into products resembling hamburgers or sausages, sometimes it is available in pieces that can be put into stews, pies and soups, and it has even been fabricated into products resembling complete cuts of meats. In all these cases it is an entire substitute for animal meat, but it can also be used as an 'extender' when mixed with natural meat in processed food products.

In terms of market share it has always been a very small competitor with animal meat. One estimate of simulated meat production in the United States in 1969 was 250 million lb, but this was insignificant compared with a natural meat (beef, veal, mutton, lamb, pigs and poultry) consumption figure of 45,000 million lb. In Japan and Europe consumption of simulated meats at this time was also very small.[21] Although they offer the advantages of controlled physical and nutritional characteristics, freedom from skin and bone and other possible wastes, as well as the cost-reducing advantages of no meat inspection, they have only had a negligible impact on the demand for animal meat. A measure that pushed forward consumption in the United States was the decision in 1971 of USDA to allow the use of 'textured vegetable protein' in the national school lunch programme. This permitted meat patties, stews and sauces, etc. to contain up to 30 per cent of soya protein; as at that time 'red meat' cost over a dollar a pound and soya protein cost less than 20 cents a pound the cost saving was significant.[22]

International interest by the 1970s was such that in 1973 more than 1,100 delegates from 46 countries attended the first World Soya Protein Conference in Munich, Germany. The United States Secretary of Agriculture estimated that by 1980 vegetable protein would account for 8 per cent of his country's total 'red meat' production, and some delegates predicted privately that this might be as high as 20 per cent of all 'meat' supply.[23] In spite of this early optimism and the stress laid on soya protein's freedom from cholesterol and animal fat, as well as the efforts of the food technologists to copy the taste and texture of animal meats, the product has had limited appeal and popularity. And although retail sales have not been entirely confined to health shops, simulated meats have failed miserably in any attempt to use them to directly compete with traditional fresh meats.[24] The product's impact has, however, been greater in the hotel and the catering industries, where its use has been more widespread, although even here it has often been as an additive to animal meat dishes. Its use as a meat 'extender' also makes it difficult to estimate the amounts consumed in relation to all animal meats.

**The Taste for Red Meats**

In the nineteenth century beef was seen on both sides of the Atlantic as the leading meat in consumer demand. Over the period as a whole the increased per capita consumption of all meats was an important function of the rise in personal income levels. The strength and profitableness of the meat industry was very often measured by its relative price and, as the most expensive to produce and the most desirable to consume, beef was always the price leader. In times of depression, with low wages and high unemployment, people would turn to cheaper mutton and pig meat that is if they were still able to afford meat at all – but beef was still the first preference among Western consumers. By the 1970s beef consumption had come to symbolize the good life throughout the western world. In the United States steak had become to meat what Cadillac was to cars.[25] In Europe and the United Kingdom the contrast with the enforced austerity of meat rationing in the wartime and immediate post-war years was particularly sharp. In the United States annual per-capita consumption peaked in the mid-1970s, but declined thereafter.[26] Prior to that time, writers on the industry viewed future changes in the demand for beef purely in terms of its traditional determining factors, such as fluctuations in personal income levels, changes in production costs, farmers' responses to the state of the cattle cycle and possible alterations in trade policies.[27] There was certainly no suggestion that producers might have to face a serious long-term fall in consumer demand for this meat.

When it did occur, the decline in beef consumption occurred at about the same time in all developed countries, and at some time in the 1970s. It can be seen from Table 8.1 below that its exact timing and extent varied. In this table the per capita estimates of supplies of bovine meat for the United States, United Kingdom, the 12 countries that made up the European Union from 1986, Australia, New

Zealand and Argentina have been used as proxies for their beef consumption per head. The five-yearly averages have been used to iron out some of the extreme annual fluctuations seen in some of these countries, particularly Australia and New Zealand. A peak in beef consumption occurred first in the United Kingdom in 1963, but its experience was unusual. For the rest their peaks were in the second half of the 1970s, with New Zealand in 1976, the United States in 1976 and 1977, Australia in 1978 and the twelve countries of the EU in 1978 and 1979 although they also included the United Kingdom.

**Table 8.1  Per capita beef consumption of developed countries, 1961–2000 (kilos)**

|           | United States | United Kingdom | European Union (12) | Australia | New Zealand | Argentina |
|-----------|------|------|------|------|------|------|
| 1961–65   | 44.1 | 25.0 | 19.9 | 49.8 | 49.4 | 77.7 |
| 1966–70   | 50.4 | 24.2 | 22.2 | 46.4 | 53.7 | 82.3 |
| 1971–75   | 52.3 | 24.0 | 23.0 | 50.8 | 51.5 | 68.4 |
| 1976–80   | 52.9 | 23.7 | 23.4 | 70.8 | 66.1 | 86.1 |
| 1981–85   | 48.0 | 22.0 | 22.8 | 50.9 | 48.5 | 75.3 |
| 1986–90   | 46.1 | 22.0 | 23.0 | 46.2 | 43.2 | 68.4 |
| 1991–95   | 42.8 | 18.7 | 21.0 | 43.1 | 34.0 | 62.9 |
| 1996–2000 | 43.4 | 16.5 | 19.3 | 39.8 | 31.4 | 57.2 |

*Source:* FAOSTAT August 2004

Table 8.1 demonstrates that the greatest decline in beef's popularity was in English-settled countries, where New Zealand and Australia's per capita consumption fell by 53 and 44 per cent, respectively. The next largest fall was in the United Kingdom with a drop of 34 per cent, followed by the United States and Europe with 19 and 18 per cent, respectively. Although not shown in Table 8.1, a decline in Canada's beef consumption of approximately 30 per cent also took place over roughly the same time period.[28] Even in Argentina, where the volatile weather and economic fluctuations caused strong short-term fluctuations in stocking and slaughtering figures, people were eating less beef by the 1990s than forty years earlier. By the 1990s their average consumption was some 25 per cent less than what Argentines had been eating in the 1960s. But as beef is the most readily available of all meats in Argentina, consumers were still eating almost half as much again as in the United States and three times as much as in Europe.

A number of reasons have been put forward to explain the long-term fall in per capita consumption, as it represents an extremely important change in the industry. Before the 1970s, any decline in per capita beef consumption was caused either by a fall in income levels, something usually experienced in recessions, or else caused by the very obvious constraints on supply experienced in time of war. But in the 1970s there were no restrictions on supply caused by global warfare, and although that decade did experience recession it did not herald in any long-term decline in income levels – in fact the reverse has been the case as living standards in the developed world have risen over the last thirty years. But beef consumption levels of the mid-1970s can be seen as unusually high for a number of reasons. Increases in beef output in Europe had been encouraged in the 1960s because cattle prices had increased relative to those of grain and other meat producing animals, thus encouraging farmers to intensify cattle feeding. In addition European levels of meat consumption had been low in the 1950s and income increases in the 1960s raised the demand for beef.[29] The increase in output slowed in the late 1970s, after the general setback to production due to the worldwide recession caused by the 1973 rise in oil prices and remained at low levels in the 1980s.[30] The rise in oil prices also raised the price of fertilizers and higher fertilizer costs fed back into grain prices and pushed up the price of grain-fed beef in America and Europe. Increased beef prices and lower incomes did cause some consumers to have second thoughts and look for cheaper alternatives.[31] There was a similar pattern of events in other Western countries, although in all cases the precise timings and the extent of the slowdown in production were influenced by local conditions, such as the state of a country's cattle production cycle.

But in all Western countries the failure of beef consumption to keep pace with the increase in population has been associated with two factors that have both had a long-term influence: the rise in poultry consumption and health scares. The increase in poultry consumption pre-dates much of the anxiety about beef on health grounds. Before 1940 poultry meat was regarded as a luxury and only eaten by most families on special occasions such as Christmas and sometimes Easter in Britain and Europe, and Christmas and Thanksgiving in the United States. Wartime beef and other red meat rationing did something to raise the consumption of poultry, whenever it was available. But it was from the 1950s onwards that large-scale broiler farms reduced poultry prices significantly, so that it became a strong competitor with beef, pork and sheep meat. The high rates of growth in world output from 1970 onwards are shown in table 7.5 above, when poultry output grew faster than any other meat. Boosted by low feed grain prices, increased demand, and the emergence of well-integrated industry in a number of countries world output rose by about 30 per cent in the 1980s. By far the largest producer was the United States with around 30 per cent of world output, followed by the EU with a 20 per cent share of world production.[32]

Growth continued into the 1990s and the United States remained the world's largest producer with around 30 per cent of output. The position of Europe slipped from second place to third, as it was overhauled by China. Output growth in all countries was explained by poultry meat's widespread consumer appeal, and the increasingly efficient (capitalist) production systems that continued to take advantage of low feed costs (essentially maize and soya) to lower the real cost of the final output. Although there were wide differences in per capita consumption, the United States retained its premier position, but Argentina and Brazil increased both output and consumption. Brazil became the world's fourth largest producer, and Argentina's increase in consumption was mainly at the expense of beef.[33] As in all other developed nations the Argentine diet became more varied, and the population more health conscious, as fears about red meat became a global anxiety. Even in the 1980s a salad bar had been an unusual eating place in Buenos Aires, but by the 1990s they had become much more popular, and by 2000 even such exotic establishments as sushi bars had become the latest thing.[34]

But although the per capita consumption of beef did not increase in the developed countries, the continued rise in population meant that overall consumption in these markets never declined to anything like the same extent. After failing to increase between 1975 and 1984, world beef output resumed its growth in the second half of the 1980s and in the 1990s (see Table 7.5 above). This growth was also assisted by increased beef production in the countries of Asia, and in other minor producers.

The other red meat that faced strong sales problems and declining per capita consumption was mutton and lamb. This was never as popular as beef and the major market since the nineteenth century had always been the United Kingdom. The main suppliers, as we have seen in Chapters 2 and 3 above, were New Zealand followed by South America and Australia. While this meat with its high fat content shared some of the long-term health scares associated with beef, its strong taste and the comparatively small size of its joints and cuts making preparation time-consuming may also have helped account for its decline in popularity.

**Table 8.2 Per capita mutton and lamb consumption of developed countries, 1961–2000 (kilos)**

|  | Australia | New Zealand | United Kingdom | European Union (12) |
|---|---|---|---|---|
| 1966–70 | 38.4 | 39.4 | 10.6 | 3.5 |
| 1971–75 | 33.8 | 40.6 | 8.9 | 3.4 |
| 1976–80 | 19.4 | 32.2 | 7.3 | 3.3 |
| 1981–85 | 21.5 | 27.9 | 7.2 | 3.6 |
| 1986–90 | 22.8 | 33.0 | 7.0 | 3.8 |
| 1991–95 | 20.4 | 32.3 | 6.9 | 3.9 |
| 1996–2000 | 16.7 | 28.7 | 6.7 | 3.7 |

*Source:* FAOSTAT August 2004

Table 8.2 shows the declining per capita consumption of sheep meat in its three major markets, and the EU 12 (the consumption of goat meat in all of these was negligible). The overall trend for the United Kingdom was downwards after 1965, with consumption stabilising at around 7 kilos per head from about 1976, its lowest level for at least forty years.[35] But mutton and lamb were also becoming less popular in both the two major producers of this meat, New Zealand and Australia after 1970. Both countries were, and still are, in a class by themselves for consumption of this meat. In 1968 although a small market in global terms, the next largest per capita consumer of sheep meat was Uruguay with 26 kg, followed by Greece with 14 kg, whereas in the United States only 1.8 kg per person was eaten, although this was a larger market than the other two by virtue of its aggregate size.[36] Although it is impossible to make a precise separation, the sheep meat sector has always produced two quite separate products – mutton and lamb – each catering for different markets and having quite different characteristics. Approximately two-thirds of the volume of output is made up of mutton, but mutton is not produced to suit the requirements of the consumer, as it is a by-product of wool. Lamb, which makes up the remaining one-third of output, accounts for 90 per cent of the total *value* of sheep meat. By the 1980s the Western world's lamb industry had become a highly specialised sector, largely separate from the wool industry, and existed directly to provide meat for consumers.

Lamb has faced a number of severe problems in the late twentieth century. Firstly, its price rose faster than other meats. Even in Australia lamb prices increased by 90 per cent between 1980 and 2000, whereas the price of chicken rose by only 50 per cent. Lamb has also tended to remain the most expensive meat in all markets. In the United States in 2000 the retail price of lamb was 15 per cent more than beef, around 40 per cent more than pork, and more than double the price of poultry.[37] Persistent high prices contributed to the low and falling consumption levels that posed another serious problem. For beef, as can be seen from Table 8.3 below, the per capita decline in supplies and consumption in Western countries was counterbalanced by its rising consumption in Asia, but although sheep meat consumption increased in Asia it never did so to the same extent as beef or any other meats. But one feature of this higher Asian preference for sheep meat that did slightly assist its sales in the United Kingdom was the increasing number of ethnic restaurants that opened from the late 1970s.[38]

**Table 8.3 Percentage changes in per capita meat supplies in Asia between 1980 and 2000**

|            | 1980–1990 | 1990–2000 | 1980–2000 |
|------------|-----------|-----------|-----------|
| Beef       | 35        | 52        | 105       |
| Sheep meat | 30        | 31        | 70        |
| Poultry    | 54        | 100       | 209       |
| Pork       | 56        | 43        | 123       |

*Source:* FAOSTAT August 2004

The two ways for the industry to counter sheep meat's very unfavourable market situation in the 1980s and 1990s were by adopting measures to increase productivity to drive down lamb prices, and paying closer attention to quality control in an attempt to raise its appeal to the consumer. In Australia and New Zealand technical changes such as scanning sheep before lambing, culling dry ewes, and providing better feeding for those carrying multiple lambs all helped to increase lambing percentages. They also allowed the quantities of lamb to increase at a time when flock numbers were falling. But there were extra cost implications here as scanning required extra equipment, and as twins are generally smaller than single lambs they involved a higher cost of care. But although these measures generally helped to stabilise the price situation, the industry also had to face a variety of marketing problems. One of the most worrying features for producers was that lamb's greatest appeal was to older consumers. In the UK 70 per cent of all lamb consumed in the 1990s was by people over 45, and in Australia 62 per cent of lamb was eaten by this age group. There was also evidence that lamb was regarded as inconvenient to prepare, particularly when general meal preparation times were reduced from over two hours in the 1960s to around 30 minutes, or less, in the 1990s. In the 1960s the housewife was prepared to spend the time required to roast a whole joint of lamb, but younger consumers by the 1990s preferred lighter meals where smaller amounts of meat were combined with pastas and stir-fries, rather than relying on traditional roasts, steaks or chops.[39]

But the most serious problem facing New Zealand sheep farmers was the 1972 decision of their largest customer, the United Kingdom, to join the EC. The eventual exclusion of the major part of New Zealand mutton and lamb exports from the British market caused a major upheaval in its meat industry. But anxieties among New Zealand meat producers about their ability to trade with Britain began in the 1950s with the United Kingdom's termination of the wartime bulk purchasing agreements in 1954, even before the formal agreement with the EU was concluded.[40] New Zealand had hoped that all of Europe would provide an expanding market for sheep meat, but in addition to exclusion from those markets its farmers had to face up to the fact that they were producing a meat that was becoming less desirable in most markets. The decline in the British market for New Zealand lamb was neither immediate nor complete. In 1977 Britain was still the main market for New Zealand lamb, but there were fears it would face increased pressure when the EEC duty on lamb rose from 16 to 20 per cent in June of that year.[41]

As the effect of the common level of EU duties was to remove the favoured status of the New Zealand meat farmer in the British market, the hope from New Zealand was that they might also make the European market more accessible. This gave the New Zealand meat industry an initial encouragement to try and sell more mutton and lamb in Europe if possible. However, Table 8.2 shows the European taste for mutton and lamb did not increase but remained stable, and with the exception of Britain (which had its own sizeable industry) and minor customers like Greece and Belgium, it remained only a small item of meat consumption in the 12 countries of the whole Community.

But new markets, as well as general changes in consumer preferences, forced the industry to pay more attention to quality control and local market requirements to retain as much of its sales as possible. For instance as lamb tended to be seen as an expensive and unhealthy meat because of its high fat and bone, concerted efforts were made to reduce fat and increase lean meat. In 1984 the New Zealand Meat Producers Board introduced a new grading scheme to encourage its members to produce more lean lamb carcases. Up to that time the normal pattern of production contained around only 35 per cent of the leaner carcases, but the Board aimed to raise that figure to 60 per cent. Under the new scheme the highest returns within the most popular 13 to 16 kg lamb carcase range were paid for the relatively fat free YM grade of lamb than for the fatter YP grade that required more trimming of excess fat.[42]

Although the production of leaner carcases may have helped to reduce the decline in demand for lamb, it certainly could not hope to reverse the process. Access to the EU was no easier after 1973 than before with tariff barriers to outsiders such as New Zealand as high as 40 per cent in order to preserve as much of this market as possible for European lamb producers. The anxieties within the New Zealand industry led to the question 'are sheep meats doomed?' being asked in the mid-1980s, while some producers wondered if they should swing their production towards wool at the expense of meat.[43]

**Table 8.4  Per capita pig meat consumption of developed countries, 1961–2000 (kilos)**

|  | United States | United Kingdom | European Union (12) | Australia | New Zealand | Argentina |
|---|---|---|---|---|---|---|
| 1961–65 | 28.1 | 27.2 | 23.6 | 10.7 | 15.1 | 7.8 |
| 1966–70 | 28.6 | 27.6 | 26.5 | 12.4 | 12.9 | 8.8 |
| 1971–75 | 28.7 | 27.5 | 30.6 | 14.3 | 12.7 | 9.5 |
| 1976–80 | 28.6 | 26.2 | 34.5 | 13.2 | 11.8 | 8.9 |
| 1981–85 | 29.4 | 25.8 | 38.2 | 15.7 | 13.1 | 7.4 |
| 1986–90 | 28.6 | 25.6 | 40.4 | 17.6 | 14.2 | 5.8 |
| 1991–95 | 29.7 | 24.7 | 40.2 | 18.9 | 14.7 | 6.5 |
| 1996–2000 | 29.3 | 24.8 | 42.5 | 18.9 | 17.5 | 7.1 |

*Source:* FAOSTAT August 2004

The per capita consumption of pig meat, as can be seen from Table 8.4 above, remained stable in the United States, New Zealand, and Argentina, declined slightly in the United Kingdom, and only experienced a marked long-term increase in the 12 countries of the European Union and Australia. The increase in Europe, which would be greater if the United Kingdom were excluded from the 12, was accounted for mainly by the rising living standards in the lower-income countries like Spain, Portugal, Greece, Italy and Ireland from the 1960s onwards.[44] In the 1960s the bulk of world trade in pig meat was between the countries of Western Europe, supplied principally by Denmark, but also from Holland and Belgium. The really high European consumer of pig meat was Germany, maintaining the position it had always held since the nineteenth century. In 1971 the consumption in West Germany was 41 kilos per head, followed by France with 29 kilos.[45] In all countries the consumption of pig meat in the form of bacon, ham, sausages and processed meats has always exceeded the amount eaten as joints and each country had varying preferences for different types of pork product. In Germany there was a strong preference for sausages and pickled pork, but the consumption of bacon, though not of hams, was largely confined to Britain.[46]

In spite of the long-term expansion since the 1960s, even the European pig meat industry felt it faced a crisis after the mid-1980s, as the growth of per capita consumption and overall production slowed down. Consumers came increasingly to regard pig meat as being fatty, boring and having limited versatility. Like lamb, as changing lifestyles meant more meals were eaten outside the home and less time was devoted to preparing meals at home, the demand for a pork roast that took over an hour to cook naturally declined. Even the market for British bacon, the fastest of all pig meats to prepare, experienced a decline from 222,000 tonnes in 1976 to 187,000 in 1994 as a result of 'the growing awareness of healthy eating with the traditional daily cooked breakfast being substituted by cereals'.[47] Producers were so concerned about stagnation that some of the industry's policy makers from the United Kingdom, Denmark, Holland, France, Germany and Spain held an international conference at Warwick in 1992 to discuss overall strategies for the future. In summing up at the end, Mick Sloyan, the chief economist to the United Kingdom's Meat and Livestock Commission stressed among other things the industry's need to develop a strong positive image in the mind of the consumer that pig meat was a quality item, produced to the highest standards of hygiene and welfare.[48]

Part of the problem seems to have been that whilst the British and European industry had increasingly concentrated on producing lean pig meat since the 1960s, taking as its standard the Danish model of pig and bacon grading, this was not enough to meet the changed requirements of the consumer by the 1980s. With the general reaction against what were seen as the excesses of factory farming, particularly intensive indoor fattening, consumers now needed to be reassured that their meat, besides being as free as possible from unnecessary and potentially harmful fat, was also 'naturally produced'. This new emphasis on image as well as substance was not always easy for the industry to accept, and as one authority put it:[49]

... the term 'natural' is, romantically whatever the consumer chooses to define as natural, and there are undoubtedly considerable market opportunities for those who are prepared to go along with their view. Again, one must concede the right of choice to the buyer, even when such a choice involves an element of gimmick and charade. If by following this type of lead, pig meat can be reinstated in the purchase preferences of those who have otherwise lost confidence in the product, then this is all to the good.

For most people the term 'natural' food became synonymous with 'organic', implying in this case that organic meat came from animals that were reared out of doors and fed on naturally grown cereals rather than those kept in intensive feedlots and given concentrated feeds produced by the large feed milling firms. This was in spite of the fact that all objective studies in Europe and America have shown no difference between organic food and conventional food in terms of the major constituents, minerals and vitamins. Indeed, organic farming brings its own risks. Scientists were quick to point out that health hazards, such as E-coli 0157 can live just as happily in the guts of organic cattle, and Citrobacter freundii in the guts of organic pigs, as in the factory-farmed versions of those animals.[50] In addition to the pains the pig meat industry had to take to reassure the public that their product was healthy, they also needed to convince it that it was not fatty, boring and old fashioned.

In reality the organic option faced the industry with an impossible dilemma. Despite all the publicity given to it, surveys revealed that the effective demand for meat from animals kept in the open and fed on organically produced feeding stuffs was very limited. One study of the whole European pig meat industry published in 2001 found that organic pig meat only accounted for 0.5 per cent of the market. A survey of the Danish market showed that better educated, though not necessarily richer consumers, were more likely to buy organic food. The great majority of people were not interested in organic food as such, but simply bought the cheapest, and even among those who were willing to try it price considerations were still important. The higher production costs of outdoor rearing made organic pig products between 50 to 100 per cent more expensive than normal.[51] This part of the market research intro the industry suggested that it was crucial to bring down these costs as far as possible. But paradoxically the premium should not be allowed to drop too close to conventional prices, lest it undermine the 'brand' quality of the organic label.[52] The industry was forced to accept that it is impossible to compensate for the stagnation of a mass market largely driven by price by fostering a relatively expensive niche product.

A more practical alternative was to stimulate the market for the conventionally reared product but to stress that it was as fat free as possible. In 1988 the British Meat and Livestock Commission developed alternative cutting methods, which it publicised in a pamphlet. This aimed to help butchers produce cuts of meat that were attractive, convenient in size, quick and easy to cook, and above all as lean as possible to satisfy the increasing number of consumers who wanted to reduce the amount of fat they were eating.[53] This particular Meat and

Livestock Commission marketing exercise affected only the retail end of the pork food chain, because there was little scope in Europe to improve pig quality. There were similar market problems in the United States where per capita consumption had stagnated since the 1960s, but there they required a different solution. The meat producer Joseph Luter, head of the giant Smithfield Foods, was so dissatisfied with stagnating sales that he toured Europe to see if it was possible to improve them. As a result of what he saw there he decided that most American pigs were second-rate and hired a specially chartered Boeing 747 to import some 2,000 particularly fine British sows. These he used for crossbreeding in his pig units, to produce much leaner meat for his processing business.[54]

While the attempts to use improved breeding and butchering techniques to reduce the meat's fat content were both perfectly conventional and reasonable marketing strategies, some of the other marketing ploys were rather more unusual, and even showed signs of desperation. In Australia pig producers experienced a steep fall in prices in the late 1990s, caused principally by competition from imported Canadian pig meat. The Australian Pork Corporation, the statutory marketing authority for all pork produced in Australia, had been campaigning to increase the meat's popularity since 1976. Like the Meat and Livestock Commission in Britain it began by promoting better butchering techniques for boneless, attractively trimmed and largely fat free retail cuts. Collectively they were called the 'New Fashioned Pork' range, and were aimed at the health conscious as they carried the endorsement from the country's National Heart Foundation. But progress was relatively slow and in 1991, in an attempt to increase the meat's acceptability, the Corporation launched 'The Other White Meat' campaign. The idea behind the new slogan was to position pork in direct competition with chicken, conveying it as a lean, nutritional, and healthy modern meat. The Australians were not the only ones to use this device. In the United States the National Pork Producers Council also used it to portray a healthy nutritious alternative white meat to compete directly with chicken.[55]

The Australians, however, disbanded 'The Other White Meat' campaign when the Corporation became worried it implied that pork was an alternative, or even second best meat. Instead, it decided to follow a lead from the country's beef industry by including the words 'Grain Fed' in its promotional material, believing that by stressing it was fed on home-grown cereal would add to the healthy image of Australian pork. United States producers did not publicly drop the 'Other White Meat' slogan, but it became less prominent as they added other marketing schemes to it, to bring pork into direct competition with poultry. One was to work with some of the food retail chains and analyse their databases of consumer profile information taken from their store loyalty schemes. The study of addresses and postal codes allowed them to identify customers who continually bought chicken and try to tempt them away by sending them promotional material for pork as well as vouchers for pork products.[56]

**The Increased Popularity of Poultry Meat**

Although the market for red meats was either stagnant or increasing only slowly in most developed countries, this was not the case for poultry meat. From a position of minor importance in the 1940s poultry consumption rose to became one of the major meats by 2000. There is no doubt this has been the one meat that has become increasingly popular in the post-war era. It had a much shorter production time than beef and sheep meat, and even shorter than for pig meat, making it easier for producers to respond quickly to changes in demand. The industry was thus ideally suited to meet the long-term increase in demand for protein, especially in Europe, after 1945. But the response was not immediate and production was slow to expand during the 1950s. Partly this was because the public still regarded it as something for special occasions and expected it to be expensive. As most poultry production in Europe and the United States was only a secondary enterprise in addition to the main farming activity, poultry units were mainly small, usually run by farmers' wives, output was low and prices high.

Change to this system started first in the United States with the turkey fattening and by the late 1950s, turkey production was concentrated on relatively few farms with relatively large numbers of birds. These producers entered into formal contracts with processors to deliver particular types and weight of birds, and the processors often provided the farmers with feed ingredients and specialized medicines. There was a similar concentration in chicken production. In the past most chicken meat was from older birds that had finished egg production. But post war affluence and intensive feeding methods made the broiler, a young chicken bred specifically for meat, a common part of most families' diet.[57] At a later stage the meat production became even more specialised with birds bred specifically as broilers for roasting and others produced specifically for frying. As can be seen in Table 8.5 below, these developments raised American poultry consumption levels well above those of Europe.

**Table 8.5  Per capita poultry meat consumption of the United States, United Kingdom, Denmark and West Germany, pre-war to 1960 (kilos)**

|          | United States | United Kingdom | Denmark | West Germany |
|----------|---------------|----------------|---------|--------------|
| Pre-war  | 7.4  | 2.0 | 6.6 | 1.6 |
| 1945–50  | 12.4 | 2.4 | 5.1 | – |
| 1951–54  | 12.1 | 2.6 | 6.9 | – |
| 1955–60  | 14.9 | 4.3 | 6.8 | 6.7 |

*Source:* Commonwealth Economic Committee (1950–65), *Meat: A Summary of Figures of Production, Trade and Consumption*, HMSO, London.

From the 1960s Europe followed the United States in the application of large-scale intensive production systems to increase supplies and lower poultry meat prices. But not all the credit for subsequent technical change can be claimed by the United States. A substantial proportion of the research and development of technology took place in Europe, just as it did for intensive milk and pig production. By the start of the 1960s global demand for poultry meat was forecast to expand at a higher rate than any of the other major categories of meat. It was anticipated that there would be no difficulty in meeting this demand in Europe, in view of the necessary changes in production methods pioneered in America during the 1950s. The only constraining factors in Europe after the war had been shortages of feedstuffs and the necessary capital but both were readily available after 1960.[58]

As it was not an important part of meat output before the war, few countries were bothered enough to collect sufficient poultry production figures after 1945 to enable them to estimate per capita consumption. But Table 8.5 above provides some indication of the situation in the United States and Britain, as well as Denmark and West Germany, between 1945 and 1960. The United States did show some increase in consumption after 1945, but in the United Kingdom this only occurred after 1955 and in Denmark, where European consumption had been highest before the war, per capita poultry consumption was almost stationary before 1960. Denmark had been a large-scale egg producer since the late nineteenth century and this had given it a surplus of poultry meat to consume at home as well as export to its immediate neighbours.[59] As a result Danish exports partly fed West German consumption after the war as poultry became increasingly popular in that country, so that between 1955 and 1960 per capita consumption reached levels similar to Denmark.

Through the 1960s and 1970s poultry's popularity increased as consumers substituted it for red meats so that it steadily outstripped the consumption of pork and rivalled that of beef by the end of the 1980s.[60] It overtook beef and veal in popularity first in the United Kingdom in 1985 when it accounted for 27 per cent of the meat market, and went on to account for 38 per cent of the country's meat consumption by 1994.[61] In the United States beef managed to retain its premier position for only slightly longer, until 1987 when for the first time American consumers ate more poultry than beef.[62] Thereafter the popularity of the two meats was close, but with poultry definitely ahead in the 1990s.

Part of the increasing international popularity of poultry meat after 1960 that can be seen in Table 8.6 below, was undoubtedly because of its image as the (largely) fat-free healthy 'protein of choice'.[63] But it went well beyond that; as the rise in poultry consumption began long before serious health warnings about beef. In the United States awareness of possible links between cholesterol and heart disease increased sharply after 1980 when the government advised consumers to cut back on beef. However, there is evidence that the poultry industry was already responding strongly to the growth in the demand for fast foods and convenience meals well before that date. American food processors had begun to take much of the labour out of consumers' kitchens by such activities as cutting up, boning, precooking, freezing and packaging meat products, since the late 1950s. But there is evidence that it was possible to make greater changes in this direction with poultry than with beef. After the Second World War poultry was rated as less convenient than with beef. On both sides of the Atlantic it was usual for the consumer to buy a whole bird, whereas beef was already sold as joints. Poultry processors found it was relatively cheap to disassemble carcases and start selling breasts and thighs. They then started to add further refinements with minced and processed poultry products, whereas it was neither as easy nor cheap for the red meat processing chain to dream up fresh ways of adding greater convenience to beef. Although the beef industry was not completely without innovation, progress was slow. It did produce new convenience food products after 1980, but the poultry industry produced significantly more, and had been doing so since the mid-1960s.[64] As late as 1988 in the United States producers of branded products had still only a small share of total beef sales.[65]

**Table 8.6  Per capita poultry meat consumption of developed countries, 1961–2000 (kilos)**

|           | United States | United Kingdom | European Union (12) | Australia | New Zealand | Argentina |
|-----------|---------------|----------------|---------------------|-----------|-------------|-----------|
| 1961–65   | 16.9          | 6.8            | 6.8                 | 5.1       | 3.1         | 3.4       |
| 1966–70   | 20.2          | 9.6            | 8.9                 | 8.1       | 4.1         | 6.2       |
| 1971–75   | 21.7          | 11.7           | 11.7                | 12.5      | 7.4         | 9.4       |
| 1976–80   | 24.4          | 13.1           | 13.7                | 17.1      | 9.7         | 10.1      |
| 1981–85   | 28.7          | 14.8           | 15.1                | 20.1      | 11.9        | 11.8      |
| 1986–90   | 35.7          | 18.3           | 16.7                | 23.4      | 15.2        | 12.4      |
| 1991–95   | 42.5          | 23.5           | 19.1                | 25.6      | 20.6        | 19.7      |
| 1996–2000 | 45.9          | 27.6           | 21.0                | 30.8      | 25.2        | 25.9      |

*Source:* FAOSTAT August 2004

But for matters of health to be the driving force in the shift from beef to poultry one would expect the greatest increases to have been in the consumption of whole chickens and a decline in the consumption of the beef hamburger. This is because whole chickens have less saturated fat than processed beef products. But market surveys show the consumption of the beef hamburger has held up rather well, and the consumption of processed chicken products increased more than whole chickens. So it seems from the 1960s onwards the greatest shift in demand was from the relatively high quality and expensive beef table cuts to cheaper processed chicken products and chicken parts. Thus price and convenience also seem to have been important factors behind the shift in demand for poultry. Significant growth in the demand for parts and processed forms of both meats may also have been fostered by the dramatic increase in fast food outlets for both beef and chicken products.[66]

The question of health and fat content thus came into the marketing debate relatively late and reinforced a change in the relative positions of beef and poultry that was already well advanced. Meat from the typical factory farmed chicken was neutral tasting and could be readily flavoured in a number of ways to provide the meat base for a wide variety of ethnic and other dishes. It also seems unlikely that the industry ever took much trouble to worry about whether these products were particularly fat free at a time when the issue raised little concern. As with other relationships between current consumption and long-term health, such as smoking and lung cancer, repeated studies confirming the links were needed before the public completely accepted the health warning associated with red meat.

But once the anxieties over saturated fats and cholesterol were publicised, poultry processors and fast food chains readily incorporated the healthy meat image into their marketing programmes. In 1995 two of the smaller United States fast food chains, Boston Market and Kenny Rogers Roasters were locked in fierce argument over which of them served the leaner roast chicken. Kenny Rogers claimed that a skinless portion of its white-meat chicken had only 0.6 grams of saturated fat per ounce, or just over half of Boston's, which had 1.09 grams. In fact such small differences, taken to two decimal places were statistically insignificant, and the United States government food standards rated both products equally at 1.0 gram.[67]


## Changes in the Industry's Structure

Before 1945 there was still very much a two-fold division in the industry: meatpacking and wholesaling was the stronghold of the large firm, but most consumers bought their meat from small independent retail butchers. This tended to give the large packing and importing businesses in the United States and Britain a great deal of power over the retail sections of the industry which they supplied with meat through branch wholesale houses. But from the 1920s their power in the United States meat industry began to decline. Under pressure from the Federal Government the Trust firms were forced to give up control of stockyards, cold stores, and other facilities, while generally agreeing to loosen their control over the industry. This reduced barriers to entry, allowing new firms with lower production costs into the industry. Improved road transport encouraged the establishment of processing plants close to beef-producing areas, rather than transporting them by rail to Chicago. Because the new plants installed the latest technology they could reduce processing costs, and as they were non-unionised labour costs were lower than for the established firms who were all unionised. The growth of motor transport and in-store refrigerators also allowed retailers to take greater control over their own distribution. As the chain stores preferred to source more of their meat from the new firms, the market share of the old entrants inevitably declined, as did concentration ratios in the industry as a whole.[68]

The large firm was not entirely absent from the retail sector. In Britain the Vestey family's Union Cold Storage Company owned an extensive chain of butcher shops retailing almost exclusively imported meat, and other firms like Sainsbury, as well as the Co-operative societies also had their chains of shops, retailing other foods besides meat with some of them concentrating more on the sale of home-killed meat. But up to 1950 over 70 per cent of meat and meat products in the United Kingdom was still sold by the small specialist independent butcher.[69] In the United States the large multiple food retailer had made greater progress, and food supermarkets appeared in the 1920s, usually with their own specialist meat departments where meat was cut and matched to the customer's requirements. In 1929 it was estimated that 15 per cent or more of the retail sales of meat in the United States was by chain stores.[70] In Canada grocery chain stores and the larger department stores were carrying meat and meat products by the 1930s, and they and full-line supermarkets had also captured some of the retail market in meats from the traditional craft butcher.[71]

From 1950 the revolution in meat selling that had begun in the 1920s gathered force. Inexorably, the small independent craft retailer and the traditional butcher's shop lost ground in the face of the advance of the food supermarket where meat was just one of the products on sale. Even the multiple chains, like Vestey's Dewhurst butchers shops which traded very much on traditional lines, where the individual branches were run by a manager and sold joints of meat prepared in the traditional way felt the pinch. The Vestey policy had always been to close shops that made insufficient profits, and it was for this reason there was a steady reduction in the number of Dewhurst branches from the 1960s onwards. In the mid-1920s the organization operated a national chain of 2356 retail shops in Britain, but by 1990 there were only 1030 shops in the chain, though not all traded under the Dewhurst name.[72] When the firm finally disposed of the remnants of its Dewhurst chain to Lloyd Maunder, a Devon-based meat processing and retailing firm, the number had shrunk to 109, and they employed only 500 people.[73]

When Dewhursts, and other specialist butchers shops closed, their sales were replaced, but not directly by the specialist butcher. In their place there appeared a variety of supermarkets, frozen food stores, tandoori takeaways, kebab or burger bars, and different types of restaurant. This was a similar pattern of closure to that experienced by premises occupied by small independent fishmongers, bakers, and greengrocers. It was all part of the general change in food retailing where an increasing proportion of sales were taken over by large supermarkets, and fast food outlets. It was assisted by the consumer's increasing preference for ready-prepared foods and reluctance to undertake lengthy meal preparation at home, lifestyle trends that began in the United States and rapidly spread to all Western nations.

A survey conducted by the United Kingdom Meat and Livestock Commission revealed that by 1980 only 45 per cent of retail meat sales were in the hands of specialist (solus) butchers. The stores run by Co-operative societies had about 7 per cent and the supermarkets (defined as large multiple grocers) had 23.5 per cent. The remaining 24.5 per cent of sales were by smaller supermarkets, independent grocers, and what were defined as 'other residual outlets'. This last group included farm shop and market stall sales, as well as the meat sold in a variety of chain stores such as Marks & Spencer, Woolworths, and Littlewoods, who had recently opened food sections.[74] By 1990 the supermarkets, especially the large out of or edge of town ones, had increased their hold on the trade. They now held 38 per cent of the sales of red meats, and the number of specialist butchers shops had shrunk from 22,895 in 1980 to 14,181. The large supermarket had all the advantages of easy parking, a wider range of all products, and the buying power to offer prices with which the specialist high street shop could not compete.[75]

As the large supermarkets captured more of the retail trade from the craft butcher, the changes in the nature of the product accommodated this. One of the strong points about the craft butcher was the provision of personal customer service. In his shop the housewife could select the type of meat she wanted from the larger pieces on display, and then watch as the butcher cut off just the amount she required and then packaged it for her. This was in sharp contrast to the supermarkets. They relied on providing a fast, cheap, and inevitably a less personal service. In the 1970s and 1980s most supermarkets still had their own meat cutting departments who would prepare an individual piece for customers who asked. But meat was increasingly being pre-cut and ready packaged and placed in chilled display cabinets for customers to select for themselves. With an increasing amount of meat processed sold in branded packs and cartons, there was no need for any personal contact with the retailing staff from the time customers entered the store until arriving at the checkout.

These changes were underpinned by developments in the wholesale trade. In the 1950s and 1960s most slaughterhouses would send out carcases, but there was a tendency for them to do more of the meat cutting and preparation from the 1970s and 1980s. These developments started in the United States and Canada where, as in Britain, retailers had formerly received most of their meat in whole or parts of carcases, which still required the traditional skilled and time-consuming preparation. But by the 1990s an increased amount of fresh meat was received from the slaughterhouses and meat processors packed in boxes. This applied particularly to beef, where the retailer paid more for 'boxed beef' but saved time, labour and money on in-store preparation of the product for sale. Previously a carcase had to be cut up with skill and there was always the worry of not being able to dispose of the parts less in demand. With the boxed beef retailers could specify exactly what cuts and pieces they required, so that it contained just those that were most easy to sell. When it arrived at the shop – and supermarkets were the first to adopt this product because it was suited to their low cost philosophy – it was 'case ready' and required little or no further cutting or preparation before being placed in the shop's refrigerated display cabinets.[76]

Although 'case ready' meat could be fresh meat, an increased amount of meat was sold in branded product packs. One feature of both these trends was they enhanced the importance of the processor in the industry. By 2003 it was estimated that the five top beef companies in the United States (Tyson, Excel, Swift, Farmland, and Smithfield) controlled 89 per cent of the country's steer and heifer slaughter.[77] In the nineteenth century when customers purchased meat they did so with a limited amount of information about it. Broad categories of imported and home-produced were recognised, though little else. By the late twentieth century the consumer often knew exactly which manufacturer or processor was responsible for the items they had purchased. One effect of this was that some of the giant meat processing businesses of the late twentieth century could exert a level of control over the industry similar to that of the American meat trust in the nineteenth century. Firms such as Tyson Foods in the United States and Bernard Matthews in the United Kingdom came into this category. Both of these operated on a small scale in the 1950s in their national poultry industries, but by the end of the 1990s they had grown into large corporations with extensive ranges of branded products that had global sales.

Bernard Matthews began in 1952 as a Norfolk turkey farmer and by 1968 was producing over a million birds. In the 1970s innovative turkey product such as Turkey fillets and Turkey breast meats appeared and by 1985 the firm's turnover exceeded £100 million. In 1990s the firm purchased businesses in Germany, Hungary and New Zealand and opened offices in the Czech Republic, Poland and Slovakia.[78] Tyson Foods also began in the poultry sector as a modest chicken farm in Arkansas with a few delivery trucks and was built up by Don Tyson into the country's largest poultry producer when he retired in 2001. He was one of the first to recognise that if he owned the chicken throughout the production cycle from farm to grocery store he could reduce manufacturing costs, streamline production, improve quality, and increase the firm's profit margins. Along with the hamburger chain of McDonalds he developed the chicken nugget, and appealed to the working housewife with a range of convenience chicken products like boneless chicken breast and breaded chicken patties, that were sold in supermarkets. Like Bernard Matthews, the company diversified. They moved into beef and pork by acquiring processing firms in the red meat sector, so that by 2004 the Tyson Dinner Meats line included beef pot roasts and chicken breasts in various sauces, as well as pork in gravy, and glazed ham.[79] Another parallel with Matthews was that both concerns sited their manufacturing plants away from the major cities to take advantage of low cost rural labour, and as this dried up by the late 1990s both resorted to low cost immigrant labour.[80] This was in contrast to the nineteenth century when the meat packers sited their plants on the outskirts of cities.

As the large production plants became more powerful, a number of concerns were raised about the way they ran their businesses. These were similar to those expressed about the meat packers of the nineteenth century. Critics argued that the vertical integration of the industry gave such market power to the processors that it allowed them to concentrate on lowering costs without worrying about the effects this had on the other sectors of the industry. It was claimed they dictated unreasonable terms and conditions to the farmers who supplied them. They were accused of dictating to farmers the exact specifications of the animals they required, and penalising them heavily if they failed to satisfy these requirements. Their concentration on low prices, it was argued, was also one of the factors forcing farmers to neglect such things as humane treatment of the animals. In addition they were accused of exploiting employees by forcing them to work on fast-moving production lines in processing plants where little attention was paid to health and safety legislation. Finally, there were anxieties about the quality of their manufactured meat products, principally over fat contents, and that little attention was paid to the effect they had on the health of consumers.[81]

But the rise of the big multinational firm was not simply confined to processors serving the retail trade. The fast food sector of the industry also saw the emergence of global giants like McDonald's, Kentucky Fried Chicken and Burger King. They also had a strong influence over the rest of the industry that consisted mainly of smaller sized clones many of whom they acquired as these market leaders grew in size. They, and some of the other internationally recognised restaurant chains, had their origins in the various destination restaurant and hamburger stalls that had grown up alongside state highways, and in American cities from the 1920s. But the post-war chains were very much the brainchildren of new entrants who went into the industry in the 1950s. They included inspired entrepreneurs like Ray Kroc, a former milkshake machine salesman who developed MacDonald's business from 1955 and bought it from the original owners for $2.7 million in 1961, and Harland Sanders who sold his first franchise for Kentucky Fried Chicken in 1952. All of the fast food restaurant chains used flamboyant advertising and various forms of the franchise to extend their operations. Franchising allowed them to keep a close control over product quality, while the various local managers who risked their own (often borrowed) capital to open the establishment had every incentive to increase sales, as well as bring forward fresh ideas for product innovation, while also adhering to the company's rules on product preparation and quality. Ray Kroc kept a particularly close control on the McDonald's chain, barring franchisees from being absentee owners or operating other kinds of restaurants. [82]

Like the processors, with whom they sometimes cooperated to develop new meat products for their restaurants, they were keen to export the American way of eating once they had established just about as many outlets as they could in the United States. By 1987 McDonald's had a worldwide chain of 9,800 outlets with 1300 of them outside the United States. The first overseas branches appeared in Britain and Europe, but they were willing to test the potential of countries well outside the Western meat industry's normal market area.[83] This had mixed success, and some countries were more receptive to Western marketing. For instance, by 1982 both McDonald's and Kentucky Fried Chicken restaurants were huge successes in Japan, where tastes were becoming more Western.[84] But this was less true in India where, by the end of 1997, McDonald's had opened seven burger restaurants in an attempt to tap the growing middle-class market of Westernised Indians. However, in this market the firm struggled. They discovered that it was rather smaller than they had anticipated, and found it necessary to make concessions to local preferences in a country where 40 per cent of consumers were vegetarian, where meat-eaters had an aversion to either beef or pork, and where there was a dislike of frozen meat or fish. The largest concession was to the slogan that the Big Mac was 'the same the world over', as the Indian variety was minced mutton instead of beef, and had to be heavily laced with local spices, rather than laid upon a bed of fried onions.[85]

Wherever the fast food giants operated, because they were very much at the end of the food chain they decided to pay a great deal of attention to fostering customer loyalty in ways the large meat firms of the nineteenth century had never had to consider. Of McDonald's it was said, both by McDonald's and their critics, that their marketing was so intensive they were not so much selling a meat-based foodstuff, but a McDonald's food-based lifestyle. The Armours, Swifts, Vesteys, and other early barons of the industry had been accused of profiteering, but that was about as far as it went; even their strongest critics had never accused them of total social engineering.[86]

## Notes

1  Simoons, F.J., *Eat Not This Flesh: Food Avoidances from Prehistory to the Present* (Madison, 1994).

2  Atkins, P.J. and I. Bowler, *Food in Society: Economy, Culture, Geography* (London, 2001), p. 241.

3  Antrobus, D., *A Guiltless Feast: The Salford Bible Christian Church and the Rise of the Modern Vegetarian Movement* (Salford, 1997), pp. 17, 64, 116.

4  Antrobus, pp. 64–5, 69, 72, 88–90.

5  Kelogg, J.H., *Shall We Slay to Eat?* (Battle Creek, 1905), pp. 145–67, quoted in J.C. Whorton, 'Vegetarianism', in K.F. Kiple and K.C. Ornelas (eds), *The Cambridge World History of Food*, vol. 2 (Cambridge, 2000), pp. 1559–60.

6  Antrobus, p. 100; *The Times Food Number* (London, 1915), p. 83; *The Times* (27 Oct 1997), p. 8.

7  Spencer, C., *The Heretic's Feast: A History of Vegetarianism* (London, 1993), pp. 274–301.

8  *The Outlook*, 'Meat Substitutes' (3 July 1918), p. 376.

9  Dewey, P.E., *British Agriculture in the First World War* (London, 1989), p. 215.

10 'Meat Substitutes' p. 376.

11 Spencer, p. 317.

12 *The Times* (18 July 1985).

13 *Marketing* (5 Oct. 1989), p. 20.

14 Reid, R.L. and A. Hackett, 'A Database of Vegetarian Foods', *British Food Journal*, 104(11) (2002): 873.

15 Reid and Hackett, p. 876; *Marketing Week* (26 May 2005), p. 38.

16 *Marketing Magazine* (7 July 1997), p. 4.

17 A detailed summary of the argument can be found in Whorton, pp. 1561–2.

18 Heiser, C.B., Jr., *Seed to Civilization: The Story of Man's Food* (San Francisco, 1973), pp. 131–3.
19 Logan, J.R and E. Medved, 'Simulated Meats', *Journal of Home Economics*, 58(8) (1966): 677.
20 Sault, J.L. and J.B. Gale, 'A Review of Developments in Simulated Meats', *Quarterly Review of Agricultural Economics* 23(4) (1970): 209–11.
21 Sault and Gale, pp. 212–15.
22 *New Zealand Journal of Agriculture* 129 (1974): 33.
23 *Ibid.*
24 English, P.R., V.R. Fowler, S. Baxter and B. Smith, *The Growing and Finishing Pig: Improving Efficiency* (Ipswich, c.1988), p. 7.
25 Harris, M. and E.B. Ross, 'How Beef Became King', *Psychology Today* 12(5) (1978): 88; H.A. Levenstein, *Revolution at the Table: The Transformation of the American Diet* (New York, 1988), p. 174.
26 Mitchell, D., *The Politics of Food* (Toronto 1975), p. 83.
27 Reeves, G.W. and A.H. Hayman, 'Demand and Supply Forces in the World Beef Market', *Quarterly Review of Agricultural Economics*, 28(3) (1975): 121–51.
28 MacLachlan, I., *Kill and Chill: Restructuring Canada's Beef Commodity Chain*, (Toronto, 2001), p. 312
29 Roberts, I.M. and G.L. Miller, 'An Analysis of the EEC Market for Beef and Veal', *Quarterly Review of Agricultural Economics*, 24(3) (1971): 143–44.
30 Anon., 'The Outlook for Beef and Veal in the EEC for the next Five Years', *MLC International Market Review*, 2 (1981): 2– 3.
31 Levenstein, H.A., *Revolution at the Table: The Transformation of the American Diet* (New York, 1988), p. 209.
32 General Agreement on Tariffs and Trade, *The International Markets for Meat, 1987/88* (Geneva, 1988), p. 48.
33 Gordon, A.D., 'Key Aspects of World Meat Markets' (Cyclostyled paper delivered at the 13th International Meat Secretariat World Meat Congress at Belo Horizonte, Brazil: Sept. 2000): 8.
34 *The Economist* (20 Apr. 2000), p. 34.
35 Meat and Livestock Commission, *Meat Demand Trends* (Bletchley, Sept. 1982), p. 2.
36 McCoy, J.H., *Livestock and Meat Marketing* (Westport, 1972), pp. 90, 94, 96.
37 Barnard, P. (Sept. 2000), 'World Sheep Market', Cyclostyled paper delivered at the 13th World Meat Congress, Belo Horizonte, Brazil, pp. 4–5.
38 Meat and Livestock Commission, *Meat Demand Trends* (Bletchley, Sept 1982), p. 8.
39 Barnard, 'World Sheep Market', pp. 9–10.
40 Singleton, J., 'New Zealand's Economic Relations with Japan in the 1950s', *Australian Economic History Review*, 37(1) (1997): 9–10.
41 *New Zealand Journal of Agriculture*, 134(1) (1977): 7, 28.
42 *New Zealand Journal of Agriculture*, 150(2) (1985): 19–20.
43 Ibid., p. 25.
44 Farnsworth, H.C., 'National Food Consumption of Fourteen Western European Countries and Factors Responsible for their Differences', *Food Research Institute Studies*, 13 (1) (1974): 84–5, 93.
45 Commonwealth Secretariat, *Meat: A Review of Figures of Production, Trade and Consumption* (London, 1973), pp. 56–9.
46 Davidson, H.R., *The Production and Marketing of Pigs*, 3rd edn. (London, 1962), p. 7.

47 Meat and Livestock Commission, *Meat Demand Trends* (Bletchley, May 1995), p. 4.
48 Meat and Livestock Commission, *The Future of the European Pig Meat Industry: A Report of the Conference at Warwick* (Bletchley, 1992), p. 95.
49 English, Fowler, Baxter and Smith, p. 525.
50 A. Trewavas 'Science: Is Organic Food Safe?', *Independent* (30 July 1999), Features, p. 9.
51 *The Economist* (13 June 2002), p. 34; Meat and Livestock Commission, *Meat Demand Trends* (Bletchley, Aug. 1999), p. 5.
52 King, J., *The Market for Organic Pigmeat in Europe* (Uckfield, 2001), pp. 6–7.
53 Meat and Livestock Commission, *Alternative Pork Cutting Method: Providing the Lean Alternative* (Bletchley, 1988).
54 *The Economist* (29 Nov. 2001), p. 86.
55 Kemp, M., *The Promotion and Marketing of Pork and Bacon* (Uckfield, 2000), pp. 27, 32.
56 Ibid., pp. 1, 9–11, 28.
57 *Fedgazette* 10(2) (1998), p. 6.
58 Food and Agriculture Organization, *The World Meat Economy* (Rome, 1965), p. 103.
59 Nash, E.F. and E.A. Atwood, *The Agricultural Policies of Britain and Denmark: A Study in Reciprocal Trade* (London 1961), pp. 18, 20, 30.
60 *The Meat Trades Journal* (2 Dec. 1965), pp. 721, 725; Meat and Livestock Commission, *Meat Demand Trends* (Bletchley, Jan. 1981), pp. 11–12.
61 *Retail Business: Market Surveys* (June 1995), p. 9
62 *Changing Times* (Feb. 1988), p. 10.
63 *Frozen Food Age*, 42(6) (Jan. 1994), p. 33.
64 Anderson, E.W. and S.M. Shugan, 'Repositioning for Changing Preferences: The Case of Beef versus Poultry', *Journal of Consumer Research* 18 (Sept. 1981), pp. 223, 225, 229.
65 *Supermarket Business* 43(8) (1988), p. 19.
66 Eales, J.S. and L.J. Unnevehr, 'Demand for Beef and Chicken Products: Separability and Structural Change', *American Journal of Agricultural Economics*, 70 (Aug. 1988): 530–31.
67 *Fortune*, 132(2) (1995), p. 18.
68 Arnould, R.J., 'Changing Patterns of Concentration in American Meat Packing, 1880–1963', *Business History Review*, 45(1) (1971): 24–34.
69 Jefferys, J.B., *Retail Trading in Britain 1850–1950* (Cambridge, 1954), pp. 191–201.
70 Clark, F.E. and L.D.H. Weld, *Marketing Agricultural Products in the United States* (New York, 1932), pp. 196–8.
71 MacLachlan, I., *Kill and Chill: Restructuring Canada's Beef Commodity Chain* (Toronto, 2001), pp. 298–9.
72 Meat and Livestock Commission, *Meat Demand Trends* (Bletchley, Mar. 1992), p. 17.
73 Cmd 2390 (PP 1924–25, vol. XIII), *First Report of the Royal Commission on Food Prices, volume I.*, pp. 97–8; Clarke, H. and H. Binding, *The History of Lloyd Maunder 1898–1998: A West Country Business* (Tiverton, 1998): Clarke Willmott News (14 Mar. 2005) http://www.clarkewillmott.com/news.htm?Article=461.
74 Meat and Livestock Commission, *Meat Demand Trends* (Bletchley, Jan. 1981), pp. 2–4.
75 Meat and Livestock Commission, *Meat Demand Trends* (Bletchley, Mar. 1992), pp. 14, 17.
76 MacLachlan, pp. 306–9.

77  *The Economist* (2 Jan. 2003), p. 37.
78  Bernard Matthews Foods Ltd, http://www.bernardmatthews.com/CompanyHistory.asp.
79  *The Wall Street Journal (Eastern Edition)* (12 Oct. 1988), p. 1; *Fortune* (13 May 2005), p. 18; *Frozen Food Age* (May 2005), p. 18.
80  Case Studies — Bernard Matthews Foods Ltd., Employing Migrant Workers, http://www.employingmigrantworkers.org.uk/resources/5_9_3.html.
81  Rifkin, J. *Beyond Beef: The Rise and Fall of the Cattle Culture* (New York, 1992), pp. 170–75; Anon, 'Challenging Concentration of Control in the American Meat Industry', *Harvard Law Review*, 117(8) (2004): 2643.
82  Carlino, B., '75 Years: The Odyssey of Eating Out', *The Nation's Restaurant News* (Jan. 1994), pp. 11–28; *Wall Street Journal (Eastern edition)* (18 Dec. 1981), p. 1.
83  Economist Intelligence Unit, *Multinational Business*, 2 (1984): 56.
84  *Advertising Age (Midwest region edition)*, 53(52) (13 Dec. 1982): M.
85  *The Economist* (22 Nov. 1997), p. 81.
86  Ritzer, G., *The McDonaldization of Society* (Thousand Oaks, 1996), pp. 9–11.

# Chapter 9

# Governments and Questions of Welfare

Although much of the change that took place in the industry from 1945 onwards was driven by shifts in consumer demand, it can also be argued that another significant factor has been changes in governments' attitudes towards measures of control and regulation for the industry. Leaving aside trade restrictions designed to protect domestic meat producers from foreign competition already discussed in Chapter 7 above, the other area of government intervention was over matters of human and animal health. Both were strongly interlinked and had a serious impact on producers and the markets they supplied. Here the overriding concerns were animal health and food safety. In some cases it is impossible to make a neat distinction between the two, as it is possible for a number of animal diseases to infect humans. For example it has been known since the nineteenth century that bovine tuberculosis, anthrax, and trichinosis could all be transferred to humans.[1] More recently there were concerns about people becoming infected with *E Coli* O157 in cooked meat and salmonella in eggs. Also bovine spongiform encepalopathy (BSE), a disease similar to scrapie in sheep, has been linked to the appearance of new variant Creuzfeldt-Jakob disease, a fatal brain disease in humans.[2] In the late twentieth century there were strong public debates about potential risks to health in all Western nations. This meant that even if any governments had no particularly strong desire to protect the health of their own farm livestock or their own citizens, they were still forced to pay close attention to them if they wanted to participate in international trade.

In their recent study of meat safety, Spriggs and Isaac argue that governments can choose between two kinds of policy approach.[3] The first is the *Rational Actor Model* (RAM), which suggests that when meat is unsafe a government should select the most direct and efficient way of making it safe. The second policy choice involves the *Political Equilibrium Model* (PEM). This says that in its attempt to make meat safe the government also needs to balance the competing interests of the various parties involved in the industry. Although the authors are concerned with beef safety, the same line of thinking can be applied to animal health. In practice, Spriggs and Isaac acknowledge that any decision-making process will generally lie somewhere along a line between the RAM and the PEM ends of the spectrum. For a country highly dependent on imported meat, as Britain was for most of the nineteenth and twentieth centuries, the decision to exclude any imports was a question of balancing the threat they presented to human or animal health against the commercial losses that would be incurred by traders and investors participating in the trade.

Throughout the whole of the twentieth century the questions of disease and sanitary regulations were a source of friction between meat exporting and meat importing countries. Whenever exporters were denied access to an important market they frequently argued that country's government was exaggerating the problems caused by a particular disease. They were also highly suspicious that the restrictions were being used as an excuse to meet the demands of domestic livestock feeders for a ban on competing imports.

## Animal Health

Since the nineteenth century all Western nations have had to take notice of animal health. Part of this was driven by the fear that a new animal disease might be imported into a country that had hitherto been free of it. Britain had been seriously inconvenienced by outbreaks of rinderpest or cattle plague brought into the country from Eastern Europe as early as 1745.[4] The next outbreak in 1865 caused serious losses and required the government to introduce stringent restrictions on the import of animals and the movement of domestic farm livestock.[5] The first recorded outbreaks of foot-and-mouth disease in 1838–39 and pleuro-pneumonia in 1840 were widely supposed to have been introduced from Europe.[6] Anxiety about imported livestock disease became far greater as the volume of international trade in meat and livestock rose. Throughout the nineteenth century more and more countries introduced controls over this trade in order to prevent the import of animal disease. The most obvious thing to do was to ban meat and livestock imports, at least from countries where a particular disease was known to exist, but this conflicted with both the principles of free trade and the need to allow in food imports to feed the population. But there is also evidence that the opening of ports to foreign livestock had a damaging effect on British agriculture. Losses of farm stock from disease increased significantly between 1850 and 1870, and may even have made a temporary contribution to the domestic meat shortages that free trade was meant to cure.

A later refinement, under the Cattle Diseases Prevention Act of 1866, was to require imported animals to be landed only at specified ports where they could be examined to detect signs of disease. But as this was no use against animals incubating but as yet showing no sign of disease, it became the rule for animals to be slaughtered immediately on landing if they came from countries where there was a risk of disease.[7] As a result, as can be seen in Chapter 3 above, increasing restrictions were placed on the live animal trade. Thus by as early as 1889 the United Kingdom had an elaborate system of regulations that applied to virtually all its imports of cattle sheep and pigs. By then hardly any of them were allowed to be moved inland to market; the great majority had to be slaughtered at the ports where they were landed. Even those animals that were from countries free of disease were only allowed to be moved inland after veterinary inspections at the ports where they had been landed.[8] At the same time other countries introduced similar measures, so that by 1914 the international trade in livestock was very closely controlled.

Occasionally there were complaints from some producers, such as some Canadian cattle farmers who exported store cattle to the United Kingdom at the end of the nineteenth century. Although never a large trade, some of these beasts were fattened by graziers in Norfolk and parts of Scotland. This lasted until 1892 when pleuro-pneumonia was discovered among a consignment of cattle from Montreal at Dundee. This led to a ban on the trade from 1893 onwards, and Canadian cattle had to be slaughtered at the port of debarkation as United States cattle had since 1879, after the same disease had been found among a cargo a cattle from that country in 1878.[9] Slaughter at individual ports posed no problems provided that they each had adequate cold store space to cope. By the twentieth century complete restrictions of animal imports on the grounds of animal health made little difference to the overall volumes of meat traded internationally as the continuous improvement of ocean-going refrigeration technology reduced the need for livestock imports.

## Foot-and-Mouth Disease in Europe

Probably the greatest long-term concern about animal disease was over the import of meat from countries where foot-and-mouth disease was present. For the international trade in meat it has been the most economically significant animal disease in the world over the last two centuries because of the methods that have been adopted to prevent it spreading. In the nineteenth century the anxiety was about imports of live animals from countries that had the disease, but after 1900 there was increasing evidence that it might be imported in other ways. The disease is highly contagious and is caused by a virus with a number of different strains and affects all cloven-hoof animals. Vaccination against the disease is possible but provides no protection against other strains of the virus and was said to last only as long as a natural immunity that is offered when infected animals recover, between three and four months. Although rarely fatal, there is a varying loss of condition and output from recovered animals, but this varies and has been a matter of some debate. Besides direct contact, it was found it is possible for it to be transmitted by meat and bones from infected animals as well as anything that has come into direct or indirect contact with them. It can also lie dormant for long periods of time. After the initial outbreaks in the nineteenth century, Britain was always liable to re-infection, because it relied so heavily on livestock and meat imports. In the first half of the twentieth century the situation was, if anything, worse than in the previous half-century and the country was never really free of the disease until 1963. An outbreak in 1908 was traced to a consignment of hay from Holland. Another one, involving two separate outbreaks stretching over 1922 to 1924, was originally blamed on infected hay and straw used as packing material. These outbreaks were particularly serious as it was estimated that together they cost the British government almost £4 million in compensation for slaughtered livestock.[10]

Most of the interwar outbreaks of the disease in Britain were small in extent and contained by the methods evolved in the early twentieth century. These were the quarantining of infected farms, bans on the transport of livestock and closure of livestock markets plus the slaughter (with compensation) of infected and contact animals, followed by close disinfecting of affected farms. Although some countries used vaccination as a means of control, it was never employed in the United Kingdom. Abigail Woods has argued that the policy of keeping the country free of the disease was inherited from the later nineteenth century when 'stamping out' was seen as the only way to eliminate the disease. It was at that time a course of action that particularly suited the interests of a group of wealthy, influential breeders of pedigree livestock. These were men who were heavily involved in the profitable international trade in pedigree livestock and were desperate to keep the country free of foot-and-mouth disease because it would hinder the free export of their animals. This applied especially to some of their most valuable markets – the United States, Canada, Australia New Zealand and South Africa who also followed disease-free livestock policies. Woods has argued that these disease-free policies of many countries were an indirect export from Britain. They came to believe they needed to keep themselves free from the infection because of their high dependence on the disease-free British market for their meat.[11]

The special protection of the pedigree export trade was evident in the management of the 1922 epidemic by Stewart Stockman, chief veterinary officer of the Ministry of Agriculture. His firm belief in slaughter did not extend to the valuable pedigree animals infected with the disease; they were kept isolated and allowed to recover. He argued that it was in the national interest to preserve these irreplaceable products, but the cost of compensation was also a consideration. If the animals on the 65 farms that were isolated had been slaughtered this would have raised the compensation bill of £750,000 for the 1922 outbreak by 25 per cent.[12] At this time the British farming establishment became firmly set against any use of vaccination as a measure of control, believing that eradication was superior. In the meantime vaccination was employed as a control measure in Europe, though its use there was stopped after 1991. The maintenance of Britain's strict restrictions on livestock imports throughout the interwar years did cause one problem after the war. It meant that special permission had to be sought from the Ministry of Agriculture for the import of European breeds of cattle, sheep and pigs to improve native flocks and herds. Imports of stud animals had to be kept in strict quarantine for six months before they were allowed to mix with other farm livestock.

Three serious post-war outbreaks of the disease appeared in 1951–52, 1967–68 and finally in 2001. None were caused by imported livestock or infected contact material(s) but by imports of meat or meat bones. With the exception of the 2001 outbreak, there was strong suspicion that the disease originated with imports of meat from Argentina. There the disease was and is endemic in cattle, sheep and pigs and was the cause of intermittent problems for its meat exporters for most of the twentieth century. But all post-war outbreaks raised once again the general question of how to treat imported meat from foot-and-mouth infected countries, as well as the United Kingdom's continued adherence to a policy of slaughter and its rejection of vaccination. The 1951 outbreak occurred at a time when Britain was still recovering from the war and was desperately in need of cheap imports of meat. There was strong evidence that disease control among all those engaged in the Argentine meat industry, including farmers, government veterinary officials, and *frigorifico* managers were not all they could have been, but it was impossible for the British government to persuade them to invest more in this.[13] Against this background there was little opposition to resuming the trade with Argentina soon after the outbreak was under control.

The infective agent for the 1967–68 outbreak of the disease was again believed to have been meat imports from Argentina. Within a month of the first outbreak on 25 October 1967 that country voluntarily suspended exporting all meat to Britain, even before the British government announced a ban on meat imports from countries where the disease was endemic on 1 December. Argentina used as its excuse the claim that the British market price for its meat was too low, but it was the first time it had ever found it low enough to suspend its export trade. In the first eleven months of 1967 that country had sent 88,000 tons of chilled beef and 18,000 tons of chilled lamb to Britain, but in 1968 only 15,000 tons of beef arrived after the British government lifted the ban on Argentine beef from 15 April 1968. Imports of mutton and lamb from all countries where foot-and-mouth disease was endemic remained banned as the strongest circumstantial evidence suggested the outbreak was caused by infected carcases of Argentine lamb.[14]

For the next 34 years Britain remained free of the disease, and over such a long period it was alleged that the Ministry of Agriculture became rather complacent, reducing the number of officials it employed as a response to public spending cuts.[15] As a result it was slow to react when the 2001 outbreak was first noticed on 20 February 2001 when the official veterinary surgeon at an Essex abattoir noticed the symptoms in three pigs. The animals had come from a pig-finishing unit at Burnside Farm in Northumberland, which was licensed to feed waste food. Subsequent investigations indicated that the virus was probably in this waste food, but never established its precise origins. It was believed to have originated from a country where foot-and-mouth was present, and that this was somewhere in the Far East was given support by the identification of the pan-Asian form of the virus in some of the pig carcases. It was popularly supposed that it was contained in illegally imported meat products used by the restaurant and catering trade.[16]

But the virus was also blown by the wind to a neighbouring sheep farm at Prestwick Hall, and animals were sent from this farm to the nearest markets at Hexham in Northumberland and Longtown in Cumberland, before the infection was traced back to Burnside. These sheep then infected others at those markets, as well as passing it on through the marketing chain via dealers and their vehicles. In this way the disease was soon widely disseminated in England, Wales, and the bordering counties of Southern Scotland.[17] As in the past livestock markets were (eventually) closed, the movement of animals severely restricted, and practically the whole of the British countryside was closed to the general public lest they unwittingly transferred the disease on their persons.

Although the spread of the 2001 outbreak was similar to earlier ones, by a process of 'multiple seedings' from the original site of infection, it did have some differences from previous epizootics. As it was impossible to trace the source of the virus this time there was no reason for the United Kingdom to ban any meat imports, especially as the evidence pointed towards its probable origin being illegally imported meat.[18] But like past epidemics, the impact of this outbreak on the international meat trade was far from minimal, although in a different way than formerly. Since 1967, and under the protection of CAP subsidies and allowances, Britain had become an exporter of meat and livestock to the EU, and the EU had become a much larger exporter to the rest of the world. Denmark, Germany and Holland all had flourishing markets beyond the EU for products such as beef and pork. In 2000 the EU exported 1.53 million tons of pig meat, of which 408,000 tons went to Russia.[19] Once the disease appeared in the United Kingdom its exports to Europe were stopped, but not before some sheep carrying the virus had caused a few cases of the disease to appear in France, Holland and Ireland.[20] They were far more efficient in limiting its spread, but the presence of the disease immediately caused scores of countries, including disease-free ones like the United States, Canada and Australia, to ban imports of livestock and meat products from the EU.[21]

In the end, according to the official figures, the epidemic in the United Kingdom lasted for 32 weeks, affected 2,030 farms, and resulted in the slaughter of 4,068,000 cattle, sheep and pigs.[22] After this epidemic the costs were estimated rather differently from earlier ones. In the past only the direct costs to the farming community had been assessed, but this approach was inappropriate by the end of the twentieth century when agriculture was no longer a major part of the rural economy. The official assessments by the Department for Environment, Food and Rural Affairs covered the direct livestock compensation, and associated costs paid out directly by the government, other costs were estimated by academics and the press. When the costs to the whole economy were estimated it was found the severe restrictions on access to countryside designed to prevent the spread of the disease, had brought significant losses to those involved in the tourist industry. In round figures losses in the two areas were about equal: agricultural costs were about £3.1 billion and losses to the tourist industry estimated by academics were between £2.7 billion and £3.2 billion, although some press estimates put the tourism costs as high as £5.3 billion.[23] Some of the higher estimates of the cost to the tourism industry were probably unrealistic as they ignored the fact that some of spending which did not take place in the areas closed by the disease was diverted to other parts of Britain.

At this point it is necessary to issue a word of caution about the cost and the extent of the epidemic. It was certainly the most serious one that Britain had experienced, but some of the early estimates of animal losses were very much higher than the 4,068,000 in the 2005 National Audit Office report. Some of the unofficial figures suggested when the epidemic was in progress ranged from 6.5 to as high as 10 million. The main reason for this seems to have been that as no one knew exactly the extent and scale of the outbreak, rumour and exaggeration thrived. This may have been helped as Britain's policy of absolute eradication was challenged even more strongly than it had been during and after all other epidemics. Criticisms were focused on the length of time that was being taken to bring the outbreak under control, the slow response to reports of infection that was held partly to blame for the rapid spread of the disease. Some of the culls of uninfected animals on contiguous farms were regarded as unjust and unnecessary, and the effectiveness of simply relying on slaughter as a way of local containment was seen as outdated.[24]

For Europe the duration of the disease and length of time taken to bring it under control in the United Kingdom meant exports of meat were sharply reduced. In 2001 the quantities of beef, pork, mutton and lamb exported from the EU were around twenty per cent lower than 2000.[25] What this outbreak also did was to reveal how much farming systems since the 1960s had come to rely on the frequent and rapid transport of meat and animals, not only within the United Kingdom but over mainland Europe as well, thus adding to the risk of spreading the disease.

The 2001 outbreak also provoked frantic precautions on a worldwide scale against its introduction. New Zealand, desperate to preserve its disease-free status, launched a public education programme in a bid to protect its $US 5 billion worth of agricultural trade. The Agriculture Ministry intensified border surveillance and security, with disinfecting systems at airports and seaports and on-the-spot fines for any person illegally bringing food into the country. For that country the main threat was imports of the disease from South-East Asia where there had been 490 outbreaks of the disease in 2000. An outbreak of the disease in Turkey caused veterinary officials in Cyprus to set up disinfecting stations at crossing points along the ceasefire line to prevent the disease being carried across by diplomats and UN personnel travelling from Turkish occupied Northern Cyprus.[26] When the British Prime Minister attended the EU summit in Stockholm on 22 March 2001, Swedish officials impounded and burnt all the food on the aircraft.[27]

**Foot-and-mouth Disease in the Americas**

The endemic nature of the disease in South America remained a constant problem facing its meat exporters. The United States introduced a series of very stringent controls over the importation of livestock from infected countries, very similar to those in force in Britain. Nevertheless, from 1870 to 1929 the United States experienced ten different outbreaks of foot-and-mouth disease from imports from Europe and South America. Two of these, in 1914 and 1924 were particularly serious, costing tens of millions of dollars to eradicate.[28] Unlike Britain, the United

States received store cattle over its extensive land borders with Canada and Mexico. Foot-and-mouth disease was less of a problem in Canada with just one or two outbreaks that were quickly controlled, but Mexico had more and there they took longer to control. For these reasons the United States has had some of the world's toughest disease control regulations along its borders, applying not only to live animals but other sources of infection as well. Its anti foot-and-mouth measures were also influenced by the changing nature of primary outbreaks.

A 1994 study conducted by the United States Department of Agriculture (USDA) found that of 558 worldwide outbreaks of the disease between 1870 and 1993, only 2 per cent of those occurring before 1969 had been caused by imported livestock. Of the other outbreaks over the same period, 71 per cent were attributed to meat, meat products and garbage infected with foot-and-mouth disease, and 24 per cent to airborne transmission, sometimes by the wind and sometimes by birds. But since 1969 imported animals had become the major cause of the disease, accounting for 36 per cent of outbreaks, and the next largest was vaccines at 25 per cent.[29]

When the United Kingdom banned imports of live animals from the River Plate for immediate slaughter in 1900, because of the disease there it caused little damage to the meat industry of that country. It simply encouraged further investment in refrigerated meat plants and increased the growth of the trade in frozen and then chilled meat, as described in Chapter 3 above. But in 1926 the United States also prohibited the import of South American chilled and frozen beef because it was now realised that the meat itself might carry foot-and-mouth disease. At that time the United States ban on its chilled and frozen beef was not an immediate problem for Argentina as Britain was still South America's major overseas market for fresh meat in the interwar years. However, the United States ban did not extend to Argentine cured beef, which was joints of about a pound in weight that had 4 per cent salt added and were then 'ripened' for three days at 4°C. There was not much of a trade in this product in the interwar years, but after 1945 as United States population grew and prosperity increased, demand grew and the country became a major market for imported meat in the 1950s. At the same time, partly because of the slower growth of its purchasing power and partly because of the recovery of its livestock sector, the British market became less important.[30]

After 1955 the Argentine beef industry had recovered from the effects of drought and the downturn brought about by the economic policies of the Perón regime and cattle numbers increased. In the second half of the 1950s exports of cured beef to the United States rose and became a significant business for both Argentina and Uruguay. When in 1958 the United States decided that cured beef also carried a disease risk and banned it from 15 May, there were strong protests from both countries. Although scientific tests confirmed foot-and-mouth virus could survive in the lymph nodes and bones of salt-cured meat, the immediate reaction of the Argentine government was to accuse the United States of using its sanitary regulations as an excuse to exclude competition from its meat.

Arguments between the two countries then followed, as to whether imported Argentine meat ever contained lymph nodes or bone fragments. The Argentine authorities also expressed protests over the damage to the reputation of Argentine meat by the United States stating once again that the disease existed in their country. Although there was no denying the fact of its presence, it was so widespread that Argentine ranchers considered it as one of the usual risks of business, virulent outbreaks were rare and the country's livestock population was so large that it only affected a limited number of them at any one time.[31]

The split between the United States and Argentina over foot-and-mouth disease was partly a function of the way their livestock industries were managed. The extensive nature of the pampas meant that Argentina has always remained a range producer, whereas the United States had largely abandoned this method by the end of the nineteenth century. Thereafter the United States beef industry relied increasingly on feedlots with cattle concentrated in small areas, and its dairy industry was also managed in a similar way. In these circumstances the disease spreads rapidly, and is regarded as a serious matter. Countries such as Britain and the United States who relied on the slaughter, with compensation, of infected and contact animals for control were extra-vigilant to prevent the import of infected animals. They argued that for their intensively managed livestock industries the cost of the disease would be high if it ever became endemic, putting estimates of the overall loss of productivity for the industry, from infected, recovering and recovered animals at around 25 per cent.

It was always possible at any time to import Argentine cooked meats, such as corned beef, into the United States or any other country that banned its chilled and frozen meat because of the threat of disease. But as there was no great demand for cooked meats when there was a plentiful supply of fresh meat and cooked meats commanded a lower price than chilled, the Argentine producers resented this exclusion from the best markets. In the 1960s parts of the European market were still open to Argentine chilled and frozen meat, but even here controls were raised after the 1967–68 outbreak in the United Kingdom. In attempts to gain wider access to the best markets, South American countries considered introducing culling programmes designed to eliminate the disease from their best beef producing regions. But compensation expenses were difficult for governments that were often financially stretched to meet when extensive outbreaks involved the slaughter of large numbers of animals. But even if it had been possible for them to eliminate the disease they would also have been held back from the United States market by its import quotas and heavy subsidies to domestic producers.[32]

The disease was also to become a cause of friction between the United States and Mexico. In the 1940s Mexico exported around half a million cattle a year to the United States. The United States allowed this trade because both countries had signed a Sanitary Convention in 1928 mutually agreeing not to import livestock from countries that had foot-and mouth disease. But in 1946 Mexico imported for herd improvement a number of Indian Zebu bulls from Brazil – a country where the disease was endemic. Immediately the United States banned imports of

Mexican cattle, arguing there was a strong risk that the disease could appear in Mexico and then be carried northward when the United States imported Mexican cattle. An outbreak of the disease in December 1946 at Veracruz, in the area near where the bulls had been landed, and its rapid spread over seventeen of Mexico's states, were taken as signs that American policy was fully justified. United States veterinary inspectors were sent south to confirm the disease, and on 26 December the border was closed to all Mexican livestock and livestock products.[33]

The Mexican outbreak was neither a small nor isolated one; it involved some 57 million hectares and 15 million livestock. It was only brought under control and eliminated, by a policy of vaccination, slaughter of nearly a million cattle, and assistance from the United States which cost that country 120 million dollars by 1950. The effects of the United States import ban on the Mexican livestock industry were very serious. Canneries had to be built to alleviate a glut of animals on the northern ranges of the country, while special arrangements had to be made to ensure that quarantine regulations and restrictions on the movement of animals did not cause meat shortages in Mexico City. The task of removing the disease was a prolonged one. Mexico was first declared free of the virus and the livestock trade with the United States was restored in September 1952. But the disease flared up again in 1953, and it was not until 31 December 1954 that restrictions on the import of livestock from Mexico were again lifted. The Mexican outbreak was significant because for the first time United States animal disease control officials had worked with the Mexican authorities on both sides of the border to eradicate a disease in another country.[34]

## International Attempts at Animal Disease Control

One feature of the twentieth century was an attempt to control the international transfer of foot-and-mouth and other livestock diseases by international bodies. The first of these, the Office International des Epizooties (OIE) was established in Paris in 1924. By the end of the twentieth century over 160 countries had joined the organisation. It was set up to develop international guidelines for animal health based upon generally agreed scientific thinking, and then to get agreement from all its members before its guidelines were adopted. But it had no power to act as an international animal health policeman, because every member still maintained its sovereign right to develop its own individual standards for animal health and trade. All the OIE was ever able to do was provide guidance for countries, rather than hard and fast rules on matters national and international animal health. Although it was impossible for this body to perform any executive functions during the interwar years, it did begin the collection and dissemination of animal health information on an international scale as far as was possible. The strongest threat to existence came immediately after the war when, with the establishment of the FAO, there were suggestions that it was now irrelevant and should be dissolved. The challenge was fought off and it managed to survive, although immediately after the war most of its work was just involved in collecting and publishing information about the international incidence of all disease of farm livestock. Had it remained doing only this it is difficult to see how it could have survived, but as the OIE was not formally linked to any of the post-war economic and political blocs this allowed it to eventually become the main forum on international animal health.

The earliest example of the OIE helping towards an international agreement about animal health standards came with foot-and-mouth disease. After the 1951–52 epidemic, the European Commission for the Control of Foot-and-Mouth (EUFMD) was set up as a rival to the OIE. Unlike the OIE, it could actively formulate policy, so by the 1960s it was beginning to have an effect on the disease in Europe. With the subsequent widening of the EU and proper co-operation between a larger number of states, progress was made towards reducing the number of cases. By the 1990s as Europe was largely free of the disease the members of the EU agreed to abandon the policy of vaccination, except in special circumstances to control any fresh outbreak.[35] The major benefits of this move were an immediate relaxation of international trade barriers. This was also partly the result of better cooperation between EUFMD and the OIE that had been largely inactive for twenty years.

Their joint discussions resulted in an agreement about the rules on how to define a country as free from the disease. After any outbreak a country would be subject to the trade restrictions of other foot-and-mouth disease countries, and would only be declared free of the disease three months after the last case was stamped out, or 12 months after emergency vaccination ceased.[36] It was therefore not surprising that the European response was highly critical when the disease was reintroduced, causing it to lose its disease-free status, through what was seen as lax vigilance by the United Kingdom. In March 2001 Hugh Byrne, the Natural Resources Minister in the Irish Government, referred to the United Kingdom as the 'leper of Europe' and described its handling of the outbreak as 'nothing short of a scandal'.[37] The European Parliament reacted by setting up a Temporary Committee on Foot and Mouth Disease, and it issued its final report on 17 December 2002, reinforcing the criticism of the United Kingdom.[38]

As foot-and-mouth was endemic throughout the whole of South America there was also recognition that all South American states needed an organisation where they could work together to give warnings of and control the disease as much as possible. To achieve this, in 1951 the Americas Animal Health Authorities established the Pan-American Foot-and-Mouth-Disease Center. The popular name for foot-and-mouth in South America was aftosa, so this body was generally known as PANAFTOSA. Located in Rio de Janeiro the organization carried out research into new longer-lasting vaccines, and developed its surveillance and early warnings of outbreaks of the disease. The ultimate aim of PANAFTOSA was to eradicate the disease but although it was able to coordinate and encourage effective cooperation between countries that were affected by joint outbreaks, like Chile and Argentina in 1987, eradication was to prove impossible. However it had some successes with its policy of regular livestock vaccination and inspection, in freeing regions from the disease. Under its systems of management vaccinated herds have been able to gain international recognition as disease-free under the OIE definitions, thus guaranteeing the international trade in meat products from those herds, and from certain regions.[39]

But over much of the period after 1945 this disease remained a constant nuisance, flaring up at times in particular hot spots to disrupt meat exports. Even the improvements in control by the end of the 1990s did not prevent the United Kingdom's outbreak from having knock-on effects over the whole international meat trade. But although surveillance and inspections at ports could detect the disease in animals, there was no cost-effective way of efficiently monitoring its extent in legal imports of meat. There was also no chance of the OIE, or any other international surveillance body, detecting meat with this or any other infection in the increasing amounts of meat that were illegally sent from countries where this and other diseases were endemic and poorly controlled, to friends and relatives in the West.[40] The OIE could effectively monitor only the legal international trade in livestock and meat products and it was up to national governments to stop smuggling.

### BSE and the Transfer of Livestock Disease to Humans

Although the epidemics of foot-and-mouth seem to have been the most widely feared international livestock disease after 1945, its commercial impact was mainly a problem for farmers and meat processors, as the possibility of its transfer to humans is almost non-existent. However, since the 1990s there has been greater concern over the transfer of new animal diseases to humans, and this has added to the consumer reaction against meat. In 1945 most of the concern in this area was over conditions that had been known about since the nineteenth century, such as tuberculosis, trichinosis and anthrax. In order to eliminate the transfer of such diseases, central and local governments in Europe and America had started to insist that trained meat inspectors were employed in slaughterhouses since the nineteenth century. Progress was never as rapid as everyone would have liked as local inertia, vested interests and the extra public expense involved always slowed down the implementation of food inspection. But by the 1970s inspection of slaughterhouses and processing plants was pretty well universal in Western countries and gave good control of known meat-borne diseases.[41]

From the 1980s this situation changed. Up to that time there was little public anxiety about catching anything from eating meat. The only major exception since the war had been a number of outbreaks of typhoid in Britain in 1963–64. These were traced back to contaminated tins of Argentine corned beef. The animals from which the beef came were disease free, but the typhoid germ was introduced by using untreated water from the River Plate to cool cases of corned beef after cooking and sealing. In some of these containers there were fissures and it was through these that the meat became infected. Subsequent investigation found the River Plate received considerable outfalls of untreated sewage each day, thus making it an ideal medium for the spread of the typhoid bacillus. The British government's attitude was to give as little publicity as possible to the first three occurrences of infection in England in 1963 because it feared they might promote public panic. It was also a policy that ideally suited the Argentine corned beef manufacturers and the meat's British distributors, as they feared the publicity would turn consumers against their product. This policy of secrecy and evasion only ended after a fourth and much larger outbreak of the disease in Aberdeen, Scotland, in May 1964 made it impossible to continue.[42] Once again, the United Kingdom government used the country's heavy reliance on imported meat to rationalise its inaction.

There were still traces of this thinking in the 1980s when another animal infection, BSE, was first noticed in cattle.[43] It appeared to be a brain disease (encepalopathy) that caused staggering and then death in affected animals, symptoms similar to a disease in sheep called scrapie. Post-mortem examinations revealed affected cow's brains were damaged and had extensive pitted (spongiform) areas. This was in fact a new disease and it was for a time feared that it could present a far more serious threat to public health than all previous animal diseases. This was when it was finally established that it was able to jump the species barrier and infect humans. Its presence was first noticed in British cattle in November 1986, and in May 1988 the British government set up a Working Party on Bovine Spongiform Encepalopathy under Sir Richard Southwood to find out more about it and advise on any possible risk to humans. In October it was reported that it could be transmitted to mice and by the end of the year it was officially classified as an animal disease that could be passed to humans, although at that point Sir Richard thought the danger was largely theoretical rather than real. It was also thought that the primary agent in spreading the disease was in the animal protein included along with cereals in animal feeds. For generations all animal feed millers had mixed meat, blood and bone waste from slaughterhouses in their products to promote faster growth.[44]

Following the identification of a new disease there was a rising anxiety among professionals as to exactly what it was, and among consumers whether it was safe to eat beef.[45] Investigations into the disease were therefore conducted on two fronts: to establish the risk to animals, and discover the extent of the risk to humans. The situation for livestock became more serious when it was established that not only could the disease be passed on through maternal transmission, but that calves could be born to cows who were carrying the disease but displaying no symptoms at the time of calving. In 1990 the United Kingdom government banned 'bovine offal' from animal feed and in 1994 most of the EU also banned the inclusion of animal protein in animal feed, and allowed beef-on-the-bone exports only from British farms that had been free of BSE for six years. But throughout the 1990s the British Government reassured the public there was no danger from eating beef, though by 1995 BSE was linked to a new form of Creutzfeld Jacob

Disease (vCJD), a degenerative brain disease in humans whose symptoms were similar to those in cattle. Eventually in March 1996 the British government was forced to admit there was probably a connection between BSE in cattle and vCJD in humans. When this was announced the EU immediately banned all exports of British beef. Up to that time the British official policy had been to reassure the public that all beef was safe to eat, but in 1996 a 30-month slaughter scheme was introduced by the United Kingdom to prevent cows over that age from entering the human food chain.

Throughout the ten years since the disease had first been noticed the United Kingdom government had to balance its first priority, to protect the health of its citizens, against any damage that BSE might do to agriculture. Once the transmissibility of the disease had been firmly established, both government and the meat industry faced a new sequence of events. The number of fresh cases of BSE rose steadily so that thousands were being identified each year. The rise was only halted after the controls on feed milling ingredients started to take effect. The numbers of fresh cases of BSE in Britain reached a maximum of 37,280 cases in 1992, but fell thereafter so that there were only 343 in 2004.[46] But there were real fears that because of the uncertain incubation period for vCJD many thousands of people might succumb to the disease long after the prolonged BSE epidemic was over. After a time even this began to look increasingly unlikely, and epidemiologists started to revise down their predictions of future cases when the incidence of vCJD began to decline after 2000. The maximum diagnosed that year was 28, but for 2004 it was just 9, and by July 2005 the total deaths and probable infections amounted to only 156 since 1995.[47]

The economic effects of the outbreak were more serious. Unlike other animal epidemics, it took over a decade to firmly establish its nature and the danger it posed to humans. There was an immediate feeling of betrayal by the public once the government finally announced, after countering several years of growing doubt with reassurances that beef was safe to eat, that BSE had probably been transmitted to humans as vCJD. This was acknowledged in the 14-volume report from the official inquiry it was forced to set up in 1998, to investigate the way it had handled the whole episode up to 1996.[48] Although this report was not highly critical of the entire management of the epidemic, it did point out there were some shortcomings in the way the disease was investigated and findings acted upon up to that time.[49]

By 1996 it was established the chief danger of infection for humans appeared to come from eating parts of bovine offal, including mechanically recovered meat from bones and especially from around the spinal column.[50] From this it followed that the greatest danger came from eating ground beef, which was included in all the cheaper manufactured beef products such as pies, sausages and hamburgers. But as there appeared to be no danger from eating muscle tissue the safest beef was the most expensive, that is steaks and joints. However, not all British consumers made such fine distinctions and as a result the consumption of all forms of British beef fell to some extent, driven by the massive media coverage over the uncertainty of what the government statement meant for the safety of beef. Between 1995 and 1996 consumption of beef fell by 15.9 per cent, but the largest fall, of 26.5 per cent, was for mince, whereas there was a much smaller decline in demand for steaks and roasts, purchases of which fell by 3.2 per cent and 7.8 per cent, respectively. In addition, the market share of frozen beef products, including burgers and sausages suffered a decline.[51] The immediate economic effect of the 1996 announcement was to reinforce the general health anxieties over beef and force down its consumption, at least in the short-term.

As far as exports were concerned they were more seriously affected. Between 1986 and 1995 United Kingdom beef and live cattle exports more than doubled from £290 million to £720 million, most of this after 1991. This growth was in spite of the measures of control that were being imposed by EU and non-EU countries on exports of British cattle and beef from 1988 in order to protect their own herds from BSE and consumers from vCJD. When the EU prohibited all United Kingdom exports of beef and cattle at the end of March 1996 the whole of the export market in these products disappeared, causing serious financial problems for all those involved in it.[52]

The announcement's effect was not only felt in Britain.[53] The export of British cattle and beef and the knowledge that over the years British cattle had been used in Europe for herd improvement caused loss of confidence in beef in the EU as a whole. Consumption fell in 1996 in all the other major EU consuming countries and in 1997 remained below what it had been in the pre-BSE crisis levels of 1995. Germany was the worst affected as there overall consumption of the meat was down 7 per cent, whilst in France and Italy it fell by 5 per cent. An immediate reaction of all EU consumers was to substitute other meats, and in Britain and France the demand for lamb rose, while other countries ate more poultry and, to a smaller extent, pork. But EU production did not fall as a consequence because CAP support subsides still made it profitable to produce beef as intervention buying, which was almost non-existent before the crisis, was used to relieve the market of any surplus. Although France initially lost some of its markets for beef in North Africa, exports from Europe rose in 1997 although as these were now from intervention stocks this conflicted with WTO rules on export subsidies.

Cases of the disease also appeared elsewhere in Europe, but never reaching the proportions of the British epidemic. Some of the earlier cases in Denmark, Germany, Italy and Portugal were among imported cows, but later ones were diagnosed among their domestic herds.[54] The first probably originated from exports of British cattle before the infection risks were fully understood and the introduction of export controls. Between 1985 and 1989 more than 55,400 British cattle were exported from Britain to other EU countries for breeding, some of these certainly with BSE. Once the disease was present in Europe the movement of infected animals within a market largely free of border controls was relatively easy. But European countries, like Britain in the early stages of its own epidemic, found it hard to admit there was a problem. A study carried out in 1997 estimated that had these 55,400 animals remained in Britain, 1,642 of them would have contracted BSE. Yet European countries had admitted to a total of only 285 cases, most of them from Switzerland. Some of the worst offenders for under-reporting were countries that had campaigned strongly to ban exports of British beef. For example in Germany the expected number of cases was 243, yet the number actually reported was only five.[55] For years Germany held itself to be an oasis of BSE-free beef in Europe, but allegations that government ministers knew for almost a year that German beef was not safe, forced its health and agriculture ministers to resign in January 2001.[56]

Against this background there was further dispute between the United Kingdom and the rest of the EU over re-allowing its beef exports after it had taken steps to reduce the risk of BSE. In July 1999 the EU Commission set 1 August as the date for lifting the ban on specified beef imports from the United Kingdom under the Date-Based Export Scheme (DBES). Basically this would allow the export of de-boned beef from animals aged between 6 and 30 months from BSE-free herds.[57] But both France and Germany found reasons not to lift the ban. France claimed there were insufficient scientific guarantees for the safety of British beef, and Germany delayed because the German parliament was in recess and needed to approve the change. This refusal opened up a prolonged dispute between Britain and other members of the EU, particularly with France who consistently refused to accept British beef.[58] As a result of this, and the general restrictive conditions attaching to the export of British beef, the DBES made very little difference to attempts to revive the export business after 1998. As can be seen from Table 9.1 below, annual exports of boned beef and veal in 1999–2003 were worth less than 10 per cent of their pre-crisis level.

**Table 9.1 Annual Cattle and Beef Exports from the United Kingdom, 1995–2003 ($000)**

|           | Cattle  | Beef and Veal | Boned Beef and Veal | Total   |
|-----------|---------|---------------|---------------------|---------|
| 1995      | 103,157 | 531,066       | 303,570             | 937,793 |
| 1996      | 13,276  | 105,084       | 90,397              | 208,757 |
| 1997      | 5       | 832           | 17,990              | 18,827  |
| 1998      | 36      | 2,799         | 15,311              | 18,146  |
| 1999–2003 | 6       | 1,793         | 26,789              | 28,588  |

*Source:* FAOSTAT August 2004

Cases of BSE in Europe rose while its incidence was declining in the United Kingdom because it delayed the tightening regulations on meat and bone meal in feedstuffs, whereas the United Kingdom already had a watertight ban in place by 1996. This led a number of countries to prohibit beef imports from Europe, just as they had done from Britain. In December 1997 the United States took steps to ban all beef imports from Europe, just as it had done with beef from Britain in 1989, and from January 2001 Australia and New Zealand both banned beef imports from anywhere in the EU. For a time it seemed that the world trade in beef was in danger of forming into particular trading blocs, depending on the presence or absence of BSE in rather the same way the cattle trade had done over the presence or absence of foot-and-mouth.[59] But, ironically, the South American countries that had had the most serious problems with foot-and-mouth found themselves to be largely free of BSE. This seems to have been because South American cattle, like those of Australia and New Zealand, were mainly grass-fed and so did not receive rations of animal feed contaminated with protein concentrates that had been responsible for the spread of the disease in the United Kingdom and Europe.

The practice of banning the trade in cattle and beef with a country as soon as its first case of BSE was confirmed became a standard response, and it was difficult to get this reversed when subsequent ones appeared. In order to prevent low risk countries reporting just a few cases from being regarded in the same way as the United Kingdom, where the BSE outbreaks had been most numerous, the OIE began a grading scheme. After 1990 more data on the disease became available as countries started testing at abattoirs to estimate its presence in animals not yet showing symptoms. By combining this information with any reported cases from farms it became possible to assess a country's risk. The United Kingdom was naturally high risk, but a number of the European countries were only moderate, and minimal risk. The collection of this data allowed the OIE to publish a Terrestrial Animal Health Code with guidelines on how a country should be treated when it came to considering the risks from international trade in its cattle and beef products.[60] The guidelines, which were constantly updated as more knowledge about the disease became available, established the principle that the presence of BSE in a country was not necessarily a reason to discontinue beef imports from it. Provided the necessary safeguards were in place, such as using killing methods that did not cause meat contamination, and the removal of specified risk material from carcases, then its beef could still be safe to eat. This manner of thinking and risk assessment became increasingly important as the disease spread beyond Europe, even though the OIE had no power to enforce its recommendations.

Since the first appearance of the disease in Britain the United Sates had, as with foot-and-mouth, been particularly careful in erecting an elaborate system of firewalls to guard against its entry.[61] From 1990 it had a national routine surveillance programme to test for the disease in animals after slaughter. With the appearance of BSE in Europe the United States initially hoped it would open up a fresh market there for its own beef from BSE-free cattle. This was because since 1989 its beef could not be exported to Britain or any of the EU countries because it used hormone growth boosters, which were outlawed by the EU. But despite the presence of BSE and a series of WTO rulings against the EU ban on beef from cattle treated with hormones, the EU still refused to accept such beef imports from the United States, reinforcing the familiar suspicion that the hormone ban was being used as a disguised form of protection.[62] The European ban did not do much harm to United States beef exports, as its major export markets were Japan,

Mexico, Korea and Canada, but these markets were seriously affected after BSE was identified in the United States.

The first positive case, in December 2003, was an eight-year old Holstein breed dairy cow from the State of Washington sent for processing at Midway Meats in Washington State. Other countries reacted to the news in the usual way and immediately stopped importing beef from the United States. Even when subsequent investigations showed the cow did not originate from the United States but had been imported from Canada, the ban on American beef in overseas markets still remained. The largest market was Japan, which stopped importing all beef from the United States.[63] Japan had already some experience of BSE in 2001 when it was imported from South Korea, which also banned United States beef at the same time as Japan. In 2003 the Japanese and South Korean markets for United States beef exports were worth $1,167m and $749m, respectively. But they had almost vanished in 2004 when the Japanese market shrank to only $6m and the South Korean to $400,000. Up to that point the United States had, like other countries, closed its borders to all imports from countries with BSE, but from the start of 2004 it was lobbying Japan and Korea to readmit beef from cattle between 6 and 30 months.[64]

The tracing back of the disease to Canada on 20 May 2004 meant the northern border was immediately closed to beef and cattle. This posed severe problems for Canada as it made significant exports of cattle and beef to the United States. In 1999–2001 over 900,000 Canadian cattle were exported, around eighty per cent of them for immediate slaughter, but there were also some heavy steers and heifers as stores for further feeding. For a number of years there was a significant two-way flow of animals, as in 2000 when drought damage to pasture forced United States producers to export greater numbers of stores to Canada. But with the border closed, Canadian cattle and beef prices fell, causing similar problems for the Canadian industry as the closure of the southern border because of foot-and-mouth disease had done to the Mexican cattle industry in the late 1940s and early 1950s. The Canadian beef processing industry had undergone some expansion in the 1990s, mainly because United States firms had invested in capacity north of the border to supply their home market with ground beef and muscle meat. But even with this expansion the Canadian industry was not able to slaughter and process something like an extra million cattle.[65]

The effects of BSE on the global beef export business were as serious as foot-and-mouth. When isolated cases of each turned up in various parts of the world, they had the ability to profoundly disrupt international trading relations. If anything, BSE posed more serious problem, as unlike foot-and-mouth the disease can only be positively confirmed after death as there is to date (July 2005) no way of testing live animals for BSE. Once a case had been detected it was virtually impossible, at least in the short term, to get other nations to lift their import bans even if, like the EU, they already had experience of the disease. This was something the United States and Canada found to their cost in 2004 when they found themselves subject to the international trade restrictions they had pioneered in the 1990s. Countries that already had the disease had no reason to be indulgent when others were afflicted, and an immediate and complete embargo on beef from other countries with BSE was the most logical course of action. BSE always caused an initial fall in beef prices when some consumers switched their demand to other meats. In this situation any ban on beef imports reduced the amount of beef available, and this helped to counteract the disease's effect on prices and thus ease the market situation for home producers. The initial announcement of BSE was always accompanied by public anxiety, and in such situations governments had to help their own beef producers by reassuring people that home-produced beef was still safe to eat, rather than tell them other countries' was safe too.

**The International Livestock Trade**

Before 1850 the main way of supplying meat to deficit regions was by the transit of live animals, but by the end of the nineteenth century technical developments and livestock disease regulations made it appear as though the movement of livestock for food purposes would eventually wither away. But the complete elimination of all international livestock trade never happened. Even though dwarfed by the international trade in meat, it hung on and in some cases took on new forms when fresh international markets were opened up that could only be effectively supplied by import of livestock ready for immediate slaughter.

The United Kingdom, as the world's largest single market for meat for much of the nineteenth century, led the way in pioneering humane regulations to protect transported livestock both within Britain and those brought in from overseas by ocean transport. This part of the international livestock trade was difficult to regulate, because it was almost impossible to enforce controls once the ships left port. Nevertheless, by the 1890s the United Kingdom and other Western countries had imposed some legislative controls on the trade. They covered such things as the number of animals individual ships were allowed to carry, determined by the tonnage of the ship and how much space they had to allow each animal, as well as minimum care arrangements for them on the voyage. Enforcement was by official inspection at the ports, and another check on conditions could be obtained by enforcing the publication of mortality figures on the voyage. But by 1914 all foreign and colonial meat was brought to Britain on the hook rather than on the hoof. Foot-and-mouth and other animal disease controls had stopped livestock imports from Europe and South America, and the North American live cattle trade finished because its cattle surplus had dried up. All that remained was the substantial short-distance traffic of animals across the Irish Sea.

Despite this, within most countries farm animals still needed to be moved three or four times before going to slaughter, and in certain cases cross-border transit remained because it was convenient. Even at the end of the nineteenth century a substantial international trade in livestock took place in Europe. Some of this was store stock like the imports of Irish cattle for fattening in Britain, but they included meat animals going for immediate slaughter as well. [66] Central Europe was also a significant meat deficit region and in the interwar years Germany, Austria and Czechoslovakia together imported some 500,000 head of cattle. Germany's supplies came from Denmark, but Austria and Czechoslovakia received cattle from Hungary and the Balkans. Both North and South America took part in the international cattle trade with the United States, which took some 300,000 head a year from Canada and Mexico, while Chile imported around 80,000 cattle a year from Argentina and Uruguay. Besides cattle, there was a trade in sheep and pigs as well. France imported sheep from Algeria and Britain imported them from Ireland. Between the wars Poland was the greatest international exporter of live pigs, mostly to Austria and Czechoslovakia. Besides cattle and sheep, Britain imported pigs from Ireland. [67]

By 1945 most of the trade in livestock was still very localised and for the most part confined to short distances. [68] But it was a trade that continued in the post-war years, despite the advances made in meat processing, because it could satisfy a demand in certain markets that chilled, frozen or other processed meat was unable to. Even at the start of the twenty-first century freshly killed meat from imported livestock continued to be more acceptable and command a premium over refrigerated imports, just as the beef from United States cattle had over North American chilled and South American frozen had in the late nineteenth century. It also partly explained the persistence and development of the live export of cattle and sheep from Australia and New Zealand in the 1960s. But although international livestock movements were but a fraction of the international trade in meat, it roused fierce debate and forced both governments to adjudicate between the competing claims of various groups. Both livestock farmers and livestock shipping firms lobbied for its protection and assistance, whereas animal welfare groups and domestic meat processors each wanted the trade stopped. The animal activists campaigned against it on the grounds of cruelty alleging that it produced unnecessary suffering, and the meat processing industry argued that it was reducing work for them, taking jobs, and forcing some firms to close.

### Livestock Exports from Australia and New Zealand

The trade grew from the 1970s onwards partly as a response to the reduction of traditional markets. The subsidised increase in sheep numbers in the EU significantly reduced the export market for Australian and New Zealand frozen mutton and lamb in Britain and Europe. Therefore the rational response in both countries, particularly Australia, was to develop fresh markets in Asia and the Middle East. They were both regions of meat deficit with no large tradition of eating beef, and where sheep-meat was acceptable on traditional and religious grounds. But developing these markets was treading new ground, because for the first time significant exports of meat were being made by Western nations to non-Western nations. These new cross-cultural markets had a variety of differences from those of the EU, which Australian and New Zealand exporters had to accommodate. The most serious problem was they were only prepared to eat meat from animals slaughtered in accordance with religious requirements, that is, without stunning before death. This excluded chilled and frozen meat from conventional plants processing meat for export. In addition, there was a shortage of conveniently sited cold storage in these countries making stockpiling and distribution difficult. There was also a greater demand for more strong-tasting meat from slightly older animals than in Europe where the taste was very much for young lamb. Taken together, these factors encouraged the export of live sheep.

But the long-distance transport of livestock through the tropics raised objections from animal welfare lobbyists using the traditional argument that to avoid unnecessary suffering animals should be killed as near as possible to where they were to be consumed. From the 1970s they also argued against the trade on the grounds that animals received inhumane treatment once they reached their destination. There were allegations that some animals died from lack of care awaiting slaughter and that others faced further long distance journeys, this time by road to other Middle-Eastern countries. While Western governments were prepared to see that animals were transported from their shores under humane conditions, they were both unable and unwilling to attempt to intervene in the internal civil matters in the receiving country.

The trade also roused opposition from the domestic slaughter industry who saw animal exports as a loss of output for their own businesses. As far as the meat processors were concerned, governments tended to stand aside and let market forces take their course. They were aware that livestock exports reduced the impact on sheep farmers of changes in traditional export markets, as well as the fall in per capita consumption of mutton and lamb. But trade unions did have some success in pressuring Labour governments to restrict the numbers of livestock exported, as the Australian Meat Industry Employees Union did in the late 1970s and early 1980s. Trade unions were, somewhat surprisingly, also able to get a certain amount of support from sections of the animal welfare groups who recognised that the livestock exports meant loss of jobs in the meat industry.[69]

The trade was pioneered by Australia, who exported relatively small numbers each year to the Far East before the war.[70] In the immediate post-war years recovery was slow, but by the 1960s it had largely revived. In 1963 the 20-knot Blue Funnel passenger and cargo liner *MV Centaur* was fitted out for the Far Eastern trade, to carry sheep and cattle between Freemantle in Western Australia and Malaysia and Singapore. On its first voyage in 1964 this 8,000-ton vessel took 4,500 sheep and 40 dairy cows to Singapore. On arrival the sheep were, as always, slaughtered according to local custom and the cows were kept for milking for as long as possible in the hot climate before being slaughtered. Some attention had been paid to detail in order to ensure that the trade was humane and animals were cared for, as well as meeting the Australian government's own animal transport regulations. The equipment on board the *Centaur* was designed to change the air in the animal holds 30 times an hour, and there were facilities for manure removal,

washing down the animal areas and providing water and care for them on the
voyage, as well as a milking parlour for the cows.[71]

At this time the trade was small and, although the animal lobby was never
happy about it, there appear to have been no strong complaints about the conditions
under which the animals were carried. But the increased oil wealth of the Middle
East generated new markets for sheep in places like Saudi Arabia and Kuwait.[72]
There was also a seasonal element here as the demand for sheep was heavy at the
end of the Moslem fast period of Ramadan and in Saudi Arabia there was a heavy
demand for sheep for sacrifice at the time of the annual peak of the Haj.
Traditionally the countries of the Horn of Africa had supplied much of this, but
drought and war from the 1980s caused these supplies to dwindle.[73]

But exports to the Middle East involved longer journey times, and the use of
very large freight vessels, able to take over 50,000 sheep per voyage raised fresh
anxieties about animal welfare. The New Zealand live export trade recommenced
in 1985 after several years of a total ban in response to the demands of the meat
packers and with strict quotas on numbers, to satisfy the animal lobbyists and the
slaughter industry. By 1988/89 the numbers had risen to a million animals, mainly
to the Middle East where the largest market was Saudi Arabia. The trade ran into
problems in the 1990s when there were instances of heavy mortalities on some
trips.[74] The two worst appear to have been connected with a particular ship, the *MV
Cormo Express*, originally built as an 11-deck car transport with closed decks that
caused ventilations problems when temperatures were unusually high.

The first case was in 1990 when a cargo of New Zealand sheep suffered a
mortality rate of 12 per cent, the usual loss being around 1 per cent. At this time
New Zealand was exporting over a million sheep, but briefly suspended the Saudi
trade, as there were also disputes over the rejection of shipments on animal health
grounds. After resuming, this trade reached a million again in the mid-1990s but
dwindled thereafter for a number of reasons. The Haj takes place according to the
Gregorian calendar, and so moves forward 11 days each year. As this meant
younger animals were increasingly being selected mortality from pneumonia rose,
and so the New Zealand government responded to public pressure and set a
minimum age for exporting. The age restriction of lambs, falling flock numbers,
and rising transport costs all helped to reduce the country's share of this trade.[75]

But by the late 1990s Australian sheep exports had climbed to well over 4
million and it was supplying a large portion of about 600,000 animals needed each
year for the Haj. This trade was brought to an end in 2003 by an even more
unfortunate voyage for the *Cormo Express*, which left Fremantle in Western
Australia on 5 August with 58,000 sheep. When it arrived at Jeddah on 21 August
the animals were inspected by a Saudi vet and rejected on disputed health grounds.
This was followed by another eight weeks of delay during which the sheep were
shipped around the Gulf as their original owner tried without success to get other
countries to take them.[76] Eventually the embarrassed Australian government
purchased them and presented them as a present to Eritrea along with $A 1 million
to cover their feed and processing costs, where they were unloaded at the end of

October. During the time the ship was in the Gulf temperatures reached over 100F and the final number of animals that died on board was 5,581.[77]

This episode received prolonged worldwide news coverage during the weeks before the sheep were finally landed, and as a result of the public outcry Australia suspended sheep exports to Saudi Arabia for the next two years until better inspection procedures were agreed. The Australian government did not let the trade begin again until Saudi Arabia signed a Memorandum of Understanding over the veterinary inspection of livestock cargoes. Australian sheep farmers looked forward to resuming the trade as they anticipated it would provide a major boost in demand, but they were also aware that the animal welfare groups would not welcome the news. The President of the Australian National Farmers Federation claimed: 'We provide industry based expertise, and real world experience to animal welfare issues, unlike our critics who offer a breathtaking lack of understanding of Australian farming systems and have not spent a cent on improving the welfare standards.'[78]

The difficulties that this trade experienced were partly a result of the strong criticism and demonstrations at the ports by animal welfare groups that succeeded in igniting public opinion.[79] But the animal welfare groups were not alone in their protests, and the economic difficulties being experienced by meat processors in Australia and New Zealand were also used to put pressure on governments to restrict the export of live animals. This was most apparent in Western Australia from where most of the Australian sheep exports originated. In 1990 the state had 57 abattoirs but by November 2002 this had been reduced to 29, and part of this reduction was caused by the rise in sheep exports.[80] But the trade had its internal problems as well. There was a long history of disputes between the shipping firms and the governments of Gulf countries over the health status of animals and exporters often accused local officials of rejecting cargoes of perfectly healthy sheep. The problem became so serious that in 1990 they agreed to meet the expense of having an Australian government-appointed vet on board each ship to monitor the health of their sheep. They were willing to pay because the trade was worth $A 155 million a year and accounted for about half of the country's animal exports.[81] But even this did not stop disputes, as the events of 2003 proved.

**The European Livestock Trade**

As it was conducted in an entirely different socio-cultural context, the trans-national trade in animals for meat within the EU was very different from the Australian and New Zealand trade with Asia and the Gulf, but even here animal welfare became an issue. By the 1990s the intra-European trade in live animals was substantial, but here distances were much shorter and the largest individual consignments only amounted to a few thousand, rather than tens of thousands. This meant there was never the possibility of the duration of suffering animals experienced on the journeys from Australia and New Zealand. However, animal health regulations were not standardised so there was scope for international disputes over the health status of animals travelling between countries. Also the treatment of animals within different states of the EU differed and so there were complaints when animals were moved from a country where it was perceived that more attention was given to welfare issues to those who paid less attention to welfare.

Within Europe itself there had been concern before the 1960s about the long distances under which animals could be sent in appalling conditions for slaughter. As early as 1968 the Council for Europe had drafted the *European Convention for the Protection of Animals during International Transport*. After 1991 the EU accepted the need to take common action to ensure minimum standards of animal welfare. In 1991 the heads of government of the community agreed a *Declaration on the Protection of Animals*. Although this was later attached to the 1993 Maastricht Treaty on European Union, it did not mean the immediate imposition of a uniform system of welfare regulations for animals. The 1993 treaty allowed a period of time for national governments to harmonise their existing laws on these and most other matters. The problem in achieving uniformity and adherence to common codes of practice is that the movement of animals over national frontiers involved three industries; farming, transport, and the slaughter industry. All of these industries were carried on in each country under varying national animal welfare standards where tradition accorded different levels of concern for animal suffering.[82] Given this background, it is perhaps no surprise that it was very difficult to break down these differences and impose uniform standards of animal welfare over the EU as a whole.

The strongest European protests over the welfare of livestock exported within the EU came in the 1990s, and were centred on the trade in live animals from Britain to Europe. Although this trade was only a part of the total intra-European livestock movements, the protesters were almost exclusively British nationals and British animal activist groups. The trade in livestock from Britain to Europe began in the early 1950s, but in the 1950s and 1960s there was little in the way of public opposition to it, and in any case the trade then was far smaller than it was in the 1990s. Although in the 1950s there was a body called the Protection of Livestock for Slaughter Organisation it seems to have been largely ignored, although it did get a parliamentary enquiry in 1957 that resulted in the Balfour Report. This laid down several government 'assurances' governing the transport of animals. But although animal activists resorted to more forceful action from the 1970s to ensure these issues were brought to its attention, the British government never at any time considered there was ever a case for completely banning the trade on the grounds of animal welfare.[83] This was a view also upheld by the courts.[84] As there was never any prospect of permanently stopping the trade, it meant protest movements tended to be short-lived, attracting a lot of attention for a few months before eventually losing momentum.

**Table 9.2  Average Annual Livestock Exports from the United Kingdom,
1961–2003**

|           | Sheep   | Cattle  | Pigs    | Total     |
|-----------|---------|---------|---------|-----------|
| 1961–65   | 403,692 | 221,182 | 26,822  | 651,696   |
| 1966–70   | 242,277 | 209,885 | 44,144  | 496,306   |
| 1971–75   | 184,002 | 157,613 | 48,038  | 389,653   |
| 1976–80   | 426,514 | 439,920 | 80,464  | 946,898   |
| 1981–85   | 119,339 | 250,981 | 475,186 | 845,506   |
| 1986–90   | 442,967 | 309,618 | 99,188  | 851,773   |
| 1991–95   | 906,213 | 422,916 | 253,196 | 1,582,325 |
| 1996–2000 | 357,260 | 11,452  | 190,889 | 559,601   |
| 2001–03   | 52,068  | 23*     | 34,816  | 86,907    |

*Total exports, for 2001 only

*Source:* FAOSTAT August 2004

As can be seen from the annual average figures from 1961 onwards in Table 9.2 above, the extent of the trade varied. Although it does also include some pedigree animals exported for flock and herd improvement, most of them were destined for more or less immediate slaughter in Europe, though in some cases not until after long and arduous road journeys, sometimes as far as Spain or Greece. In general, Northern Europe paid greater attention to animal welfare than the South. In the early 1960s annual exports were approximately 650,000, but they dipped thereafter to under 400,000 in the early 1970s. The high point was in the early 1990s when over 1.5 million farm livestock were exported each year, the great majority of them going to Europe, at a time when the strongest opposition to it was being voiced.

The concern about this part of the European livestock trade appears to have been a peculiarly British matter, as it did not appear to cause such strong reactions in other countries of the EU. As a result of demonstrations in 1994 and 1995 at a number of British air and seaports from which cattle and sheep were shipped to Europe, further restrictions were placed on the trade. Unlike in Australia and New Zealand, there were instances of commercial concerns bowing to public pressure when some of the larger passenger and freight-carrying firms decided to withdraw. For them the fear that if they continued to carry farm animals they might be boycotted by a substantial number of passengers was enough to make them abandon the trade, as it only accounted for a minor part of their business. However, there were always smaller specialised freight carriers who saw a chance to profit from this and were willing to step in and fill the gap. In 1998 a group of livestock farmers formed their own company, Farmers Ferries Ltd, to ship animals from Dover to Dunkirk.[85] It is true that the British government made some response to public pressure, although it had no legal way of banning the trade. But it tried to improve conditions for the export of live animals for slaughter, though this was never considered to be fast enough or sufficient by its (mostly middle-class) animal activist critics.[86]

In 1997 the new Labour government overhauled the whole set of regulations governing the commercial transport of animals, largely replacing the existing series of animal movement orders going back as far as 1927.[87] Although the primary purpose of the new order was to regulate the movement of animals within the United Kingdom, there was an attempt to cater for the trade to Europe, which had caused so much of the trouble in the first place. Schedule 10 of *The Welfare of Animals (Transport) Order 1997* required transport companies taking animals to a destination outside the United Kingdom to sign a declaration agreeing 'to comply with the requirements of *Council Directive 91/626/EEC* as amended up to the place of destination.' British transport firms had also to employ competent staff to care for the animals on the whole of their journey. The EU also responded to further pressure from animal welfare groups within the European Parliament to tighten up its standards. In November 2004 there were further moves to reduce journey times for all animals and use satellite navigation systems to monitor longer journeys.[88]

In fact much of this came into force after the export of cattle from the United Kingdom had been stopped in March 1996 because of BSE and the export of sheep was briefly halted by the outbreak of foot-and-mouth disease in February 2001. The sheep export ban was not permanent and after the EU declared the United Kingdom to be disease free in February 2002 exports were resumed in August 2002 when the first consignment of 1600 animals left Dover on board the *MV Caroline*. While agreeing to the resumption, the Animal Welfare Minister, Eliot Morley emphasised that he wanted the export trade in meat to replace live animal movements. Animal welfare groups, such as Compassion in World Farming once again attempted to organise demonstrations against the trade, but as public feeling against the trade had died down the protests never had the same strong support as those of the mid-1990s. The export of livestock in Europe therefore survived, but it did so on sufferance as politicians came to view it with distaste and welfare groups continued to campaign for its removal.[89] In Australia and New Zealand the public and political support for it was stronger, particularly where the export of meat was not an option as in the case of the live sheep for the Middle East. But when in May 2005 the Australian Agriculture Minister, Warren Truss, announced that the sheep trade with Saudi Arabia was to be resumed, he also emphasised that 'The community expects the livestock trade to be conducted in a humane way.'[90]

## Notes

1   Perren, R., *The Meat Trade in Britain, 1840–1914* (London, 1977), pp. 133–8, P.A. Koolmees, J.R. Fisher and R. Perren, 'The Traditional Responsibility of Veterinarians in Meat Inspection', in F.J. Smulders (ed.), *Veterinary Aspects of Meat Production,*

*Processing and Inspection* (Utrecht, 1999). pp. 10–11, 13, 15–16, P.J. Atkins, 'The Glasgow Case: Meat, Disease and Regulation, 1889–1924', *Agricultural History Review*, 52(2) (2004): 164–7.

2   Pennington, T.H., *When Food Kills: bse, e coli and Disaster Science* (Oxford, 2003); P.J. Atkins and I. Bowler, *Food in Society: Economy, Culture, Geography* (London, 2001), pp. 201–2.

3   Spriggs, J. and Isaac, G., *Food Safety and International Competitiveness: The Case of Beef* (Wallingford, 2001), pp. 8–10.

4   Broad, J., 'Cattle Plague in Eighteenth-Century England', *Agricultural History Review* 31(2) (1983): 104–15.

5   [C] 3656 (PP 1866, Vol. XXII), *Third Report of the Cattle Plague Commissioners;* C. 362 (PP 1877, Vol. IX) *Report of the Select Committee on Cattle Plague and Importation of Livestock*, pp iii, ix–x.

6   Whitlock, R., *The Great Cattle Plague: An Account of the Foot-and Mouth Epidemic of 1967–8* (London, 1968), pp. 9–10, 12.

7   Afton, B. and M. Turner, 'The Impact of Foreign Trade', in E.J.T. Collins (ed.), *The Agrarian History of England and Wales, Vol. VII, 1850–1914 Part II* (Cambridge, 2000), pp. 2107–8.

8   Cd 4643 (PP 1909, Vol. XV), *Report of the Departmental Committee on Combinations in the Meat Trade*, Appendix IV, p. 286.

9   Floud, F.L.C., *The Ministry of Agriculture and Fisheries* (London, 1927), Chapt. 4.

10  Whitlock, pp. 14, 22; E.H. Whetham, *The Agrarian History of England and Wales, Vol. VIII, 1914–1939, II* (Cambridge, 1978), p. 202; A. Woods, *A Manufactured Plague? The History of Foot-and-Mouth Disease in Britain* (London, 2004), pp. 33–4.

11  Woods, A., 'Press Release: Foot and Mouth Disease in Britain: The History' (22 Feb. 2001), http://www.chstm.man.ac.uk/news/pressrel-fmd.htm.

12  Woods, *A Manufactured Plague?*, pp. 33–4.

13  Cmd. 9214 (PP 1953–54, Vol. XIII), *Report of the Departmental Committee on Foot-and-Mouth Disease 1952*–1954, pp. 14–16, 29–30; Woods, *A Manufactured Plague?*, pp. 119–20

14. Whitlock, pp. 56–7, 92–3; Cmnd. 3999 (PP 1968–69, Vol. XXX), *Report of the Committee of Inquiry on Foot-and-Mouth Disease 1968, Part One*, p. 53; Commonwealth Secretariat, *Meat: A Review of Figures of Production, Trade and Consumption* (London, 1973), pp. 33, 50

15. *The Economist* (3 Mar. 2001), p. 51.

16  *The Economist* (14 Apr. 2001), p. 55.

17  Department for the Environment, Food and Rural Affairs, *Origin of the UK Foot and Mouth Disease Epidemic in 2001* (June 2002), pp. 3–6.

18  *The Economist* (31 Mar. 2001), p. 63.

19  Economist.com *The Economist Global Agenda*, 'Foot, mouth and public bodies' (4 Apr. 2001).

20  Woods, A., 'Why Slaughter? The Cultural Dimensions of Britain's Foot-and-Mouth Disease Control Policy', *Journal of Agricultural and Environmental Ethics*, 17 (2004): 358.

21	Foot and Mouth Disease, France Impact Worksheet, March 2001, http://www.aphis.usda.gov/vs/ceah/cei/IW_2001_files/fmd_france0301e.htm.; *The Economist* (17 Mar. 2001), p. 57.

22	Department for Environment, Food and Rural Affairs, *Report of the Chief Veterinary Officer: Animal Health 2003* (June 2004), p.81.

23	National Audit Office, *Foot-and-Mouth Disease: Applying the Lessons* (HC 184 Session 2004–05, 2 Feb. 2005), p. 9; A. Blake, M.T. Sinclair and G. Sugiyarto, 'The Economy-Wide Effects of Foot-and-Mouth Disease in the UK Economy', (2001?) http://www.nottingham.ac.uk/~lizng/ttri/Pdf/2001/2001%203.PDF; D. Thompson, P. Muriel, D. Russell, P. Osborne, A. Bromley, M. Rowland, S. Creigh-Tyte and C. Brown, 'Economic Costs of the Foot-and-Mouth Disease Outbreak in the United Kingdom in 2001, *Scientific and Technical Review of the International Epizootics Office* 21(3) (2002): 675–87; Economist.com *The Economist Global Agenda* (25 July 2002).

24	See the Warmwell web site http://www.warmwell.com/about.html. This has a comprehensive collection of press cuttings, letters, etc., of criticisms of how the epidemic was managed; B. Nerlich, 'War on Foot-and-Mouth Disease in the UK, 2001: Towards a Cultural Understanding of Agriculture', *Agriculture and Human Values*, Vol. 21 (1) (2004): 22–3.

25	FAOSTAT December 2004.

26	Alberta Cattle Feeders' Association, Agency Reports (6 Mar. 2001), http://cattlefeeder.ab.ca/herd/fmd010308.shtml.

27	Economist.com *The Economist Global Agenda* (26 Mar. 2001).

28	Machado, M.A., *An Industry in Crisis: Mexican-United States Cooperation in the Control of Foot-and-Mouth Disease* (Berkeley, 1968), p. 1.

29	Economist.com *The Economist Global Agenda* (21 Mar. 2001); PL 107–9 Federal Inter-Agency Working Group, *Animal Disease Risk Assessment, Prevention and Control Act of 2001 (PL 107–9)*, (Washington, Jan. 2003), p. 8.

30	Gebhardt, R.C., *The River Plate Meat Industry since c.1900: Technology, Ownership, International Trade Regimes and Domestic Policy*, Unpublished PhD Thesis (London School of Economics, 2000), pp. 281–2.

31	Peffer, E.L., 'Foot-and-Mouth Disease in United States Policy', *Food Research Institute Studies*, 3(2) (1962): 168–71.

32	Economist.com, *The Economist Global Agenda* (5 Apr. 2001).

33	Machado, pp. 5–7, 13–14.

34	Ibid., pp. 79–81.

35	Woods, *A Manufactured Plague?*, pp. 131–4.

36	OIE, 'Short history of the OIE', http://www.oie.int/.; Woods, *A Manufactured Plague?*, p. 134.

37	BBC News Online: World: Europe, 'UK labelled 'leper of Europe'' (12 Mar. 2001), http://www.bbc.co.uk/1/low/world/europe/1215638.stm.

38	*Guardian* (1 Oct 2002).

39	Spatuzza, A. (2003), 'PANAFTOSA Crusaders for Animal Health', *Perspectives in Health Magazine, the Magazine of the Pan American Health Organization*, Vol. 8 (3). http://www.paho.org/English/DD/PIN/Number18_article4.htm.

40	Donaldson, A.I. (2002), 'Foot-and-mouth Disease in Western North Africa an Analysis of the risk to Europe', *The European Commission for the Control of Foot-and-Mouth*

*Disease*, Appendix 5,
http://www.fao.org/ag/againfo/commisions/en/eufmd/maison/app5.html.
41 Koolmees, Fisher, and Perren, 'The Traditional Responsibility of Veterinarians in Meat Inspection', pp. 18–19.
42 Cmnd. 2542 (PP 1964–65, Vol. XVII), *Aberdeen Typhoid Outbreak 1964;* L. Diack and D. Smith, 'Sensationalism and Secrecy: The Aberdeen Typhoid Outbreak, 1964', *History Scotland Magazine* 1(1) (2001): 57–61.
43 This paragraph relies heavily on, *The BSE Inquiry Vol. 3: The Early Years, 1986–88* and *Vol. 4: The Southwood Working Party, 1988–89* (Parliament. House of Commons: Papers; 1999–2000, 887, I–XVb, 2000), http://www.bseinquiry.gov.uk.
44 Lockwood, J.F., *Provender Milling* (Liverpool, 1945), pp. 17, 34–6, 98–9.
45 This paragraph relies heavily on, *The BSE Inquiry Vol. 5: Animal Health 1989–96* and *Vol. 6: Human Health, 1989–96* (Parliament. House of Commons: Papers; 1999–2000, 887, I–XVb, 2000) http://www.bseinquiry.gov.uk.
46 OIE, 'Number of cases of BSE reported in the United Kingdom', http://www.oie.int/eng/info/en_esbru.htm. This may be an understatement as some of the cattle slaughtered at 30-months may have been incubating the disease
47 University of Edinburgh, CJD Surveillance Unit, http://www.cjd.ad.ac.uk/figures.htm.
48 *The BSE Inquiry*, Volumes 1–16. (Parliament. House of Commons: Papers; 1999–2000 887 I–XVb, 2000), http://www.bseinquiry.gov.uk.
49 *The BSE Inquiry, Vol. 1: Findings and Conclusions* (Parliament. House of Commons: Papers; 1999–2000, 887, I–XVb, 2000), http://www.bseinquiry.gov.uk
50 *The BSE Inquiry, Vol. 1: Findings and Conclusions* (Parliament. House of Commons: Papers; 1999–2000, 887, I–XVb, 2000), pp. xxiii–xxviii. http://www.bseinquiry.gov.uk (2000).
51 Meat and Livestock Commission, *Meat Demand Trends* (Bletchley, May 1997), pp. 4, 12.
52 *The BSE Inquiry, Vol. 10: Economic Impact and International Trade*, pp. 51, 58–65 (Parliament. House of Commons: Papers; 1999–2000, 887, I–XVb, 2000), http://www.bseinquiry.gov.uk (2000).
53 The following paragraph relies heavily on: USDA Foreign Agricultural Service, 'Livestock and Poultry: World Markets and Trade March 1998', http://www.fas.usda.gov/dlp2/circular/1998-98-03LP/bse.html.
54 OIE, 'Number of reported cases of bovine spongiform encepalopathy (BSE) in farmed cattle worldwide (excluding the United Kingdom)'. http://www.oie.int/eng/info/en_esbmonde.htm.
55 Schreuder, B.E.C., J.W. Wilesmith, J.M.B. Ryan and O.C. Straub, 'Risk of BSE from the Import of Cattle from the United Kingdom into Countries of the European Union', *Veterinary Record*, 141(8) (1997): 187–90.
56 *Newsweek* (4 Dec. 2000), p. 43; *Wall Street Journal* (Eastern Edition) (10 Jan. 2001), p. A19.
57 Defra, 'UK Animal health and welfare – BSE: Export & trade', http://www.defra.gov.uk/animalh/bse/export-trade/dbes.html.
58 Defra, 'UK – Animal health and welfare – International trade: Product exports – Beef exports', http://www.defra.gov.uk/animalh/int-trd/prod-ex/q-and-a.htm.

59  MacLachlan, I., *Kill and Chill: Restructuring Canada's Beef Commodity Chain* (Toronto, 2001), p. 315.
60  OIE, 'The OIE standards on BSE: a guide for understanding and proper implementation', http://www.oie.int/eng/press_en0401109.htm.
61  United States Department of Human Health Services, 'Federal agencies take special precautions to keep "Mad Cow Disease" out of the United States' (23 Aug. 2001), http://www.hhs.gov/news/press/2001pres/01fbse.html.
62  McCoy, J.H. and Sarhan, M.E., *Livestock and Meat Marketing* (3rd edn., New York, 1988), p. 520; *Seattle Post-Intelligencer* (22 Nov. 1999); Iowa Farm Bureau, 'The Economics of the EU Beef Hormone Ban and Carousel Retaliation', www.iowafarmbureau.com/programs/commodity/pdf/eoa7.pdf.
63  United States Department of State, 'Department of State Washington File' (14 Mar. 2005), http://canberra.usembassy.bov/hyper/2005/0314/epf104.htm.
64  Food Production Daily, 'New BSE case could hurt US beef market' (27 June 2005). http://www.foodproductiondaily.com/news/news-ng.asp?id=60913-new-bse-case.
65  *Wall Street Journal* (Eastern edition) (28 July 2004), p. B3; Agriculture and Agri-Food Canada, 'Canada: hogs and cattle situation and outlook', *Bi-weekly Bulletin*, 13(18b) http://www.agr.gc.ca/mad-dam/e/bulletine/v13e/v13n18eb.htm.
66  Perren, pp. 115–16, 164, 172–3.
67  Taylor, H.C. and A.D. Taylor, *World Trade in Agricultural Products* (New York, 1943), pp. 149–50.
68  Commonwealth Economic Committee, *Meat: A Summary of Figures of Production, Trade and Consumption* (London, 1950), pp. 16, 20, 33–4, 53–4.
69  The Australasian Meat Industry Employees Union, 'Unions Campaign against Live Exports', http://vic.amieu.asn.au/pages.php?recid=34.
70  International Institute of Agriculture, *International Trade in Meat* (Rome, 1936), pp. 146, 398–9.
71  *Meat Trades Journal* (23 Jan 1964), pp. 196–7.
72  Commonwealth Economic Committee, *Meat: A Summary of Figures of Production, Trade and Consumption* (London, 1965), pp. 62–3.
73  Arab News Newspaper, 'Australia to Resume Sheep Exports' (26 Dec. 2004), http://www.arabnews.com.
74  The animal welfare group, Animals Australia, described the exports of Australian sheep and cattle to the Middle East and Asia from 1980 onwards as 'A litany of disasters'. http://www.animalsaustralia.org./default2.asp?idL1=1272.
75  Ministry of Agriculture and Forestry, 'Live Sheep Exports – What's happening?', http://www.maf.govt.nz/mafnet/publications/primarysource/february-2004/primary-source-0208.htm.
76  *The Times* (13 Oct. 2003), p. 15.
77  Animals Australia, 'Australia's Live Animal Export Trade', 'A litany of disasters', http://www.animalsaustralia.org/default2.asp?idL1=1272&2dL=1283.
78  National Farmers' Federation, 'Reopening of Saudi Trade a Win for Australian Farmers' (6 May 2005), http://www.nff.org/pages/nr05/047.html.
79  'Activists halt sheep shipment' (24 Sept. 2003), http://news.bbc.co.uk/go/pr/fr/-/1/hi/world/asia-pacific/3134286.stm.

80 Department of Agriculture, Western Australia, *Cattle and Sheep Meat Processing in Western Australia: Ministerial Taskforce Report, Dec 2003*, .p. A4, http://www.agric.wa.gov.au/pls/portal30/docs/FOLDER/1KMP/_ABT/FS/edu_meat.htm.

81 *Wall Street Journal* (Eastern edition) (9 Jan. 2000), p. B3.

82 Svendsen, G.D., 'Animal Welfare and the European Union', in R. Garner (ed.), *Animal Rights: The Changing Debate* (London, 1996), pp. 144–6, 156–7.

83 Howkins, A. and L. Merricks, '"Dewey-eyed calves": Live Animal Exports and Middle-class Opinion, 1980–1995', *Agricultural History Review* 48(1) (2000): 88.

84 Defra, 'Live Sheep Exports' (3 Feb. 2003), http://www.defra.gov.uk/corporate/ministers/statements/em030203.htm.

85 Advocates for Animals, 'The Facts about Live Animal Transportation', http://www.advocatesforanimals.org.uk/resources/farmed/transportation.html.

86 *The Economist* (21 Jan. 1995), p. 58; Howkins and Merricks, '"Dewey-eyed calves"': 90–94.

87 Statutory Instrument No. 1480, *The Welfare of Animals (Transport) Order 1997*, ISBN 0 11 063764 X.

88 EUROPA, 'Animal Welfare during Transport', (11 Jan. 2005), http://europa.eu.int/comm/food/animal/welfare/trnsport/index_en.htm.

89 DEFRA News release, 'Morley Calls for Fewer Live Sheep Exports' (26 Feb 2002), http://www.defra.gov.uk/news/2002/020226a.htm; BBC News, UK, 'Lumley rallies against live exports' (9 Feb 2002), http://news.bbc.co.uk/1/hi/uk/1809738.stm; Compassion in World Farming, 'The Export of Live Farm Animals from the UK' (Mar. 2003), http://www.ciwf.org.uk/publictions/Briefings%5CBR7577.pdf.

90 Warren Truss MP Media Release, 'Welfare of livestock put first in resuming trade with Saudi Arabia' (4 May 2005), http://www.maff.gov.au/releases/05/05108wt.html.

# Conclusion

Since the 1970s the meat industry has met with a generally critical reception. The intensive methods of factory livestock farming on animal welfare have evoked keen debate. In addition, the effects of modern livestock farming on the environment, and the appearance of animal diseases that can be transmissible to humans have also provoked a deep distrust of the farming community. In a number of ways the industry has also been seen as one that has been afforded special government assistance with production subsidies and guaranteed home markets. But these are not the traditional ways in which the industry has always been viewed. In the nineteenth century there was some concern for animal welfare but it was less prominent, and a better understanding of the health risks that animal disease posed for humans only began after 1880. For much of the nineteenth century the greatest concern was over obtaining sufficient quantities of meat to feed the rising population of Western Europe. In the search for further territories on which to keep livestock, as well as grow more grain, the frontiers of settlement were pushed to their limits in North and South America, and Australia and New Zealand. In doing so hundreds of thousands of indigenous people were displaced from their lands, but this was a process that evoked hardly any adverse comment in the Western world. As increased supplies of cheap meat and other foodstuffs were made available from the New World, the industry was able to present itself as a social benefactor as well as a pioneer of new technology and business methods.

The experiences from the middle of the nineteenth to the start of the twenty-first century largely reflect many of the changes that have taken place in Western living standards. In the nineteenth century Europe became a region of overall shortages of most things, except people. But even though its population growth outran that of internal food resources, international trade and investment flourished and allowed the regions of recent settlement and development to make good any shortages. This applied especially to the United Kingdom who relied heavily on external suppliers, not only for its meat but all temperate foodstuffs. Probably no country, either before or since, has been so continually dependent on external sources for such a range of essentials as the United Kingdom in 1914 and thereafter. For Britain and Europe in the nineteenth century, meat was both an essential food for the poor as well as a luxury food for the rich. This meant that the industry had to supply a number of distinctive qualities of meat with different price ranges to the various income groups. Because of this a number of separate industries grew up, each providing a particular type and quality of meat product, sourced from different parts of the world. As beef was regarded as the top quality and was most expensive meat, it meant that chilled beef from the United States was purchased by a different class of customers from those who bought frozen South American, Australian or New Zealand mutton, or others who had to make do with cheap salted bacon from the United States.

For the nineteenth and much of the twentieth century the public image of all of these products was eventually very favourable, once initial doubts and consumer prejudice about the new technologies had been overcome. Meat was regarded as an essential and healthy food by all classes, and demand was always buoyant and it commanded a high price in times of full employment. The quantity available for each person to consume was regarded as one of the convenient yardsticks to measure a country's material progress and current prosperity. Whenever there were potential shortages, as in the two World Wars, arrangements were made to try and ensure that supplies were maintained, and at no time was it ever relegated to the category of a luxury or inessential food, even though many non-Western nations were able to perform perfectly well on traditional diets that were low in fat and meat content.[1] This view still held good in the years after the wars as efforts were made in all Western countries to restore personal consumption to its pre-war levels, and then to increase it further. Against this background of success in solving chronic shortages that had worried those who had written about food supplies in the nineteenth century, the industry found it hard to accept their product's eventual fall from grace.

Concern over meat was shown in a number of ways. The continuous criticisms after 1960 on environmental, humanitarian, and health grounds were not always answered in a direct way. Sometimes they could not be as they were applied to different aspects of the industry at different times. For instance, the growing suspicion about the danger to health was partly a question of nutrition. But nutrition is a complex matter. In the interwar and wartime years the concern of commentators like Boyd Orr was that those on low incomes risked malnutrition because they could not afford sufficient protein.[2] But in the post-war world this changed, and it became a concern about whether the current level of nutrition matched the reduced energy requirements of modern living, or was excessive. However, meat only made up a part of the surplus calories and anxieties were voiced about possibly excessive amounts of other foodstuffs consumed, ranging from dairy products to genetically modified soya bean and cereals.

But the worries about the long-term effects of eating red meat and its possible links to the likelihood of heart disease and cancer applied principally to the traditional parts of the industry. However, the disquiet about the effects of methods of factory farming applied also to the emerging poultry industry This was the one sector of meat production which was most favourably regarded by consumers seeking to reduce cholesterol intakes. At the same time it was also the one that made the greatest use of what were, for some observers, the most environmentally suspect management and processing practices that came to be associated with factory farming. But to satisfy the rising overall demand for all foodstuffs, it is difficult to see what else farmers could do in the late twentieth century other than employ the most cost-effective methods to raise output and satisfy the demand for cheap food.

This is not to say that even in the nineteenth century the industry was regarded as anything like perfect. As early as the middle of the nineteenth century the Goldner scandal and other complaints about internationally traded canned meat products were an indication that this was an industry that would require constant monitoring. In the nineteenth century the industry's defenders were careful to stress that the product itself was basically sound and that any fault was due to mismanagement and human error, rather than something that was systemic to the whole industry as twentieth-century critics argued.

As a result, towards the end of the twentieth century the industry was required to defend itself on a number of fronts. Firstly there was the criticism of the basic product itself. But in addition, modern farming techniques, factory production, and marketing methods were all subject to criticism. A great deal of attention was paid to the first of these and the urgent attempts to reduce the fat content of all red meats were largely effective. Between the 1950s and 1990s the best breed improvement programmes, early-maturing animals and scientific feeding techniques had all helped to reduce the fat content of cattle, sheep and pigs by anything up to 40 per cent. This was probably the easiest thing for the industry to achieve, as it was just a further stage in the continuous history of livestock improvement that stretched back to the eighteenth century.

When challenges were directed at the industry's organisation and management, they proved to be more intractable. As far back as the nineteenth century the large multinational meat companies had attracted the criticism of farmers, governments, and the smaller players in the industry. Its most extreme form was the fear that they would take control and dominate the entire international trade in meat, just as they had done in the United States. Such anxieties became particularly acute during and immediately after the First World War. Allied governments helped this process because they had to make arrangements with them to ensure that essential supplies were kept flowing to Europe – arrangements that were highly profitable for the meat firms. During the war there was a real fear that once hostilities were over they might use their power and expertise, as well as their experience in dealing with governments, to take control over ranches and other livestock farmers in all meat-exporting countries.[3] In the event this never happened and, like other sectors of industry, the meat giants found sales and profits reduced in the depression, as wages slipped, unemployment rose and the growth of consumer demand slowed. Nevertheless, they remained the most powerful forces both within the industry in the United States and on the international meat scene.[4]

As an industry, meat processing, wholesaling and retailing experienced a similar range of criticisms and accusations to a number of others industries where economies of scale conferred particular benefits. As with all food industries, people could always make comparisons between the situation before and after the arrival of big business. It would have been remarkable if participants in the industry before their arrival had regarded every aspect of their activities with favour. But as far as the consumer was concerned they were responsible for a more or less assured supply, ironing out seasonal shortage as far as possible, and also a guarantee of product quality. This became easier as the large firms learnt to work together and achieved at least some control over parts of the market. It was also helped when some of them also had direct ownership of retail stores. But even if ownership was not always direct the advertising power of the industry's giants kept names like 'Armour', 'Swift' and other large owners of processing and refrigeration works, constantly in the minds of customers.

As the industry changed after 1945 and the big names of the nineteenth century were overhauled by the new names of the late twentieth century the whole image of the industry was also transformed. As an increasing amount of the consumption of meat shifted away from the home to the restaurant and fast food outlet an increasing amount of the preparation of what remained to be consumed at home was also shifted elsewhere. As consumers were eating more pre-packaged and prepared meat cuts the housewife placed a greater reliance on the processor and supermarket to select the family's meat for it. This meant that as consumers became cautious and wary about eating red meat from 1960 onwards, it was the retailers who noticed these changes first, before they were transmitted back down the food chain to the farmer and grazier. As the last link in the chain restaurant owners and food retailers were in the best position to absorb any shifts in demand without any serious loss, as all they had to do was to switch from serving steak to serving chicken or from selling beef to selling more poultry. Very rarely did people react to even the most serious health scares over meat by permanently selecting the vegetarian option.

For the meat producer the options were less appealing. For those parts of the Western world specialising in beef and lamb there were few alternatives when consumer demand for them fell. The standard response was to reduce costs and, if possible, to look for additional markets. But the first option did not necessarily trim output to meet the reduced demand, and the search for alternative markets had a limited likelihood of success. Australian and New Zealand cattle and sheep farmers did develop new markets in Asia, Japan and the Middle East for some of their output. But the industry continued to produce a high cost food product that could only be afforded by the developed world. As the process of development after 1945 was limited to a few nations, and it was only those that had the money to widen their traditional diets and consume more protein, there was limited scope to develop completely new world markets. Most of the international trade in meat remained one between the Western industrialised nations, linked by common cultures and similar lifestyles.

Another reaction, as with all producers facing difficulties, was to appeal to governments for assistance. Government help to the industry went back to the interwar years when meat producers and marketing boards had been set up in a number of countries to regulate the surpluses and low prices immediately after the First World War, and nurse parts of the industry through the difficulties

experienced in periods of depression in the 1920s and 1930s. But as much of the
long-term increase in meat output in the period after 1945 had been made easier by
increased state assistance in the way of generous subsidies, guaranteed minimum
prices, and protected markets, the willingness of governments to undertake further
assistance was very limited indeed. In the 1950s the first concern had been to
eliminate the shortages in the immediate aftermath of the war, but by the 1980s
governments and taxpayers grew alarmed at the prospect of paying for unnecessary
surpluses. For the most part from then on meat-producers, like all other farmers,
were left very much to make their own adjustments to changed conditions, and
they achieved this with varying degrees of success.

## Notes

1   British Medical Association, *Report of the Committee on Nutrition* (London, 1947), pp.
    54–5, 102–3.
2   Orr, J.B., *Food Health and Income: Report on A Survey of Diet in Relation to Income*
    (London, 1936), pp. 38–48.
3   Cd 7896 (PP 1914–16, Vol. XLVI), *Report of the Royal Commission on the Meat Export
    Trade of Australia.*
4   Rifkin, J., *Beyond Beef: The Rise and Fall of the Cattle Culture* (New York, 1992), p.
    116.

# Bibliography

**Books**

Abel, W., *Agricultural Fluctuations in Europe from the Thirteenth to the Twentieth Centuries* (London: Methuen, 1980).

Adelman, J., *Frontier Development: Land Labour, and Capital on the Wheatlands of Argentina and Canada, 1890–1914* (Oxford: Clarendon Press, 1994).

Albert, B. with the assistance of Henderson, P., *South America and the First World War: The Impact of the War on Brazil, Argentina, Peru and Chile* (Cambridge: Cambridge University Press, 1988).

Alejandro, C.D., *Essays on the Economic History of the Argentine Republic* (New Haven: Yale University Press, 1970).

Anderson, G., *The Frozen Meat Industry: A Paper Read before the Otago Agricultural and Pastoral Society, Dunedin, 15 June 1905* (Dunedin: Otago Daily Times, 1905).

Anthony, D.J. and Blois, W.G.T., *The Meat Industry* (London: Baillière, Tindall & Cox, 1931).

Antrobus, D., *A Guiltless Feast: The Salford Bible Christian Church and the Rise of the Modern Vegetarian Movement* (Salford: City of Salford Education and Leisure, 1997).

Ashton, T.S., *Economic Fluctuations in England 1700–1800* (London: Oxford University Press, 1959).

Atkin, M., *Snouts in the Trough: European Farmers, the Common Agricultural Policy and the Public Purse* (Abingdon: Woodhead Publishing, 1993).

Atkins, P.J. and Bowler, I., *Food in Society: Economy, Culture, Geography* (London: Arnold, 2001).

Augé-Laribé, M. and Pinot, P., *Agriculture and Food Supply in France During the War* (New Haven: Yale University Press, 1927).

Barton, R.A. (ed.), *A Century of Achievement: A Commemoration of the First 100 Years of the New Zealand Meat Industry* (Palmerston North: Dunmore Press, 1984).

Belshaw, H. (ed.), *Agricultural Organization in New Zealand* (Melbourne: Melbourne University Press, 1936).

Bethell, L. (ed.), *The Cambridge History of Latin America, vol. III, From Independence to c.1870* (Cambridge: Cambridge University Press, 1985).

———— (ed.), *Argentina Since Independence* (Cambridge: Cambridge University Press, 1993).

Beveridge, W.H., *British Food Control* (London: Oxford University Press, 1928).

Beveridge, W.H., et al., *Tariffs: The Case Examined* (London: Longmans, 1931).

Boorstin, D.J., *American Railroads* (Chicago: University of Chicago Press (1961).

Brandt, K. et. al., *Management of Agriculture and Food in the German-Occupied and Other Areas of Fortress Europe: A Study in Military Government* (Stanford: Stanford University Press, 1953).

Brannon, R.H., *The Agricultural Development of Uruguay* (New York: Praeger, 1967).

British Medical Association, *Report of the Committee on Nutrition* (London: British Medical Association, 1947).

Butlin, N.G., *Investment in Australian Economic Development 1861–1900* (London: Cambridge University Press, 1964).

Cairncross, A.K., *Years of Recovery: British Economic Policy 1945–51* (London: Methuen, 1985).

Cecil, R., *The Development of Agriculture in Germany and the UK: 1. German Agriculture 1870–1970* (Ashford: Wye College, 1979).

Chaloner, W.H., *People and Industries* (London: Frank Cass, 1963).

Chandler, A.D., Jr., *Strategy and Structure: Chapters in the History of the Industrial Enterprise* (Cambridge, Mass.: Harvard University Press, 1962).

———, *The Visible Hand: The Managerial Revolution in American Business* (Cambridge, Mass.: Belknap Press, 1977).

———, *Scale and Scope: The Dynamics of Industrial Capitalism* (Cambridge, Mass.: Belknap Press, 1990).

Clark, F.E. and Weld, L.D.H., *Marketing Agricultural Products in the United States* (New York: The Macmillan Company, 1932).

Clarke, H. and Binding, H., *The History of Lloyd Maunder 1898–1998: A West Country Business* (Tiverton: Halsgrove, 1998).

Clemen, R.A., *The American Livestock and Meat Industry* (New York: Ronald Press Company, 1923).

Collinge, G.H., et al., *The Retail Meat Trade*, 2 vols (London: The Gresham Publishing Co., 1929).

Condliffe, J.B., *New Zealand in the Making: A Study of Economic and Social Development* (London: George Allen & Unwin, 1936).

Crasweller, R.D., Perón and the Enigmas of Argentina (New York: W.W. Norton & Co., 1987).

Critchell, J.T. and Raymond, J., *A History of the Frozen Meat Trade* (London: Constable and Company, 1912).

Curtis-Bennet, N., *The Food of the People: The History of Industrial Feeding* (London: Faber & Faber, 1949).

Davidson, B.R., *European Farming in Australia: An Economic History of Australian Farming* (Amsterdam: Elsevier, 1981).

Davidson, H.R., *The Production and Marketing of Pigs*, 3rd edn. (London: Longmans, 1962).

Dewey, P.E., *British Agriculture in the First World War*, (London: Routledge, 1989).

————, *War and Progress: Britain 1914–945*, (London: Longman, 1997).

Díaz Alejandro, C.F., *Essays on the Economic History of the Argentine Republic* (New Haven: Yale University Press, 1970).

Dodd, G. *The Food of London*, (London: Longmans, Brown, Green and Longmans, 1856).

Domville-Fife, C., *The States of South America: The Land of Opportunity* (London: G. Bell and Sons, 1920).

Drummond, I. M., *British Economic Policy and the Empire, 1919–1939* (London: Allen & Unwin, 1972).

———— *Imperial Economic Policy 1917–1939: Studies in Expansion and Protection* (London: Allen & Unwin, 1974).

English, P.R., Fowler, V.R., Baxter, S. and Smith, B., *The Growing and Finishing Pig: Improving Efficiency* (Ipswich: Farming Press, c.1988).

Farrer, K.T.H., *A Settlement Amply Supplied: Food Technology in Nineteenth Century Australia* (Melbourne: Melbourne University Press, 1980).

————, *Australian Meat Exports to Britain in the Nineteenth Century: Technology Push and Market Pull, Working Paper No. 38* (London: Sir Robert Menzies Centre for Australian Studies Institute of Commonwealth Studies, University of London, 1988).

Fenelon, K.G., *Britain's Food Supplies* (London: Methuen, 1952).

Fennell, R., *The Common Agricultural Policy of the Agricultural Community: Its Institutional and Administrative Organization* (London: Granada, 1979).

Ferns, H.S., *Argentina* (New York: Praeger, 1969).

Finch, M.H.J., *A Political Economy of Uruguay Since 1870* (London: Macmillan, 1981).

Fishlow, A., *American Railroads and the Transformation of the Ante-Bellum Economy* (Cambridge, Mass.: Harvard University Press, 1965).

Floud, F.L.C., *The Ministry of Agriculture and Fisheries* (London: Putnam, 1927).

Fogel, R.W. *Railroads and Economic Growth: Essays in Econometric History* (Baltimore: The Johns Hopkins Press, 1970).

Foreman-Peck, J., *A History of the World Economy* (Brighton: Harvester Press, 1983).

Gamgee, J.S., *The Cattle Plague and Diseased Meat, in their Relations with the Public Health and the Interests of Agriculture* (London: T. Richards, 1857).

Gerrard, F., *The Book of the Meat Trade* (2 vols, London: Caxton Publishing Company, 1949).

Gradish, S.F., *The Manning of the British Navy During the Seven Years' War* (London: Royal Historical Society, 1980).

Grattan, C.H., *The Southwest Pacific Since 1900* (Ann Arbor: The University of Michigan Press, 1963).

Gravil, R., *The Anglo-Argentine Connection, 1900–1939* (Boulder: Westview Press, 1975).

Greg, I.M. and Towers, S.H., *Cattle Ships and our Meat Supply*, The Humanitarian League Publication No. 15 (London: William Reeves, 1894).

Grunwald, J. and Musgrove, P., *Natural Resources in Latin American Development* (Baltimore: Johns Hopkins, 1970).

Gunther, J., *Inside Latin America* (London: Hamish Hamilton, 1942).

Hadfield, W., *Brazil and the River Plate in 1868: By William Hadfield, Showing the Progress of those Countries since his Former Visit in 1853* (London: Bates, Hendry and Co., 1869).

Haldane, A.R.B., *The Drove Roads of Scotland* (Newton Abbot: David & Charles, 1973).

Hammond, R.J., *Food and Agriculture in Great Britain: Aspects of Wartime Control* (Stanford: Stanford University Press, 1954).

Hancock, W.K. and Gowing, M.M., *The British War Economy* (London: HMSO, 1949).

Hanson, S.G., *Argentine Meat and the British Market: Chapters in the History of the Argentine Meat Industry* (Stanford: Stanford University Press, 1938).

Harberler, G., *Prosperity and Depression*: *A Theoretical Analysis of Cyclical Movements*, 3rd edn. (New York: United Nations, 1946).

Harrison, G., *Borthwicks: A Century in the Meat Trade, 1863–1963* (London: Thomas Borthwick and Sons, 1963).

Hays, S.P., *Conservation and the Gospel of Efficiency: The Progressive Conservation Movement, 1890–1920* (Cambridge, Mass.: Harvard University Press, 1959).

Hawke, G.R., *The Making of New Zealand* (Cambridge: Cambridge University Press, 1985).

Heiser, C.B., Jr., *Seed to Civilization: The Story of Man's Food* (San Francisco: W.H. Freeman and Company, 1973).

Hibbard, B.H., *Effects of the Great War upon Agriculture in the United States and Great Britain* (New York: Oxford University Press, 1919).

Hutchinson, T.J., *The Paraná; with Incidents of the Paraguayan War and South American Recollections from 1861 to 1868* (London: Edward Stanford, 1868).

Jackson, A.J., *Official History of the National Association of Meat Traders* (Plymouth: Oakfield Press, 1956).

Jackson, R.V., *Australian Economic Development in the Nineteenth Century* (Canberra: Australian National University Press, 1977).

Jefferys, J.B., *Retail Trading in Britain 1850–1950* (Cambridge: Cambridge University Press, 1954).

Johnson, A.M. and Supple, B.E., *Boston Capitalists and Western Railroads: A Study in the Nineteenth Century Railroad Process* (Cambridge, Mass.: Harvard University Press, 1967).

Jones, C.F., *South America* (London: George Allen & Unwin, 1931).

Josling, T.E., Tangerman, S. and Warley, T.K., *Agriculture in the GATT* (Basingstoke: Macmillan Press, 1996).

Keen, B., *A History of Latin America* (Boston: Houghton Mifflin Company, 1996).

Kemp, M., *The Promotion and Marketing of Pork and Bacon* (Uckfield: Nuffield Farming Scholarship Trust, 2000).

King, J., *The Market for Organic Pigmeat in Europe* (Uckfield: Nuffield Farming Scholarship Trust, 2001).

Kingston, B., *The Oxford History of Australia, vol. 3, 1860–1900, Glad, Confident Morning* (Melbourne: Oxford University Press, 1988).

Kiple, K.F., *Blacks in Colonial Cuba* (Gainsville: University Press of Florida, 1976).

Knightley, P., *The Vestey Affair* (London: Macdonald, 1981).

Knox, F., *The Common Market and World Agriculture: Trade–Patterns in Temperate Zone Foodstuffs* (New York: Praeger, 1972).

Koebel, W.H., *Argentina: Past and Present* (London: Kegan Paul & Co. Ltd., 1910).

Lawrie, R.A., *Meat Science* (Oxford: Pergamon Press, 1974).

Lamartine Yates, P., *Food Production in Western Europe* (London: Longmans, Green and Co., 1940).

Latham, W., *The States of the River Plate: Their Industries and Commerce* (London: Longmans, Green, and Co., 1866).

Leffingwell, A., *American Meat and Its Influence Upon the Public Health* (London: George Bell & Sons, 1910).

Leighton, G.R. and Douglas, L.M., *The Meat Industry and Meat Inspection* (5 vols, London: The Educational Book Company, 1911).

Levenstein, H.A., *Revolution at the Table: The Transformation of the American Diet* (New York: Oxford University Press, 1988).

Lewis, C., *British Railways in Argentina 1857–1914: A Case Study of Foreign Investment* (London: Athlone, 1983).

Lewis, M., *The Navy in Transition 1814–1864: A Social History* (London: Hodder and Stoughton, 1965).

Liebig, J. von, *Researches on the Chemistry of Food ... Edited from the manuscript of the author by W. Gregory* (London: Taylor & Walton, 1847).

Lindberg, J., *Food, Famine and Relief 1940–1946* (Geneva: Economic, Financial and Transit Department League of Nations, 1946).

Linge, G.J.R., *Industrial Awakening: A Geography of Australian Manufacturing 1788 to 1890* (Canberra: Australian National University Press, 1979).

Lloyd, C., *The British Seaman 1200–1800: A Social* Survey (London: Collins, 1968).

Lloyd Prichard, M.F., *An Economic History of New Zealand to 1939* (London: Collins, 1970).

Lockwood, J.F., *Provender Milling* (Liverpool: Northern Publishing Co., 1945).

Macdonald, J., *Food From the Far West* (London: William P. Nimmo, 1878).

Macdonald, N., *Canada: Immigration and Colonization, 1841–1903* (Aberdeen: Aberdeen University Press, 1966).

Machado, M.A., *An Industry in Crisis: Mexican-United States Cooperation in the Control of Foot-and-Mouth Disease* (Berkeley: University of California Press, 1968).

MacLachlan I., *Kill and Chill: Restructuring Canada's Beef Commodity Chain* (Toronto: University of Toronto Press, 2001).

Macrosty, H.W., *The Trust Movement in British Industry* (London: Longmans, Green and Co., 1907).

Malthus, T.R., *An Essay on the Principle of Population* (London, 1798).

Martin, J., *The Development of Modern Agriculture: British Farming since 1931* (Basingstoke: Macmillan Press, 2000).

McCoy, J.H., *Livestock and Meat Marketing* (Westport: The AVI Publishing Co., 1972).

McCoy, J.H. and Sarhan, M.E., *Livestock and Meat Marketing* (3rd edn., New York: Van Nostrand Reinhold, 1988).

McFall, R.J., *The World's Meat* (New York: D. Appleton and Co., 1927).

McLintock, A.H., *An Encyclopaedia of New Zealand* (3 vols, Wellington: R.E. Owen, 1966).

Michael, P., *Settlers and the Agrarian Question: Foundations of Capitalism in Colonial Australia* (Cambridge: Cambridge University Press, 1984).

Middleton, T.H., *The Recent Development of German Agriculture* (London: HMSO, 1917).

Middleton, T.H., *Food Production in War* (London: Clarendon Press, 1923).

Mitchell, B.R., 'Statistical Appendix', in C.M. Cipolla (ed.), *The Fontana Economic History of Europe:* vol. 4 (2), *The Emergence of Industrial Societies* (London: Collins, 1973).

Mitchell, D., *The Politics of Food* (Toronto: James Lorimer & Company, 1975).

Mottram, R.F., *Human Nutrition* (3rd edn., London: Edward Arnold, 1979).

Murray, K.A.H., *Agriculture* (London: HMSO and Longmans Green, 1955).

Nash, E.F. and Atwood, E.A., *The Agricultural Policies of Britain and Denmark: A Study in Reciprocal Trade* (London: Land Books, 1961).

Nicol, J., *Vital, Social, and Economic Statistics of the City of Glasgow* (Glasgow: J. Maclehose, 1885).

Nourse, E.G., *American Agriculture and the European Market* (New York: McGraw-Hill, 1924).

O'Connor, P.S., *Mr Massey and the American Meat Trust: Some sidelights on the Origins of the Meat Board* (Palmerston North: Massey University, 1973).

Offer, A., *The First World War: An Agrarian Interpretation* (Oxford: Oxford University Press, 1989).

Ohlin, H., *The Course and Phases of the World Depression* (Geneva: League of Nations, 1931).

Oliver, W.H. with Williams, B.R. (eds), *The Oxford History of New Zealand* (Oxford: The Clarendon Press, 1981).

Orr, J.B., *Food Health and Income: Report on A Survey of Diet in Relation to Income* (London: Macmillan, 1936).

Osgood, E.S, *The Day of the Cattleman: The Legend of the Wild West viewed against the Truth of History* (Chicago: University of Chicago Press, 1929).

Pearse, A.W., *The World's Meat Future* (London: Constable and Company, 1920).

Pennington, T.H., *When Food Kills: bse, e coli and Disaster Science* (Oxford: Oxford University Press, 2003).

Perren, R., *The Meat Trade in Britain, 1840–1914* (London: Routledge & Kegan Paul, 1977).

Platt, D.C.M., *Latin America and British Trade 1806–1914* (London: Adam and Charles Black, 1972).

Platt, D.C.M. and Di Tella, G. (eds), *Argentina, Australia and Canada: Studies in Comparative Development, 1870–1965* (Oxford: Macmillan, 1985).

Pollard, S., *The Development of the British Economy 1914–90* (London: Edward Arnold, 1992).

Putnam, G.E., *Supplying Britain's Meat* (London: George G. Harrap, 1923).

Reber, V.B., *British Mercantile Houses in Buenos Aires 1810–1880* (Cambridge, Mass.: Harvard University Press, 1979).

Rifkin, J., *Beyond Beef: The Rise and Fall of the Cattle Culture* (New York: Penguin, 1992).

Ritzer, G., *The McDonaldization of Society* (Thousand Oaks: Pine Forge Press, 1996).

Robertson, R.M., *History of the American Economy* (3rd edn., New York: Harcourt Brace, 1973).

Rock, D., *Argentina in the Twentieth Century* (London: Duckworth, 1975).

Russell, E.J., *World Population and Food Supplies* (London: Allen & Unwin, 1954).

Schwartz, H., *In the Dominions of Debt: Historical Perspectives on Dependent Development* (Ithaca: Cornell University Press, 1989).

Simoons, F.J., *Eat Not This Flesh: Food Avoidances from Prehistory to the Present* (Madison: University of Wisconsin Press, 1994).

Simkin, G.G.F., *The Instability of a Dependent Economy: Economic Fluctuations in New Zealand 1840–1914* (Oxford: Oxford University Press, 1951).

Sinclair, K., *A History of New Zealand* (London: Allen Lane, 1980).

Sinclair, U., *The Jungle* (New York: Doubleday & Co., 1906).

Smith, J.R., *The World's Food Resources* (London: Williams and Norgate, 1919).

Smith, P.H., *Politics and Beef in Argentina: Patterns of Conflict and Change* (New York: Columbia University Press, 1969).

Solberg, C.E., *The Prairies and the Pampas: Agrarian Policy in Canada and Argentina, 1880–1930* (Stanford: Stanford University Press, 1987).

Spencer, C., *The Heretic's Feast: A History of Vegetarianism* (London: Fourth Estate, 1993).

Spriggs, J. and Isaac, G., *Food Safety and International Competitiveness: The Case of Beef* (Wallingford: CABI Publishing, 2001).

Stewart, I.A.D. (ed.), *From Caledonia to the Pampas: Two Accounts of Early Scottish Emigrants to the Argentine* (East Linton: Tuckwell Press, 2000).

Stone, R.C.J., *Makers of Fortune: A Colonial Business Community and its Fall* (Dunedin: Auckland University Press, 1973).

Surface, F.M. and Bland, R.L., *American Food in the World War and Reconstruction Period* (Stanford: Stanford University Press, 1931).

The Times, *The Times Book on Argentina* (London: Times Newspapers, 1927).

Weddel, W., *Memorandum on the Imported Meat Trade of the United Kingdom (Frozen and Refrigerated) of the United Kingdom With suggestions for fostering production within the Empire* (London: W. Weddel & Co., Ltd., April 1917).

Taylor, H.C. and Taylor, A.D., *World Trade in Agricultural Products* (New York: The Macmillan Company, 1943).

Tibbles, W., *Foods: their Origin, Composition and Manufacture* (London: Baillière, Tindall and Cox, 1912).

Tracy. M., *Government and Agriculture in Western Europe 1880–1988* (London: Harvester Wheatsheaf, 1989).

Walsh, M., *The American Frontier Revisited* (London: Macmillan, 1981).

———, *The Rise of the Midwestern Meat Packing Industry* (Lexington Ky.: The University Press of Kentucky, 1982).

Whetham, E.H., *The Agrarian History of England and Wales, vol. VIII, 1914–1939, II* (Cambridge: Cambridge University Press (1978).

Whitlock, R., *The Great Cattle Plague: An Account of the Foot-and-Mouth Epidemic of 1967–8* (London: John Baker, 1968).

Woods, A., *A Manufactured Plague? The History of Foot-and-Mouth Disease in Britain* (London: Earthscan, 2004).

Wright, W.R., *British-Owned Railways in Argentina: Their Effect on Economic Nationalism 1854–1948* (Austin: University of Texas Press, 1974).

Yeager, M., *Competition and Regulation: The Development of Oligopoly in the Meat Packing Industry* (Greenwich Conn.: JAI Press Inc., 1981).

**Articles in Edited Books**

Afton, B. and Turner, M., 'The Impact of Foreign Trade', in E.J.T. Collins (ed.), *The Agrarian History of England and Wales, vol. VII, 1850–1914 Part II*, (Cambridge: Cambridge University Press, 2000), pp. 2106–40.

Alhadeff, P., 'Public Finance and the Economy in Argentina, Australia and Canada during the Depression of the 1930s', in D.C.M. Platt and G. Di Tella (eds), *Argentina, Australia and Canada: Studies in Comparative Development, 1870–1965* (Oxford: Macmillan, 1985), pp. 53–75.

Beattie, D., 'The Opening of the Totara Estate Industrial Park', in R.A. Barton (ed.), *A Century of Achievement: A Commemoration of the First 100 Years of the New Zealand Meat Industry* (Palmerston North: Dunmore Press, 1984), pp. 15–23.

Berensztein, A. and Spector, H., 'Business, Government and Law', in G.D. Paolera and A.M. Taylor (eds), *A New Economic History of Argentina* (Cambridge: Cambridge University Press, 2003), pp. 324–68.

Bogue, A.G., 'An Agricultural Empire', in C.A Milner II, C.A. O'Connor, and M.A. Sandweiss (eds), *The Oxford History of the American West* (New York: Oxford University Press, 1994), pp. 275–313.

Brewster, J.A., 'The South American Trade', in F. Gerrard (ed.), *The Book of the Meat Trade* (2 vols, London: Caxton Publishing Company, 1949), vol. 1, pp. 202–20.

Brooking, T., 'Economic Transformation', in W.H. Oliver with B.R. Williams (eds), *The Oxford History of New Zealand* (Oxford: The Clarendon Press, 1981), pp. 226–49.

Bryant, L.B. Jr., 'Entering the Global Economy', in C.A Milner II, C.A. O'Connor, and M.A. Sandweiss (eds), *The Oxford History of the American West* (New York: Oxford University Press, 1994), pp. 203–35.

Capie, F., 'The Demand for Meat in England and Wales Between the Two World Wars', in D.J. Oddy and D.S. Miller (eds), *Diet and Health in Modern Britain* (London: Croom Helm, 1985), pp. 66–80.

de Garis, B.K., '1890–1900', in F.K. Crowley (ed.), *A New History of Australia* (Melbourne: William Heinemann, 1974), pp. 216–59.

Collins, E.J.T., 'Rural and Agricultural Change' in E.J.T. Collins (ed.), *The Agrarian History of England and Wales*, vol. VII, *1850–1914, Part I* Cambridge (Cambridge: University Press, (2000), pp. 72–223.

Crossley, C and Greenhill, R., 'The River Plate Beef Trade', in D.C.M. Platt (ed.), *Business Imperialism 1840–1930, An Inquiry Based on British Experience in Latin America* (Oxford: Oxford University Press 1977), pp. 284–334.

Drummond, J.C., 'Historical Introduction', in J.C. Drummond (ed.), *Historic Tinned Foods* (Publication No 85, Greenford: International Tin Research and Development Council, 1939), pp. 8–33.

Elbaum, W., 'An Institutional Perspective on British Decline', in B. Elbaum and W. Lazonick (eds), *The Decline of the British Economy* (Oxford: Clarendon Press, 1986), pp. 1–17.

Fodor, J., 'Perón's Policies for Agricultural Exports 1946–48: Dogma or Commonsense?', in D. Rock (ed.), *Argentina in the Twentieth Century* (London: Duckworth, 1975), pp. 135–61.

———, 'The Origin of Argentina's Sterling Balances, 1939–43', in G. di Tella and D.C.M. Platt (eds), *The Political Economy of Argentina 1880–1946* (London: MacMillan, 1986), pp. 154–82.

Freebairn, J.W., 'Natural Resource Industries', in R. Maddock and I.W. McLean, (eds), *The Australian Economy in the Long Run* (Cambridge: Cambridge University Press, 1987), pp. 133–64.

Gardner, W.J., 'A Colonial Economy', in W.H. Oliver with B.R. Williams (eds), *The Oxford History of New Zealand* (Oxford: The Clarendon Press, 1981), pp. 57–86.

Graham, J., 'Settler Society' in W.H. Oliver with B.R. Williams (eds), *The Oxford History of New Zealand* (Oxford: The Clarendon Press, 1981), pp. 112–139.

262 *Taste, Trade and Technology*

Grant, R., 'The Australian Meat Industry', in R. Ramsay (ed.), *The Frozen and Chilled Meat Trade: A Practical Treatise by Specialists in the Trade* (2 vols, London: The Gresham Publishing Company, 1929), vol. 1, pp. 31–97.

Gravil, R., 'Anglo-U.S. Trade Rivalry in Argentina and the D'Abernon Mission of 1929', in D. Rock (ed.), *Argentina in the Twentieth Century* (London: Duckworth, 1975), pp. 41–65.

Greenhill, R.G., 'Shipping and the Refrigerated Meat Trade from the River Plate 1900-1930', in K. Friedland (ed.), *Maritime Food Transport* (Köln: Böhlau Verlag, 1994), pp. 417–34.

Harley, C.K., 'The World Food Economy and pre-World War I Argentina', in S.N. Broadberry and N.F.R. Crafts (eds), *Britain and the International Economy 1870–1939* (Cambridge: Cambridge University Press, 1992), pp. 244–68.

Jones, D., 'New Zealand Trade', in R. Ramsay (ed.), *The Frozen and Chilled Meat Trade: A Practical Treatise by Specialists in the Trade* (2 vols, London: The Gresham Publishing Company, 1929), vol. 1, pp. 101–55.

King, M., 'Between Two Worlds', in W.H. Oliver with B.R. Williams (eds), *The Oxford History of New Zealand* (Oxford: The Clarendon Press, 1981), pp. 279–301.

Koolmees, P.A., Fisher, J.R. and Perren, R., 'The Traditional Responsibility of Veterinarians in Meat Inspection', in F.J. Smulders (ed.), *Veterinary Aspects of Meat Production, Processing and Inspection* (Utrecht: ECCEAMST, 1999), pp. 7–30.

Lewis, C., 'Anglo-Argentine Trade, 1945–1965', in D. Rock (ed.), *Argentina in the Twentieth Century* (London: Duckworth, 1975), pp. 114–34.

Lintner, V., 'The European Community – 1958 to the 1990s, in M.S. Schultz (ed.), *Western Europe: Economic and Social Change Since 1945* (London: Longman, 1998), pp. 140–57.

Lynch, J., 'The River Plate Republics from Independence to the Paraguayan War', in L Bethell (ed.), *The Cambridge History of Latin America, vol. III, From Independence to c.1870* (Cambridge: Cambridge University Press, 1985), pp. 615–76.

———, 'From Independence to National Organization' in L. Bethell (ed.), *Argentina Since Independence* (Cambridge: Cambridge Universty Press, 1993), pp. 1–46.

Maddock, R and Maclean, I.W., 'Introduction: The Australian Economy in the Very Long Run', in R. Maddock and I.W. Maclean (eds), *The Australian Economy in the Long Run* (Cambridge: Cambridge University Press (1987), pp. 5–29.

Nugent, W., 'Comparing Wests and Frontiers', in C.A Milner II, C.A. O'Connor, and M.A. Sandweiss (eds), *The Oxford History of the American West* (New York: Oxford University Press, 1994), pp. 803–33.

Oddone, J.A., 'The Formation of Modern Uruguay. c.1870–1930', in L. Bethell (ed.), *The Cambridge History of Latin America, vol. V, c.1970 to 1930* (Cambridge: Cambridge University Press, 1986), pp. 453–74.

Olson, E., 'Towards a New Society', in W.H. Oliver with B.R. Williams (eds), *The Oxford History of New Zealand* (Oxford: The Clarendon Press, 1981), pp. 250–78.

Perren, R., 'The Retail and Wholesale Meat Trade, 1880–1939', in D. Oddy and D. Miller (eds), *Diet and Health in Modern Britain* (London: Croom Helm, 1985), pp. 46–65.

——, 'Food Manufacturing', in E.J.T. Collins (ed.), *The Agrarian History of England and Wales, vol. VII, 1850–1914 Part II* (Cambridge: Cambridge University Press, 2000), pp. 1085–1100.

Pope, D., 'Population and Australian Economic Development', in R. Maddock and I.W. McLean, *The Australian Economy in the Long Run* (Cambridge: Cambridge University Press, 1987), pp. 33–60.

Prebish, R., 'Argentine Economic Policies since the 1930s: Recollections', in G. di Tella, and D.C.M. Platt (eds), *The Political Economy of Argentina 1880–1946* (London: MacMillan, 1986), pp. 133–53.

Ramsay, R., 'The World's Frozen and Chilled Meat Trade', in R. Ramsay (ed.), *The Frozen and Chilled Meat Trade: A Practical Treatise by Specialists in the Trade* (2 vols, London: The Gresham Publishing Company, 1929), vol. 1, pp. 3–27.

Richelet, J.E., 'The Argentine Trade', in R. Ramsay (ed.), *The Frozen and Chilled Meat Trade: A Practical Treatise by Specialists in the Trade* (2 vols, London: The Gresham Publishing Company, 1929), vol. 1, pp. 191–242.

Richelet, J.E., 'The Argentine Meat Trade', in R. Ramsay (ed.), *The Meat Trade* (3 vols, London: The Gresham Publishing Company, 1935), vol. 3, pp. 151–202.

Robbins L.C., 'Agriculture', in W. H. Beveridge, et al., *Tariffs: The Case Examined* (London: Longmans, 1931), pp. 148–69.

Rock, D., 'The Argentine Economy, 1890–1914: Some Salient Features', in G. di Tella and D.C.M Platt (eds), *The Political Economy of Argentina 1880–1946* (Basingstoke: Macmillan, 1986), pp. 60–73.

Sánchez-Albornoz, N., 'The Population of Latin America, 1850–1930', in Bethell, L. (ed.), *The Cambridge History of Latin America, vol. IV, c.1870 to 1930* (Cambridge: Cambridge University Press, 1986), pp. 121–52.

Solberg, C.E., 'Land Tenure and Land Settlement: Policy and Patterns in the Canadian Prairies and the Argentine Pampas, 1880–1930', in D.C.M. Platt and G. Di Tella (eds), *Argentina, Australia and Canada: Studies in Comparative Development, 1870–1965* (London: Macmillan, 1985), pp.53–75.

Sorrenson, M.P.K., 'Maori and Pakeha', in W.H. Oliver with B.R. Williams (eds), *The Oxford History of New Zealand* (Oxford: The Clarendon Press, 1981), pp. 168–93.

Svendsen, G.D., 'Animal Welfare and the European Union', in R. Garner (ed.), *Animal Rights: The Changing Debate* (London:Macmillan, 1996), pp. 143–65.

Thompson, F.M.L., 'Agriculture and Economic Growth in Britain', in P. Mathias and J. Davies (eds), *Agriculture and Industrialization: From the Eighteenth Century to the Present Day* (Oxford: Blackwell, 1996), pp. 40–85.

West, E., 'The American Frontier', in C.A Milner II, C.A. O'Connor, and M.A. Sandweiss (eds), *The Oxford History of the American West* (New York: Oxford University Press, 1994), pp. 115–119.

White, R., 'Animals and Enterprise', in C.A Milner II, C.A. O'Connor, and M.A. Sandweiss (eds), *The Oxford History of the American West* (New York: Oxford University Press, 1994), pp. 237–75.

Whorton, J.C., 'Vegetarianism', in K.F. Kiple and K.C. Ornelas (eds), *The Cambridge World History of Food vol. II* (Cambridge: Cambridge University Press, 2000), pp. 1553–64.

Wynter, A., 'Preserved Meats', in A. Wynter, *Our Social Bees: Or Pictures of Town and Country Life and Other Places* (London: Robert Hardwicke, 1865), pp. 191–207.


**Articles in Journals**

Allen, G., 'Agricultural Policies in the Shadow of Malthus', *Lloyds Bank Review*, 117 (1975): 14–31.

Alvord, H.E., 'The American Cattle Trade', *Journal of the Royal Agricultural Society of England*, Series 2, 13 (1877): 356–74.

Anderson, E.W. and Shugan, S.M., 'Repositioning for Changing Preferences: The Case of Beef versus Poultry', *Journal of Consumer Research*, 18 (Sept. 1981): 219–32.

Anon., 'Challenging Concentration of Control in the American Meat Industry', *Harvard Law Review*, 117(8) (2004): 2643.

Anon., 'On the Price of Butcher-Meat, and the Increase of Home Supplies of Cattle and Sheep', *Journal of Agriculture*, 25 (July 1865 to June 1866): 358–70.

Anon., 'The Economic Effects of Cattle Disease Legislation', *Economic Journal*, 15 (1905): 156–63.

Anon., 'The Outlook for Beef and Veal in the EEC for the next Five Years', *MLC International Market Review*, 2 (1981): 2–7.

Arnould, R.J., 'Changing Patterns of Concentration in American Meat Packing, 1880–1963', *Business History Review*, 45(1) (1971): 18–34

Atkins, P.J., 'The Glasgow Case: Meat, Disease and Regulation, 1889–1924', *Agricultural History Review*, 52(2) (2004): 161–82.

Bansback, B., 'Towards a Broader Understanding of Meat Demand', *Journal of Agricultural Economics* 46(3) (1995): 287–308

Byrne, A.C., 'The Common Agricultural Policy of the EEC', *Quarterly Review of Agricultural Economics*, 24(2) (April 1971): 82–95.

Capie, F., 'Australian and New Zealand Competition in the British Market 1920–39', *Australian Economic History Review*, 18(1) (1978): 46–63.

———, 'The First Export Monopoly Control Board', *Journal of Agricultural Economics*, 29 (1978): 133–41.

Carlino, B., '75 Years: The Odyssey of Eating Out', *The Nation's Restaurant News* (Jan 1994): 11–28.

Craigie, P.G., 'Twenty Years' Changes in Our Foreign Meat Supplies', *Journal of the Royal Agricultural Society of England*, Series 2, 23 (1887): 465–500.

Crawford, R.F., 'The Food Supply of the United Kingdom', *Journal of the Royal Agricultural Society of England*, Series 3, 11 (1900): 19–34.

David, R., 'The Demise of the Anglo-Norwegian Ice Trade', *Business History*, 37(3) (1995): 52–69.

Diack, L. and Smith, D., 'Sensationalism and Secrecy: The Aberdeen Typhoid Outbreak, 1964', *History Scotland Magazine*, 1(1) (2001): 57–61.

Duckham, T. and Brown, G. T., 'The Progress of Legislation Against Contagious Diseases of Livestock', *Journal of the Royal Agricultural Society of England*, Series 3, 4 (1893): 262–86.

Duncan, R., 'The Demand for Frozen Beef in the United Kingdom, 1880–1940', *Journal of Agricultural Economics*, 12(1) (1956): 82–8.

Dyck, J and Nelson, K., 'World Meat Trade Shaped by Regional Preferences and Reduced Barriers', *Agricultural Outlook*, (Mar. 2000): 7–10.

Eales, J.S. and Unnevehr, L.J., 'Demand for Beef and Chicken Products: Separability and Structural Change', *American Journal of Agricultural Economics*, 70 (Aug. 1988): 521–32.

Edwards, R. and Perren, R., 'A Note on Regional Differences in British Meat Prices, 1825–1865', *Economy and History*, 22(2) (1979): 123–34.

Erickson, A.B., 'The Cattle Plague in England, 1865–1867', *Agricultural History*, 35(2) (1961): 94–103.

Farnsworth, H.C., 'National Food Consumption of Fourteen Western European Countries and Factors Responsible for their Differences', *Food Research Institute Studies*, 13(1) (1974): 77–94.

Ford, A.G., 'British Investment in Argentina and Long Swings, 1880–1914', *Journal of Economic History*, 31(3) (1971): 650–63.

Frost, L., 'The Contribution of the Urban Sector to Australian Economic Development before 1914', *Australian Economic History Review*, 38(1) (1998): 42–73.

Gamgee, J., The System of Inspection in Relation to the Traffic in Diseased Animals or their Produce', *Edinburgh Veterinary Review*, 5 (Nov. 1863): 663–70.

Gibson, C., 'The British Army, French Farmers and the War on the Western Front 1914–1918', *Past & Present*, 180 (2003): 175–239.

Gibson, H., 'The Foreign Meat Supply', *Journal of the Royal Agricultural Society of England*, Series 3, 2 (1896): 206–19.

Grundy, J.E., 'The Hereford Bull: His Contribution to New World and Domestic Beef Supplies', *Agricultural History Review*, 50 (2002): 69–88.

Guild, J.B., 'Variations in the Numbers of Live Stock and in the Production of Meat in the United Kingdom During the War', *Journal of the Royal Statistical Society*, 88(4) (1920): 533–71.

Hall, S.A., 'The Cattle Plague of 1865', *Medical History*, 6 (1962): 45–58.

Harris, M. and Ross, E.B., 'How Beef Became King', *Psychology Today*, 12(5) (Oct. 1978): 88–94.

Hau, M. and Selig, J.M. 'Malnutrition in XIX[th] Century Alsace', *Journal of European Economic History*, 32(1) (2003): 61–75.

Hendrick, J., 'The Growth of International Trade in Manures and Foods', *Transactions of the Highland and Agricultural Society*, Series 5, 29 (1917): 1–36.

Herbert, R., 'Statistics of Live Stock and Dead Meat for Consumption in the Metropolis', *Journal of the Royal Agricultural Society of England*, 22 (1861): 131–5; 413–16.

—— 'Statistics of Live Stock and Dead Meat for Consumption in the Metropolis', *Journal of the Royal Agricultural Society of England*, Series 2, 3 (1867): 91–6.

Howkins, A. and Merricks, L., '"Dewey-eyed calves": Live Animal Exports and Middle-class Opinion, 1980–1995', *Agricultural History Review*, 48 (2000): 85–103.

Hudson, P., 'English Emigration to New Zealand, 1839–1850: Information Diffusion and Marketing a New World', *Economic History Review*, 54(4) (2001): 680–98.

Hunt, K.E., 'Notes on the Shortage of Meat in the United Kingdom and on Costs of Overcoming it', *The Farm Economist*, 6 (1949): 83–9.

Jackson, R.V., 'The Colonial Economies: An Introduction', *Australian Economic History Review*, 18(1) (1998): 1–15.

Libecap, G.D., 'The Rise of the Chicago Packers and the Origin of Meat Inspection and Antitrust', *Economic Inquiry*, 30 (1992): 242–62.

Logan, J.R and Medved, E., 'Simulated Meats', *Journal of Home Economics*, 58(8) (October 1966): 677–78.

Long, J., 'The Sources of our Meat Supply', *Co-operative Wholesale Societies Annual*, (1891): 380–444.

Macrosty, H.W., 'Army Meat Supplies', *The Board of Trade Journal*, New Series 99(1357) (30 Nov. 1922): 603-605.

Nerlich, B., 'War on Foot-and-Mouth Disease in the UK, 2001: Towards a Cultural Understanding of Agriculture', *Agriculture and Human Values*, 21(1) (2004): 15–25.

Olmstead, A.M. and Rhode, P.W., 'An Impossible Undertaking: The Eradication of Bovine Tuberculosis in the United States', *Journal of Economic History*, 64(3) (2004): 734–72.

——, 'The "Tuberculous Cattle Trust": Disease Contagion in an Era of Regulatory Uncertainty', *Journal of Economic History*, 64(4) (2004): 929–63.

Peffer, E.L., 'Foot-and-Mouth Disease in United States Policy', *Food Research Institute Studies*, 3(2) (1962): 141–80.

Perren, R., 'The North American Beef and Cattle Trade with Great Britain, 1870–1914', *Economic History Review*, 24(3) (1971): 430–44.

————, 'Big business and its customers: the European market for American meat from 1840 to 1939', *Journal of European Economic History*, 32(2) (2003): 591–620.

————, 'Farmers and Consumers Under Strain: Allied Meat Supplies in the First World War', *Agricultural History Review*, 53(2) (2005): 212–28.

Philpott, B. P. and Stewart, J.D., 'Capital, Income and Output in New Zealand Agriculture 1922–1956', *Economic Record*, 34 (1958): 223–37.

Reeves, G.W. and Hayman, A.H., 'Demand and Supply Forces in the World Beef Market', *Quarterly Review of Agricultural Economics*, 28(3) (1975): 121–51.

Reid, R.L. and Hackett, A., 'A Database of Vegetarian Foods', *British Food Journal*, 104(11) (2002): 873–80.

Rew, R.H., 'The Nation's Food Supply', *Journal of the Royal Statistical Society*, 76(1) (1912): 98–105.

Roberts, I.M. and Miller, G.L., 'An Analysis of the EEC Market for Beef and Veal', *Quarterly Review of Agricultural Economics*, 24(3) (July 1971): 131–49.

Sauerbeck, A., 'Prices of Commodities and the Precious Metals', *Journal of the Statistical Society*, 49 (1886): 581–648.

Sault, J.L. and Gale, J.B., 'A Review of Developments in Simulated Meats', *Quarterly Review of Agricultural Economics*, 23(4) (1970): 209–21.

Schreuder, B.E.C., Wilesmith, J.W., Ryan, J.M.B. and Straub, O.C., 'Risk of BSE from the Import of Cattle from the United Kingdom into Countries of the European Union', *Veterinary Record*, 141(8) (1997): 187–190.

Schwartz, H., 'Foreign Creditors and the Politics of Development in Australia and Argentina 1880–1913', *International Studies Quarterly*, 33(3) (1989): 281–301.

Sheldon, J.P., 'Report on the American and Canadian Meat Trade', *Journal of the Royal Agricultural Society of England*, Series 2, 13 (1877): 295–355.

Simon, J.L., 'Demographic Causes and Consequences of the Industrial Revolution', *Journal of European Economic History*, 23(1) (1994) 141–58.

Simkin, G.G.F., 'Wartime Changes in the New Zealand Economy', *Economic Record*, 24 (June 1948): 18–31.

Singleton, J. (1997), 'New Zealand's Economic Relations with Japan in the 1950s', *Australian Economic History Review*, 37(1): 1–18

Taylor, A.M., 'Peopling the Pampa: On the Impact of Mass Migration to the River Plate, 1870–1914', *Explorations in Economic History*, 34 (1997): 100–132.

Thompson, D., Muriel, P., Russell, D., Osborne, P., Bromley, A., Rowland, M., Creigh-Tyte, S. and Brown, C., 'Economic Costs of the Foot-and Mouth Disease Outbreak in the United Kingdom in 2001', *Scientific and Technical Review of the International Epizootics Office*, 21(3) (2002): 675–87.

Thompson, H.S., 'On the Management of Grass Land, with Especial Reference to the Production of Meat', *Journal of the Royal Agricultural Society of England*, Series 2, 8 (1872): 153–79.

Ville, S., 'Business Development in Colonial Australia', *Australian Economic History Review*, 38(1) (1998): 16–41.

Voelcker, A., 'On Australian Concentrated Mutton-soup as a Food for Pigs', *Journal of the Royal Agricultural Society of England*, Series 2, 9 (1873): 428–37.

Wagstaff, H., 'EEC Food Surpluses: Controlling Production by Two-Tier Prices, *National Westminster Bank Quarterly Review* (Nov 1982): 30–41.

Walton, J.R., 'Pedigree and the National Cattle Herd circa 1750–1950', *Agricultural History Review*, 34(2) (1986): 149–70.

Whetham, E.H., 'The Trade in Pedigree Livestock 1850–1910', *Agricultural History Review*, 27(1) (1979): 47–50.

Whitechurch, V.L., *Railway Magazine*, 'The London and North Western Railway and American Meat', 5 (1899): 358–63.

Woods, A., 'Why Slaughter? The Cultural Dimensions of Britain's Foot-and-Mouth Disease Control Policy', *Journal of Agricultural and Environmental Ethics*, 17 (2004): 341–62.

## British Government Publications

Board of Agriculture, *Agricultural Statistics* (London: HMSO, 1867–).

[C] 3591 (PP 1866, Vol. XXII), *First Report of the Commissioners appointed to enquire into the Origin and Nature of the Cattle Plague.*

[C] 3600 (PP 1866, Vol. XXII), *Second Report of the Cattle Plague Commissioners.*

[C] 3656 (PP 1866, Vol. XXII), *Third Report of the Cattle Plague Commissioners.*

[C] 3747 (PP 1866, vol. LXXI), *Report from Her Majesty's Diplomatic Agents in South America on Schemes for Curing Meat for the British Market.*

C 362 (PP 1877, Vol. IX) *Report of the Select Committee on Cattle Plague and Importation of Livestock.*

C 6350 (PP 1890–91, Vol. LXXVIII) *Report of the Departmental Committee of the Board of Trade and the Board of Agriculture on the Transatlantic Cattle Trade*

Cd 2643 (PP 1905, LXXIX), *Report of the Royal Commission on Supply of Food and Raw Materials in Time of War.*

Cd 4643 (PP 1909, Vol. XV), *Report of the Departmental Committee on Combinations in the Meat Trade.*

Cd 7896 (PP 1914–16, Vol. XLVI), *Report of the Royal Commission on the Meat Export Trade of Australia.*

Cd 8358 (PP 1916, Vol. XIV), *Departmental Committee on Increase of Prices of Commodities since the Beginning of the War, Interim Report, Meat Milk and Bacon.*

Cmd 456 (PP 1919, Vol. XXV), *Inter-Departmental Committee on Meat Supplies. Report of the Committee appointed by the Board of Trade to Consider the Means of Securing Sufficient Meat Supplies for the United Kingdom.*

Cmd 1057 (PP 1920, Vol. XXIII), *Profiteering Acts, 1919–1920, Interim Report on Meat (Standing Committee on Trusts).*

Cmd 1356 (PP 1921, Vol. XVI), *Profiteering Acts, 1919–1920, Final Report on Meat (Standing Committee on Trusts)*.

Cmd 2390 (PP 1924–25, Vol. XIII), *First Report of the Royal Commission on Food Prices, volume I*.

Cmd 2499 (PP 1924–25, Vol. XIII), *Report of the Imperial Economic Committee on Marketing and Preparing for Market of Foodstuffs Produced in the Overseas Parts of the Empire, Second Report – Meat*.

Cmd 4174–4175 (PP 1931–32, Vol. X), *Imperial Economic Conference at Ottawa, 1932. Summary of Proceedings and copies of Trade Agreements. Appendices*.

Cmd 4492 (PP. 1933–34, Vol. XXVII), *Convention between the Government of the United Kingdom and the Government of the Argentine Republic Relating to Trade and Commerce, with Protocol*.

Cmd 5839 (PP 1937–38, Vol. VIII), *Report of Joint Committee of Enquiry into the Anglo-Argentine Meat Trade*.

Cmd 6879 (PP 1945–46, Vol. XX), *Second Review of the World Food Shortage July 1946*.

Cmd 7203 (PP 1946–47, Vol. XI), *Food Consumption Levels in the United Kingdom*.

Cmd 9214 (PP 1953–54, Vol. XIII), *Report of the Departmental Committee on Foot-and-Mouth Disease 1952–1954*.

Cmnd 2542 (PP 1964–65, Vol. XVII), *Aberdeen Typhoid Outbreak 1964*.

Cmnd 3999 (PP 1968–69, Vol. XXX), *Report of the Committee of Inquiry on Foot-and-Mouth Disease 1968, Part One*.

Cmnd 4225 (PP 1969–70, Vol. V), *Report of the Committee of Inquiry on Foot-and-Mouth Disease 1968, Part Two*.

Commonwealth Economic Committee, *Meat: A Summary of Figures of Production, Trade and Consumption*, (London: HMSO, 1948–67).

Commonwealth Secretariat, *Meat: A Review of Figures of Production, Trade and Consumption*, (London, HMSO, 1968–1973).

Department for Environment, Food and Rural Affairs, *Origin of the UK Foot and Mouth Disease Epidemic in 2001* (June 2002).

Department for Environment, Food and Rural Affairs, *Report of the Chief Veterinary Officer: Animal Health 2003* (June 2004).

Empire Marketing Board, [Compiler] *Meat*, (London: HMSO, July 1932).

Imperial Economic Committee, *Meat: A Summary of Figures of Production and Trade* (London: HMSO, 1932–38).

Intelligence Branch of the Imperial Economic Committee, *Cattle and Beef Survey: A Summary of Production and Trade in British Empire and Commonwealth Countries* (London: HMSO, 1934).

Meat and Livestock Commission, *Alternative Pork Cutting Method: Providing the Lean Alternative* (Bletchley, 1988).

Meat and Livestock Commission, *MLC International Market Survey* (Bletchley, 1978–80).

Meat and Livestock Commission, *MLC International Market Review* (Bletchley, 1981–86).

Meat and Livestock Commission, *MLC International Meat Market Review* (Bletchley, 1987–2003).

Meat and Livestock Commission, *Meat Demand Trends* (Bletchley, 1976–2000).

Meat and Livestock Commission, *The Future of the European Pig Meat Industry: A Report of the Conference at Warwick* (Bletchley, 1992).

Ministry of Agriculture and Fisheries Economic Series, *Report on the Trade in Refrigerated Beef, Mutton and Lamb* (London: HMSO, 1925).

Ministry of Agriculture and Fisheries Economic Series, *Report on the Marketing of Pigs in England and Wales* (London: HMSO, 1926).

Ministry of Agriculture and Fisheries Economic Series, *Report on the Pork and Bacon Trades in England and Wales* (London: HMSO, 1928).

Ministry of Agriculture and Fisheries Economic Series, *Report on the Marketing of Cattle and Beef in England and Wales* (London: HMSO, 1929).

Ministry of Agriculture and Fisheries Economic Series, *Report on the Committee Appointed to Review the Working of the Agricultural Marketing Acts* (London: HMSO, 1947).

Ministry of Agriculture, Fisheries, and Food, *Animal Health, 1865–1965* (London: HMSO, 1965).

Ministry of Agriculture, Fisheries, and Food, *A Century of Agricultural Statistics 1866–1966* (London: HMSO, 1968).

National Audit Office, *Foot-and-Mouth Disease: Applying the Lessons* (HC 184 Session 2004–05, 2 Feb. 2005).

National Consumer Council, *Consumers and the Common Agricultural Policy* (London: HMSO, 1988).

(PP 1852, Vol. XXX), *Date and Terms of Contract for Preserved Meat for the Use of the Navy entered into with Goldner and others; the Quantities issued since the commencement of the Contracts; Quantities returned into Store as unfit for use; Complaints made; also Contract Prices of Beef and Pork for the years 1848, 1849, 1850, and 1851.*

(PP 1866, Vol. XLVI), *Names of newspapers in which advertisements of May 1866, relating to contracts for ox beef and vegetables were inserted; letter on the subject by the Provincial Newspaper Society to the Admiralty; and reply.*

(PP 1867–8, Vol. LV), *Return Relating to the Past and Present Supply of Dead Meat to the Country and the Metropolis.*

(PP 1893–94, Vol. XII), *Report from the Select Committee House of Lords on the Marking of Foreign Meat.*

(PP 1897, Vol. VIII), *Report and Special Report from the Select Committee on the Agricultural Produce [Meat, &c.] Marks Bill.*

*Royal Commission on Food Prices, Volume II, Minutes of Evidence* (London: HMSO, 1925).

Statutory Instrument No. 1480, *The Welfare of Animals (Transport) Order 1997*, ISBN 0 11 063764 X.

## Overseas Government Publications

Bergman, A.M., *A Review of the Frozen and Chilled Trans-Oceanic Meat Industry* (Uppsala: Swedish Government, 1916).

Bureau of Agricultural Economics, *The Meat Situation*, 1 (Canberra: Australian Government Publishing Service, August 1972): 28–31.

Census of Canada.

Consulate-General of Uruguay, *The Republic of Uruguay; Its Geography, History, Rural Industries, Commerce, and General Statistics* (London, Edward Stanford, 1883).

New Zealand Department of Agriculture, *Ninth Report of the Department of Agriculture* (Wellington, 1901).

New Zealand Department of Agriculture (1902), *Tenth Report of the Department of Agriculture* (Wellington, 1902).

PL 107–9 Federal Inter-Agency Working Group, *Animal Disease Risk Assessment, Prevention and Control Act of 2001 (PL 107–9)* (Washington, Jan. 2003).

Regmi, A., ed, *Changing Structure of Global Food Consumption and Trade* (Washington: Agriculture and Trade Report WRS–01–1, Economic Research Service, U.S. Department of Agriculture, May 2001).

Rommel, G.H., 'Notes on the Animal Industry of Argentina', United States Department of Agriculture, *Twenty–Fifth Annual Report of the Bureau of Animal Industry for the Year 1908* (Washington: Government Printing Office, 1910): 315–33.

United States Department of Agriculture, *Annual Reports of the Bureau of Animal Industry* (Washington: Government Printing Office, 1884–).

United States Department of Agriculture, *Reports of the Commissioner of the Operations of the Department for the Year* (Washington: Government Printing Office, 1862–).

United States Department of Agriculture: Section of Foreign Markets, *Agricultural Imports of the United Kingdom, 1896–1900* (Bulletin 26, Washington: Government Printing Office, 1902).

United States Department of Agriculture: Section of Foreign Markets, *Distribution of the Agricultural Exports of the United States, 1897–1901* (Bulletin 29, Washington: Government Printing Office, 1903).

United States Department of Agriculture, *Yearbook of the Department of Agriculture 1897* (Washington: Government Printing Office, 1898).

Wrenn, J.E., *International Trade in Meats and Animal Fats* (Trade Promotion Series 26, Washington: United States Bureau of Foreign and Domestic Commerce, 1925).

## Publications of Non-Governmental Organizations

American Institute Foundation, *The Science of Meat and Meat Products* (San Francisco: W.H. Freeman and Co., 1960).

Food and Agriculture Organization, *Trade in Agricultural Commodities in the United Nations Development Decade* (Part 1, Rome, 1964).

Food and Agriculture Organization, *The World Meat Economy* (Rome: United Nations, 1965).

Food and Agriculture Organization, *FAO Commodity Review* (Rome, 1961–68).

Food and Agriculture Organization, *Commodity Review and Outlook* (Rome, 1968–95).

Food and Agriculture Organization, *FAO Commodity Market Review* (Rome, 1996–).

General Agreement on Tariffs and Trade, *The International Markets for Meat, 1987/88* (Geneva, 1988).

International Institute of Agriculture, *International Trade in Meat* (Rome, 1936)

International Institute of Agriculture, *World Production in Meat* (Rome, 1938).

International Institute of Agriculture, *International Yearbook of Agricultural Statistics 1940–41, vol. II, Numbers of the Principal Species of Livestock and Poultry* (Rome, 1941).

International Institute of Agriculture: Bureau of the F.A.O., *International Yearbook of Agricultural Statistics 1941–42 to 1945–46, vol. 1, Agricultural Production and Numbers of Livestock* (Rome, 1947).

International Labour Office, *Food Control in Great Britain* (Montreal, 1942).

League of Nations, *Food, Famine and Relief 1940–1946* (Geneva, 1946).

Royal Institute of International Affairs, *World Agriculture: An International Survey. A Report by a Study Group* (London: Oxford University Press, 1932).


## Non-Published Sources

Barnard, P., 'World Sheep Market' (Cyclostyled paper delivered at the 13th International Meat Secretariat World Meat Congress at Belo Horizonte, Brazil, Sept. 2000): 1–13.

Gebhardt, R.C., *The River Plate Meat Industry since c.1900: Technology, Ownership, International Trade Regimes and Domestic Policy* (London: London School of Economics Unpublished PhD Thesis, 2000).

Gordon, A.D., 'Key Aspects of World Meat Markets' (Cyclostyled paper delivered at the 13th International Meat Secretariat World Meat Congress at Belo Horizonte, Brazil, Sept. 2000): 1–16.

PRO, MUN 4/6541 (SGS/2295) War Office. Comparative Army rations, 31 July 1915 to 31 May 1917.

**Web Sources**

Agriculture and Agri-Food Canada, 'Canada: hogs and cattle situation and outlook', *Bi-weekly Bulletin*, 13(18b), http://www.agr.gc.ca/mad-dam/e/bulletine/v13e/v13n18eb.htm.

Alberta Cattle Feeders' Association, Agency Reports (6 Mar. 2001), http://cattlefeeder.ab.ca/herd/fmd010308.shtml.

Animals Australia, http://www.animalsaustralia.org./default2.asp?idL1=1272.

Animals Australia, 'Australia's Live Animal Export Trade', 'A litany of disasters', http://www.animalsaustralia.org/default2.asp?idL1=1272&2dL=1283.

Arab News Newspaper, 'Australia to Resume Sheep Exports' (26 Dec. 2004), http://www.arabnews.com.

The Australasian Meat Industry Employees Union, 'Unions Campaign against Live Exports', http://vic.amieu.asn.au/pages.php?recid=34.

Australian Hereford Society, http://www.hereford.com.au/index.html.

BBC News, UK, 'Lumley rallies against live exports' (9 Feb. 2002), http://news.bbc.co.uk/1/hi/uk/1809738.stm

BBC News Online: World: Europe, 'UK labelled 'leper of Europe' (12 Mar. 2001), http://www.bbc.co.uk/1/low/world/europe/1215638.stm.

*The BSE Inquiry, Volumes 1–16* (Parliament. House of Commons: Papers; 1999–2000, 887, I–XVb, 2000). http://www.bseinquiry.gov.uk.

Compassion in World Farming, 'The Export of Live Farm Animals from the UK' (Mar 2003), http://www.ciwf.org.uk/publictions/Briefings%5CBR7577.pdf.

Bernard Matthews Foods Ltd, http://www.bernardmatthews.com/CompanyHistory.asp.

Blake, A., Sinclair, M.T. and Sugiyarto, G., 'The Economy-Wide Effects of Foot-and-Mouth Disease in the UK Economy', (2001?) http://www.nottingham.ac.uk/~lizng/ttri/Pdf/2001/2001%203.PDF.

Case Studies – Bernard Matthews Foods Ltd., Employing Migrant Workers, http://www.employingmigrantworkers.org.uk/resources/5_9_3.html.

Clarke Willmott News (14 Mar. 2005), http://www.clarkewillmott.com/news.htm?Article=461.

Defra, 'Live Sheep Exports' (3 Feb. 2003), http://www.defra.gov.uk/corporate/ministers/statements/em030203.htm.

DEFRA News release, 'Morley Calls for Fewer Live Sheep Exports' (26 Feb. 2002), http://www.defra.gov.uk/news/2002/020226a.htm.

Defra, 'UK – Animal health and welfare – BSE: Export & trade', http://www.defra.gov.uk/animalh/bse/export-trade/index.html.

Defra, 'UK – Animal health and welfare – International trade: Product exports – Beef exports', http://www.defra.gov.uk/animalh/int-trd/prod-ex/q-and-a.htm.

Department of Agriculture, Western Australia, *Cattle and Sheep Meat Processing in Western Australia: Ministerial Taskforce Report, Dec. 2003*, http://www.agric.wa.gov.au/pls/portal30/docs/FOLDER/1KMP/_ABT/FS/edu_meat.htm.

Donaldson, A.I., 'Foot-and-Mouth Disease in Western North Africa ... an Analysis of the risk to Europe', *The European Commission for the Control of Foot-and-Mouth Disease*, Appendix 5 (2002),
   http://www.fao.org/ag/againfo/commisions/en/eufmd/maison/app5.html.
EUROPA, 'Animal Welfare during Transport', (11 Jan. 2005), http://europa.eu.int/comm/food/animal/welfare/trnsport/index_en.htm.
Food and Agriculture Organization, FAOSTAT data, 2004, http://apps.fao.org/faostat/form?collection=FS.NonPrimaryLivestockAndProducts&Domain=FS&servlet=1&hasbulk=0&version=ext&language=EN.
Food Production Daily, 'New BSE case could hurt US beef market' (27 June 2005), http://www.foodproductiondaily.com/news/news-ng.asp?id=60913-new-bse-case.
Foot and Mouth Disease, France Impact Worksheet, March 2001, http://www.aphis.usda.gov/vs/ceah/cei/IW_2001_files/fmd_france0301e.htm.
Hereford Cattle Society,
   http://www.herefordwebpages.co.uk/herdsoc.shtml#.address.
Iowa Farm Bureau, 'The Economics of the EU Beef Hormone Ban and Carousel Retaliation', www.iowafarmbureau.com/programs/commodity/pdf/eoa7.pdf.
Irish Hereford Breed Society, http://www.irishhereford.com/aboutus.html.
Ministry of Agriculture and Forestry, 'Live Sheep Exports – What's happening?', http://www.maf.govt.nz/mafnet/publications/primarysource/february-2004/primary-source-0208.htm.
National Farmers' Federation, 'Reopening of Saudi Trade a Win for Australian Farmers' (6 May 2005), http://www.nff.org/pages/nr05/047.html.
OIE, 'Number of cases of BSE reported in the United Kingdom', http://www.oie.int/eng/info/en_esbru.htm.
OIE, 'Number of reported cases of bovine spongiform encepalopathy (BSE) in farmed cattle worldwide (excluding the United Kingdom)'. http://www.oie.int/eng/info/en_esbmonde.htm.
OIE, 'Short history of the OIE', http://www.oie.int/.
OIE, 'The OIE standards on BSE: a guide for understanding and proper implementation', http://www.oie.int/eng/press_en0401109.htm.
Spatuzza, A., 'PANAFTOSA Crusaders for Animal Health', *Perspectives in Health Magazine, the Magazine of the Pan American Health Organization*, vol. 8 (3) (2003), http://www.paho.org/English/DD/PIN/Number18_article4.htm.
USDA Foreign Agricultural Service, 'Livestock and Poultry: World Markets and Trade March 1998', http://www.fas.usda.gov/dlp2/circular/1998–98–03LP/bse.html.
United States Department of Human Health Services, 'Federal agencies take special precautions to keep "Mad Cow Disease" out of the United States' (23 Aug. 2001), http://www.hhs.gov/news/press/2001pres/01fbse.html.
United States Department of State, 'Department of State Washington File' (14 Mar. 2005), http://canberra.usembassy.bov/hyper/2005/0314/epf104.htm.
University of Edinburgh, CJD Surveillance Unit,
   http://www.cjd.ad.ac.uk/figures.htm.

Warmwell web site has a comprehensive file of criticisms of how the UK managed
foot-and-mouth disease in 2001, http://www.warmwell.com/about.html
Warren Truss MP Media Release, 'Welfare of livestock put first in resuming trade
with Saudi Arabia' (4 May 2005),
http://www.maff.gov.au/releases/05/05108wt.html.
Woods, A., 'Press Release: Foot and Mouth Disease in Britain: The History', (22
Feb. 2001), http://www.chstm.man.ac.uk/news/pressrel-fmd.htm.


**Magazines and Newspapers**

*Advertising Age (Midwest region edition)* (Chicago).
*Agricultural Gazette* (London, 1846–1912).
*Annual Review of the (Chilled and) Frozen Meat Trade* (London, W. Weddel and
Co., 1899–1927).
*Changing Times* (Washington, Feb. 1988).
*Cold Storage and Ice Trades Review* (London, 1898–1910).
*The Economist* (London, 1843–).
*Multinational Business* (London: Economist Intelligence Unit, 1971–1992)
*Fedgazette* (Minneapolis, Apr. 1998).
*Fortune* (New York, 1930–).
*Frozen Food Age* (New York, Aug. 1952–).
*Guardian* (London).
*Independent* (London).
*Journal of Agriculture*, Series 2 (Edinburgh: William Blackwood & Sons, 1843–
66), continued as *Journal of Agriculture*, Series 3 (1866–68).
*Journal of the Society of Arts* (London).
*Marketing* (London, 1989).
*Marketing Magazine* (Toronto, 1997).
*Marketing Week* (London, 1979–).
*Meat and Provision Trades Review* (London, 1877–78, 1880–81).
*Meat Trades' Journal and Cattle Salesman's Gazette* (Manchester, 5 May 1888–
June 1892); (London, July 1892–).
*The Nation's Restaurant News* (New York).
*New Zealand Journal of Agriculture* (Wellington, 1927–87).
*Pastoral Review* (Melbourne, 1890–).
*Pharmaceutical Journal*.
*Quarterly Journal of Agriculture* (Edinburgh: William Blackwood & Sons, 1829–
43), continued as *Journal of Agriculture*, Series 2 (1843–66), continued as
*Journal of Agriculture*, Series 3 (1866–68).
*Retail Business: Market Surveys* (New York, June 1995).
*Seattle Post-Intelligencer* (Seattle).
*Supermarket Business*, (New York, 1979–).
*The Times* (London).

# Index

**Modern Economic and Social History Series**

*General Editor*
Derek Aldcroft, University Fellow, Department of Economic and Social History,
University of Leicester, UK

Derek H. Aldcroft
*Studies in the Interwar European Economy*
ISBN 1 85928 360 8 (1997)

Michael J. Oliver
*Whatever Happened to Monetarism?: Economic Policy Making and Social
Learning in the United Kingdom Since 1979*
ISBN 1 85928 433 7 (1997)

R. Guerriero-Wilson
*Disillusionment or New Opportunities?: The Changing Nature of Work in Offices,
Glasgow 1880–1914*
ISBN 1 84014 276 6 (1998)

Barry Stapleton and James H. Thomas
*Gales: A Study in Brewing, Business and Family History*
ISBN 0 7546 0146 3 (2000)

Derek H. Aldcroft and Michael Oliver
*Trade Unions and the Economy: 1870–2000*
ISBN 1 85928 370 5 (2000)

Patrick Duffy
*The Skilled Compositor, 1850–1914: An Aristocrat Among Working Men*
ISBN 0 7546 0255 9 (2000)

Roger Lloyd-Jones and M. J. Lewis with the assistance of M. Eason
*Raleigh and the British Bicycle Industry: An Economic and Business History,
1870–1960*
ISBN 1 85928 457 4 (2000)

Ted Wilson
*Battles for the Standard: Bimetallism and the Spread of the Gold Standard in the
Nineteenth Century*
ISBN 1 85928 436 1 (2000)

Andrew D. Popp
*Business Structure, Business Culture and the Industrial District:
The Potteries, c. 1850–1914*
0 7546 0176 5 (2001)

Bernard Cronin
*Technology, Industrial Conflict and the Development of Technical Education in 19th-Century England*
ISBN 0 7546 0313 X (2001)

Geoffrey Channon
*Railways in Britain and the United States, 1830–1940: Studies in Economic and Business History*
ISBN 1 84014 253 7 (2001)

Sam Mustafa
*Merchants and Migrations: Germans and Americans in Connection, 1776–1835*
ISBN 0 7546 0590 6 (2001)

Robert Conlon and John Perkin
*Wheels and Deals: The Automotive Industry in Twentieth-Century Australia*
ISBN 0 7546 0405 5 (2001)

Michael Ferguson
*The Rise of Management Consulting in Britain*
ISBN 0 7546 0561 2 (2002)

Scott Kelly
*The Myth of Mr Butskell: The Politics of British Economic Policy, 1950–55*
ISBN 0 7546 0604 X (2002)

Alan Fowler
*Lancashire Cotton Operatives and Work, 1900-1950: A Social History of Lancashire Cotton Operatives in the Twentieth Century*
ISBN 0 7546 0116 1 (2003)

John F. Wilson and Andrew Popp (eds)
*Industrial Clusters and Regional Business Networks in England, 1750-1970*
ISBN 0 7546 0761 5 (2003)

John Hassan
*The Seaside, Health and the Environment in England and Wales since 1800*
ISBN1 84014 265 0 (2003)

Andrew Dawson
*Lives of the Philadelphia Engineers: Capital, Class and Revolution, 1830–1890*
ISBN 0 7546 3396 9 (2004)

Anne Clendinning
*Demons of Domesticity: Women and the English Gas Industry, 1889–1939*
ISBN 0 7546 0692 9 (2004)

Armin Grünbacher
*Reconstruction and Cold War in Germany:*
*The Kreditanstalt für Wiederaufbau (1948–1961)*
ISBN 0 7546 3806 5 (2004)

Joseph Harrison and David Corkill
*Spain: A Modern European Economy*
ISBN 0 7546 0145 5 (2004)

Lawrence Black and Hugh Pemberton (eds)
*An Affluent Society?: Britain's Post-War 'Golden Age' Revisited*
ISBN 0 7546 3528 7 (2004)

Marshall J. Bastable
*Arms and the State: Sir William Armstrong and the*
*Remaking of British Naval Power, 1854–1914*
ISBN 0 7546 3404 3 (2004)

Robin Pearson
*Insuring the Industrial Revolution: Fire Insurance in Great Britain, 1700–1850*
ISBN 0 7546 3363 2 (2004)

Ross E. Catterall and Derek H. Aldcroft (eds)
*Exchange Rates and Economic Policy in the 20th Century*
ISBN 1 84014 264 2 (2004)

Till Geiger
*Britain and the Economic Problem of the Cold War: The Political Economy and*
*the Economic Impact of the British Defence Effort, 1945–1955*
ISBN 0 7546 0287 7 (2004)

Julian Greaves
*Industrial Reorganization and Government Policy in Interwar Britain*
ISBN 0 7546 0355 5 (2005)

Timothy Cuff
*The Hidden Cost of Economic Development: The Biological Standard of Living*
*in Antebellum Pennsylvania*
ISBN 0 7546 4119 8 (2005)

Derek H. Aldcroft
*Europe's Third World: The European Periphery in the Interwar Years*
ISBN 0 7546 0599 X (2006)

James P. Huzel
*The Popularization of Malthus in Early Nineteenth-Century England:*
*Martineau, Cobbett and the Pauper Press*
ISBN 0 7546 5427 3 (2006)